SCHOLASTIC

Student Thesaurus

SCHOLASTIC

Student Thesaurus

JOHN K. BOLLARD

SCHOLASTIC REFERENCE
An imprint of
SCHOLASTIC

Editorial Assistant: Catrin Lloyd-Bollard
Curriculum Consultant: Bob Stremme
Book design: Nancy Sabato
Composition: Kevin Callahan / BNGO Books

Library of Congress Cataloging-in-Publication Data

Bollard, John K.
    Scholastic student thesaurus/John K. Bollard
        p.   cm.
    Includes index.
    Summary: Provides synonyms and antonyms for thousands of English words.
    1. English language—Synonyms and antonyms—Juvenile literature.
    [1. English language—Synonyms and antonyms.] I. Title
    PE1591 .B586 2002
    423'.1—dc21
    2001045766

ISBN-10: 0-439-02588-5
ISBN-13: 978-0-439-02588-1

18 17 16 15 14 13 12   13 14 15 16 17

Printed in China,   38
First Scholastic printing, August 2002
Updated edition, May 2007

Contents

Introduction

The Web of Words

Imagine a large, beautiful spiderweb. Its strands run from point to point creating intricate and fascinating patterns wherever you look. The English language is just such a web, but it is a web of words. Many words are connected by strands of meaning to other similar words, called *synonyms*. Those words, in turn, are connected to still other synonyms, moving you gradually from one idea to another. How can you find your way around this web of words? How can you find just the right word when you need it? A thesaurus helps you to do just that. The *Scholastic Student Thesaurus* is designed to move you around in the web of words. If you start with a word you know, your thesaurus will help you find synonyms to choose from.

Why Use a Thesaurus?

You already know thousands of words. These words are usually all you need. But sometimes, even though you know you have a good idea, you just can't think of quite the right word to express it the way you want. Here are some of the ways in which the *Scholastic Student Thesaurus* can be helpful:

To avoid repetition. Suppose you have used the same word three or four times in one paragraph or page. Rather than use that word again, you would like to find a different way to express the same idea. Your thesaurus provides you with a variety of synonyms.

To make your meaning clear and precise. When you speak or write, you usually think about what you *mean,* not about the words you are using. But sometimes the meaning doesn't come out as easily or as clearly as you had hoped. Your thesaurus can help you find words that express your idea more effectively than the words you began with. You may find that looking through the synonyms of a word brings to mind different ways to express your idea. It may even help you understand the idea better yourself. Sometimes a word you have used may be too vague. Sometimes its meaning or its tone is not exactly what you want. You want your readers to understand exactly how you felt, what you saw, or what you thought. Your thesaurus can give you synonyms that are more precise and effective.

To avoid overused terms. There are a few words that get used so often in so many different ways that they have run out of energy. They no longer have a sharply defined meaning, even though they give a general impression of what we want to say. It may be easier just to use these words, but they don't say anything specific. Often they lead us into clichés or vague thinking. If you find yourself using such general words as **nice** or **pretty** or **good,** try to pin down your thoughts with synonyms that more specifically describe what you are talking about. Your thesaurus can help you replace those words with synonyms like "delightful," "striking," or "favorable." This will make your writing more energetic and original.

To achieve the proper tone. Sometimes the word you thought of is too informal to be used in a school assignment or for a letter you want to write. You want a more serious word, but can't think of one. Or the opposite may be true. You may be writing a story or poem in a conversational or informal style. The synonyms in your thesaurus cover a broad range of vocabulary from informal to colloquial to formal. Some words are labeled as *informal* in your thesaurus. You should avoid using these in your serious writing. For example, "chicken" and "yellow" are informal synonyms of **cowardly.** You may not want to use them in an essay or assignment, but they might be just right for a character's speech in a story. When selecting any synonym, you should always take a moment to consider whether it is suitable for the style in which you are writing or speaking.

You already know many of the words in the *Scholastic Student Thesaurus,* but you will also find many new words here. Your thesaurus will guide you through this web of words in order to make your writing more clear, more mature, and even more elegant. Most importantly, the *Scholastic Student Thesaurus* will help you to write accurately and precisely. In this way, you can communicate your thoughts more easily to others. And that is what you are always trying to do when you speak or write.

At-a-Glance

A thesaurus is a reference book that lists words that mean the same thing or almost the same thing. Such words are called *synonyms*. In some cases, your thesaurus also helps you find words that mean the opposite or almost the opposite. These words are called *antonyms*. The different parts of your *Scholastic Student Thesaurus* are identified in the sample page below.

Guide words give the first and last words alphabetically on each page, including both the main entries and the on-the-page index.

Main entries are listed in alphabetical order.

Main entry words are set in blue type. Main entry words jut out a bit from the entry. This makes it easier for you to find the word you are looking for.

The **on-the-page index** alphabetically lists every synonym that is not a main entry. If a word you are looking up is not a main entry, you should look for it here. The black arrow points to the main entry word or words where you will find it and other synonyms.

slam ▸ smear

slant 1. *vb* tilt, lean, list, incline, slope, bank, sag, pitch, cant ➡ **bend**
2. *n* slope, incline, climb, ascent, rise, descent, declivity, grade, hill

slavery *n* bondage, servitude, enslavement, serfdom, subjugation, vassalage ⇨ *freedom*

sleep 1. *vb* slumber, doze, snooze, nod, nap, hibernate ➡ **rest**
2. *n* slumber, doze, rest, repose, siesta, nap, catnap, shut-eye (*informal*)

slide 1. *vb* glide, skim, coast, skid, slip, skate ➡ **push**
2. *n* ➡ **channel**
3. *n* ➡ **photograph**
4. *n* ➡ **avalanche**

slippery *adj* smooth, slick, glassy, icy, waxy, soapy

slow 1. *adj* leisurely, gradual, sluggish, deliberate, moderate, torpid ⇨ *fast*
2. *adj* dilatory, lackadaisical ➡ **passive, lazy, listless**
3. *adj* ➡ **dull, stupid**

sly 1. *adj* devious, crafty, cunning, shrewd, subtle, tricky, sneaky, wily, slick, shifty, artful, scheming, underhanded ➡ **dishonest**
2. *adj* secretive, furtive, sneaky, surreptitious, stealthy, elusive ➡ **private**

small 1. *adj* little, tiny, miniature, minute, diminutive, Lilliputian, compact ➡ **trivial** ⇨ *big*
2. *adj* scanty, meager, slight, spare, skimpy, stingy, paltry ➡ **inadequate**

smart 1. *adj* intelligent, clever, bright, wise, learned, brilliant, keen, acute, quick, alert, apt, astute, perceptive, insightful, discerning, incisive, canny, shrewd ➡ **precocious, educated, profound** ⇨ *foolish, stupid*
2. *adj* ➡ **fashionable**
3. *vb* ➡ **hurt**
In general, **smart, clever,** *and* **bright,** *which all suggest quickness in learning, are more often applied to young people than are* **intelligent, wise,** *and* **learned,** *which suggest the wisdom that comes from experience, education, and age.*

If the word you want is not a main entry above, look below to find it.

slam ➡ close
slammer ➡ jail
slander ➡ insult
slang ➡ dialect
slap ➡ punch, blow[1]
slash ➡ cut, decrease
slat ➡ board
slate ➡ gray, ballot
slather ➡ rub
slaughter ➡ kill, murder
slave ➡ servant, prisoner, work
slavish ➡ servile
slay ➡ kill
slayer ➡ killer
slaying ➡ murder
sled ➡ vehicle

sledge ➡ hammer
sledgehammer ➡ hammer
sleek ➡ shiny
sleeping ➡ asleep
sleepless ➡ awake
sleepy ➡ tired
sleet ➡ ice
slender ➡ thin, narrow, light[2]
slew ➡ abundance
slice ➡ cut, block
slick ➡ slippery, sly
slight ➡ small, thin, short, light[2], insult
slightest ➡ least
slightly ➡ partly
slim ➡ thin, narrow
slime ➡ dirt

sling ➡ throw
slink ➡ sneak
slip ➡ mistake, trip, dock, ticket, slide, fall
slip by ➡ elapse
slit ➡ cut
slither ➡ crawl
slogan ➡ saying
slop ➡ dirt
slope ➡ slant
sloppy ➡ messy
slosh ➡ splash
sloth ➡ laziness
slothful ➡ lazy
slouch ➡ bend
slough ➡ shed
slovenly ➡ messy

sludge ➡ dirt
slug ➡ hit, missile
sluggard ➡ loafer
sluggish ➡ slow, listless
sluice ➡ channel
slumber ➡ sleep
slumbering ➡ asleep
slump ➡ depression, fall, drop, bend
slush ➡ snow
slushy ➡ wet
smack ➡ hit, kiss, blow[1]
smaller ➡ less
smallest ➡ least
small-minded ➡ mean
smash ➡ break, hit, collide
smear ➡ rub, insult

170   *n* = noun • *vb* = verb • *adj* = adjective • *adv* = adverb • *prep* = preposition • *conj* = conjunction

Thesaurus Entries Close-up

Sense numbers separate the different meanings of an entry. This makes it easier for you to find the word use you are looking for.

slant 1. *vb* tilt, lean, list, incline, slope, bank, sag, pitch, cant ➡ **bend**
2. *n* slope, incline, climb, ascent, rise, descent, declivity, grade, hill

slavery *n* bondage, servitude, enslavement, serfdom, subjugation, vassalage ⇨ *freedom*

Black arrows point to **synonym cross-references.** These synonyms have their own main entry. You can find more synonyms by looking up these entries.

Part-of-speech labels in *italic (slanted)* type give the part of speech for each entry or sense.
n = noun
vb = verb
adj = adjective
adv = adverb
prep = preposition
conj = conjunction
interj = interjection
pron = pronoun

smart 1. *adj* intelligent, clever, bright, wise, learned, brilliant, keen, acute, quick, alert, apt, astute, perceptive, insightful, discerning, incisive, canny, shrewd ➡ **precocious, educated, profound** ⇨ *foolish, stupid*
2. *adj* ➡ **fashionable**
3. *vb* ➡ **hurt**

In general, **smart**, **clever**, *and* **bright**, *which all suggest quickness in learning, are more often applied to young people than are* **intelligent**, **wise**, *and* **learned**, *which suggest the wisdom that comes from experience, education, and age.*

White arrows point to **antonym cross-references.** Look up these entries to find more antonyms.

Usage notes in *italic* type give information about how some synonyms are used.

slender ➡ thin, narrow, light²
slew ➡ abundance
slice ➡ cut, block
slick ➡ slippery, sly
slight ➡ small, thin, short, light², insult
slightest ➡ least

slogan ➡ saying
slop ➡ dirt
slope ➡ slant
sloppy ➡ messy
slosh ➡ splash
sloth ➡ laziness
slothful ➡ lazy

Small raised numbers tell you which entry to look up if two headwords are spelled the same.

9

How to Use This Book

The *Scholastic Student Thesaurus* will help you find synonyms for a word that you have in mind. The three main features of the thesaurus are explained below: **main entries**, **cross-references**, and the **on-the-page index**.

Main Entry Words

Synonyms are grouped together after **main entry words**. These **main entries** are listed alphabetically and printed in **blue boldface** type. Suppose you need a synonym for **exaggerate**. Your thesaurus has a main entry for **exaggerate** with nine synonyms:

exaggerate *vb* overstate, overdo, inflate, embellish, embroider, elaborate, gild, magnify, dramatize

If a main entry word has more than one sense or use, the synonyms are grouped in numbered senses, as in the entry for **boast**, which can be either a verb or a noun:

boast 1. *vb* brag, gloat, crow, show off, vaunt, swagger, exult
  2. *n* brag, bragging, vaunt, claim, assertion, bluster, swagger, bravado

If two main entries have the same spelling, a small raised number is used to tell them apart, as at **live¹** and **live²**. The same raised numbers are used in the index.

live¹ 1. *vb* exist, be, thrive, subsist, breathe ➡ **experience**
  2. *vb* survive, outlive, outlast, persevere, persist ➡ **continue** ⇨ *die*
  3. *vb* reside, dwell, stay, abide, inhabit, lodge, room, sojourn ➡ **occupy**

live² *adj* ➡ **lively, alive, active**

Part-of-speech labels

Each entry or numbered sense has a **part-of-speech label** that identifies the part of speech of the main entry and the synonyms of each sense. The part-of-speech labels are:

n	noun	*prep*	preposition
vb	verb	*conj*	conjunction
adj	adjective	*interj*	interjection
adv	adverb	*pron*	pronoun

Usage labels and usage notes

Some synonyms are followed by a **usage label** printed in *italics* inside parentheses. A usage label helps you recognize how that synonym is used. For example, there are two usage labels at the entry for **wig**:

wig *n* hairpiece, fall, toupee, periwig *(historical)*, rug *(informal)* ➡ **hair**

The *(historical)* label indicates that "periwig" is used in historical contexts. You can learn from a dictionary that it is a term for a type of wig popular in the 17th and 18th centuries. The *(informal)* label is the most common usage label in this thesaurus. It warns you that a synonym should not be used in serious or formal writing or speech. Other usage labels may indicate the language of origin of a term, such as "*adios (Spanish), au revoir (French)*" at the entry **good-bye**, or a field of reference to which it is restricted, such as "petrol *(British)*" at **gasoline**.

Some entries are followed by a usage note, which gives information about how the synonyms are used or how they are different from each other. For an example, see the usage note at **maybe**:

All of these words express uncertainty about something.
Maybe *and* **perhaps** *are very close synonyms and it usually makes no difference which one you use.*
Possibly *stresses the uncertainty more than* **maybe.**
Conceivably *and* **feasibly** *suggest even greater uncertainty.* **Perchance** *is a more formal and less common synonym.*

Cross-references

Many entries include a boldface cross-reference, indicated by an arrow, that directs you to a related main entry. If you don't find a synonym that you want at one main entry, the cross-references direct you to other entries where you will find more choices. There are two types of cross-references: ➡ **synonym cross-references** and ⇨ *antonym cross-references.*

➡ Synonym cross-references

Synonym cross-references direct you to other main entries that are related to the main entry you looked up. Synonym cross-references are printed in **boldface** type following a black arrow ➡, as at the entry for **patriotic:**

patriotic *adj* loyal, zealous, nationalistic, chauvinistic ➡ **faithful**

If the main entry you looked up does not have a synonym you want, the synonym cross-reference points you to another main entry that might be helpful.

Sometimes more than one synonym cross-reference is given, as at **tolerant:**

tolerant *adj* permissive, lenient, indulgent, easygoing ➡ **liberal, kind, patient**

In these cases, look first at the entry that seems closest to the idea you have in mind. And remember that the cross-reference itself may be a synonym for you to use.

In some main entries, you will find a sense number with only a cross-reference and no other synonyms. This cross-reference indicates that the synonyms for that sense are given at the cross-reference entry, as at the entry for **house:**

house 1. *n* ➡ **home**
  2. *vb* accommodate, board, lodge, put up, shelter, quarter, billet

At the entry for **home,** you will find the noun "house" with 17 other synonyms and two more cross-references.

⇨ Antonym cross-references

Sometimes you can find a clearer way to express your idea by putting it in opposite terms. **Antonym cross-references** direct you to main entries that are approximate opposites, or *antonyms,* of the entry where they are found. If you are not quite satisfied with any of the synonyms you have found, it may be helpful to check the antonym cross-references. Antonym cross-references are printed in **boldface italic** type following a white arrow ⇨, as at **punctual**:

punctual *adj* timely, prompt, precise, expeditious, punctilious ⇨ *late*

On-the-page Index

All of the synonyms in the *Scholastic Student Thesaurus* are listed alphabetically in the **on-the-page index** in the bottom portion of the page. Each word in the index is followed by a black arrow ➡ with one or more **main entries** where the index word is listed as a synonym:

class ➡ course, elegance
classic ➡ masterpiece, model
classified ➡ secret
classify ➡ arrange

If a word you are looking for is not a main entry, you should look in the **on-the-page index** on the same page where you looked for it as a main entry. Having the **on-the-page index** on the same pages as the main entries means that you will not have to look in two parts of the book just to get started in your search for the right word. For example, if you look up the word **silly**, you will find that it is not a main entry on page 169. The main entries go from **signature** to **skeptic**. On the bottom of that same page, however, you will find "silly" in the **on-the-page index**:

silly ➡ foolish

All you need to do now is turn to the main entry for **foolish**, where there are 10 synonyms, including "silly," and three more cross-references.

Guide Words

The **guide words** at the top left and right corners of the pages give the first and last words alphabetically on each page, including both the **main entries** and the **on-the-page index**.

An Important Reminder

Teachers have one common complaint about the way thesauruses are used. They complain that often students will pick an unfamiliar synonym without realizing that it does not fit properly into the sentence where they put it. Remember that **no two synonyms mean *exactly* the same thing**. Sometimes synonyms are used in different grammatical constructions. If you have a feeling that a synonym is not quite right, trust your instincts. You can either look in a dictionary to find out more about it or pick another synonym that you are more sure of. Anytime you are not certain whether a synonym is just the one you want, or if you are not sure what it means, look it up in a dictionary. Or ask someone whose judgment and knowledge of the language you can trust.

A

abandon 1. *vb* quit, cease, discontinue, concede, abdicate, renounce, resign, forfeit, scuttle ➡ **surrender, discard**
2. *vb* ➡ **leave, betray**

abandoned *adj* deserted, desolate, forsaken, uninhabited, neglected, rejected, derelict ➡ **empty**

abbreviation *n* acronym, initialism, contraction, abridgment, shortening

ability *n* capability, capacity, competence, aptitude, proficiency, ingenuity, faculty, power, efficacy ➡ **strength, talent**

able 1. *adj* capable, competent, qualified, eligible, authorized, suitable, fit
2. *adj* accomplished, proficient, skillful, adept, clever, handy, dexterous, deft ➡ **smart, expert, practical**

abolish *vb* end, eradicate, exterminate, eliminate, revoke, cancel, obliterate, repeal, rescind, annul, nullify, countermand, disallow, veto, overrule ➡ **finish, destroy, erase** ⇨ *save*

about 1. *adv* approximately, around, roughly, nearly, almost ➡ **practically**
2. *adv* around, round, all around, everywhere, nearby
3. *prep* concerning, regarding, touching, relating to
4. *prep* around, near, at

above 1. *prep* over, on, higher than, upon ⇨ *under*
2. *prep* over, more than, beyond, exceeding
3. *adv* over, overhead, up, upward, upwards, aloft ⇨ *under*

abroad *adj* overseas, away, traveling, touring

abrupt 1. *adj* blunt, hurried, impetuous, brusque, curt, short, gruff ➡ **rude, thoughtless**
2. *adj* ➡ **steep**
3. *adj* ➡ **sudden, sharp**

absence 1. *n* nonattendance, truancy, absenteeism ⇨ *presence*
2. *n* deficiency, dearth, lack ➡ **want**

absent *adj* away, missing, elsewhere, astray, AWOL ➡ **lost** ⇨ *present*

If the word you want is not a main entry above, look below to find it.

abase ➡ shame

abash ➡ embarrass, confuse

abashed ➡ ashamed

abate ➡ decrease

abbess ➡ religious

abbey ➡ monastery

abbot ➡ religious

abbreviate ➡ condense

abbreviated ➡ short

abdicate ➡ abandon

abdication ➡ surrender

abdomen ➡ stomach

abduct ➡ seize

aberration ➡ oddity, departure

abhor ➡ hate

abhorrence ➡ hatred

abide ➡ bear, live[1], wait

abiding ➡ permanent

abject ➡ poor, servile

ablaze ➡ burning

abnormal ➡ strange

abnormality ➡ oddity

abode ➡ home

abominable ➡ bad

abominate ➡ hate

aboriginal ➡ primitive, native

abortive ➡ useless

abounding ➡ abundant

above all ➡ best

abrade ➡ rub

abrasion ➡ friction

abreast ➡ parallel

abridge ➡ condense

abridged ➡ short

abridgment ➡ abbreviation, summary

abscess ➡ sore

absentee ➡ runaway

absenteeism ➡ absence

➡ = synonym cross-reference • ⇨ = antonym cross-reference

15

absentminded *adj* forgetful, preoccupied, distracted, inattentive, oblivious, scatterbrained, spacey (*informal*) ➡ **absorbed**

absorb 1. *vb* soak (up), digest, suck up, sop up
2. *vb* ➡ **learn, interest**

absorbed *adj* engrossed, engaged, intent, involved, preoccupied, immersed ➡ **thoughtful, absent-minded**

abstain *vb* refrain, forbear, forgo, renounce, shun, eschew ➡ **avoid**

abstinence *n* temperance, forbearance, denial, self-denial, self-restraint, austerity, moderation, celibacy

abundance *n* profusion, wealth, surplus, plethora, excess, plenty, lot, peck, slew, load, ton, glut

abundant *adj* plentiful, copious, ample, profuse, plenteous, generous, voluminous, abounding, bountiful, bounteous, prodigal, much ➡ **big, enough**

abuse 1. *vb* misuse, mistreat, torment, oppress, suppress, repress, ill-treat, maltreat, torture, persecute, victimize, molest, harass ➡ **hurt, insult, punish**
2. *n* misuse, mistreatment, ill-treatment, injury, harm, punishment, torture

accent 1. *n* stress, emphasis, prominence, beat, cadence, diacritic
2. *n* pronunciation, inflection, drawl, twang, burr ➡ **dialect**
3. *n* ➡ **decoration**
4. *vb* ➡ **emphasize**

accident 1. *n* mishap, setback ➡ **collision, disaster, emergency**
2. *n* ➡ **chance**

accidental *adj* incidental, coincidental, unintentional, fortuitous, inadvertent, unplanned, chance ➡ **lucky**

accidentally *adv* unintentionally, inadvertently, unwittingly, unconsciously, fortuitously, incidentally ⇨ *purposely*

accompany *vb* escort, attend, chaperon, chaperone, convoy ➡ **lead**

accuracy *n* exactness, precision, correctness, exactitude ➡ **truth**

If the word you want is not a main entry above, look below to find it.

absolute ➡ complete, certain, unconditional, dictatorial

absolutely ➡ very, certainly

absolution ➡ forgiveness

absolutism ➡ tyranny

absolve ➡ forgive

absorbing ➡ interesting

abstinent ➡ celibate

abstract ➡ theoretical, summary

abstruse ➡ obscure

absurd ➡ foolish, illogical

absurdity ➡ nonsense

abut ➡ border

abutting ➡ adjacent

abyss ➡ hole

academic ➡ theoretical, intellectual, teacher

academy ➡ school

accede ➡ agree, surrender

accelerate ➡ hurry

acceleration ➡ speed

accentuate ➡ emphasize

accept ➡ agree, approve, believe, receive, bear

acceptable ➡ fair

acceptance ➡ approval

access ➡ door

accessible ➡ available, open

accession ➡ acquisition

accessory ➡ partner

acclaim ➡ approve, praise

acclamation ➡ praise

acclimatize ➡ adjust

accommodate ➡ adjust, house, contain, condescend

accommodation ➡ loan

accomplice ➡ partner

accomplish ➡ do

accomplished ➡ able, successful

accomplishment ➡ act, work, success

accord ➡ agree, agreement

accordingly ➡ therefore

accost ➡ approach, call

account ➡ story, description, supply

accoutrement ➡ equipment

accumulate ➡ gather

accurate ➡ correct, careful

accurately ➡ correctly

acquisition 1. *n* attainment, procurement, takeover, appropriation
2. *n* purchase, inheritance, possession, accession ➡ **property**

acrobat *n* gymnast, tumbler, aerialist, trapeze artist ➡ **athlete**

act 1. *vb* perform, work, function, operate, execute, stage, carry out, ply, serve, go ➡ **do**
2. *vb* behave, seem, appear
3. *vb* perform, play, enact, stage, portray, dramatize, impersonate, pose, render ➡ **pretend**
4. *n* deed, action, feat, accomplishment, achievement, exploit, undertaking, step ➡ **work**
5. *n* bill, law, decree, statute, ordinance, legislation ➡ **rule**
6. *n* performance, routine, number, sketch, bit, skit ➡ **pretense**

active *adj* animated, spirited, dynamic, busy, vibrant, bustling, frenetic, hyperactive, strenuous, athletic ➡ **lively, alive** ⇨ *passive*

activity 1. *n* action, motion, liveliness, commotion, bustle ➡ **movement** ⇨ *calm*
2. *n* ➡ **pastime, exercise**

actor *n* actress, performer, player, entertainer, star, thespian, ham ➡ **celebrity, comic, artist**

add 1. *vb* sum, total, calculate, compute, tally, count, score ⇨ *subtract*
2. *vb* combine, include, append, annex, supplement, incorporate, integrate ➡ **join**

addition 1. *n* reckoning, computing, summation, tabulating, counting ⇨ *subtraction*
2. *n* extension, expansion, annex, enlargement, appendix, complement, supplement, amendment, rider, codicil

adhesive 1. *n* glue, paste, mucilage, cement, epoxy, tape, Scotch tape (*trademark*), adhesive tape, masking tape, duct tape
2. *adj* ➡ **sticky**

adjacent 1. *adj* adjoining, neighboring, bordering, abutting, tangent, next, next door ➡ **near**
2. *prep* ➡ **beside**

If the word you want is not a main entry above, look below to find it.

accusation ➡ **complaint**
accuse ➡ **blame**
accused ➡ **defendant**
accustomed ➡ **usual**
ace ➡ **expert**
ache ➡ **pain, hurt**
achieve ➡ **do, win**
achievement ➡ **act, event, success**
acid ➡ **sour**
acidic ➡ **sour**
acknowledge ➡ **admit, answer, believe**
acknowledgment ➡ **gratitude, apology**

acme ➡ **top**
acquaint ➡ **introduce**
acquaintance ➡ **friend, introduction**
acquiesce ➡ **surrender**
acquiescence ➡ **surrender**
acquire ➡ **get**
acquisitive ➡ **greedy**
acquit ➡ **forgive**
acrid ➡ **smelly**
acrobatics ➡ **gymnastics**
acronym ➡ **abbreviation**
across from ➡ **opposite**
acting ➡ **temporary**

action ➡ **act, activity, fight, suit**
action figure ➡ **doll**
activate ➡ **start**
actress ➡ **actor**
actual ➡ **real**
actuality ➡ **certainty, event**
actually ➡ **really**
acute ➡ **sharp, smart, urgent**
ad ➡ **advertisement**
adage ➡ **saying**
adamant ➡ **resolute, hard**
adapt ➡ **adjust, prepare**
adaptation ➡ **translation**

added ➡ **more**
addict ➡ **fan**
addiction ➡ **habit**
additional ➡ **more**
additionally ➡ **more, besides**
address ➡ **approach, welcome, speech, destination**
adept ➡ **able**
adequate ➡ **enough, fair**
adequately ➡ **well**
adhere ➡ **stick, obey**
adhesive tape ➡ **adhesive**
adieu ➡ **good-bye**
adios ➡ **good-bye**

---

adjust *vb* alter, modify, regulate, adapt, tailor, accommodate, conform, acclimatize, orient ➡ **change, fix, arrange**

admit 1. *vb* acknowledge, confess, own, concede, confirm, allow ➡ **reveal**
2. *vb* ➡ **receive**

adopt 1. *vb* embrace, appropriate, assume, espouse ➡ **approve, choose, use**
2. *vb* foster, take in, raise, rear

adult 1. *adj* grown-up, mature, full-grown, ripe
2. *n* grown-up, man, woman ⇨ *child, baby*

advantage *n* benefit, profit, superiority, convenience, vantage, upper hand, asset, virtue, plus, avail

adventure *n* exploit, escapade, venture, enterprise, spree, lark, fling ➡ **event**

advertise *vb* publicize, announce, promote, proclaim, declare, broadcast, pitch, parade, flaunt, plug ➡ **tell, show**

advertisement *n* commercial, ad, notice, circular, flier, billboard, poster, promotion, pitch, plug ➡ **announcement**

advertising *n* promotion, publicity, hype, propaganda ➡ **advertisement**

advice *n* guidance, counsel, recommendation, suggestion, caution, admonition ➡ **tip, warning**

adviser *n* advisor, counselor, counsel, consultant, attorney, lawyer, advocate ➡ **teacher**

affect 1. *vb* influence, impress, move, sway
2. *vb* ➡ **act, pretend**
3. *n* ➡ **emotion**
*In the most common or frequent uses of **affect** and **effect**, **affect** is a verb and **effect** is a noun. There is also a verb **effect**, which you should be careful not to confuse with the verb **affect**. See* **effect.**

If the word you want is not a main entry above, look below to find it.

adjoin ➡ border

adjoining ➡ adjacent, beside

adjudge ➡ decide

adjudicate ➡ try

adjustment ➡ repair, correction

ad-lib ➡ invent

administer ➡ lead, govern

administration ➡ government, leadership

administrator ➡ official, principal

admirable ➡ good

admiration ➡ respect

admire ➡ love, respect

admission ➡ ticket

admonish ➡ scold, warn

admonition ➡ warning, advice

adolescence ➡ childhood

adolescent ➡ teenager, young

adorable ➡ cute

adoration ➡ love

adore ➡ love, worship

adoring ➡ loving

adorn ➡ decorate

adornment ➡ decoration

adroit ➡ expert

adroitness ➡ talent, agility

adulate ➡ flatter

adulation ➡ praise, worship

adulterate ➡ weaken

adulthood ➡ maturity

advance ➡ approach, go, promote, lend, progress, loan, forward

advanced ➡ gifted

advancement ➡ progress, promotion

advantageous ➡ useful

advent ➡ approach

adventuresome ➡ brave

adventurous ➡ brave

adversary ➡ enemy, opponent

adverse ➡ unfortunate, destructive

adversity ➡ hardship

advise ➡ suggest, warn

advisor ➡ adviser

advocate ➡ prefer, adviser

aerate ➡ fan

aerialist ➡ acrobat

aerobatics ➡ gymnastics

aerobics ➡ gymnastics

aeronaut ➡ pilot

aeronautics ➡ flight

affable ➡ nice

affair ➡ business

affectation ➡ pretense, habit

affection ➡ love

affectionate ➡ loving

affidavit ➡ document

affiliate ➡ member, department

affiliation ➡ link

n = noun • *vb* = verb • *adj* = adjective • *adv* = adverb • *prep* = preposition • *conj* = conjunction

afford *vb* pay for, support, bear, manage

afraid *adj* scared, frightened, alarmed, terrified, petrified, aghast, scared, timorous ➡ **anxious, nervous, cowardly** ⇨ *brave*

afternoon *n* p.m., midday, lunchtime, teatime ➡ **day, evening**

again *adv* once more, anew, afresh, over ➡ **encore**

agent 1. *n* representative, intermediary, middleman, broker, executor, liaison, delegate, spokesperson, go-between, handler ➡ **seller**
2. *n* ➡ **spy**

agile *adj* nimble, spry, quick, sprightly, dexterous, supple, limber ➡ **active**

agility *n* dexterity, nimbleness, adroitness, spryness ➡ **talent**

agree 1. *vb* consent, assent, concur, accept, accede ⇨ *argue, object*

2. *vb* match, correspond, coincide, harmonize, accord, jibe ➡ **suit**

agreement 1. *n* bargain, deal, contract, lease, treaty, pact, accord, covenant, compact, arrangement, compromise, understanding
2. *n* consent, assent, consensus, concurrence, compliance, conformity, sympathy, harmony ➡ **unity**

air 1. *n* sky, heaven, atmosphere, stratosphere, troposphere ➡ **space**
2. *n* breath, ventilation, oxygen ➡ **wind**
3. *n* ➡ **quality, appearance**
4. *vb* ➡ **broadcast, play, say**

airplane *n* aircraft, plane, flying machine ➡ **vehicle**

alert 1. *adj* attentive, wide-awake, watchful, vigilant, aware, conscious ➡ **awake**
2. *adj* ➡ **smart**
3. *vb* ➡ **warn**

If the word you want is not a main entry above, look below to find it.

affinity ➡ link, similarity, relationship

affirm ➡ believe, testify, approve

affirmative ➡ yes

afflict ➡ hurt, trouble

affliction ➡ hardship, illness, disability

affluence ➡ wealth

affluent ➡ rich

affordable ➡ cheap

affront ➡ insult

aficionado ➡ fan

afire ➡ burning

afresh ➡ again

aft ➡ back

after ➡ past

aftermath ➡ effect

aftershock ➡ earthquake

afterword ➡ conclusion

against ➡ beside, opposite

age ➡ period, weather

aged ➡ old

agency ➡ department

agenda ➡ list

aggravate ➡ bother

aggravated ➡ angry

aggregate ➡ total

aggression ➡ violence, anger

aggressive ➡ belligerent, ambitious

aghast ➡ afraid

agitate ➡ disturb, fan, excite

agitated ➡ tense

agitation ➡ excitement

agnostic ➡ atheist

agonizing ➡ uncomfortable

agony ➡ misery

agrarian ➡ farming

agreeable ➡ nice, pleasant, compatible

agricultural ➡ farming

agriculture ➡ farming

ahead ➡ forward

ahead of ➡ before

aid ➡ help, back

aide ➡ helper

ail ➡ trouble

ailing ➡ sick

ailment ➡ illness

aim ➡ object, plan, intend

aimless ➡ indiscriminate

aircraft ➡ airplane

airfield ➡ field

airless ➡ stuffy

airman ➡ pilot

airport ➡ field

airtight ➡ tight

airy ➡ windy

ajar ➡ open

akin ➡ alike

alarm ➡ fear, scare, warning

alarmed ➡ afraid

alcohol ➡ drink

alcoholic ➡ drunkard

alcove ➡ bay

alertness ➡ attention

➡ = synonym cross-reference • ⇨ = antonym cross-reference

alibi *n* defense, excuse, cover story

alike 1. *adj* similar, like, analogous, comparable, equivalent, parallel, close, akin ➡ **same** ⇨ *different*
2. *adv* similarly, likewise, comparably, analogously

alive *adj* living, live, animate, animated, vital, viable, quick, organic ➡ **lively, active** ⇨ *dead*

all 1. *n, pron* everything, everyone, everybody, sum, whole, totality ➡ **total**
2. *adj* every, entire, each, complete, whole, total
3. *adv* ➡ **completely**

alone *adj* lone, solitary, isolated, unaccompanied, unattended, solo, single-handed ➡ **lonely, single**

alternate 1. *vb* reciprocate, oscillate, fluctuate, switch
2. *adj* alternating, every other ➡ **periodic**
3. *n* substitute, replacement, backup, surrogate, double

amateur 1. *n* nonprofessional, novice, beginner, dilettante, apprentice, neophyte
2. *adj* amateurish, unskilled, inexperienced, untrained, inexpert, unpaid, green ➡ **clumsy, incompetent, naive**

ambition 1. *n* aspiration, drive, enterprise, eagerness, desire, will, get-up-and-go, initiative ➡ **hope, enthusiasm, energy**
2. *n* ➡ **object**

ambitious 1. *adj* eager, zealous, enterprising, determined, aggressive, industrious, resourceful ➡ **competitive** ⇨ *lazy*
2. *adj* ➡ **hard**

If the word you want is not a main entry above, look below to find it.

alfalfa ➡ hay

alfresco ➡ outside

alias ➡ pseudonym

alien ➡ foreign, foreigner

alight ➡ descend

align ➡ straighten

aligned ➡ parallel

alignment ➡ order

all around ➡ about

allay ➡ relieve

allegation ➡ complaint

allege ➡ argue

allegiance ➡ loyalty

alleviate ➡ relieve

alley ➡ road

alliance ➡ union

allocate ➡ budget

allot ➡ budget

allotment ➡ share, budget

allow ➡ let, admit

allowable ➡ legal

allowance ➡ share, wage, budget, loan

all right ➡ cool

allude ➡ mention

allure ➡ attraction, enchantment, personality

alluring ➡ attractive

ally ➡ friend

almighty ➡ strong

almost ➡ about

alms ➡ gift

aloft ➡ above

alongside ➡ beside, parallel

aloof ➡ cool

alphabetical ➡ consecutive

already ➡ before

also ➡ besides

alter ➡ change, adjust

alteration ➡ change

altercation ➡ fight

alternately ➡ instead

alternating ➡ alternate

alternative ➡ choice

alternatively ➡ instead

although ➡ but

altitude ➡ height

altogether ➡ completely

altruistic ➡ generous

always ➡ forever, regularly

a.m. ➡ morning

amalgam ➡ mixture

amalgamation ➡ union, mixture

amass ➡ gather

amateurish ➡ amateur

amaze ➡ surprise

amazed ➡ dumbfounded

amazement ➡ surprise

amazing ➡ awesome

ambassador ➡ diplomat, messenger

ambiance ➡ setting

ambiguity ➡ problem

ambiguous ➡ obscure

ambivalent ➡ doubtful

amble ➡ walk

ambush ➡ attack

amen ➡ yes

amend ➡ perfect, correct

amendment ➡ addition

amiability ➡ hospitality

amiable ➡ friendly

amicable ➡ peaceful

amid ➡ between

amidst ➡ between

n = noun • *vb* = verb • *adj* = adjective • *adv* = adverb • *pron* = pronoun • *conj* = conjunction

ammunition *n* munitions, matériel, ammo (*informal*), bullets, shells

ancestor *n* forebear, forefather, progenitor, forerunner, predecessor, antecedent, patriarch, matriarch, elder ➡ **parent**

ancestry *n* lineage, birth, descent, extraction, blood ➡ **family**

anchor 1. *n* mooring, grapnel, stay, mainstay ➡ **support, protection**
2. *n* ➡ **reporter**
3. *vb* ➡ **dock, join**

angel *n* spirit, sprite, archangel, seraph, cherub

anger 1. *n* rage, fury, wrath, temper, indignation, hostility, animosity, annoyance, ire, aggression, belligerence
2. *vb* infuriate, enrage, madden, incense, exasperate, outrage, upset, provoke, rile, antagonize, embitter ➡ **bother**

angry *adj* mad, furious, upset, annoyed, irritated, aggravated, exasperated, indignant, irate, infuriated, livid, bitter, sore ➡ **cross, belligerent, violent**

animal 1. *n* creature, beast, brute, being, organism ➡ **monster**
2. *adj* bestial, beastly, brutish

announcement *n* declaration, notice, notification, proclamation, report, statement, pronouncement, news, revelation, bulletin, message, tidings
➡ **advertisement**

anonymous *adj* unsigned, unnamed, unknown, pseudonymous, nameless, secret

---

If the word you want is not a main entry above, look below to find it.

amigo ➡ friend
amiss ➡ wrong
amity ➡ friendship, peace
ammo ➡ ammunition
amnesty ➡ forgiveness
among ➡ between, through
amongst ➡ between
amorous ➡ loving
amount ➡ number, total, price, measure
amphibian ➡ reptile
amphitheater ➡ hall
ample ➡ enough, abundant
amplify ➡ strengthen, lengthen, grow

amputate ➡ cut
amuse ➡ entertain
amusement ➡ entertainment, pleasure, humor, toy
amusement park ➡ carnival
amusing ➡ funny
analogous ➡ alike
analogously ➡ alike
analogue ➡ duplicate
analogy ➡ similarity
analysis ➡ study, reason
analyze ➡ study
anarchy ➡ confusion
anatomy ➡ body
anchorage ➡ harbor

ancient ➡ old
anecdote ➡ story
anesthetic ➡ drug
anew ➡ again
angelic ➡ innocent
angle ➡ corner, perspective
angleworm ➡ worm
anguish ➡ misery, sorrow
animal farm ➡ zoo
animals ➡ livestock
animate ➡ alive
animated ➡ alive, active
animation ➡ life
animosity ➡ anger, hatred

annex ➡ add, addition
annihilate ➡ destroy, kill
annihilation ➡ murder
announce ➡ tell, advertise
annoy ➡ bother
annoyance ➡ anger, nuisance
annoyed ➡ angry
annoying ➡ inconvenient
annual ➡ flower
annuity ➡ pension
annul ➡ abolish
anoint ➡ rub, bless
anomaly ➡ oddity
anon ➡ soon

➡ = synonym cross-reference • ⇨ = antonym cross-reference

answer 1. *n* reply, response, retort, rejoinder, riposte, reaction, reciprocation ⇨ **question**
2. *n* solution, key, result, explanation, resolution, product ⇨ **problem, question**
3. *vb* reply, respond, retort, acknowledge, echo, counter, react, reciprocate ⇨ **question**
4. *vb* ➡ **solve**
5. *vb* ➡ **satisfy**

anticipate 1. *vb* foresee, expect, look forward to ➡ **predict**
2. *vb* ➡ **hope**

antique 1. *n* heirloom, relic, curio, artifact, antiquity
2. *adj* ➡ **old**

anxious 1. *adj* worried, apprehensive, uneasy, disturbed, insecure ➡ **afraid, nervous, tense**
2. *adj* ➡ **eager**

any *pron* each, some, every, either ➡ **few**

anyway *adv* anyhow, nevertheless, nonetheless, however, regardless, notwithstanding, still

apart *adv* asunder, separately, independently ⇨ **together**

apathetic *adj* indifferent, unconcerned, unresponsive, uncaring, disinterested, nonchalant ➡ **listless, lazy, cool** ⇨ **eager**

apathy *n* indifference, unconcern, nonchalance, disinterest ➡ **boredom** ⇨ **enthusiasm**

apology *n* excuse, acknowledgment, regrets, explanation

apparently 1. *adv* evidently, seemingly, presumably, supposedly, reputedly ➡ **probably**
2. *adv* clearly, obviously, plainly, patently

appeal 1. *vb* petition, pray, supplicate, sue, invoke ➡ **beg, ask**
2. *vb* ➡ **fascinate**
3. *n* request, plea, claim, petition, application ➡ **invitation**
4. *n* ➡ **attraction**

appear 1. *vb* emerge, arise, rise, surface, materialize, come into view, show up, turn up, form ➡ **come**
2. *vb* ➡ **act**
3. *vb* ➡ **look**

If the word you want is not a main entry above, look below to find it.

another ➡ more, different

antagonism ➡ opposition, competition

antagonist ➡ enemy, opponent

antagonistic ➡ unfriendly, competitive

antagonize ➡ anger

antarctic ➡ cold

ante ➡ bet

antecedent ➡ ancestor, past

antedate ➡ precede

anteroom ➡ hall

anthem ➡ hymn

antibiotic ➡ drug

antic ➡ joke, funny

anticipated ➡ due

anticipation ➡ foresight, suspense

antidepressant ➡ drug

antidote ➡ cure

antipathy ➡ opposition, hatred

antiquated ➡ old

antiquity ➡ antique, past

antiseptic ➡ sterile

antisocial ➡ unfriendly

antithesis ➡ opposite

antithetical ➡ opposite

anxiety ➡ worry, fear

anyhow ➡ anyway

apartment ➡ home, room

ape ➡ boor, imitate

aperture ➡ hole

apex ➡ top

aphorism ➡ saying

apocryphal ➡ legendary

apogee ➡ top

apologetic ➡ sorry

apologize ➡ regret

appall ➡ shock, disgust

appalling ➡ awful, scary

apparatus ➡ equipment, tool

apparel ➡ clothes

apparent ➡ obvious, likely

apparition ➡ ghost, illusion

appealing ➡ pleasant, attractive

n = noun • *vb* = verb • *adj* = adjective • *adv* = adverb • *pron* = pronoun • *conj* = conjunction

appearance 1. *n* look, looks, aspect, features, countenance, demeanor, air, atmosphere, bearing, mien, visage
2. *n* ➡ **approach**

appetite *n* hunger, thirst, craving ➡ **desire**

appointment 1. *n* selection, nomination, election, designation, assignment, delegation, installation, investiture, ordination ➡ **choice**
2. *n* ➡ **meeting, visit**
3. *n* ➡ **profession**

appreciate 1. *vb* value, prize, cherish, treasure, relish, savor ➡ **respect**
2. *vb* thank, enjoy ➡ **welcome**
3. *vb* ➡ **understand**

approach 1. *vb* come near, draw near, near, advance, loom, gravitate toward ➡ **come**
2. *vb* address, accost, speak to ➡ **talk**
⇨ *avoid*
3. *n* coming, arrival, appearance, advent, entry
4. *n* ➡ **method, treatment**

approval 1. *n* acceptance, passage, ratification, enactment ➡ **support, praise**
2. *n* ➡ **permission**

approve 1. *vb* endorse, support, authorize, sanction, certify, ratify, validate, legalize, affirm ➡ **agree, back**
2. *vb* accept, favor, applaud, recommend, acclaim, commend ➡ **appreciate**

approximate 1. *adj* rough, inexact, estimated, close, near, ballpark, general
2. *vb* ➡ **estimate**
3. *vb* ➡ **resemble**

arbitrary 1. *adj* chance, random, subjective, unpredictable, unscientific, haphazard, unplanned, careless, stray ➡ **indiscriminate**
2. *adj* capricious, frivolous, impulsive, whimsical ➡ **illogical**
3. *adj* willful, unreasonable ➡ **dictatorial**

If the word you want is not a main entry above, look below to find it.

appease ➡ pacify, soften, satisfy
appellation ➡ name
append ➡ add
appendage ➡ limb
appendix ➡ addition, table
appertain ➡ concern
appetizing ➡ delicious
applaud ➡ approve, clap
applause ➡ praise
appliance ➡ tool
applicable ➡ fit[1], relevant
applicant ➡ candidate
application ➡ use, diligence, appeal

apply ➡ belong, use, ask
appoint ➡ name, hire
apportion ➡ share, divide
apposite ➡ relevant, fit[1]
appraisal ➡ estimate
appreciation ➡ gratitude, wisdom
appreciative ➡ grateful
apprehend ➡ arrest, know
apprehension ➡ worry, fear, suspense, arrest
apprehensive ➡ anxious, suspicious
apprentice ➡ amateur
apprise ➡ introduce
approaching ➡ future

appropriate ➡ fit[1], correct, take, adopt
appropriately ➡ correctly
appropriation ➡ acquisition
approved ➡ official
approvingly ➡ well
approximately ➡ about
approximation ➡ estimate
apricot ➡ orange
apropos ➡ relevant
apt ➡ likely, fit[1], smart
aptitude ➡ talent, ability
aquarium ➡ zoo
aqueduct ➡ channel
aqueous ➡ liquid

arbiter ➡ judge
arbitrate ➡ negotiate, decide
arboretum ➡ greenhouse
arc ➡ curve
arcane ➡ secret
arch ➡ bend, curve
archaic ➡ old, early
archangel ➡ angel
archetypal ➡ model
archetype ➡ model
archfiend ➡ devil
archipelago ➡ island
architect ➡ creator
arctic ➡ cold

➡ = synonym cross-reference • ⇨ = antonym cross-reference

argue 1. *vb* quarrel, debate, dispute, disagree, bicker, squabble, quibble, wrangle ➡ **fight**
⇨ *agree*
2. *vb* claim, maintain, plead, assert, contend, allege, charge, protest

argument *n* quarrel, dispute, debate, controversy, discussion, squabble, row, fuss, falling-out, disagreement, misunderstanding, spat, tiff ➡ **fight, disagreement**

aristocracy *n* nobility, gentry, elite, upper class, society, high society, haut monde (*French*), jet set, rich

arm 1. *n* forelimb, forearm ➡ **limb**
2. *n* ➡ **branch**
3. *n* ➡ **bay**

arms *n* weapons, weaponry, armament, ordnance, artillery, matériel, armor ➡ **gun**

army 1. *n* force, armed force, troops, military, service, militia, legion ➡ **troop, soldier**
2. *n* ➡ **crowd**

arrange 1. *vb* organize, sort, classify, order, file, systematize, categorize, determine, array, structure, place, rank, orient, orientate ➡ **adjust, straighten**
2. *vb* plan, devise, set up, schedule

arrest 1. *vb* apprehend, detain, take prisoner, bust (*informal*), collar (*informal*), nab (*informal*) ➡ **catch, seize**
2. *vb* ➡ **stop**
3. *n* capture, seizure, detention, apprehension

art *n* skill, craft, technique, artistry, craftsmanship, creativity, artifice ➡ **talent**

articulate 1. *adj* intelligible, understandable, eloquent, lucid, fluent, clear, coherent
2. *vb* ➡ **pronounce**

artist *n* painter, sculptor, artisan, craftsman ➡ **musician, actor, photographer, writer, creator**

If the word you want is not a main entry above, look below to find it.

ardent ➡ eager, loving

ardor ➡ enthusiasm

arduous ➡ hard

area ➡ space, zone, field

arena ➡ field, hall

argot ➡ dialect

arid ➡ dry, sterile

arise ➡ ascend, descend, appear, happen

aristocrat ➡ noble

aristocratic ➡ noble

armada ➡ navy

armament ➡ arms

armed ➡ military

armed force ➡ army

armistice ➡ truce

armoire ➡ closet

armor ➡ arms

armory ➡ warehouse

aroma ➡ smell

aromatic ➡ fragrant

around ➡ about, through

arouse ➡ wake, excite, fan

arraign ➡ try

arrangement ➡ order, structure, display, bouquet, agreement, score

array ➡ assortment, display, arrange, deploy, dress

arrears ➡ debt

arrival ➡ approach, return

arrive ➡ come

arrivederci ➡ good-bye

arrogance ➡ pride

arrogant ➡ proud, dogmatic

arrow ➡ missile

arroyo ➡ canyon

arsenal ➡ warehouse

artery ➡ blood vessel, channel, road

artful ➡ sly

art gallery ➡ gallery

article ➡ object, report

articulation ➡ speech, word

artifact ➡ antique

artifice ➡ art, trick

artificial ➡ fake, manufactured

artillery ➡ arms

artisan ➡ artist

artistic ➡ talented

artistry ➡ art

artless ➡ naive

n = noun • *vb* = verb • *adj* = adjective • *adv* = adverb • *prep* = preposition • *conj* = conjunction

ascend *vb* climb, rise, mount, arise ⇨ *descend*

ashamed *adj* humiliated, mortified, chagrined, embarrassed, shamed, abashed ➡ **sorry**

ask *vb* inquire, request, question, interrogate, query, quiz, examine, interview, grill, petition, apply ➡ **beg**

asleep *adj* sleeping, dozing, napping, resting, dreaming, somnolent, slumbering, dormant, hibernating ➡ **unconscious** ⇨ *awake*

assembly 1. *n* ➡ **meeting, committee, government**
2. *n* construction, building, creation, erection, fabrication, production, manufacture, formation

assortment *n* variety, mix, selection, collection, compilation, array, miscellany, range, series, gamut, medley, potpourri, hash ➡ **pile, mess**

assume 1. *vb* presume, postulate, presuppose, surmise, gather ➡ **guess, believe, pretend**
2. *vb* ➡ **adopt, bear**

atheist *n* agnostic, deist, freethinker, unbeliever, nonbeliever, infidel, heathen ➡ **skeptic**

athlete *n* player, competitor, contender, sportsman, sportswoman, jock (*informal*) ➡ **contestant**

atom *n* molecule

If the word you want is not a main entry above, look below to find it.

as ➡ because

ascendancy ➡ victory

ascension ➡ climb

ascent ➡ slant, climb

ascertain ➡ learn, verify, infer

ascetic ➡ hermit

ascot ➡ tie, scarf

ascribe ➡ attribute

ashen ➡ pale

ashram ➡ monastery

asinine ➡ foolish

askance ➡ sideways

askew ➡ zigzag

aspect ➡ appearance, part

asphyxiate ➡ choke

aspirant ➡ candidate

aspiration ➡ ambition, hope

aspire ➡ hope

assail ➡ attack

assailant ➡ enemy

assassin ➡ killer

assassinate ➡ kill

assassination ➡ murder

assault ➡ attack

assemble ➡ build, gather

assembly plant ➡ factory

assent ➡ agree, agreement

assert ➡ insist, argue

assertion ➡ boast

assertive ➡ certain

assess ➡ estimate, charge

assessment ➡ estimate, tax

asset ➡ advantage

assets ➡ property, wealth

assiduous ➡ patient, diligent

assign ➡ name, attribute, place

assignment ➡ appointment, job, lesson

assimilate ➡ learn

assist ➡ help

assistance ➡ support, help

assistant ➡ helper

associate ➡ friend, partner, join, mix

association ➡ organization, union, link

assonant ➡ musical

assorted ➡ different

assuage ➡ soften

assumption ➡ theory, conclusion

assurance ➡ promise, certainty

assure ➡ guarantee, promise, verify

assured ➡ certain, resolute

asteroid ➡ meteor

astonish ➡ surprise

astonished ➡ dumbfounded

astonishing ➡ awesome

astonishment ➡ surprise

astound ➡ shock

astounding ➡ great

astray ➡ absent

astrologer ➡ prophet

astute ➡ smart

asunder ➡ apart

asylum ➡ protection

at ➡ about

athletic ➡ strong, active

athletic field ➡ field

atmosphere ➡ air, appearance, quality

atoll ➡ island

atone ➡ pay

atrium ➡ court

atrocious ➡ awful

attach ➡ join, attribute

attaché ➡ diplomat

attached ➡ married

attachment ➡ link, love

➡ = synonym cross-reference • ⇨ = antonym cross-reference

attack 1. *vb* invade, assault, charge, ambush, waylay, mug, storm, raid, beseige, harry, assail, ravage, bombard, ravage, strike ➡ **fight, argue, pillage** ⇨ *protect*
2. *n* assault, raid, invasion, charge, offensive, offense, incursion, strike, sally, sortie, foray, onset, onslaught, counterattack, operation, sack
3. *n* ➡ **fit²**

attention 1. *n* concentration, awareness, alertness, thought, consideration ➡ **diligence**
2. *n* ➡ **notice**

attic *n* loft, garret, dormer ➡ **room**

attraction *n* allure, appeal, charm, draw, fascination, enticement, temptation, lure, seduction ➡ **pull, personality**

attractive *adj* appealing, fascinating, captivating, magnetic, alluring, inviting, desirable, intriguing, charming, charismatic, winning ➡ **pretty, pleasant**

attribute 1. *n* ➡ **quality**
2. *vb* ascribe, assign, attach, credit ➡ **join**

audacity 1. *n* ➡ **courage**
2. *n* nerve, cheek, impertinence, insolence, temerity, gall

audible *adj* perceptible, discernible, distinct, clear ➡ **loud** ⇨ *quiet*

audience *n* spectators, viewers, onlookers, readers, listeners, patrons, congregation, gallery ➡ **meeting, patron**

automatic 1. *adj* automated, mechanical, mechanized, motorized, self-starting, self-acting, computerized
2. *adj* habitual, involuntary, instinctive, mechanical, spontaneous, reflex, unintentional

---

If the word you want is not a main entry above, look below to find it.

attacker ➡ enemy

attain ➡ finish, come

attainment ➡ acquisition, success

attempt ➡ try

attend ➡ accompany, frequent, concentrate, listen

attendance ➡ presence

attendant ➡ servant, doorman

attendants ➡ court

attentive ➡ alert, loving

attentiveness ➡ diligence

attenuate ➡ weaken

attest ➡ testify

attire ➡ clothes, dress

attitude ➡ belief, perspective, posture

attorney ➡ adviser

attract ➡ pull, fascinate

attractiveness ➡ beauty

auction ➡ sale

audacious ➡ brave, rude

audiobook ➡ book

audition ➡ tryout

auditorium ➡ hall

auf Wiedersehen ➡ good-bye

augment ➡ strengthen, grow

augur ➡ predict

augury ➡ prediction

august ➡ grand, dignified

au revoir ➡ good-bye

aurora ➡ halo

auspicious ➡ lucky, successful

austere ➡ empty, hard, plain, strict

austerity ➡ abstinence, economy

authentic ➡ real, correct, official

authenticate ➡ verify

authentication ➡ proof

authenticity ➡ truth

author ➡ writer, creator, write

authoritarian ➡ dictator, dictatorial

authoritative ➡ infallible,

model

authorities ➡ police

authority ➡ basis, right, expert, permission, rule

authorization ➡ permission

authorize ➡ approve, let

authorized ➡ official, able

autocrat ➡ dictator

autocratic ➡ dictatorial

autograph ➡ signature, sign

automated ➡ automatic

automobile ➡ vehicle

autonomous ➡ free

autonomy ➡ freedom

auxiliary ➡ subordinate

avail ➡ help, advantage

n = noun • *vb* = verb • *adj* = adjective • *adv* = adverb • *prep* = preposition • *conj* = conjunction

available *adj* accessible, usable, convenient, handy ➡ **ready**

avalanche *n* slide, landslide, mudslide, rockslide

average 1. *adj* unexceptional, mediocre, unremarkable, standard, routine, medium, modest ➡ **common, normal**
2. *n* mean, median, midpoint, standard, medium, par, norm

avoid *vb* shun, dodge, evade, shirk, duck, sidestep, elude, avert, bypass, circumvent ➡ **escape**

awake 1. *adj* conscious, up, sleepless, wakeful ➡ **alert** ⇨ *asleep*
2. *vb* ➡ **wake**

award 1. *n* honor, decoration, medal, ribbon, citation ➡ **prize**
2. *n* grant, scholarship, fellowship ➡ **prize**
3. *vb* ➡ **give**

awesome 1. *adj* amazing, impressive, astonishing, miraculous, terrific, sensational ➡ **grand, great**
2. *adj* ➡ **scary**

awful *adj* terrible, horrible, dreadful, dire, ghastly, appalling, wretched, grievous, disagreeable, atrocious, outrageous, disgraceful, hateful, odious ➡ **bad, gruesome**

ax, axe *n* hatchet, tomahawk, broadax, pickax, poleax

axis *n* pivot, fulcrum, swivel, hinge ➡ **middle**

If the word you want is not a main entry above, look below to find it.

avarice ➡ greed

avaricious ➡ greedy

avenge ➡ revenge

avenging ➡ revengeful

avenue ➡ road

averse ➡ reluctant

aversion ➡ opposition, hatred

avert ➡ prevent, avoid

aviary ➡ zoo

aviation ➡ flight

aviator ➡ pilot

avid ➡ eager

avocation ➡ pastime, profession

await ➡ wait

awaken ➡ wake

aware ➡ alert

awareness ➡ attention, knowledge

away ➡ absent, abroad

awe ➡ respect, shock

awe-inspiring ➡ grand

awfully ➡ very

awkward ➡ clumsy, inconvenient

AWOL ➡ absent

awry ➡ wrong

axiom ➡ saying, rule

aye ➡ yes

azure ➡ blue

➡ = synonym cross-reference • ⇨ = antonym cross-reference

B

baby 1. *n* infant, newborn, toddler, babe, tot
➡ **child** ⇨ *adult*
2. *vb* ➡ **pamper**

back 1. *n* rear, posterior, end, rear end, backside, stern (*of a boat or ship*), aft (*of a boat or ship*), tail (*of an animal or plane*), hindquarters (*of an animal*), rump (*of an animal*), haunch (*of an animal*), reverse (*of a coin or page*) ⇨ *front*
2. *vb* aid, finance, sponsor, fund, promote
➡ **approve, support, help**
3. *vb* back up, reverse ➡ **retreat**
4. *adj, adv* ➡ **backward**

background 1. *n* backdrop, distance, landscape
➡ **setting**
2. *n* ➡ **experience**

backward 1. *adj* backwards, rearward, reversed, behind, retrograde, regressive
➡ **underdeveloped** ⇨ *forward*
2. *adv* backwards, back, rearward, behind, regressively, reversed

bad 1. *adj* evil, sinful, naughty, infamous, villainous, nefarious, incorrigible, disreputable
➡ **wicked, improper, mischievous, dishonest, immoral** ⇨ *good*
2. *adj* unpleasant, disagreeable, undesirable, objectionable, miserable, lousy, nasty, offensive, abominable, repulsive, detestable, despicable, vile, nauseating, sickening, unsavory, disgusting, obnoxious, distasteful ➡ **awful**
3. *adj* rotten, spoiled, rancid, decayed, putrid, moldy ➡ **stale**
4. *adj* ➡ **sad**
5. *adj* ➡ **unhealthy**
6. *adj* ➡ **wrong**

badge *n* insignia, emblem, shield, medallion, escutcheon

bag 1. *n* sack, pouch, purse, handbag, pocketbook, satchel, tote bag, tote, backpack, pack, knapsack, fanny pack ➡ **container, luggage, wallet**
2. *n* ➡ **base**
3. *vb* ➡ **catch**

balance 1. *n* stability, equilibrium, footing, poise
2. *n* symmetry, harmony, counterbalance, proportion, equilibrium
3. *n* ➡ **remainder**
4. *vb* stabilize, counterbalance, steady, poise, counterpoise, neutralize, equalize, redeem, compensate, coordinate, offset

---

If the word you want is not a main entry above, look below to find it.

babble ➡ chatter

babe ➡ baby

baby blue ➡ blue

baby doll ➡ doll

babyhood ➡ childhood

back down ➡ retreat

backdrop ➡ background, setting

backer ➡ support

backing ➡ support

back out ➡ retreat

backpack ➡ bag

backside ➡ back

backslide ➡ relapse

backup ➡ alternate

backwards ➡ backward

backwoods ➡ country, rural

backwoodsman ➡ pioneer

badger ➡ bother

badlands ➡ desert

bad-tempered ➡ cross

baffle ➡ confuse

bafflement ➡ confusion

baffling ➡ mysterious

baggage ➡ luggage

baggage carrier ➡ porter

baguette ➡ bread

bailiwick ➡ field

bait ➡ tempt

bake ➡ cook

baked goods ➡ pastry

baker ➡ cook

n = noun • *vb* = verb • *adj* = adjective • *adv* = adverb • *prep* = preposition • *conj* = conjunction

bald 1. *adj* hairless, bald-headed, bare ➡ **naked**
2. *adj* flagrant, outright, unadorned, blunt, forthright ➡ **obvious**

ball 1. *n* globe, sphere, orb, globule, drop, pellet, bead, pearl
2. *n* ➡ **dance**
3. *n* ➡ **foot**

ballot *n* slate, ticket, lineup ➡ **vote, choice**

ban 1. *vb* ➡ **forbid**
2. *n* prohibition, embargo, proscription, restriction, injunction, boycott, sanction

band 1. *n* ➡ **group**
2. *n* group, orchestra, ensemble, combo
3. *n* stripe, ribbon, belt, girdle, sash, tape, border, strip, streak, seam, vein ➡ **row, zone, ring**

bandage 1. *n* dressing, compress, Band-Aid (*trademark*), gauze
2. *vb* dress, bind, wrap, swathe

bang 1. *n* crash, crack, pop, boom, blast, explosion, report, thud, detonation, clang, rumble, clap, thunder ➡ **noise, knock**
2. *vb* rattle, clatter, clash, clank, bump ➡ **knock, hit, collide**

banish *vb* deport, exile, expel, expatriate, drive out, drive away, dispel, evict, ostracize ➡ **exclude, oust**

bank 1. *n* ➡ **hill, shore, cliff**
2. *n* savings bank, credit union, trust company, savings and loan, treasury, exchequer, repository, depository
3. *vb* save, deposit, invest
4. *vb* ➡ **slant**

bar 1. *n* rod, shaft, pole, crossbar, boom, rib, rail, stake, stripe, strip ➡ **stick**
2. *n* tavern, saloon, barroom, pub, cocktail lounge, lounge, nightclub, cabaret, brewery
3. *n* ➡ **block**
4. *n* ➡ **table**
5. *n* ➡ **court**
6. *vb* ➡ **lock**
7. *vb* block, obstruct, impede, thwart, hinder, restrict, handicap ➡ **prevent, exclude, forbid, delay**

bargain 1. *n* ➡ **agreement**
2. *n* discount, deal, good deal, buy, reduction, steal (*informal*) ➡ **sale**
3. *vb* ➡ **negotiate**

bark 1. *vb, n* yelp, yap, yip, howl, snarl, growl, woof ➡ **cry**
2. *n* ➡ **boat**
3. *n* ➡ **peel**

If the word you want is not a main entry above, look below to find it.

balanced ➡ sane

balderdash ➡ nonsense

bald-headed ➡ bald

baleful ➡ ominous

balk ➡ hesitate

ballad ➡ song

balloon ➡ swell

ballpark ➡ approximate

ball-peen hammer ➡ hammer

ballpoint ➡ pen

baloney ➡ nonsense

banal ➡ trite, common

banality ➡ cliché

Band-Aid® ➡ bandage

bandanna ➡ scarf

bandit ➡ criminal

bane ➡ poison

banishment ➡ exile, suspension

bankrupt ➡ ruin

banner ➡ flag

banquet ➡ feast, meal

banter ➡ joke

baptize ➡ bless

barb ➡ thorn

barbarian ➡ vandal

barbecue ➡ cook, fireplace

bard ➡ musician

bare ➡ empty, naked, bald, reveal

barely ➡ only, seldom

barf ➡ vomit

baritone ➡ low

barkeep ➡ host

➡ = synonym cross-reference • ⇨ = antonym cross-reference

barn *n* stable, stall, cow barn, cowshed, byre ➡ **shed, pen, building**

barrel *n* keg, vat, drum, cask, tub, hogshead, tun ➡ **container**

barrier *n* obstacle, obstruction, hindrance, hurdle, difficulty, impediment, barricade, roadblock, blockade, palisade, clog ➡ **divider**

base 1. *n* foundation, bottom, support, footing, foot, root ➡ **floor** ⇨ *top*
2. *n* ➡ **basis**
3. *n* headquarters, home, home base, base camp, camp, station, terminal
4. *n* plate, goal, bag, sack
5. *vb* found, ground, predicate, establish
6. *vb* locate, station, post, situate

basement *n* cellar, crypt, bunker, storm cellar, crawl space ➡ **room**

basic *adj* elemental, elementary, fundamental, staple, rudimentary, primitive, introductory, primary ➡ **necessary**

basis *n* foundation, support, justification, grounds, authority, underpinning, raison d'être, cornerstone, rudiment ➡ **base, cause**

bat 1. *n* club, stick, pole, mallet
2. *vb* ➡ **hit**

bathrobe *n* robe, dressing gown, negligee, peignoir

bathroom *n* washroom, rest room, lavatory, toilet, bath, women's room, men's room, latrine, head, facilities ➡ **room**

bay 1. *n* inlet, cove, bayou, lagoon, estuary, gulf, arm ➡ **harbor**
2. *n* alcove, niche, nook, recess
3. *vb* ➡ **cry**
4. *adj* ➡ **brown**

beam 1. *n* timber, rafter, stud, joist ➡ **bar, board**
2. *n* ➡ **light**[1]
3. *vb* ➡ **shine**
4. *vb* ➡ **smile**
5. *vb* ➡ **broadcast**

bear 1. *vb* endure, stand, tolerate, abide, stomach, suffer, accept, brook, take, shoulder, assume, undertake ➡ **experience**
2. *vb* ➡ **carry**
3. *vb* ➡ **support, afford**
4. *vb* ➡ **give**

beard *n* whiskers, goatee, Vandyke, stubble, five o'clock shadow, sideburns ➡ **hair**

bearing 1. *n* carriage, demeanor, manner, deportment, presence, mien ➡ **behavior, personality**
2. *n* ➡ **relevance**
3. *n* ➡ **course**
4. *n* ➡ **appearance, posture**

If the word you want is not a main entry above, look below to find it.

barrage ➡ flood	bash ➡ hit	bathing ➡ swim	bazaar ➡ market
barren ➡ sterile	bashful ➡ shy	baton ➡ stick	be ➡ live[1]
barrens ➡ desert	basically ➡ chiefly, practically	batter ➡ hit	beach ➡ shore
barricade ➡ barrier, wall	basin ➡ bowl, sink, valley	battle ➡ fight	beacon ➡ light[1]
barring ➡ but	bass ➡ low	battlefield ➡ field	bead ➡ trinket, drop, ball
barroom ➡ bar	bassinet ➡ bed	battleground ➡ field	beak ➡ nose
barrow ➡ grave	baste ➡ sew	bauble ➡ trinket	beaker ➡ glass
bartender ➡ host	batch ➡ number	bawdy ➡ dirty	bear on ➡ concern
barter ➡ trade, buy, sell	bath ➡ bathroom, cleaning	bawl ➡ cry	beast ➡ animal, monster
base camp ➡ base	bathe ➡ clean, swim	bayou ➡ bay, swamp	beastly ➡ animal

n = noun • *vb* = verb • *adj* = adjective • *adv* = adverb • *prep* = preposition • *conj* = conjunction

beautiful *adj* gorgeous, glamorous, exquisite, beauteous, elegant, stunning, ravishing, dazzling, magnificent ➡ **pretty** ⇨ *ugly*

beauty *n* attractiveness, loveliness, prettiness, elegance, winsomeness, pulchritude, grace, charm, good looks

because *conj* since, due to, for, as, on account of

bed 1. *n* couch, cot, futon, mattress, bedstead, bunk, berth, crib, cradle, bassinet, gurney, stretcher, litter
2. *n* ➡ **floor**

bedroom *n* bedchamber, boudoir, dormitory, guest room, nursery ➡ **room**

before 1. *adv* previously, formerly, earlier, already, beforehand, yet
2. *prep* prior to, ahead of, preceding ➡ **until**

beg *vb* implore, entreat, beseech, plead, urge, solicit, importune ➡ **ask**

beggar 1. *n* panhandler, tramp, bum, hobo, pauper, wretch, derelict, vagrant
2. *vb* ➡ **ruin**

beginning *n* origin, source, outset, onset, commencement, initiation, inauguration, start, birth, conception, genesis, infancy, threshold ➡ **front** ⇨ *finish, conclusion*

behavior 1. *n* conduct, manners, etiquette, decorum ➡ **bearing**
2. *n* performance, function, operation, execution

belief 1. *n* conviction, opinion, view, notion, mind, instinct, hunch, suspicion, attitude, sentiment ➡ **theory, idea, feeling, perspective**
2. *n* faith, trust, confidence, credit, credence, understanding ➡ **certainty**
3. *n* creed, doctrine, dogma, credo, principle ➡ **religion, philosophy, superstition**

believe 1. *vb* accept, think, hold, deem, trust, acknowledge, affirm, view ⇨ *deny*
2. *vb* ➡ **guess**

bell *n* chime, gong, carillon, buzzer, signal

belligerent *adj* hostile, aggressive, combative, contentious, bellicose, pugnacious, militant ➡ **angry, violent, unfriendly**

If the word you want is not a main entry above, look below to find it.

beat ➡ hit, defeat, mix, tick, accent, rhythm, round
beatify ➡ bless
beating ➡ defeat
beauteous ➡ beautiful
beautification ➡ decoration
beautify ➡ decorate
beckon ➡ call, wave
become ➡ suit
becoming ➡ pretty, correct
bed-and-breakfast ➡ hotel
bedazzle ➡ surprise
bedchamber ➡ bedroom
bedeck ➡ decorate

bedraggled ➡ messy
bedspread ➡ blanket
bedstead ➡ bed
bedtime ➡ night
befall ➡ happen
befit ➡ suit
be fond of ➡ like
beforehand ➡ before
befoul ➡ dirty
befuddle ➡ confuse
beget ➡ reproduce
begin ➡ start
beginner ➡ amateur
begrudge ➡ envy

begrudging ➡ jealous
beguile ➡ cheat, entertain, enchant
behave ➡ obey, act
behemoth ➡ giant
behest ➡ order
behind ➡ backward, late, past
behindhand ➡ late
behold ➡ see
beholden ➡ grateful
beige ➡ brown
being ➡ life, existence, animal, human being

belated ➡ late
belatedly ➡ late
belfry ➡ tower
believable ➡ possible
belittle ➡ ridicule, underestimate
bellboy ➡ porter
belles lettres ➡ literature
bellhop ➡ porter
bellicose ➡ belligerent, military
belligerence ➡ anger
bellow ➡ yell, cry
belly ➡ stomach

➡ = *synonym cross-reference* • ⇨ = *antonym cross-reference*

belong *vb* fit, go, fit in, pertain, apply, relate, concern

bend 1. *vb* twist, curve, wind, arch, warp, flex, buckle, bow, droop, veer, meander, thread, contort, distort ➡ **turn, slant** ⇨ *straighten*
2. *vb* bow, curtsy, genuflect, stoop, kneel, crouch, squat, duck, hunch, slouch, slump
3. *n* twist, kink, crimp, curl, tangle ➡ **curve, corner**

bent *adj* curved, twisted, warped, bowed, crooked, contorted, misshapen, gnarled ⇨ *straight*

beside *prep* next to, alongside, adjoining, adjacent to, against, near, with

besides 1. *adv* moreover, furthermore, plus, also, too, additionally
2. *prep* ➡ **but**

best 1. *adj* finest, choicest, first, prime, premium, optimum, preeminent, leading, unparalleled, unsurpassed, superlative, foremost, ultimate, supreme, prime, top, upper ➡ **good** ⇨ *worst*
2. *adv* most, above all ⇨ *least*
3. *vb* ➡ **defeat, exceed**

bet *n, vb* wager, venture, gamble, risk, stake, ante

betray 1. *vb* deceive, trick, tell on, inform on, double-cross, abandon ➡ **cheat**
2. *vb* ➡ **reveal**

better 1. *adj* finer, greater, preferable, improved, superior ➡ **good, best**
2. *adj* improved, improving, convalescent, convalescing ➡ **healthy**
3. *adv* ➡ **more**
4. *vb* ➡ **exceed**
5. *vb* ➡ **defeat**

between *prep* among, amid, amongst, amidst, betwixt ➡ **through**
  Note that **among** *refers to more than two people or things, and* **between** *most often refers to two, but sometimes more than two.*

big *adj* large, generous, substantial, considerable, giant, stout, stocky, great ➡ **huge, heavy, fat, infinite, abundant, high** ⇨ *small*

If the word you want is not a main entry above, look below to find it.

belongings ➡ property
beloved ➡ love, valuable
below ➡ under
belowground ➡ underground
belt ➡ band, zone, punch
bemoan ➡ regret
bench ➡ seat, court
benchmark ➡ measure
bendable ➡ flexible
beneath ➡ under
benefactor ➡ patron
beneficial ➡ useful
benefit ➡ worth, advantage, pension, help, prosper

benevolence ➡ generosity
benevolent ➡ kind
benign ➡ kind
bequeath ➡ leave, give
bequest ➡ inheritance, will
berate ➡ scold
berry ➡ fruit
berserk ➡ violent, insane
berth ➡ dock, bed
beseech ➡ beg
beseige ➡ attack
beset ➡ infest
besotted ➡ drunk
bestial ➡ animal

best-liked ➡ favorite
bestow ➡ give, leave
betrayal ➡ treason
betrothed ➡ married
betting ➡ gambling
betwixt ➡ between
beverage ➡ drink
bevy ➡ herd
bewail ➡ grieve, regret
bewilder ➡ confuse
bewildered ➡ dumbfounded
bewilderment ➡ confusion
bewitch ➡ enchant
bewitching ➡ magic

beyond ➡ above, past
bias ➡ prejudice, tendency
biased ➡ prejudiced
bicker ➡ argue
bicyclist ➡ rider
bid ➡ order, offer, try, estimate
bidding ➡ invitation
bifocals ➡ glasses
big house ➡ jail
bigoted ➡ prejudiced
bigotry ➡ prejudice

bill 1. *n* check, tab, invoice, charge, tally, statement ➡ **price, debt**
2. *n* ➡ **act**
3. *n* ➡ **nose**
4. *n* visor, peak, brim
5. *vb* ➡ **charge**

binge *n* spree, bout, fling

bird *n* fowl, songbird, seagull, waterfowl, wader, chick, fledgling ➡ **animal**

birth 1. *n* childbirth, delivery, nativity ⇨ *death*
2. *n* ➡ **beginning**
3. *n* ➡ **ancestry**

bit 1. *n* piece, fragment, particle, scrap, shred, chip, flake, fleck, trifle, snippet, snatch ➡ **bite, block, part**
2. *n* trace, hint, suggestion, shade, touch, lick, glimmer, dash, pinch, tang, modicum, jot, iota, shred
3. *n* ➡ **role, act**

bite 1. *vb* chew, gnaw, nibble, munch, taste, chomp, nip, snap
2. *n* morsel, taste, mouthful, nibble, scrap ➡ **bit, meal**

black *adj, n* ebony, jet, sable, raven, inky, pitch-black, coal-black ➡ **dark** ⇨ *white*

blame 1. *vb* censure, criticize, condemn, denounce, accuse, implicate, charge ➡ **try, scold** ⇨ *forgive*
2. *n* ➡ **guilt**

blank 1. *adj* ➡ **empty, clean**
2. *adj* expressionless, vacuous, impassive, vacant, deadpan, poker-faced

blanket 1. *n* cover, quilt, comforter, duvet, featherbed, bedspread, sheet, shroud
2. *n* ➡ **coat**
3. *adj* ➡ **comprehensive**
4. *vb* ➡ **cover**

bleach *vb* fade, whiten, blanch, lighten, pale

bleak *adj* dreary, desolate, somber, grim, depressing, drear, hopeless, cheerless, gloomy, oppressive, dismal, dour ➡ **sad, sterile, pessimistic**

bless *vb* consecrate, sanctify, dedicate, exalt, hallow, beatify, glorify, anoint, baptize, ordain

blind 1. *adj* sightless, visually impaired, visionless, eyeless, unseeing
2. *adj* ➡ **unaware**

If the word you want is not a main entry above, look below to find it.

billboard ➡ **advertisement**
billet ➡ **house**
billfold ➡ **wallet**
billow ➡ **wave, cloud**
bind ➡ **tie, wrap, bandage**
binocular ➡ **glass**
biographer ➡ **writer**
birthplace ➡ **source**
biscuit ➡ **bread**
bishop ➡ **priest**

bistro ➡ **restaurant**
biting ➡ **sharp**
bitter ➡ **sour, sharp, hard, angry**
bizarre ➡ **strange**
blackfly ➡ **fly**
blackness ➡ **dark**
blade ➡ **knife**
blameless ➡ **innocent**
blameworthy ➡ **guilty**

blanch ➡ **bleach**
bland ➡ **insipid**
blasé ➡ **bored**
blaspheme ➡ **curse**
blasphemy ➡ **curse**
blast ➡ **bang, blow[1], wind, shoot**
blatant ➡ **obvious**
blather ➡ **chatter**
blaze ➡ **burn, fire**

blazer ➡ **coat**
blazing ➡ **bright, burning**
bleached ➡ **fair**
bleachers ➡ **seat**
bleeding ➡ **bloody**
blemish ➡ **spot, defect, scar**
blend ➡ **mix, mixture**
blessed ➡ **holy**
blight ➡ **disease, fungus, destroy**

---

blink *vb* wink, flicker, flash, twinkle
➡ **shine**

block 1. *n* piece, chunk, cube, cake, slice, slab, bar, hunk, wedge ➡ **bit, part**
2. *n* ➡ **neighborhood, building**
3. *vb* ➡ **hide**
4. *vb* ➡ **bar**

blood vessel *n* artery, vein, capillary, duct

bloody *adj* bleeding, gory, bloodstained

blossom 1. *n* ➡ **flower**
2. *vb* bloom, flower, bud ➡ **grow, prosper**

blow¹ 1. *n* hit, stroke, strike, punch, slap, jab, lick, swat, kick, stab, poke, whack, thwack, smack ➡ **push**
2. *n* blast, impact, concussion, shock, wallop, jolt
3. *n* ➡ **shock**

blow² 1. *vb* waft, float, sail, drift ➡ **wave**
2. *vb* honk, toot, sound ➡ **play**
3. *vb* ➡ **breathe**
4. *n* ➡ **wind**

blue 1. *adj, n* navy, azure, turquoise, royal blue, powder blue, baby blue, sky blue
2. *adj* ➡ **sad**

blush *vb* flush, redden, color, glow

board 1. *n* plank, beam, slat, timber, lumber, rafter, joist, two-by-four
2. *n* meals, fare, keep ➡ **food**
3. *n* ➡ **committee**
4. *vb* ➡ **enter**
5. *vb* ➡ **house**

boast 1. *vb* brag, gloat, crow, show off, vaunt, swagger, exult
2. *n* brag, bragging, vaunt, claim, assertion, bluster, swagger, bravado

boat *n* ship, vessel, craft, bark

body 1. *n* build, physique, frame, anatomy, figure, form, torso, trunk
2. *n* corpse, carcass, cadaver, remains, skeleton, bones
3. *n* ➡ **human being**
4. *n* ➡ **group**
5. *n* ➡ **matter**
6. *n* ➡ **density**

bogeyman *n* bogey, bugaboo, goblin, hobgoblin, bugbear

boil 1. *vb* simmer, stew, seethe, parboil, bubble, poach ➡ **cook**
2. *n* ➡ **sore**

If the word you want is not a main entry above, look below to find it.

bliss ➡ heaven, pleasure

blissful ➡ ecstatic

blizzard ➡ storm, snow

blob ➡ lump

bloc ➡ group, party

blockade ➡ barrier

blockhead ➡ fool

blond, blonde ➡ fair, yellow

blood ➡ ancestry

bloodshed ➡ murder

bloodstained ➡ bloody

bloodthirsty ➡ predatory

bloom ➡ flower, blossom

blooper ➡ mistake

blot ➡ spot

blotch ➡ spot

blow up ➡ explode

blue-blooded ➡ noble

bluebottle ➡ fly

blueprint ➡ pattern

bluff ➡ cheat, cliff

blunder ➡ mistake

blunderbuss ➡ gun

blunt ➡ dull, bald, abrupt, straightforward

blurry ➡ dim

blushing ➡ red

bluster ➡ boast

blustery ➡ stormy, windy

B.O. ➡ sweat

boards ➡ stage

boating ➡ nautical

boatman ➡ sailor

bobby pin ➡ pin

bodily ➡ physical

body odor ➡ sweat

bog ➡ swamp

bogey ➡ bogeyman

bogus ➡ fake

boiler ➡ furnace

boiling ➡ hot

boisterous ➡ loud

bold ➡ brave, rude

boldness ➡ courage

bolster ➡ cushion, support

bolt ➡ lock, nail, missile, run, escape, eat

bombard ➡ attack

bombardment ➡ fire

bombastic ➡ pompous

bond 1. *n* shackle, chain, fetter, manacle, handcuff, restraint
2. *n* ➡ **link**

book *n* volume, publication, text, paperback, hardcover, work, tome, manual, handbook, audiobook, manuscript, script, libretto ➡ **pamphlet**

boor *n* lout, oaf, churl, bumpkin, yahoo, Philistine, ape, lummox, dullard

booth *n* stall, counter, kiosk, stand, cubicle, compartment, enclosure

booty *n* loot, plunder, spoils, winnings, contraband, pillage ➡ **prize**

border 1. *n* frontier, boundary, march, borderland ➡ **edge, circumference, band**
2. *vb* abut, adjoin, neighbor, bound, skirt, flank ➡ **join**

bored *adj* uninterested, jaded, blasé ➡ **tired**

boredom *n* ennui, apathy, tedium, monotony

borrow *vb* rent, hire, bum (*informal*), scrounge (*informal*), mooch (*informal*) ➡ **adopt, get, use**

boss 1. *n* chief, leader, head, director, employer, foreman, manager, supervisor, superior, captain, commander, skipper ➡ **principal, chairperson**
2. *vb* ➡ **lead, control**

bother 1. *vb* annoy, vex, tease, plague, pester, needle, aggravate, irk, nag, hound, badger, harass, bug, irritate, chafe, rankle ➡ **disturb, worry**
2. *n* ➡ **nuisance**

bottle *n* jug, pitcher, flask, canteen, carafe, ewer, crock, cruet ➡ **container**

bouquet 1. *n* bunch, posy, nosegay, arrangement, spray, garland
2. *n* ➡ **smell**

bowl *n* dish, vessel, basin, tureen, crock ➡ **container, kettle, plate**

If the word you want is not a main entry above, look below to find it.

bona fide ➡ real
bondage ➡ slavery
bones ➡ body
bonfire ➡ fire
bong ➡ ring
bonjour ➡ hello
bon mot ➡ joke
bonnet ➡ hat
bonus ➡ prize, tip
boo ➡ yell
boo-boo ➡ mistake
bookish ➡ educated
booklet ➡ pamphlet
boom ➡ bang, bar
boon ➡ gift
boondocks ➡ country

boorishness ➡ rudeness
boost ➡ lift, strengthen
boot ➡ shoe, kick
bordering ➡ adjacent
borderland ➡ border
bore ➡ dig, well, tire
boring ➡ dull
borough ➡ town, neighborhood
bosom ➡ chest
botch ➡ fumble
bothersome ➡ inconvenient
bottom ➡ base, floor, essence
bottomland ➡ swamp
boudoir ➡ bedroom

bough ➡ limb
boulder ➡ rock
boulevard ➡ road
bounce ➡ jump, reflect
bound ➡ jump, border
boundary ➡ edge, border, hedge
boundless ➡ infinite
bounteous ➡ abundant
bountiful ➡ abundant
bounty ➡ generosity
bourgeoisie ➡ people
bout ➡ game, period, binge
bow ➡ bend, curve, play, surrender, front
bowed ➡ bent

bow tie ➡ tie
box ➡ container, square, punch
boy ➡ child, man
boycott ➡ ban, forbid
boyfriend ➡ friend, love
boyhood ➡ childhood
boyish ➡ young
brace ➡ support, strengthen, pair
bracing ➡ brisk, cool
brackish ➡ salty
brad ➡ nail
brag ➡ boast
bragging ➡ boast

➡ = synonym cross-reference • ⇨ = antonym cross-reference

braid 1. *n* plait, pigtail, queue, twist
2. *vb* ➡ weave

branch 1. *n* limb, arm, wing, offshoot, fork, projection, tributary ➡ **stick, department**
2. *vb* ➡ **divide**

brave 1. *adj* courageous, heroic, fearless, valiant, valorous, gallant, bold, stalwart, daring, audacious, intrepid, dauntless, undaunted, adventurous, adventuresome, plucky, dashing
⇨ *afraid*
2. *vb* ➡ **face**

bread *n* loaf, biscuit, roll, baguette, tortilla ➡ **cake, pastry**

break 1. *vb* crack, shatter, smash, fracture, split, snap, crash, splinter, burst, rupture, crush, squash, chip ➡ **destroy, explode, separate**
2. *n* fracture, split, crack, rift, breach, gap, opening, chip, schism
3. *n* pause, recess, intermission, breather, respite, delay, interlude, interruption, lull, hiatus, suspension, disruption ➡ **vacation, rest, truce**
4. *vb* ➡ **disobey**

5. *vb* ➡ **defeat**
6. *n* ➡ **luck**

breakable *adj* fragile, delicate, dainty, brittle, flimsy, friable, crumbly ➡ **weak** ⇨ *unbreakable*

breath 1. *n* respiration, inhalation, exhalation, breathing
2. *n* ➡ **life**
3. *n* ➡ **air, wind**

breathe 1. *vb* inhale, exhale, respire, expire, pant, gasp, wheeze, puff, huff, gulp ➡ **mumble**
2. *vb* ➡ **live**[1]

brevity *n* conciseness, concision, succinctness, economy, terseness

bridge 1. *n* span, overpass, catwalk, gangway, gangplank, viaduct
2. *n* ➡ **link**
3. *vb* cross, connect, span ➡ **join**

bright 1. *adj* brilliant, glowing, radiant, sunny, dazzling, glaring, blazing, intense, luminous, colorful, gay, vivid, flashy ➡ **fair, shiny**
⇨ *dim, dull*
2. *adj* ➡ **happy**
3. *adj* ➡ **smart**

If the word you want is not a main entry above, look below to find it.

brain ➡ mind, genius
brake ➡ stop
bramble ➡ thorn
brand ➡ make, label
brandish ➡ swing
brand name ➡ make
brand-new ➡ new
brash ➡ rude
brat ➡ urchin
brava ➡ encore
bravado ➡ boast
bravery ➡ courage

bravissimo ➡ encore
bravo ➡ encore
brawl ➡ fight
brawny ➡ fat
breach ➡ break
breadth ➡ width
breadwinner ➡ worker
breaker ➡ wave
breakfast nook ➡ dining room
break out ➡ escape
breakthrough ➡ event, invention

break up ➡ separate
breakwater ➡ jetty
breast ➡ chest
breather ➡ break
breathing ➡ breath
breathtaking ➡ exciting
breed ➡ reproduce, grow, type
breeder ➡ farmer
breeding ➡ class, civilization
breeze ➡ wind

breezeway ➡ porch
breezy ➡ windy
brew ➡ cook
brewery ➡ bar
briar ➡ thorn
bride ➡ spouse
brief ➡ short
brier ➡ thorn
brig ➡ jail
brighten ➡ light[1]
brightness ➡ light[1]

bring *vb* fetch, deliver, lead, conduct, escort
➡ **take, lead, carry, pull**

brisk 1. *adj* crisp, bracing, invigorating
➡ **cold, cool**
2. *adj* ➡ **lively**

broach *vb* mention, bring up, introduce, raise ➡ **say**

broad *adj* wide, thick, deep, expansive, extensive, capacious ➡ **big** ⇨ *narrow*
Note that **broad** and **wide** are close synonyms in that both refer to the distance across something, as in "a **broad** street" or "a **wide** street." However, **broad** suggests the whole area or expanse of the surface itself and **wide** stresses more the distance from one side to the other. If you want to give the actual distance, use **wide**: three feet **wide, a yard wide.**

broadcast 1. *vb* transmit, beam, air, televise, telecast, relay ➡ **send, play**
2. *vb* ➡ **advertise**
3. *vb* ➡ **plant**
4. *n* ➡ **program**

broken 1. *adj* cracked, shattered, fractured, damaged, defective, faulty, malfunctioning, disabled, broken-down, down, unusable, out of order ➡ **useless**
2. *adj* ➡ **tame**

brown *adj, n* tan, chestnut, beige, fawn, tawny, khaki, bay, bronze, chocolate, taupe, umber ➡ **dark**

brush 1. *n* underbrush, undergrowth, shrubbery, scrub, thicket, bushes ➡ **hedge**
2. *n* ➡ **meeting**
3. *vb* ➡ **clean, sweep, rub**
4. *vb* ➡ **comb**

budget 1. *n* finances, expenses, allotment, allowance, resources
2. *vb* allot, allocate, ration, estimate ➡ **share**
3. *adj* ➡ **cheap**

bug 1. *n* insect, beetle, spider, vermin, pest
2. *n* ➡ **disease, germ**
3. *vb* ➡ **bother**

If the word you want is not a main entry above, look below to find it.

brilliance ➡ light[1]

brilliant ➡ bright, smart, jewel

brim ➡ bill, edge

brimful ➡ full

bring up ➡ broach

brink ➡ edge

briny ➡ salty

brittle ➡ breakable

broadax ➡ ax, axe

broad-minded ➡ liberal

broadside ➡ sideways

broadsword ➡ sword

brochure ➡ pamphlet

broil ➡ cook

broiling ➡ hot

broke ➡ poor

broken-down ➡ broken, shabby

broker ➡ agent

bromide ➡ cliché

bronze ➡ brown, statue

brooch ➡ pin

brood ➡ worry, mope, herd

brook ➡ river, bear

brother ➡ religious

brotherhood ➡ friendship

brownie ➡ fairy

browse ➡ read, eat

bruise ➡ hurt

bruised ➡ sore

brunette ➡ dark

brusque ➡ abrupt

brutal ➡ sharp, mean

brutality ➡ violence

brute ➡ animal, monster

brutish ➡ animal

bubble ➡ boil

bubbles ➡ foam

buccaneer ➡ pirate

bucket ➡ container

buckle ➡ clasp, join, bend

bud ➡ flower, blossom, shoot

buddy ➡ friend

budge ➡ move

budgetary ➡ financial

buff ➡ shine

buffer ➡ cushion, protection

buffet ➡ hit, cupboard

buffoon ➡ fool

bugaboo ➡ bogeyman

bugbear ➡ bogeyman

buggy ➡ wagon

build 1. *vb* construct, erect, assemble, raise, fabricate, fashion ➡ **form, invent, make**
⇨ *destroy*
2. *vb* ➡ **strengthen**
3. *n* ➡ **body**

building 1. *n* structure, edifice, block, shelter ➡ **house, hall**
2. *n* ➡ **assembly**

bulge 1. *n* bump, lump, hump, knob, swelling, protrusion, protuberance
2. *vb* ➡ **swell**

bully 1. *n* ruffian, troublemaker, tyrant, tormentor, tough, rowdy, hooligan ➡ **rascal, criminal**
2. *vb* ➡ **threaten**

burn 1. *vb* blaze, flare, incinerate, scorch, singe, sear, char, glow ➡ **smoke, cook**
2. *vb* ➡ **hurt**

burning *adj* flaming, fiery, blazing, ablaze, afire, inflamed, smoldering ➡ **hot**

bury *vb* inter, entomb, lay to rest, enshrine, mummify, cremate ➡ **hide**

business 1. *n* industry, commerce, trade, traffic, manufacturing, finance, economics
2. *n* affair, matter, concern, transaction ➡ **job**
3. *n* company, firm, establishment, corporation, enterprise, outfit, partnership, concern ➡ **factory**

but 1. *conj* however, although, though, yet, except, nevertheless
2. *prep* except, besides, save, excluding, barring

buy 1. *vb* purchase, pay for, barter, shop ➡ **get, hire**
2. *n* ➡ **bargain**

If the word you want is not a main entry above, look below to find it.

bulb ➡ seed, flower, light[1]

bulk ➡ size, density, most

bulky ➡ clumsy, heavy

bulldoze ➡ dig

bullet ➡ missile

bulletin ➡ announcement

bullets ➡ ammunition

bullfrog ➡ frog

bullish ➡ optimistic

bullwhip ➡ whip

bulwark ➡ jetty

bum ➡ beggar, borrow

bumbling ➡ clumsy

bump ➡ hit, bang, bulge

bumpkin ➡ boor

bumpy ➡ rough

bunch ➡ group, number, bouquet

buncombe ➡ nonsense

bundle ➡ package, number

bung ➡ top

bungalow ➡ home

bungle ➡ fumble

bunk ➡ bed, nonsense

bunker ➡ basement

buoyant ➡ light[2]

burden ➡ load, worry

bureau ➡ chest, department

bureaucrat ➡ official

burglar ➡ criminal

burglarize ➡ steal

burglary ➡ theft

burial ground ➡ cemetery

buried ➡ underground

burlesque ➡ parody

burly ➡ strong

burnable ➡ inflammable

burner ➡ furnace

burnish ➡ shine

burr ➡ accent

burro ➡ donkey

burrow ➡ dig, den

burst ➡ break, explode

bush ➡ country, plant

bushes ➡ brush, hedge

businessman, businessperson, businesswoman ➡ tycoon

buss ➡ kiss

bust ➡ chest, statue, arrest

bustle ➡ activity

bustling ➡ active

busy ➡ active, employed

n = noun • *vb* = verb • *adj* = adjective • *adv* = adverb • *prep* = preposition • *conj* = conjunction

C

cake 1. *n* layer cake, coffee cake, fruitcake, cupcake, torte ➡ **pastry, bread**
2. *n* ➡ **block**
3. *vb* ➡ **harden**

call 1. *vb* summon, beckon, invite, page, accost ➡ **welcome, visit**
2. *vb, n* ➡ **yell**
3. *vb* phone, telephone, ring, dial, buzz
4. *vb* ➡ **name**
5. *n* ➡ **attraction**
6. *n* ➡ **reason**

calm 1. *adj* peaceful, serene, tranquil, placid, undisturbed, untroubled, composed, self-possessed, relaxed, poised ➡ **quiet, gentle**

2. *n* quiet, tranquility, peacefulness, serenity, stillness, composure, silence, hush ➡ **peace** ⇨ *activity*
3. *vb* quiet, relax, soothe, ease, comfort, compose, lull ➡ **pacify** ⇨ *excite*

candidate *n* nominee, aspirant, applicant, office-seeker, front-runner, dark horse, favorite son ➡ **contestant**

canyon *n* ravine, gorge, gully, arroyo, crevasse, crevice, chasm, gulch ➡ **valley**

cape 1. *n* peninsula, promontory, point, headland, neck, spit
2. *n* ➡ **wrap**

If the word you want is not a main entry above, look below to find it.

cab ➡ taxi

cabal ➡ party

cabaret ➡ bar

cabin ➡ shack, home

cabinet ➡ cupboard, committee

cable ➡ rope

cache ➡ supply

cackle ➡ laugh

cacophonous ➡ loud

cadaver ➡ body

cadence ➡ rhythm, accent

cadet ➡ soldier

café ➡ restaurant

cafeteria ➡ restaurant

cage ➡ pen

cajole ➡ persuade

calamitous ➡ destructive

calamity ➡ disaster

calcify ➡ harden

calculate ➡ add, estimate

calculation ➡ mathematics

calendar ➡ diary

caliber ➡ class

caliph ➡ emperor

caller ➡ visitor

calligraphy ➡ handwriting

calling ➡ profession

callous ➡ insensitive

camaraderie ➡ friendship

Camelot ➡ utopia

cameraman ➡ photographer

camouflage ➡ hide, disguise

camp ➡ base

campaign ➡ movement

campanile ➡ tower

campfire ➡ fire

can ➡ container, fire

canal ➡ channel

canard ➡ lie

cancel ➡ abolish

cancer ➡ growth

candid ➡ straightforward

candor ➡ truth, honesty

cane ➡ stick, whip

canine ➡ dog

cannon ➡ gun

canny ➡ smart

canon ➡ rule

canopy ➡ tent

cant ➡ slant, dialect

cantankerous ➡ cross

cantata ➡ hymn

canteen ➡ restaurant, bottle

canter ➡ run

canto ➡ stanza

cantor ➡ singer

canvass ➡ study

cap ➡ top, hat, climax

capability ➡ ability, sense

capable ➡ able

capacious ➡ broad

capacity ➡ function, ability, size, measure

caper ➡ joke, dance

capillary ➡ blood vessel

capital ➡ property, money, good

capitalist ➡ tycoon

capitulate ➡ surrender

capitulation ➡ surrender

caprice ➡ fancy, impulse

capricious ➡ arbitrary

capsize ➡ upset

capsule ➡ medicine

captain ➡ boss, control

caption ➡ headline

captivate ➡ fascinate

captivating ➡ attractive

captive ➡ prisoner

capture ➡ catch, arrest

---

carefree *adj* lighthearted, easygoing, nonchalant, casual, informal, untroubled, devil-may-care, laid-back, mellow ➡ **happy, calm**

careful 1. *adj* painstaking, thorough, exact, accurate, particular, precise, meticulous, conscientious, studious, scrupulous, nice
2. *adj* cautious, wary, prudent, concerned, circumspect, politic, discreet, judicious, guarded ➡ **alert, suspicious** ⇨ *thoughtless*

carefully 1. *adv* precisely, meticulously, deliberately, faithfully, thoroughly
2. *adv* cautiously, warily, prudently, discreetly, mindfully, gingerly, delicately

carnival *n* fair, circus, festival, amusement park, theme park

carry 1. *vb* move, transport, convey, bear, cart, pack, haul, transfer, tote, lug (*informal*) ➡ **take**
2. *vb* ➡ **sell**
3. *vb* ➡ **support**

carve *vb* sculpt, sculpture, whittle, etch, inscribe, engrave, incise, hew, chisel ➡ **cut**

cash register *n* register, till, cash box ➡ **safe**

castle *n* fortress, fort, garrison, fortification, stronghold, citadel, keep, donjon, palace

casualty 1. *n* victim, death, injury, fatality, dead
2. *n* ➡ **disaster**

catch 1. *vb* capture, trap, grasp, take, bag, snag, clasp, snare, ensnare, entangle, mire, enslave ➡ **seize, arrest** ⇨ *free*
2. *vb* pass, overtake, outrun, outstrip
3. *vb* contract, develop, come down with, incur ➡ **get**
4. *n* grab, snag, scoop
5. *n* ➡ **clasp, lock**
6. *n* ➡ **trap**

If the word you want is not a main entry above, look below to find it.

car ➡ vehicle

carafe ➡ bottle

carapace ➡ shell

carbine ➡ gun

carcass ➡ body

card ➡ letter

cardinal ➡ important, priest

care ➡ worry, diligence, protection, treatment

career ➡ profession, life

care for ➡ like

carefulness ➡ diligence

careless ➡ thoughtless, arbitrary

caress ➡ pet, embrace, touch

caretaker ➡ guardian, doorman

cargo ➡ load

caricature ➡ parody, imitate

carillon ➡ bell

caring ➡ loving

carjack ➡ seize

carmine ➡ red

carnage ➡ murder

carnivorous ➡ predatory

carol ➡ hymn

carouse ➡ celebrate

carpet ➡ rug, cover

carpeting ➡ rug

carport ➡ garage

carriage ➡ wagon, posture, bearing, gait

carrier ➡ messenger

carry on ➡ continue

carry out ➡ do, act, commit

cart ➡ carry, wagon

cartel ➡ monopoly

carton ➡ container

cartoon ➡ picture

cascade ➡ flood, flow

case ➡ container, example, suit

cash ➡ money

cash box ➡ cash register

casing ➡ shell

cask ➡ barrel

cast ➡ throw, form

castigate ➡ scold

cast off ➡ shed

castrate ➡ sterilize

casual ➡ carefree, spontaneous

cataclysm ➡ disaster

catacomb ➡ grave, cemetery

catalog ➡ list, table

catalogue ➡ list

catapult ➡ throw

catastrophe ➡ disaster

catastrophic ➡ destructive, unfortunate

catching ➡ contagious

categorization ➡ stereotype

categorize ➡ arrange, stereotype

category ➡ type

caterpillar ➡ larva

cathedral ➡ church

catholic ➡ universal

catnap ➡ sleep

cat-o'-nine-tails ➡ whip

cattle ➡ livestock

catwalk ➡ bridge

cauldron ➡ pot

n = noun • *vb* = verb • *adj* = adjective • *adv* = adverb • *prep* = preposition • *interj* = interjection

cause 1. *vb* produce, create, effect, generate, prompt, inspire, motivate, engender ➡ **start, make, do**
2. *n* origin, source, stimulus, basis ➡ **reason**
3. *n* principle, conviction ➡ **movement**

cave *n* cavern, tunnel, grotto, chamber ➡ **hole, den**

celebrate 1. *vb* observe, commemorate, keep, solemnize, honor ➡ **praise**
2. *vb* rejoice, carouse, revel, party

celebrity 1. *n* ➡ **fame**
2. *n* notable, luminary, personage, personality, name, star, superstar, dignitary, VIP ➡ **actor**

celibate *adj* abstinent, chaste, virginal, unmarried

cemetery *n* graveyard, burial ground, memorial park, churchyard, crypt, sepulcher, catacomb ➡ **grave, monument**

ceremony 1. *n* service, ritual, rite, celebration, tradition, commemoration, festival
2. *n* formality, pomp, solemnity, protocol

certain 1. *adj* sure, positive, confident, definite, assertive, forceful, vehement, self-confident, assured, convinced
2. *adj* undeniable, unquestionable, definite, absolute, inevitable, inescapable, unavoidable ➡ **reliable, conclusive, infallible**
3. *adj* ➡ **special**
4. *adj* ➡ **reliable**

certainly *adv, interj* absolutely, positively, definitely, perfectly, completely, surely, truly, undoubtedly, unquestionably, indeed, really ➡ **finally**

certainty 1. *n* certitude, assurance, conviction, confidence, self-confidence ➡ **belief**
2. *n* fact, reality, truth, actuality, truth, foregone conclusion, sure thing

chairperson *n* chair, chairman, chairwoman, head ➡ **boss, host**

chance 1. *n* fate, fortune, luck, destiny, lot, accident, coincidence, happenstance, serendipity
2. *n* ➡ **possibility**
3. *n* ➡ **opportunity**
4. *adj* ➡ **arbitrary, accidental**
5. *vb* ➡ **happen**

If the word you want is not a main entry above, look below to find it.

caustic ➡ sharp, sarcastic

caution ➡ warn, warning, advice, protection

cautious ➡ careful

cautiously ➡ carefully

cavalcade ➡ parade

caveat ➡ warning

cavern ➡ cave

cavity ➡ hole

cavort ➡ dance

cay ➡ island

cease ➡ stop, abandon

cease-fire ➡ truce

celebrated ➡ famous

celebration ➡ party, ceremony

celerity ➡ speed

celestial ➡ heavenly

celestial body ➡ planet

celibacy ➡ abstinence

cell ➡ jail

cellar ➡ basement

cement ➡ adhesive, join

censor ➡ forbid

censure ➡ blame

census ➡ study

center ➡ middle

central ➡ middle

ceramics ➡ pottery

cerebral ➡ intellectual, profound

ceremonious ➡ dignified

certificate ➡ document

certification ➡ proof

certify ➡ guarantee, approve, testify

certitude ➡ certainty

chafe ➡ rub, bother

chagrin ➡ embarrass, shame

chagrined ➡ ashamed

chain ➡ bond, row

chair ➡ seat, chairperson, lead

chairman ➡ chairperson

chairwoman ➡ chairperson

chalet ➡ home

chalky ➡ pale

challenge ➡ contradict, face, dare

challenger ➡ opponent

chamber ➡ room, cave

chamois ➡ hide, cloth

champ ➡ winner

champion ➡ winner, savior, support

chandelier ➡ light[1]

change 1. *vb* alter, vary, modify, transform, convert, mutate, shift, innovate ➡ **correct, adjust, distort, tinker**
2. *vb* switch, exchange, replace, interchange, substitute, swap, reverse, invert, transpose ➡ **trade**
3. *n* alteration, variation, shift, deviation, evolution, mutation, transformation, revolution, modification, metamorphosis, transition, vicissitude

channel *n* trough, chute, gutter, sluice, shaft, ramp, slide, groove, furrow, trench, rut, ditch, moat, aqueduct, canal, waterway, artery ➡ **pipe, course**

charge 1. *vb* bill, assess, invoice
2. *vb* ➡ **attack**
3. *vb* ➡ **argue, blame, try**
4. *n* ➡ **bill, price**
5. *n* ➡ **duty**
6. *n* ➡ **rule, order**
7. *n* ➡ **complaint**

chatter *vb* prattle, babble, gibber, jabber, gossip, tattle, ramble, prate, blather ➡ **talk**

cheap 1. *adj* inexpensive, reasonable, affordable, economical, low-priced, cut-rate, budget ⇨ *expensive*
2. *adj* inferior, shoddy, mediocre, second-rate, chintzy
3. *adj* thrifty, frugal, prudent, stingy, miserly, niggardly, tight-fisted, penny-pinching, cheeseparing, penurious, tight

cheat 1. *vb* trick, deceive, swindle, chisel, hoodwink, beguile, bluff, defraud, dupe, con, gyp, prey on ➡ **fool**
2. *n* cheater, swindler, quack, charlatan, fraud, shyster, imposter, fake, humbug ➡ **criminal, hypocrite**

chest 1. *n* trunk, footlocker, locker, bureau, dresser, chiffonier ➡ **container, safe**
2. *n* breast, bosom, bust, ribcage, ribs, trunk, thorax

If the word you want is not a main entry above, look below to find it.

changeable ➡ variable, fickle

change purse ➡ wallet

chant ➡ sing, hymn

chaos ➡ confusion

chaotic ➡ frantic

chap ➡ man

chapeau ➡ hat

chapel ➡ church

chaperon, chaperone ➡ accompany, host

chaplain ➡ minister

chaplet ➡ crown

chapter ➡ division, department

char ➡ burn

character ➡ personality, reputation, quality, role

characteristic ➡ quality

characterization ➡ description, stereotype

characterize ➡ describe, stereotype

chargé d'affaires ➡ diplomat

charisma ➡ personality

charismatic ➡ attractive

charitable ➡ generous, kind

charitableness ➡ generosity

charity ➡ kindness, generosity

charlatan ➡ cheat, rascal

charm ➡ beauty, attraction, personality, curse, enchantment, enchant, fascinate

charmed ➡ magic

charming ➡ nice, attractive, cute, suave

chart ➡ table, plan

charter ➡ hire, license

chartreuse ➡ green

chase ➡ follow, hunt

chasm ➡ canyon, hole

chassis ➡ framework

chaste ➡ innocent, celibate

chastise ➡ scold

chastity ➡ virtue

chat ➡ talk

chateau ➡ home

chatty ➡ talkative

chauvinistic ➡ patriotic

cheapskate ➡ miser

cheater ➡ cheat

check ➡ prevent, stop, try, bill, tick

check mark ➡ tick

cheek ➡ audacity

cheeky ➡ rude

cheep ➡ peep

cheer ➡ clap, entertain

cheerful ➡ happy, optimistic

cheerio ➡ good-bye

cheerless ➡ bleak

cheeseparing ➡ cheap

chef ➡ cook

cherish ➡ love, appreciate, respect

cherished ➡ valuable

cherub ➡ angel

chestnut ➡ brown

chew ➡ bite

chiefly *adv* mainly, primarily, essentially, principally, particularly, substantially, especially, notably, importantly, fundamentally, predominantly, basically, generally, mostly

child 1. *n* juvenile, youngster, minor, kid (*informal*), youth, boy, girl ➡ **baby, teenager, urchin** ⇨ *adult*
2. *n* daughter, son, offspring, progeny, descendant

childhood *n* infancy, babyhood, youth, minority, boyhood, girlhood, adolescence, puberty, immaturity

childish *adj* childlike, infantile, immature, juvenile, puerile, sophomoric ➡ **young**

choice 1. *n* alternative, option, selection, pick, preference, way, recourse, vote, voice ➡ **preference**
2. *adj* ➡ **good, favorite, special**

choir *n* chorus, chorale, glee club, ensemble ➡ **singer**

choke *vb* strangle, suffocate, asphyxiate, stifle, smother, drown ➡ **die, kill**

choose *vb* select, pick, elect, opt, name, take, designate, vote ➡ **decide, prefer** ⇨ *exclude*

choosy *adj* finicky, fussy, particular, picky, dainty, fastidious

chorus 1. *n* ➡ **choir**
2. *n* refrain, theme, strain, motif, leitmotif

church 1. *n* cathedral, temple, synagogue, mosque, chapel, mission ➡ **building**
2. *n* congregation, parish, parishioners, flock

circle 1. *n* ring, loop, hoop, disk, coil, circuit, circumference, perimeter, periphery, revolution, orbit ➡ **round**
2. *vb* ➡ **ring**

circumference *n* perimeter, periphery, circuit, outline, contour, silhouette ➡ **edge, border, circle**

If the word you want is not a main entry above, look below to find it.

chic ➡ fashionable

chick ➡ bird

chicken ➡ cowardly

chide ➡ scold

chief ➡ boss, important

chiffonier ➡ chest

childbirth ➡ birth

childless ➡ sterile

childlike ➡ childish

chill ➡ cool

chilly ➡ cool

chime ➡ bell, ring

chimney ➡ fireplace

china ➡ plate, pottery

chintzy ➡ cheap

chip ➡ bit, break

chirp ➡ peep, sing

chisel ➡ carve, cheat

chitchat ➡ talk

chivalric ➡ noble

chivalrous ➡ polite, noble

chocolate ➡ brown

choicest ➡ best

chomp ➡ bite

chop ➡ cut

choppy ➡ rough

chorale ➡ choir

chore ➡ job

chorister ➡ singer

christen ➡ name

chronic ➡ continual, frequent

chronicle ➡ diary, story

chronograph ➡ clock

chronometer ➡ clock

chubby ➡ fat

chuck ➡ throw

chuckle ➡ laugh

chum ➡ friend

chunk ➡ block, lump

churchgoing ➡ religious

churchyard ➡ cemetery

churl ➡ boor

churn ➡ mix

chute ➡ channel

ciao ➡ good-bye, hello

cicatrix ➡ scar

cinema ➡ movies

cinematographer ➡ photographer

cipher ➡ zero, number

circlet ➡ crown, ring

circuit ➡ circle, circumference, round

circuitous ➡ indirect

circular ➡ round, advertisement

circulate ➡ spread

circulation ➡ flow

circumspect ➡ careful

circumspection ➡ tact

circumstance ➡ event, state

➡ = synonym cross-reference • ⇨ = antonym cross-reference

circumstantial *adj* indirect, inferential, inconclusive, incidental

citizen *n* inhabitant, subject, native, resident, national, denizen ➡ **occupant**

civilization 1. *n* cultivation, culture, enlightenment, refinement, breeding, polish ➡ **progress**
2. *n* ➡ **people**

clap 1. *vb* applaud, cheer, root ➡ **praise**
2. *n* ➡ **bang**

clarity *n* clearness, lucidity, simplicity, transparency, definition, focus, sharpness, resolution

clasp 1. *n* fastener, clamp, buckle, zipper, button, catch, snap, clip ➡ **lock**
2. *vb* ➡ **join, squeeze, embrace, catch**

class 1. *n* ➡ **type, group, grade**
2. *n* refinement, polish, quality, panache, grace, style, breeding, cultivation, caliber ➡ **elegance**
3. *n* ➡ **lesson, course**

clean 1. *vb* wash, cleanse, rinse, scrub, scrape, scour, launder, bathe, brush, tidy, purify, sterilize, filter ➡ **shine, sweep**
2. *adj* spotless, washed, unblemished, unused, unsoiled, fresh, blank, pristine, immaculate ➡ **neat, sterile** ⇨ *dirty*

cleaning *n* washing, wash, bath, shower, rinse, soak, scrub ➡ **laundry**

cliché *n* platitude, truism, commonplace, bromide, banality ➡ **saying, stereotype**

cliff *n* bluff, crag, precipice, escarpment, bank, promontory, palisade ➡ **hill, mountain**

climax 1. *n* ➡ **top**
2. *vb* crest, peak, culminate, cap, consummate, crown ➡ **finish**

climb 1. *vb* scale, clamber, scramble, crawl ➡ **ascend**
2. *n* ascent, ascension, rise ➡ **growth, slant**

If the word you want is not a main entry above, look below to find it.

circumvent ➡ avoid
circus ➡ carnival
cistern ➡ well
citadel ➡ castle
citation ➡ award, document
cite ➡ quote
citizenry ➡ people
city ➡ town, urban
civic ➡ public, urban
civil ➡ polite, public
civil servant ➡ official
clack ➡ tick
claim ➡ boast, argue, appeal, interest
clairvoyant ➡ prophet
clamber ➡ climb
clammy ➡ damp
clamor ➡ noise

clamorous ➡ loud
clamp ➡ clasp
clan ➡ family
clandestine ➡ secret
clang ➡ bang, ring
clank ➡ bang
claptrap ➡ nonsense
clarify ➡ explain
clash ➡ bang, fight
classic ➡ masterpiece, model
classified ➡ secret
classify ➡ arrange
clatter ➡ bang
clause ➡ term, excerpt
claustrophic ➡ stuffy
claw ➡ foot
clawhammer ➡ hammer

clean out ➡ empty
cleanse ➡ clean
clear ➡ transparent, fair, legible, obvious, articulate, audible, open, forgive
clearance ➡ sale
clearing ➡ field
clearly ➡ apparently
clearness ➡ clarity
cleave ➡ cut, separate, stick
cleaver ➡ knife
cleft ➡ cut, hole
clemency ➡ pity, forgiveness
clementine ➡ orange
clench ➡ tighten, embrace
clergy ➡ minister
clergyman ➡ minister
clergywoman ➡ minister

cleric ➡ minister
clerical ➡ religious
clever ➡ able, smart
clichéd ➡ trite
click ➡ peep, tick
client ➡ patron
climate ➡ weather, setting
clime ➡ weather
clinch ➡ finish, join
cling ➡ stick
clinic ➡ hospital
clink ➡ peep, jail
clip ➡ cut, pin, clasp
clique ➡ group
cloak ➡ wrap, hide
cloakroom ➡ closet
clobber ➡ hit

clock n timepiece, watch, wristwatch, stopwatch, chronometer, chronograph, timer, hourglass, egg timer, sundial

close 1. vb shut, fasten, slam ➡ **lock**
2. vb plug, seal, stop, clog, obstruct, fill
3. adj ➡ **near**
4. adj ➡ **alike, approximate**
5. adj ➡ **narrow**
6. adj ➡ **friendly**
7. adj ➡ **thick**
8. adj ➡ **stuffy**
In general, **shut** is a stronger or more forceful word than **close,** and it suggests the action of moving the door, lid, cover, etc., to a closed and fastened position.

closet n armoire, wardrobe, cloakroom, locker, storeroom, pantry, larder ➡ **cupboard**

cloth 1. n fabric, material, textile, weave
2. n dustcloth, dishrag, dishcloth, washcloth, chamois, rag, remnant

clothes n clothing, dress, apparel, wardrobe, garments, attire, garb, vestments, finery, habit
Note that **clothes** is a plural noun and always takes a plural verb: "My **clothes** are on fire!" **Clothing** is a collective noun; it may refer to clothes in general or to all of the clothes you are wearing, but it always takes a singular verb: "Warm **clothing** is necessary in the winter."

cloud 1. n haze, mist, billow, vapor ➡ **fog, smoke**
2. n shadow, pall, gloom

cloudy 1. adj overcast, hazy, lowering ➡ **dim**
⇨ **fair**
2. adj ➡ **obscure**

clumsy 1. adj (in reference to people) awkward, ungraceful, ungainly, inept, fumbling, bumbling, uncoordinated, gauche ➡ **amateur**
2. adj (in reference to objects) awkward, bulky, cumbersome, unwieldy, unmanageable

coat 1. n overcoat, jacket, blazer, sport coat, sport jacket, raincoat, windbreaker, parka, trench coat
2. n fur, wool, fleece ➡ **hair, hide**
3. n coating, film, covering, blanket, mantle, veneer, crust, scale ➡ **layer**
4. vb ➡ **cover**

If the word you want is not a main entry above, look below to find it.

clog ➡ close, barrier
clogged ➡ stuffy
cloister ➡ court, monastery
clone ➡ reproduce
closed ➡ impassable
close-fitting ➡ tight
closeness ➡ presence
closeout ➡ sale
closing ➡ last
clot ➡ lump, harden
clothe ➡ dress, wrap
clothing ➡ clothes

cloudburst ➡ rain
clown ➡ comic, fool
clowning ➡ play
cloying ➡ rich
club ➡ bat, stick, organization
clue ➡ sign
clump ➡ lump, pile
cluster ➡ group, flower
clutch ➡ seize, touch
clutter ➡ mess
coach ➡ teach, teacher, wagon

coagulate ➡ harden
coal-black ➡ black
coarse ➡ rough, common, rude, dirty
coarseness ➡ rudeness
coast ➡ shore, slide
coating ➡ coat
coax ➡ persuade, urge
cobblestone ➡ rock
cocktail lounge ➡ bar
coda ➡ conclusion
coddle ➡ pamper

code ➡ rule
codicil ➡ addition
coerce ➡ force
coffee cake ➡ cake
coffeehouse ➡ restaurant
coffeepot ➡ pot
coffer ➡ safe
cogent ➡ valid
cogitate ➡ think
cohere ➡ stick
coherent ➡ articulate

➡ = synonym cross-reference • ⇨ = antonym cross-reference

cold *adj* frosty, icy, freezing, frigid, arctic, polar, antarctic, raw ➡ **cool** ⇨ *hot*

college *n* university, institute, institution, community college, junior college
➡ **school**

collide *vb* crash, smash, impact, sideswipe, rear-end ➡ **hit, knock**

collision *n* crash, impact, wreck, fender-bender (*informal*) ➡ **accident**

colony 1. *n* possession, dependency, settlement, satellite ➡ **state, country**
2. *n* ➡ **herd**

color 1. *n* shade, hue, tinge, tone, tint
2. *vb* ➡ **draw**
3. *vb* ➡ **blush**

comb 1. *vb* brush, untangle, disentangle, straighten, groom, tease, curry

2. *vb* ➡ **hunt**

come *vb* arrive, reach, appear, attain ➡ **approach, descend** ⇨ *go*

comfort 1. *n* contentment, ease, relaxation, repose ➡ **pleasure**
2. *n* succor, consolation, solace ➡ **pity, help, support, kindness**
3. *vb* console, solace, condole, reassure ➡ **calm, support**
4. *vb* ➡ **pity**

comfortable 1. *adj* cozy, snug, comfy, restful, homey, roomy, spacious ⇨ *uncomfortable*
2. *adj* ➡ **rich**

comic 1. *n* comedian, comedienne, joker, humorist, clown ➡ **actor**
2. *adj* ➡ **funny**

If the word you want is not a main entry above, look below to find it.

coil ➡ **turn, circle**

coin ➡ **money**

coincide ➡ **agree**

coincidence ➡ **chance**

coincident ➡ **simultaneous**

coincidental ➡ **accidental**

coinciding ➡ **simultaneous**

Coke® ➡ **soda**

cola ➡ **soda**

cold-blooded ➡ **mean, insensitive**

coldhearted ➡ **insensitive**

coliseum ➡ **field**

collaborate ➡ **help**

collaborative ➡ **common**

collapse ➡ **fall**

collar ➡ **arrest**

collateral ➡ **parallel**

colleague ➡ **member, worker**

collect ➡ **gather, earn**

collection ➡ **assortment**

collective ➡ **common**

collectively ➡ **together**

colloquium ➡ **course**

colonist ➡ **pioneer**

colonizer ➡ **pioneer**

colorful ➡ **bright**

colors ➡ **flag**

colossal ➡ **huge**

colossus ➡ **giant**

colt ➡ **horse**

column ➡ **post, row**

comatose ➡ **unconscious**

combat ➡ **fight**

combatant ➡ **soldier**

combative ➡ **belligerent, unfriendly, military**

combination ➡ **mixture, union**

combine ➡ **mix, add**

combo ➡ **band**

combustible ➡ **inflammable**

combustion ➡ **fire**

come across ➡ **find**

come back ➡ **return**

comedian ➡ **comic**

comedienne ➡ **comic**

come down with ➡ **catch**

comedy ➡ **humor, play**

come into view ➡ **appear**

comely ➡ **pretty**

come near ➡ **approach**

comet ➡ **meteor**

comforter ➡ **blanket**

comfy ➡ **comfortable**

comical ➡ **funny**

coming ➡ **approach**

command ➡ **control, order, rule**

commandeer ➡ **take**

commander ➡ **boss**

commanding ➡ **grand**

commandment ➡ **order**

commemorate ➡ **celebrate, remember**

commemoration ➡ **ceremony**

commence ➡ **start**

commencement ➡ **beginning**

commend ➡ **praise, approve**

commendable ➡ **praiseworthy**

comment ➡ **remark**

commentary ➡ **remark**

commerce ➡ **business**

commercial ➡ **advertisement, financial**

commiserate ➡ **pity**

commiseration ➡ **pity**

commission ➡ **committee**

n = noun • *vb* = verb • *adj* = adjective • *adv* = adverb • *prep* = preposition • *conj* = conjunction

commit 1. *vb* perpetrate, enact, carry out
➡ **act, do**
2. *vb* ➡ **entrust**
3. *vb* ➡ **dedicate**
4. *vb* ➡ **jail**

committee *n* board, council, panel, commission, subcommittee, delegation, mission, cabinet, assembly

common 1. *adj* ordinary, typical, familiar, everyday, widespread, average, unpretentious, humble, commonplace, pedestrian, popular, prevalent ➡ **general, normal, usual, plain**
⇨ *strange*
2. *adj* vulgar, coarse, commonplace, crass, crude, banal, plebeian ➡ **cheap, dirty**
3. *adj* communal, mutual, joint, collective, collaborative, shared ➡ **unanimous, public**
4. *n* ➡ **park**

compare *vb* contrast, juxtapose, parallel, liken, match, correlate ➡ **study, distinguish**

compatible *adj* similar, harmonious, agreeable, congruous ➡ **friendly**

compete *vb* contend, rival, play, contest, vie
➡ **fight, face**

competition 1. *n* rivalry, contention, antagonism ➡ **fight, game**
2. *n* ➡ **opponent**

competitive *adj* rival, contentious, antagonistic, vying ➡ **ambitious**

complain *vb* protest, gripe, grouch, grumble, whine, nag, fuss, moan, groan, squawk (*informal*) ➡ **mumble, object**

complaint 1. *n* objection, grievance, criticism, lament, charge, accusation, allegation, indictment, denunciation, reproach, outcry, grudge ➡ **protest**
2. *n* ➡ **illness, hardship**

complete 1. *adj* entire, full, total, whole, absolute, utter, uncut, intact, unbroken, exhaustive, thorough, unabridged, uncensored
➡ **all, comprehensive, perfect**
2. *vb* ➡ **finish**

If the word you want is not a main entry above, look below to find it.

commitment ➡ promise

committed ➡ faithful

commodity ➡ product

commonplace ➡ common, cliché

common sense ➡ wisdom

commonwealth ➡ country, state

commotion ➡ disturbance, noise, activity

communal ➡ common, public

communicable ➡ contagious

communicate ➡ talk, tell

communication ➡ speech, mail

communications ➡ media

community ➡ town, neighborhood, people

community college ➡ college

commute ➡ travel

commuter ➡ traveler

compact ➡ firm, small, short, thick, agreement

companion ➡ friend

companionship ➡ friendship

company ➡ business, friendship, visitor, team, troop

comparable ➡ alike

comparably ➡ alike

comparison ➡ similarity, estimate

compartment ➡ booth

compass ➡ range

compassion ➡ pity, kindness

compassionate ➡ kind

compatibility ➡ relationship

compeer ➡ equal

compel ➡ force

compelling ➡ interesting, urgent

compensate ➡ pay, balance, refund

compensation ➡ wage, refund, revenge

competence ➡ ability

competent ➡ able, efficient

competently ➡ well

competitor ➡ athlete, contestant, opponent

compilation ➡ assortment

compile ➡ gather, write

complacent ➡ satisfied

complement ➡ suit, addition

---

completely 1. *adv* fully, totally, entirely, utterly, wholly, altogether, quite, thoroughly, stark
2. *adv* ➡ **certainly**

complicated *adj* complex, intricate, elaborate, sophisticated, involved, subtle ➡ **hard**

comprehensive *adj* thorough, inclusive, exhaustive, blanket ➡ **complete, general**

concentrate 1. *vb* focus, devote, attend ➡ **meditate, think, study**
2. *vb* focus, converge, consolidate, condense, compress, intensify, thicken, distill ➡ **gather**

concern 1. *vb* involve, touch, pertain, appertain, regard, bear on, refer to, encompass ➡ **affect, belong**
2. *vb* ➡ **worry**

3. *n* ➡ **worry, interest**
4. *n* ➡ **business**

conclusion 1. *n* inference, assumption, deduction ➡ **decision** ⇨ *beginning*
2. *n* afterword, epilogue, postscript, postlude, coda ⇨ *introduction*
3. *n* ➡ **finish**

conclusive *adj* decisive, definitive, undeniable ➡ **certain**

condense *vb* shorten, contract, abbreviate, abridge, compress, telescope, cut, prune ➡ **decrease, shrink, concentrate** ⇨ *lengthen*

condescend *vb* stoop, deign, vouchsafe, demean, degrade, humble, accommodate, patronize

---

If the word you want is not a main entry above, look below to find it.

completion ➡ finish

complex ➡ complicated

compliance ➡ agreement

compliant ➡ passive

complicate ➡ confuse

compliment ➡ praise

complimentary ➡ free

comply ➡ obey

component ➡ part, division

compose ➡ calm, make, write

composed ➡ calm

composer ➡ musician

composite ➡ mixture

composition ➡ structure, work, report, score

composure ➡ calm

compound ➡ mix, mixture

comprehend ➡ know, read

comprehension ➡ wisdom

compress ➡ concentrate, condense, squeeze, bandage

comprise ➡ contain

compromise ➡ agreement

compulsion ➡ obsession

compulsory ➡ necessary

compunction ➡ regret

computation ➡ mathematics

compute ➡ add

computerized ➡ automatic

computing ➡ addition

comrade ➡ friend

comradeship ➡ friendship

con ➡ cheat

con artist ➡ hypocrite

conceal ➡ hide

concealed ➡ invisible

concede ➡ admit, surrender, abandon

conceit ➡ pride

conceited ➡ proud

conceivable ➡ possible

conceivably ➡ maybe

conceive ➡ imagine, invent

concentration ➡ attention

concept ➡ idea

conception ➡ beginning

concerned ➡ careful

concerning ➡ about

concert ➡ program

concerted ➡ unanimous

concession ➡ surrender

conciliatory ➡ peaceful

concise ➡ short

conciseness ➡ brevity

concision ➡ brevity

conclude ➡ finish, decide, infer

concluding ➡ last

conclusively ➡ finally

concoct ➡ invent

concoction ➡ mixture, lie

concord ➡ peace, unity

concordance ➡ dictionary

concrete ➡ real

concur ➡ agree

concurrence ➡ agreement

concurrent ➡ simultaneous

concurrently ➡ together

concussion ➡ blow[1]

condemn ➡ blame

condensation ➡ summary

condensed ➡ thick

n = noun • *vb* = verb • *adj* = adjective • *adv* = adverb • *prep* = preposition • *conj* = conjunction

confuse *vb* perplex, puzzle, bewilder, confound, complicate, baffle, disconcert, disorient, befuddle, abash, stymie, mystify, throw, stump

confusion 1. *n* disorder, chaos, anarchy, turmoil, discord, mayhem, lawlessness
➡ **excitement, hysteria, violence**
2. *n* perplexity, bewilderment, bafflement, puzzlement, consternation, nervousness
➡ **misunderstanding**

consecutive *adj* successive, continuous, progressive, ensuing, numerical, alphabetical, sequential, serial

conservative *adj* conventional, traditional, orthodox, moderate, reactionary, right-wing, illiberal ➡ **stuffy** ⇨ *liberal*

consider *vb* reflect, weigh, entertain, contemplate ➡ **study, think**

If the word you want is not a main entry above, look below to find it.

condescending ➡ pompous

condition ➡ state, health, exercise, term

conditioning ➡ exercise

conditions ➡ weather

condo ➡ home

condole ➡ comfort

condolence ➡ pity

condominium ➡ home

condone ➡ forgive

conduct ➡ behavior, lead, bring

conductor ➡ guide

conduit ➡ pipe

confederate ➡ partner

confer ➡ talk, negotiate, give

conference ➡ meeting

confess ➡ admit, reveal

confide ➡ entrust

confidence ➡ certainty, secrecy, secret, belief

confident ➡ certain, optimistic

confidential ➡ secret

configuration ➡ pattern

confine ➡ jail

confinement ➡ privacy

confirm ➡ verify, admit

confirmation ➡ proof

confiscate ➡ take

conflagration ➡ fire

conflict ➡ fight

conflicting ➡ opposite

confluence ➡ union

conform ➡ adjust

conformity ➡ agreement

confound ➡ confuse

confront ➡ face

confrontation ➡ fight, meeting

confronting ➡ opposite

confused ➡ delirious

congeal ➡ harden, cool

congenial ➡ pleasant

congenital ➡ natural

congested ➡ stuffy

congratulate ➡ praise

congratulations ➡ praise

congregate ➡ gather

congregation ➡ audience, church

congress ➡ government

congruity ➡ similarity

congruous ➡ compatible

conifer ➡ tree

conjectural ➡ theoretical

conjecture ➡ theory

conjurer ➡ magician

connect ➡ join, bridge

connection ➡ link, junction, relevance

conniption ➡ fit²

connive ➡ plan

connoisseur ➡ expert

connotation ➡ meaning

connote ➡ mean

conquer ➡ defeat

conqueror ➡ winner

conquest ➡ defeat, victory

conscientious ➡ reliable, careful

conscious ➡ alert, awake

consciously ➡ purposely

consciousness ➡ life, mind

conscript ➡ soldier

consecrate ➡ bless

consecrated ➡ holy

consensus ➡ agreement

consent ➡ agree, agreement, permission

consequence ➡ effect, importance, punishment

consequently ➡ therefore

conservation ➡ economy

conservatory ➡ greenhouse

conserve ➡ save

considerable ➡ big

considerably ➡ far

considerate ➡ kind, thoughtful

consideration ➡ kindness, attention, price

consign ➡ entrust

consistency ➡ density

consistent ➡ same, continual

consist of ➡ contain

consolation ➡ comfort

console ➡ comfort

consolidate ➡ concentrate, mix, unify

consolidation ➡ union

consort ➡ mix, spouse

consortium ➡ monopoly

conspicuous ➡ obvious, striking

conspiracy ➡ plan

conspire ➡ plan

constable ➡ police officer

constant ➡ continual, faithful

constantly ➡ regularly

consternation ➡ confusion, fear

constituent ➡ matter, member

constitute ➡ make

constitutional ➡ legal

---

contagious *adj* infectious, catching, communicable, transmissible, transmittable, spreadable, epidemic

contain 1. *vb* hold, include, consist of, comprise, accommodate ➡ **carry, embody**
2. *vb* restrain, limit, suppress, curb, quell, quash, quench, control, repress, swallow
➡ **stop, extinguish, prevent**

container *n* receptacle, box, carton, case, crate, can, jar, cup, glass, bucket, pail, tank, tub, tube ➡ **bag, bowl, barrel, chest, package, bottle, wrapper**

contestant *n* competitor, participant, contender, player, entry ➡ **athlete, opponent, candidate**

continual *adj* continuous, incessant, unceasing, constant, persistent, relentless, steady, chronic, unvarying, invariable, unchanging, ongoing, consistent, nonstop, unbroken ➡ **frequent, permanent**

continue 1. *vb* last, endure, remain, persist, persevere, carry on, proceed
2. *vb* resume, recommence, renew, pick up ➡ **start**

contradict *vb* deny, refute, challenge, dispute ➡ **object, discredit**

contradiction *n* disagreement, discrepancy, inconsistency, incongruity, paradox, oxymoron ➡ **problem, disagreement**

control 1. *vb* command, direct, manage, dominate, subject, regulate, engineer, tame, captain, cope, handle, harness
➡ **govern, lead, contain**
2. *vb* ➡ **contain**
3. *n* ➡ **rule, discipline**

If the word you want is not a main entry above, look below to find it.

constrain ➡ force
constrict ➡ shrink
constricted ➡ narrow
constricting ➡ tight
construct ➡ build
construction ➡ assembly
consul ➡ diplomat
consult ➡ talk
consultant ➡ adviser
consultation ➡ talk
consume ➡ eat, use
consummate ➡ climax
consumption ➡ use
contact ➡ touch, link
contact lenses ➡ glasses
contacts ➡ glasses
contagion ➡ disease
contaminate ➡ dirty
contaminated ➡ dirty
contemplate ➡ consider, meditate

contemplative ➡ thoughtful
contemporaneous ➡ simultaneous
contemporaneously ➡ together
contemporary ➡ modern, fashionable, simultaneous
contempt ➡ hatred
contemptible ➡ shameful
contend ➡ argue, compete
contender ➡ athlete, contestant
content ➡ part, pleasure, please, satisfied
contented ➡ satisfied
contention ➡ competition, disagreement
contentious ➡ belligerent, competitive
contentment ➡ satisfaction, comfort
contest ➡ game, compete

context ➡ setting
continually ➡ regularly
continuous ➡ continual, consecutive
contort ➡ bend
contorted ➡ bent
contour ➡ circumference
contraband ➡ booty
contract ➡ agreement, catch, condense, shrink, tighten
contraction ➡ abbreviation
contradictory ➡ opposite
contrary ➡ opposite
contrast ➡ compare, differ, difference
contrasting ➡ opposite
contribute ➡ give
contribution ➡ gift
contributor ➡ patron
contrite ➡ sorry

contrition ➡ shame
contrivance ➡ invention
contrive ➡ invent, plan
controls ➡ wheel
controversy ➡ argument
controvert ➡ disprove
conundrum ➡ problem
convalescence ➡ cure
convalescent ➡ better, patient
convalescing ➡ better
convene ➡ gather
convenience ➡ advantage
convenient ➡ available
convent ➡ monastery
convention ➡ meeting
conventional ➡ normal, conservative, stuffy
converge ➡ concentrate
convergence ➡ junction

---

n = noun • *vb* = verb • *adj* = adjective • *adv* = adverb • *prep* = preposition • *conj* = conjunction

cook 1. *vb* fry, bake, broil, roast, grill, stew, sauté, steam, barbecue, microwave, brew
➡ **boil, prepare**
2. *n* chef, sous-chef, pastry chef, baker
➡ **servant**

cool 1. *adj* chilly, chill, brisk, fresh, bracing, nippy ➡ **cold**
2. *adj* remote, aloof, distant, reserved, chilly, impersonal ➡ **calm, apathetic, unfriendly**
3. *adj* excellent, all right, fashionable ➡ **good**
4. *vb* chill, refrigerate, freeze, congeal ➡ **fan**

copy 1. *n* reproduction, facsimile, photocopy, likeness ➡ **duplicate**
2. *vb* ➡ **reproduce, imitate**

corner 1. *n* angle, turn ➡ **bend, curve**
2. *n* intersection, turn, junction, juncture, crossroad
2. *n* ➡ **monopoly**
3. *vb* ➡ **catch**

correct 1. *adj* accurate, right, exact, precise, true, faultless, flawless, authentic, faithful, factual ➡ **perfect** ⇨ *wrong*
2. *adj* respectable, decent, proper, fitting, appropriate, seemly, decorous, becoming
➡ **fit, prim**
3. *vb* remedy, rectify, revise, edit, amend, emend, reconcile, improve, reform, redress
➡ **fix, adjust, perfect, change**
4. *vb* ➡ **punish**

correction *n* revision, remedy, adjustment, emendation, reparation, rectification ➡ **repair**

correctly *adv* properly, accurately, appropriately, right, satisfactorily ➡ **precisely**

corrode *vb* erode, rust, rot, oxidize, tarnish
➡ **decay, melt**

cosmopolitan 1. *adj* ➡ **urban**
2. *adj* sophisticated, worldly, experienced
➡ **suave**

If the word you want is not a main entry above, look below to find it.

conversation ➡ talk

converse ➡ talk, opposite

convert ➡ change, translate

convey ➡ carry, give, send, take, tell

conveyance ➡ movement

convict ➡ criminal, decide

conviction ➡ belief, cause, certainty, will

convince ➡ persuade

convinced ➡ certain

convincing ➡ valid

convivial ➡ friendly

convoy ➡ accompany

convulsion ➡ fit²

cookhouse ➡ kitchen

cookie ➡ pastry

cooler ➡ refrigerator

coop ➡ pen

cooperate ➡ help

cooperation ➡ help

cooperatively ➡ together

coordinate ➡ balance

cop ➡ police officer

cope ➡ control

copious ➡ abundant

copse ➡ forest

copyright ➡ license

coral ➡ orange

cord ➡ string

cordial ➡ friendly

cordiality ➡ hospitality

core ➡ middle, essence

cork ➡ top

cornerstone ➡ basis

cornfield ➡ field

corona ➡ halo

coronet ➡ crown

corporal ➡ physical

corporation ➡ business, organization

corporeal ➡ physical

corps ➡ troop

corpse ➡ body

corpulent ➡ fat

corral ➡ pen

correctional facility ➡ jail

correctness ➡ accuracy

correlate ➡ compare

correlation ➡ link

correspond ➡ agree, resemble

correspondence ➡ mail, similarity

correspondent ➡ reporter

corresponding ➡ same

corridor ➡ hall

corroborate ➡ verify

corroboration ➡ proof

corroded ➡ rusty

corrosion ➡ decay

corrupt ➡ dishonest, wrong

corruption ➡ dishonesty

corsair ➡ pirate

cortege ➡ court

cosmetic ➡ superficial

cosmic ➡ universal

cosmos ➡ space

cost ➡ price

cost-effective ➡ efficient

costly ➡ expensive

costume ➡ disguise, dress, suit

cot ➡ bed

coterie ➡ following

➡ = synonym cross-reference • ⇨ = antonym cross-reference

country 1. *n* nation, republic, kingdom, dominion, realm, commonwealth, land, domain, homeland, fatherland, motherland ➡ **state, colony**
2. *n* countryside, landscape, hinterland, wilderness, wild, backwoods, frontier, bush, boondocks (*informal*), sticks (*informal*)
3. *n* ➡ **music**

courage *n* bravery, valor, fortitude, boldness, spirit, gallantry, heroism, daring, audacity, nerve, mettle, grit, stomach, guts (*informal*)

course 1. *n* path, route, direction, heading, bearing, way, itinerary
2. *n* track, racetrack, trail ➡ **road**
3. *n* class, subject, seminar, program, major, minor, colloquium, elective

court 1. *n* courtyard, square, quadrangle, quad, atrium, patio, plaza, piazza, cloister

2. *n* ➡ **field**
3. *n* tribunal, law court, bench, bar, judiciary, forum
4. *n* courthouse, courtroom
5. *n* retinue, entourage, cortege, royal household, attendants
6. *vb* woo, date, romance, flirt ➡ **love**

cover 1. *vb* cover up, blanket, carpet, spread, coat, overspread, surface, pave, flag ➡ **wrap, protect, plate**
2. *vb* ➡ **hide**
3. *n* ➡ **top**
4. *n* ➡ **blanket, wrapper**
5. *n* ➡ **protection**

cowardly *adj* timid, timorous, fearful, cowering, fainthearted, yellow (*informal*), chicken (*informal*) ➡ **afraid** ⇨ *brave*

If the word you want is not a main entry above, look below to find it.

cottage ➡ home
cotter pin ➡ pin
couch ➡ seat, bed
council ➡ committee, meeting
counsel ➡ advice, adviser, suggest, warn
counselor ➡ adviser
count ➡ add, matter, score
countenance ➡ appearance, face
counter ➡ answer, booth, shelf, table, opposite
counterattack ➡ attack
counterbalance ➡ balance
counterespionage ➡ spying
counterfeit ➡ fake, invent
counterintelligence ➡ spying
countermand ➡ abolish

counterpart ➡ duplicate
counterpoise ➡ balance
counterproductive ➡ useless
countersign ➡ sign
counterspy ➡ spy
counting ➡ addition
countless ➡ infinite, many
count on ➡ depend
countryside ➡ country
coup ➡ revolution
coup d'état ➡ revolution
couple ➡ pair, few, join
coupling ➡ union
courageous ➡ brave
courier ➡ messenger
courteous ➡ polite
courtesy ➡ kindness, respect, hospitality

courthouse ➡ court
courtly ➡ noble
courtroom ➡ court
courtyard ➡ court
cove ➡ bay
covenant ➡ agreement, promise
covered ➡ underground
covering ➡ coat, wrapper
cover story ➡ alibi
covert ➡ secret, den
covet ➡ envy
covetous ➡ greedy
covetousness ➡ envy
cow ➡ scare
cow barn ➡ barn
cower ➡ fear, jump
cowering ➡ cowardly
co-worker ➡ partner

cowshed ➡ barn
coxswain ➡ pilot
cozy ➡ comfortable
crack ➡ hole, bang, break
cracked ➡ broken
crackle ➡ rustle
cradle ➡ bed, source
craft ➡ art, profession, boat
craftsman ➡ artist
craftsmanship ➡ art
crafty ➡ sly
crag ➡ cliff
cram ➡ load
crammed ➡ full
cramp ➡ pain
cramped ➡ uncomfortable
cranky ➡ cross
crash ➡ bang, break, collide, collision, depression

n = noun • *vb* = verb • *adj* = adjective • *adv* = adverb • *prep* = preposition • *conj* = conjunction

crawl 1. *vb* creep, squirm, wiggle, wriggle, slither, grovel, drag, inch ➡ **walk, climb**
2. *n* ➡ **swim**

creator *n* author, originator, architect, framer, designer, engineer, inventor, pioneer, innovator, founder ➡ **artist**

crime *n* offense, violation, sin, evil, wrong, wrongdoing, misdeed, trespass, transgression, infraction, felony, misdemeanor ➡ **theft, treason, murder**

criminal 1. *n* crook, thief, bandit, outlaw, desperado, convict, felon, offender, robber, burglar, perpetrator, wrongdoer, malefactor, lawbreaker, culprit ➡ **cheat, vandal, pirate**
2. *adj* ➡ **illegal**

cross 1. *adj* grouchy, irritable, disagreeable, cranky, fussy, peevish, cantankerous, ill-tempered, bad-tempered, ill-natured, petulant, grumpy, testy, sullen, surly ➡ **angry, rude, abrupt** ⇨ *happy*
2. *n* ➡ **tick**
3. *n* ➡ **hybrid**
4. *vb* ➡ **bridge**

crowd *n* mob, multitude, host, throng, army, legion, horde, swarm, flock ➡ **band, group, troop**

crown 1. *n* diadem, coronet, tiara, circlet, garland, chaplet, wreath
2. *vb* enthrone, invest, install, induct, inaugurate ➡ **bless**
3. *vb* ➡ **climax**

If the word you want is not a main entry above, look below to find it.

crass ➡ rude, common

crate ➡ container

crater ➡ hole

cravat ➡ tie

crave ➡ want

craving ➡ appetite

crawl space ➡ basement

craze ➡ fashion

crazed ➡ insane

crazy ➡ insane, foolish

creak ➡ squeak

creamy ➡ rich, fair, white

crease ➡ fold, wrinkle

create ➡ cause, make

creation ➡ invention, work, assembly, earth

creative ➡ talented

creativity ➡ art, imagination

creature ➡ animal

credence ➡ belief

credentials ➡ document

credible ➡ possible

credit ➡ loan, belief, attribute

credit union ➡ bank

creditable ➡ praiseworthy

credo ➡ belief

credulous ➡ naive, superstitious

creed ➡ belief

creek ➡ river

creep ➡ crawl, sneak, tingle

cremate ➡ bury

creole ➡ dialect

crepe paper ➡ paper

crescent ➡ curve

crest ➡ climax, top

crevasse ➡ canyon, hole

crevice ➡ hole, canyon

crew ➡ group, team

crib ➡ bed

crimp ➡ bend, wrinkle

crimson ➡ red

cringe ➡ jump

crinkle ➡ wrinkle

cripple ➡ paralyze, weaken

crippled ➡ lame

crisis ➡ emergency

crisp ➡ brisk

criterion ➡ measure

critic ➡ judge

critical ➡ important

criticism ➡ complaint

criticize ➡ blame, study

croak ➡ grunt

crock ➡ bottle, bowl

crook ➡ criminal, curve

crooked ➡ bent, zigzag, dishonest

crookedness ➡ dishonesty

croon ➡ sing

crop ➡ growth, whip

crossbar ➡ bar

crossbreed ➡ hybrid

crossroad ➡ corner

crouch ➡ bend

crow ➡ boast

crowded ➡ full

crucial ➡ urgent

crude ➡ primitive, common, rude

crudeness ➡ rudeness

crude oil ➡ oil

crudity ➡ rudeness

cruel ➡ mean

cruet ➡ bottle

cruise ➡ patrol, travel, trip

---

cry 1. *vb* weep, sob, wail, bawl, whimper, whine, moan, groan
2. *n, vb* shout, scream, howl, screech, bellow, shriek, roar, whoop, squeal, bay, yowl, wail, squawk ➡ **noise, yell, bark**

cupboard *n* cabinet, sideboard, buffet, locker ➡ **closet**

cure 1. *n* remedy, treatment, antidote, curative, therapy ➡ **medicine**
2. *n* recovery, recuperation, healing, rehabilitation, convalescence
3. *vb* ➡ **heal**

curious 1. *adj* inquisitive, prying, nosy, inquiring ➡ **meddlesome**
2. *adj* ➡ **strange**

curse 1. *n* oath, profanity, blasphemy, expletive
2. *n* hex, charm, spell, jinx
3. *vb* swear, blaspheme, damn, revile, vilify, cuss (*informal*)

curve 1. *n* bow, bend, turn, arch, arc, crook, trajectory, curvature, crescent, horseshoe, oxbow
2. *vb* ➡ **bend**

cushion 1. *n* pad, mat, pillow, bolster, pallet
2. *n* padding, buffer, shock absorber ➡ **protection**
3. *vb* ➡ **protect**

cut 1. *vb* chop, slice, dice, mince, shred, grate, carve, cleave, gouge, hew, hack, lacerate, amputate ➡ **rip, peel, carve**
2. *vb* trim, shave, clip, snip, shear, prune, mow, reap
3. *vb* ➡ **condense, decrease**
4. *n* gash, slash, wound, injury, incision, laceration, scrape, scratch, nick, gouge, cleft, notch, slit ➡ **rip, hole, sore**

cute *adj* adorable, charming, quaint, cutesy ➡ **pretty**

If the word you want is not a main entry above, look below to find it.

crumble ➡ **decay, grind**
crumbly ➡ **breakable**
crumple ➡ **fall, wrinkle**
crumpled ➡ **rough**
crusade ➡ **movement**
crush ➡ **break, grind, trample, defeat**
crust ➡ **coat**
crypt ➡ **cemetery, grave, basement**
cryptic ➡ **obscure, secret**
crystalline ➡ **transparent**
cube ➡ **block**
cubicle ➡ **booth**
cuddle ➡ **embrace, snuggle**
cue ➡ **reminder**
cuisine ➡ **food**
culminate ➡ **climax**
culmination ➡ **finish**

culpability ➡ **guilt**
culpable ➡ **guilty**
culprit ➡ **criminal, defendant**
cult ➡ **religion**
cultivate ➡ **dig, grow**
cultivation ➡ **farming, civilization, class**
culture ➡ **civilization**
cultured ➡ **suave**
cumbersome ➡ **clumsy, heavy**
cunning ➡ **sly, dishonesty**
cup ➡ **container, glass**
cupcake ➡ **cake**
cur ➡ **dog**
curative ➡ **medicinal, cure**
curator ➡ **guardian**
curb ➡ **contain**
curio ➡ **novelty, antique**

curiosity ➡ **interest, novelty**
curious ➡ **strange**
curl ➡ **bend, lock**
currency ➡ **money**
current ➡ **energy, flood, modern**
curry ➡ **comb**
cursive ➡ **handwriting**
cursory ➡ **superficial, fast**
curt ➡ **abrupt**
curtail ➡ **decrease**
curtain ➡ **divider**
curtsy ➡ **bend**
curvature ➡ **curve**
curved ➡ **bent**
cuss ➡ **curse**
custodian ➡ **guardian**
custody ➡ **possession**
custom ➡ **habit, rule**

customarily ➡ **usually**
customary ➡ **usual**
customer ➡ **patron**
cutesy ➡ **cute**
cutlass ➡ **sword**
cut-rate ➡ **cheap**
cutting ➡ **sharp**
cycle ➡ **period, round, periodic**
cyclical ➡ **periodic**
cyclist ➡ **rider**
cyclone ➡ **storm**
cylindrical ➡ **round**
cynic ➡ **skeptic**
cynical ➡ **pessimistic**
cyst ➡ **growth**
czar ➡ **emperor**
czarina ➡ **empress**

n = noun • *vb* = verb • *adj* = adjective • *adv* = adverb • *prep* = preposition • *conj* = conjunction

D

dam *n* embankment, dike, levee, weir ➡ **wall**

damage 1. *n* destruction, wreckage, wear, devastation, desolation, ruin, havoc, mayhem, injury, sabotage ➡ **decay, harm**
2. *vb* impair, mar, deface, scratch, scrape, scar, disfigure, deform, distort ➡ **hurt, break, destroy**

damp *adj* moist, humid, clammy, dank, muggy, sultry, sticky ➡ **wet, liquid**

dance 1. *n* ball, prom, social, mixer, gala ➡ **party**
2. *vb* step, trip, glide, pirouette, whirl
3. *vb* gambol, frolic, scamper, caper, cavort, romp ➡ **jump**

danger *n* risk, threat, peril, hazard, menace, jeopardy

dangerous *adj* harmful, perilous, hazardous, unsafe, risky, treacherous, precarious, explosive ➡ **deadly, destructive** ⇨ *safe*

dare 1. *vb* hazard, presume, risk ➡ **try**
2. *vb* defy, challenge, provoke ➡ **face**

dark 1. *adj* gloomy, murky, dusky, shady, unlit, somber, overcast, pitch-black, black, opaque ➡ **dim**
2. *adj* brunette, brown, tan, black, swarthy, sable, ebony
3. *n* darkness, dusk, gloom, blackness, shade, shadow ➡ **night**

day *n* daylight, daytime, light, midday, date ➡ **morning, afternoon** ⇨ *night*

dead 1. *adj* deceased, departed, late, lifeless, extinct, defunct, inanimate ⇨ *alive*
2. *adj* inert, still, stagnant, motionless ➡ **calm**
3. *adj* ➡ **tired**
4. *adv* ➡ **completely**
5. *n* ➡ **casualty**

deadly 1. *adj* fatal, mortal, lethal, deathly, murderous, homicidal, terminal, incurable
2. *adj* poisonous, venomous, virulent, malignant, toxic, noxious ➡ **dangerous**
3. *adj* ➡ **dull**
4. *adv* terminally ➡ **completely**

If the word you want is not a main entry above, look below to find it.

dab ➡ rub
dabble ➡ tinker
dagger ➡ knife
daily ➡ paper
dainty ➡ breakable, choosy
dais ➡ platform
dale ➡ valley
dally ➡ wait
damaged ➡ broken
damaging ➡ destructive
damn ➡ curse
dampen ➡ wet

dampness ➡ humidity
dangle ➡ hang
Danish ➡ pastry
dank ➡ damp
dapper ➡ fashionable
dappled ➡ speckled
daring ➡ brave, courage
dark horse ➡ candidate
darkness ➡ dark
darling ➡ favorite, love
dart ➡ run, missile
dash ➡ bit, race, hurry, run

dashing ➡ fashionable, brave
data ➡ knowledge, proof
date ➡ day, period, meeting, court
datebook ➡ diary
daub ➡ rub
daughter ➡ child
daunt ➡ discourage
dauntless ➡ brave
dawdle ➡ lag
dawn ➡ morning
daybook ➡ diary

daybreak ➡ morning
daydream ➡ dream
daylight ➡ day
daytime ➡ day
daze ➡ dream, surprise
dazed ➡ dizzy
dazzle ➡ surprise
dazzling ➡ bright, beautiful, striking
deadbeat ➡ loafer
deadlock ➡ tie
deadpan ➡ blank, dry

---

deaf 1. *adj* hearing-impaired, unhearing, hard of hearing ➡ **disabled**
2. *adj* ➡ **unaware**

death *n* decease, demise, dying, passing, expiration, loss ➡ **casualty, fate, finish** ⇨ *birth*

debt *n* liability, obligation, debit, arrears, deficit, indebtedness ➡ **bill**

decay 1. *vb* deteriorate, disintegrate, crumble, decompose, wear, rot, molder, spoil, putrefy ➡ **corrode, destroy**
2. *n* deterioration, degeneration, decomposition, spoilage, disrepair, disintegration, corrosion ➡ **damage**

decide *vb* settle, resolve, determine, rule, conclude, reconcile, negotiate, mediate, arbitrate, judge, adjudge, convict ➡ **choose**

decision *n* judgment, determination, resolution, ruling, finding, verdict, sentence, decree, declaration ➡ **choice, conclusion**

decorate 1. *vb* adorn, beautify, ornament, embellish, trim, garnish, bedeck, redecorate, refurbish, festoon
2. *vb* ➡ **praise**

decoration 1. *n* adornment, ornamentation, embellishment, redecoration, beautification
2. *n* ornament, garnish, trim, accent, flourish
3. *n* ➡ **prize, award**

decrease 1. *vb* lessen, diminish, abate, decline, wane, subside, ebb, dwindle, taper, shrink, shrivel, reduce, depress, lower, slash, curtail, cut ➡ **condense, weaken, shrink**
2. *n* ➡ **drop**

dedicate *vb* devote, commit, set apart, pledge ➡ **bless**

If the word you want is not a main entry above, look below to find it.

deafening ➡ loud

deal ➡ agreement, bargain, sale

dealer ➡ seller

deal out ➡ share

dean ➡ principal

dear ➡ expensive, valuable, love

dearly ➡ much

dearth ➡ absence, want

deathless ➡ eternal

deathly ➡ deadly

debacle ➡ disappointment

debase ➡ shame

debate ➡ argue, argument

debit ➡ debt

debonair ➡ suave

debris ➡ trash

debunk ➡ disprove

debut ➡ introduction

decayed ➡ rusty, shabby, bad

decease ➡ death, die

deceased ➡ dead

deceit ➡ dishonesty, pretense

deceitful ➡ dishonest

deceive ➡ betray, cheat, lie

deceiver ➡ liar, hypocrite

decency ➡ kindness, virtue

decent ➡ correct, fair, kind

deception ➡ lie, pretense, trick

deceptive ➡ dishonest, unreliable

decipher ➡ solve, translate, read

decipherable ➡ legible

decisive ➡ conclusive, resolute

decisively ➡ finally

deck ➡ floor, dress

declaim ➡ quote

declaration ➡ announcement, decision

declare ➡ tell, advertise

decline ➡ decrease, drop, refuse, depression

declivity ➡ slant

decode ➡ solve, translate, read

decompose ➡ decay

decomposition ➡ decay

decorative ➡ fancy

decorous ➡ correct, dignified, prim

decorum ➡ behavior

decoy ➡ tempt

decree ➡ act, decision, order

decrepit ➡ old

dedication ➡ loyalty, inscription

deduce ➡ infer

deduct ➡ subtract

deduction ➡ conclusion, reason, subtraction

deed ➡ act, document

deem ➡ believe

deep ➡ broad, profound, ocean

deepness ➡ depth

deface ➡ damage

n = noun • *vb* = verb • *adj* = adjective • *adv* = adverb • *prep* = preposition • *conj* = conjunction

defeat 1. *vb* conquer, beat, overcome, surmount, overpower, vanquish, best, better, top, break, overthrow, throw, upset, down, whip, crush ► **subdue, win**
2. *n* loss, downfall, failure, conquest, destruction, rout, upset, beating, thrashing ⇨ *victory*

defect 1. *n* imperfection, flaw, blemish, shortcoming, drawback, minus ► **fault, mistake, spot**
2. *vb* ► **leave**

defendant *n* accused, suspect, culprit ► **prisoner**

delay 1. *vb* postpone, defer, put off, deter, stall, procrastinate ► **wait, hesitate**
2. *vb* hamper, detain, impede, hinder, retard ► **prevent**
3. *n* ► **break**

delicate 1. *adj* ► **breakable, weak**
2. *adj* ► **thin**
3. *adj* sensitive, touchy, ticklish, tricky, sticky ► **dangerous, doubtful**

delicious *adj* tasty, delectable, appetizing, luscious, savory, mouth-watering, flavorful, scrumptious ► **rich**

delirious *adj* incoherent, hysterical, confused, hallucinating ► **frantic, insane**

delivery 1. *n* shipment, transfer, transmission, dispatch, distribution, transportation ► **flow**
2. *n* ► **birth**
3. *n* ► **salvation**
4. *n* enunciation, pronunciation, elocution, diction, presentation, performance

---

If the word you want is not a main entry above, look below to find it.

defame ► insult

defective ► broken

defector ► runaway

defend ► protect, verify

defense ► protection, justification, alibi

defenseless ► vulnerable

defer ► delay, surrender

deference ► respect

deferential ► shy, passive

defiance ► disobedience, fight

defiant ► rebellious

deficiency ► absence, want

deficient ► inadequate, partial, poor

deficit ► debt

defile ► dirty

define ► describe, specify

definite ► certain

definitely ► certainly

definition ► meaning, clarity

definitive ► conclusive, model

deflate ► empty, shrink

deflect ► distract

deform ► damage

defraud ► cheat

deft ► able

defunct ► dead

defy ► disobey, rebel, face, dare

degenerate ► immoral

degeneration ► decay

degrade ► condescend

degree ► grade

dehydrate ► dry

dehydrated ► dry

deign ► condescend

deist ► atheist

deity ► god

déjà vu ► memory

dejected ► sad

dejection ► depression

delayed ► late

delectable ► delicious

delegate ► agent, entrust, name

delegation ► appointment, committee

delete ► erase

deli ► restaurant

deliberate ► slow, voluntary, think

deliberately ► carefully, purposely

delicacy ► tact, pastry

delicately ► carefully

delight ► please, pleasure

delighted ► happy

delightful ► pleasant, nice

delight in ► like

delineate ► draw

delinquent ► late, negligent, vandal

delirium ► hysteria

deliver ► bring, take, give, free, save

deliverance ► escape, salvation

deliverer ► savior

dell ► valley

delude ► fool

deluge ► flood

delusion ► illusion

delve ► dig, hunt

demand ► insist, order

demanding ► hard

demean ► condescend, shame

demeanor ► appearance, bearing

demented ► insane

demigod ► god

demise ► death

---

den 1. *n* lair, burrow, nest, hole, warren, covert ➡ **cave**
2. *n* study, office, library, family room, recreation room, rec room, playroom ➡ **room**

density *n* substance, bulk, body, consistency, mass ➡ **weight**

dent 1. *n* indentation, depression, impression, dimple, pit, nick, notch ➡ **hole**
2. *vb* indent, pit, nick, notch ➡ **bend**

department *n* section, division, branch, bureau, agency, chapter, subsidiary, affiliate ➡ **field, business, job, arm**

departure 1. *n* exit, going, leaving, withdrawal, farewell, embarkation, exodus ➡ **escape**
2. *n* deviation, divergence, digression, aberration, irregularity ➡ **change, difference**

depend 1. *vb* trust, rely, count on ➡ **believe**
2. *vb* hang, hinge, rest ➡ **turn**

deploy *vb* position, array, marshal ➡ **arrange**

depression 1. *n* ➡ **dent**
2. *n* desolation, despair, despondency, dejection ➡ **sorrow, misery**
3. *n* recession, slump, decline, downturn, crash

deprive *vb* withhold, divest, rob ➡ **refuse**

depth 1. *n* deepness, lowness, extent ➡ **measure** ⇨ *height*
2. *n* ➡ **middle**
3. *n* profundity, gravity, insight, profoundness ➡ **wisdom**

descend 1. *vb* swoop, stoop, dip ➡ **fall, decline, sink** ⇨ *ascend*
2. *vb* dismount, land, light, alight, settle, perch
3. *vb* issue, derive, come, spring, arise

describe *vb* characterize, define, depict, represent, recount, detail ➡ **explain, draw**

If the word you want is not a main entry above, look below to find it.

demolish ➡ **destroy**

demon ➡ **devil**

demonic ➡ **wicked**

demonstrate ➡ **explain, verify, protest**

demonstration ➡ **experiment, protest, parade, movement**

demonstrative ➡ **emotional, loving**

demoralize ➡ **discourage**

demur ➡ **hesitate**

demure ➡ **shy**

denial ➡ **abstinence, rejection**

denizen ➡ **citizen**

denomination ➡ **religion**

denotation ➡ **meaning**

denote ➡ **mean**

denounce ➡ **blame**

dense ➡ **dull, firm, thick**

denseness ➡ **ignorance**

denunciation ➡ **complaint**

deny ➡ **refuse, contradict**

depart ➡ **leave, die**

departed ➡ **dead**

dependability ➡ **loyalty**

dependable ➡ **reliable**

dependency ➡ **habit, colony**

depict ➡ **draw, describe**

depiction ➡ **description**

deplane ➡ **leave**

deplete ➡ **use**

deplorable ➡ **shameful, unfortunate**

deplore ➡ **hate, regret**

deport ➡ **banish**

deportation ➡ **exile**

deportee ➡ **exile**

deportment ➡ **bearing**

depose ➡ **oust**

deposit ➡ **put, bank**

depository ➡ **warehouse, bank**

depot ➡ **warehouse**

depraved ➡ **immoral**

depravity ➡ **immorality**

deprecate ➡ **ridicule, underestimate**

depress ➡ **sadden, decrease**

depressed ➡ **sad, underdeveloped**

depressing ➡ **bleak, sorry**

deprived ➡ **poor, underdeveloped**

deputy ➡ **helper**

deranged ➡ **insane**

derby ➡ **race**

derelict ➡ **abandoned, negligent, guilty, homeless, beggar**

deride ➡ **ridicule**

derision ➡ **ridicule**

derisive ➡ **sarcastic**

derivation ➡ **source, product**

derivative ➡ **product**

derive ➡ **descend, extract**

descendant ➡ **child**

descending ➡ **down**

descent ➡ **drop, slant, ancestry**

n = noun • *vb* = verb • *adj* = adjective • *adv* = adverb • *prep* = preposition • *conj* = conjunction

description *n* portrayal, characterization, account, depiction, portrait, profile
➡ **picture, story**

desert 1. *n* wasteland, wilderness, waste, barrens, badlands ➡ **country, plain**
2. *adj* ➡ **sterile**
3. *vb* ➡ **leave**

deserve *vb* merit, earn, warrant, justify, rate

desire 1. *n* ➡ **ambition**
2. *n* ➡ **hope**
3. *n* passion, lust, infatuation, appetite, urge, hunger, longing, nostalgia, wistfulness, yearning, yen, itch ➡ **love, greed, envy**
4. *vb* ➡ **want, envy**

destination *n* end, terminus, terminal, station, address, target

destroy *vb* wreck, spoil, demolish, ruin, annihilate, damage, devastate, ravage, raze, level, blight ➡ **abolish, break, mutilate**
⇨ *build*

destructive 1. *adj* ruinous, calamitous, catastrophic, devastating ➡ **violent, dangerous**
2. *adj* harmful, injurious, adverse, unfavorable, damaging

detail 1. *n* particular, trait, feature, factor, specific, peculiarity, fact, point
2. *vb* ➡ **specify, describe**

detour 1. *n* bypass, diversion, byway, digression, deviation ➡ **departure**
2. *vb* divert, redirect, skirt, bypass

development 1. *n* ➡ **growth**
2. *n* ➡ **invention**
3. *n* subdivision, project, housing estate

If the word you want is not a main entry above, look below to find it.

descry ➡ discover

deserted ➡ abandoned, open

deserter ➡ runaway

desertion ➡ escape

deserts ➡ punishment

deserving ➡ praiseworthy

design ➡ pattern, plan, intend, invent

designate ➡ choose, name

designation ➡ name, appointment

designer ➡ creator

desirable ➡ attractive, pleasant, useful

desk ➡ table

desolate ➡ abandoned, bleak, sadden

desolation ➡ damage, depression

despair ➡ depression

desperado ➡ criminal

desperate ➡ frantic, urgent, useless

despicable ➡ bad

despise ➡ hate

despised ➡ unpopular

despondency ➡ depression

despondent ➡ sad

despot ➡ dictator

despotic ➡ dictatorial

despotism ➡ tyranny

dessicated ➡ dry

destiny ➡ chance, fate, future

destitute ➡ poor

destitution ➡ poverty

destruction ➡ damage, violence, defeat

destructiveness ➡ violence

detach ➡ separate

detached ➡ fair

detachment ➡ division

detain ➡ delay, arrest, jail

detainee ➡ prisoner

detect ➡ discover

detection ➡ discovery

detective ➡ police officer

detention ➡ arrest

deter ➡ delay, prevent

deteriorate ➡ decay, relapse

deteriorated ➡ shabby

deterioration ➡ decay

determination ➡ will, decision

determine ➡ decide, arrange, verify, learn

determined ➡ ambitious, resolute

deterred ➡ disabled

detest ➡ hate

detestable ➡ bad

dethrone ➡ oust

detonate ➡ explode

detonation ➡ bang

detrain ➡ leave

detriment ➡ harm

devastate ➡ destroy, shock

devastating ➡ destructive

devastation ➡ damage

develop ➡ grow, invent, prepare, catch

developing ➡ early

developmental ➡ experimental

deviate ➡ differ, swerve, wander

deviation ➡ change, departure, detour

device ➡ equipment, tool, object, trick

➡ = synonym cross-reference • ⇨ = antonym cross-reference

devil *n* demon, fiend, archfiend

dialect *n* idiom, vernacular, patois, slang, lingo, argot, jargon, cant, creole, pidgin ➡ **accent, language**

diary *n* journal, chronicle, memoir, datebook, daybook, calendar

dictator *n* despot, tyrant, autocrat, fascist, totalitarian, authoritarian ➡ **ruler**

dictatorial *adj* despotic, tyrannical, autocratic, fascist, totalitarian, authoritarian, absolute, arbitrary ➡ **dogmatic**

dictionary *n* glossary, lexicon, vocabulary, concordance, thesaurus, encyclopedia ➡ **book**

die 1. *vb* decease, expire, pass away, pass on, perish, succumb, depart, starve ➪ *live*
2. *n* ➡ **form**

differ *vb* vary, contrast, deviate, diverge, disagree ➡ **change**

difference *n* dissimilarity, contrast, distinction, disparity, variation, variance, discrepancy, irregularity, inequality, nuance, gulf ➡ **departure** ➪ *similarity*

different 1. *adj* distinct, other, else, another, separate, dissimilar, unlike, irregular, uneven, unequal ➡ **unique** ➪ *same, similar*
2. *adj* diverse, various, assorted, miscellaneous, disparate, eclectic, assorted, varied, heterogeneous, motley ➡ **many**
3. *adj* ➡ **strange**

differently *adv* variously, diversely, separately, else, otherwise

dig *vb* shovel, delve, scoop, excavate, burrow, tunnel, drill, bore, bulldoze, plow, hoe, cultivate, harrow, rake, grub

dignified *adj* formal, stately, solemn, decorous, ceremonious, lofty, imperious, august ➡ **serious, grand**

diligence *n* perseverance, industry, persistence, application, care, carefulness, thoroughness, attentiveness

---

If the word you want is not a main entry above, look below to find it.

devilish ➡ wicked

devil-may-care ➡ carefree

devilment ➡ mischief

devious ➡ indirect, sly

devise ➡ arrange, invent

devoid ➡ empty

devote ➡ dedicate, concentrate

devoted ➡ faithful, loving

devotee ➡ fan

devotion ➡ love, loyalty, worship

devour ➡ eat

devout ➡ religious

dew ➡ humidity

dexterity ➡ agility

dexterous ➡ able, agile

diabolical ➡ wicked

diacritic ➡ accent

diadem ➡ crown

diagram ➡ pattern, picture, draw

dial ➡ call

dialogue ➡ talk

diameter ➡ width

diamond ➡ field

diaphanous ➡ thin, transparent

dice ➡ cut

dictate ➡ say, order

dictatorship ➡ tyranny

diction ➡ speech, delivery

diet ➡ food

differentiate ➡ distinguish

differently abled ➡ disabled

difficult ➡ hard, intolerable, stubborn

difficulty ➡ trouble, barrier

diffident ➡ shy, reluctant

digest ➡ absorb, learn, summary

digit ➡ number

dignitary ➡ celebrity

dignity ➡ pride, respect, importance

digress ➡ wander

digression ➡ detour, departure

dike ➡ dam, jetty

dilapidated ➡ shabby

dilate ➡ swell

dilatory ➡ slow, negligent

dilemma ➡ problem

dilettante ➡ amateur

n = noun • *vb* = verb • *adj* = adjective • *adv* = adverb • *prep* = preposition • *conj* = conjunction

diligent *adj* industrious, hardworking, assiduous, tireless, inexhaustible, unflagging, dogged ➡ **patient, careful**

dim *adj* faint, indistinct, obscure, hazy, blurry, shadowy, murky, foggy ➡ **dark, dull** ⇨ *bright*

dining room *n* dining hall, eating area, breakfast nook ➡ **room, restaurant**

diplomat *n* ambassador, consul, emissary, statesman, attaché, envoy, minister, chargé d'affaires ➡ **official**

dirge *n* lament, requiem, funeral march, elegy, threnody ➡ **hymn**

dirt 1. *n* earth, soil, loam, humus, turf, topsoil, sand, gravel, grit, land, ground
2. *n* filth, grime, dust, mud, muck, slime, ooze, slop, sludge, mire ➡ **trash**

dirty 1. *adj* filthy, grimy, soiled, dingy, grubby, unclean, impure, unsanitary, contaminated, polluted, foul, dusty, squalid ➡ **messy** ⇨ *clean*
2. *adj* obscene, lewd, pornographic, ribald, vulgar, bawdy, coarse, earthy, salty, risqué, racy ➡ **common**
3. *vb* soil, stain, sully, pollute, contaminate, infect, defile, tarnish, taint, foul, befoul, smudge, muddy, mess ⇨ *clean*

disability *n* handicap, disadvantage, impairment, impediment, affliction, hindrance ➡ **defect**

disabled 1. *adj* handicapped, physically challenged, differently abled, impaired, incapacitated
2. *adj* hampered, thwarted, encumbered, deterred, handicapped, disadvantaged, stymied
3. *adj* ➡ **broken**

disagreement *n* contention, friction, discord, strife, dissent, dissension, heresy ➡ **argument, contradiction, fight, opposition**

disappear *vb* vanish, fade, lift, dissipate, dissolve, evaporate, fizzle, disperse, thin ➡ **melt, stop**

disappoint *vb* let down, fail, discourage, dishearten, dissatisfy, disillusion, frustrate ➡ **sadden**

disappointment 1. *n* failure, discouragement, dissatisfaction, frustration, disillusionment ➡ **regret**
2. *n* letdown, failure, disaster, debacle, fiasco, flop, dud (*informal*)

If the word you want is not a main entry above, look below to find it.

dilute ➡ weaken

dimension ➡ measure

diminish ➡ decrease, subtract

diminished ➡ less

diminished by ➡ minus

diminution ➡ subtraction

diminutive ➡ small

dimple ➡ dent

din ➡ noise

dine ➡ eat

diner ➡ restaurant

ding ➡ ring

dingy ➡ dirty, dull

dining hall ➡ dining room

dinnerware ➡ plate

dip ➡ descend, drop, sink, swim

diploma ➡ document

diplomacy ➡ tact

diplomatic ➡ suave

dipper ➡ spoon

dire ➡ awful, urgent

direct ➡ control, lead, order, straight

direction ➡ course, perspective, leadership, order

directions ➡ recipe

directive ➡ order

directly ➡ now, precisely

director ➡ boss

disable ➡ mutilate, paralyze

disadvantage ➡ harm, disability

disadvantaged ➡ disabled, underdeveloped

disagree ➡ argue, differ, object

disagreeable ➡ cross, awful, bad, thankless, uncomfortable

disallow ➡ abolish, forbid

---

disaster 1. *n* catastrophe, calamity, tragedy, casualty, cataclysm, misfortune, pity, evil
➡ **accident, emergency**
2. *n* ➡ **disappointment**

discard *vb* throw away, dispose, reject, dump, scrap, junk, jettison ➡ **abandon, shed** ⇨ *save*

discipline 1. *n* self-control, self-restraint, willpower, control ➡ **will**
2. *n* training, regimen, regimentation ➡ **practice, science**
3. *n* ➡ **field**
4. *n* ➡ **punishment**
5. *vb* ➡ **punish**

discourage 1. *vb* dispirit, dismay, demoralize, intimidate, unnerve, daunt ➡ **disappoint**
2. *vb* dissuade ➡ **prevent** ⇨ *persuade, urge*

discover 1. *vb* detect, unearth, uncover, strike, descry, ferret out ➡ **find, notice**
2. *vb* ➡ **learn**

discovery *n* finding, detection, unearthing, identification, sighting, disclosure ➡ **invention**

disease *n* infection, virus, fever, contagion, blight, syndrome, bug (*informal*), blight ➡ **illness, epidemic**

disguise 1. *n* mask, camouflage, guise, costume, masquerade, makeup ➡ **pretense**
2. *vb* ➡ **hide**

disgust 1. *vb* repel, revolt, offend, nauseate, sicken, appall
2. *n* loathing, revulsion, repugnance, distaste ➡ **hatred**

dishonest *adj* untruthful, untrustworthy, deceitful, crooked, lying, deceptive, corrupt, unprincipled, unscrupulous ➡ **fake, sly, bad**

dishonesty *n* deceit, corruption, fraudulence, vice, crookedness, duplicity, cunning, guile, hypocrisy ➡ **lie, trick**

If the word you want is not a main entry above, look below to find it.

disapproval ➡ opposition
disapprove ➡ object, refuse
disarrange ➡ disturb
disastrous ➡ unfortunate
disband ➡ finish
disbelief ➡ doubt
disbelieve ➡ doubt
disburse ➡ pay
discern ➡ see
discernible ➡ audible, visible
discerning ➡ smart, profound
discernment ➡ wisdom
discharge ➡ fire, explode, shoot, free, relieve, suspension
disciple ➡ student
disclose ➡ reveal, tell
disclosure ➡ discovery
discoloration ➡ scar

discomfit ➡ embarrass
discomfited ➡ uncomfortable
discomfort ➡ pain
disconcert ➡ confuse, disturb, embarrass
discontinue ➡ stop, abandon
discord ➡ disagreement, confusion
discount ➡ bargain, sale, subtraction
discouragement ➡ disappointment
discourse ➡ speech
discourteous ➡ rude
discourtesy ➡ rudeness
discredit ➡ disprove, shame
discreet ➡ careful
discreetly ➡ carefully
discrepancy ➡ contradiction, difference

discretion ➡ tact
discriminate ➡ distinguish, separate
discrimination ➡ prejudice
discriminatory ➡ prejudiced
discuss ➡ talk
discussion ➡ talk, argument
disdain ➡ hatred, ridicule, hate
disembark ➡ leave
disentangle ➡ comb
disfigure ➡ damage, mutilate
disfigurement ➡ scar
disgrace ➡ shame
disgraceful ➡ awful, shameful
disgusting ➡ bad
dish ➡ bowl, plate, meal
dishcloth ➡ cloth
dishearten ➡ sadden, disappoint

dishevel ➡ disturb
disheveled ➡ messy
dishonor ➡ shame
dishonorable ➡ shameful
dish out ➡ give
dishrag ➡ cloth
disillusion ➡ disappoint
disillusionment ➡ disappointment
disinclined ➡ reluctant
disinfected ➡ sterile
disinformation ➡ lie
disintegrate ➡ decay
disintegration ➡ decay
disinterest ➡ apathy
disinterested ➡ apathetic
disk ➡ circle
dislike ➡ hate, hatred, opposition

---

n = noun • *vb* = verb • *adj* = adjective • *adv* = adverb • *prep* = preposition • *conj* = conjunction

disobedience *n* defiance, rebellion, insubordination, transgression, waywardness ➡ **revolution**

disobey *vb* defy, disregard, violate, break, misbehave, transgress ➡ **rebel, refuse, fight, sin** ⇨ *obey*

display 1. *n* exhibit, exhibition, presentation, arrangement, array ➡ **show**
2. *n* ➡ **show**
3. *vb* ➡ **show**

disprove *vb* discredit, refute, rebut, invalidate, controvert, expose, debunk ➡ **contradict**

distance 1. *n* stretch, length, interval, gap, way, expanse, extent ➡ **measure**
2. *n* ➡ **background**

distinguish *vb* differentiate, discriminate, identify, recognize ➡ **separate, compare**

distort 1. *vb* ➡ **bend, damage**
2. *vb* misrepresent, pervert, misconstrue, stretch ➡ **change, lie**

distract *vb* divert, sidetrack, deflect ➡ **bother, disturb**

disturb 1. *vb* disarrange, displace, dislocate, disorder, mess, muss, dishevel, rumple, garble ➡ **move**
2. *vb* interrupt, disrupt, intrude, interfere, impose ➡ **bother, distract**
3. *vb* agitate, upset, perturb, unnerve, unsettle, disconcert, ruffle, jar ➡ **worry, bother**

If the word you want is not a main entry above, look below to find it.

disliked ➡ unpopular

dislocate ➡ disturb, hurt

dislodge ➡ move

disloyal ➡ unfaithful

disloyalty ➡ treason

dismal ➡ bleak, sad

dismay ➡ discourage, fear, shock

dismember ➡ mutilate

dismiss ➡ refuse, fire, relieve

dismissal ➡ rejection

dismount ➡ descend

disobedient ➡ mischievous, rebellious

disorder ➡ confusion, illness, disturb

disorderly ➡ messy, wild

disorient ➡ confuse

disparage ➡ ridicule

disparate ➡ different

disparity ➡ difference

dispatch ➡ delivery, letter, speed, send, kill

dispel ➡ banish

dispense ➡ give, inflict

dispersal ➡ flow

disperse ➡ spread, disappear

dispirit ➡ discourage

displace ➡ disturb

displaced ➡ homeless

displacement ➡ movement

disport ➡ play

dispose ➡ discard, persuade

disposed ➡ likely, ready, vulnerable

disposition ➡ mood, personality, tendency, order

dispossessed ➡ homeless

dispute ➡ argument, argue, contradict, object

disregard ➡ disobey, forget, neglect

disregarded ➡ unnoticed

disrepair ➡ decay

disreputable ➡ shameful, bad

disrespect ➡ rudeness, neglect

disrespectful ➡ rude

disrobe ➡ undress

disrupt ➡ disturb

disruption ➡ disturbance, break

dissatisfaction ➡ disappointment

dissatisfy ➡ disappoint

dissemble ➡ lie

dissembler ➡ hypocrite

dissembling ➡ hypocritical

disseminate ➡ spread

dissemination ➡ flow

dissension ➡ disagreement

dissent ➡ disagreement, object

dissertation ➡ report

dissident ➡ rebel

dissimilar ➡ different

dissimilarity ➡ difference

dissipate ➡ disappear, waste

dissolute ➡ immoral

dissolve ➡ melt, disappear, finish

dissuade ➡ discourage

distant ➡ far, foreign, cool

distaste ➡ disgust

distasteful ➡ thankless, bad

distend ➡ swell, lengthen

distill ➡ concentrate

distinct ➡ different, special, obvious, audible, legible

distinction ➡ difference, excellence

distinctive ➡ special

distinguished ➡ famous

distracted ➡ absentminded

distraught ➡ frantic

distress ➡ misery, sorrow, trouble

distressful ➡ uncomfortable

distressing ➡ pitiful

distribute ➡ spread, share, give

distribution ➡ delivery, division, flow

district ➡ zone

distrust ➡ doubt

distrustful ➡ suspicious

➡ = synonym cross-reference • ⇨ = antonym cross-reference

disturbance *n* commotion, uproar, riot, disruption, fracas, upheaval, turbulence, unrest, rampage ➡ **noise, confusion, protest, violence, fight**

divide 1. *vb* part, split, partition, segment, subdivide, portion, apportion, halve, quarter, zone ➡ **cut, separate, share**
2. *vb* diverge, branch, fork
3. *vb* ➡ **arrange**

divider *n* partition, barrier, screen, curtain, veil ➡ **wall**

division 1. *n* separation, detachment, partition, distribution, divorce, severance, subdivision
2. *n* section, component, chapter, passage, paragraph, scene, episode ➡ **part, share, department**

dizzy *adj* light-headed, giddy, woozy, faint, dazed, tipsy

do 1. *vb* accomplish, achieve, carry out, render ➡ **act, cause, work**
2. *vb* ➡ **solve**
3. *vb* ➡ **satisfy**

dock 1. *n* pier, wharf, quay, landing, slip ➡ **harbor**
2. *vb* moor, land, anchor, berth ➡ **descend** ⇨ *leave*

doctor 1. *n* physician, M.D., GP, professor, Ph.D.
2. *vb* ➡ **heal**

document *n* record, certificate, form, file, diploma, citation, affidavit, passport, deed, credentials, manuscript ➡ **report, agreement, license, ticket**

dog *n* hound, mongrel, mutt, cur, puppy, canine, whelp

dogmatic *adj* opinionated, doctrinaire, dictatorial, arrogant, overbearing, imperious ➡ **stubborn**

doll *n* dolly, baby doll, figurine, mannequin, action figure ➡ **puppet, toy**

door *n* doorway, entrance, entry, exit, gate, gateway, access, portal, passage, outlet, opening, mouth ➡ **threshold**

If the word you want is not a main entry above, look below to find it.

disturbed ➡ anxious

ditch ➡ channel

ditty ➡ song

dive ➡ fall, jump

diverge ➡ differ, divide, swerve, wander

divergence ➡ departure

diverse ➡ different, many

diversely ➡ differently

diversion ➡ detour, entertainment

divert ➡ distract, entertain, detour

divertissement ➡ entertainment

divest ➡ deprive, undress

divination ➡ prediction

divine ➡ holy, heavenly, religious, predict

diviner ➡ prophet

divinity ➡ god

divorce ➡ separate, division

divorced ➡ single

divulge ➡ reveal

docile ➡ gentle, passive, tame

doctrinaire ➡ dogmatic

doctrine ➡ belief

documentation ➡ proof

dodder ➡ limp

dodge ➡ avoid, escape, swerve, trick

dogged ➡ diligent, stubborn

dogma ➡ belief

doleful ➡ sad

dolly ➡ doll

dolt ➡ fool

domain ➡ country, field

domestic ➡ native, family, tame, servant

domesticated ➡ tame

domicile ➡ home

dominant ➡ predominant

dominate ➡ control, excel

dominion ➡ country, state, rule

don ➡ dress, teacher

donate ➡ give

donation ➡ gift

done ➡ past

donjon ➡ castle

donor ➡ patron

doom ➡ fate

doorkeeper ➡ doorman

---

n = noun • *vb* = verb • *adj* = adjective • *adv* = adverb • *prep* = preposition • *conj* = conjunction

doorman *n* doorkeeper, porter, gatekeeper, caretaker, watchman, attendant ➡ **porter, servant**

dose *n* dosage, treatment, teaspoonful ➡ **measure**

doubt 1. *vb* suspect, mistrust, distrust, disbelieve, wonder ➡ **question**
2. *n* uncertainty, suspicion, skepticism, distrust, misgiving, disbelief, doubtfulness, reservation, question, qualm ➡ **suspense**

doubtful *adj* dubious, questionable, uncertain, indefinite, unclear, unsure, skeptical, ambivalent, perplexed, incredulous, vague, tentative ➡ **suspicious, unbelievable, unresolved**

down 1. *adv* downward, downhill, descending
2. *adj* ➡ **sad**
3. *adj* ➡ **broken**

4. *n* ➡ **hill**
5. *vb* ➡ **defeat**
6. *vb* ➡ **drink**

draw 1. *vb* ➡ **pull**
2. *vb* ➡ **earn**
3. *vb* sketch, paint, color, portray, depict, illustrate, picture, trace, delineate, draft, diagram ➡ **describe**
4. *n* ➡ **attraction**
5. *n* ➡ **tie**

dream *n* reverie, daydream, trance, daze, spell, stupor, study, swoon ➡ **hope**

dress 1. *vb* wear, clothe, don, robe, attire, costume, outfit, deck
2. *vb* trim, groom, array ➡ **decorate**
3. *vb* ➡ **bandage**
4. *n* gown, frock, jumper, sheath, skirt, shift, shirtwaist, pinafore, smock, sari, sarong, muumuu ➡ **clothes**

If the word you want is not a main entry above, look below to find it.

doorsill ➡ threshold
doorstep ➡ threshold
doorway ➡ door
do-rag ➡ scarf
dormant ➡ asleep, latent
dormer ➡ attic
dormitory ➡ bedroom
dosage ➡ dose
dot ➡ spot
dote on ➡ love, pamper
double ➡ duplicate, alternate, fold
double agent ➡ spy
double-cross ➡ betray
doubter ➡ skeptic
doubtfulness ➡ doubt

doubting Thomas ➡ skeptic
dour ➡ bleak
douse ➡ extinguish, wet
dowel ➡ nail
downcast ➡ sad
downfall ➡ defeat, fate
downhearted ➡ sad
downhill ➡ down
downpour ➡ rain
downs ➡ plain
down-to-earth ➡ practical
downturn ➡ drop, depression
downward ➡ down
downy ➡ fuzzy
doze ➡ sleep

dozing ➡ asleep
drab ➡ dull, plain, gray
draft ➡ draw, hire, write, drink, wind
draftee ➡ soldier
drafty ➡ windy
drag ➡ pull, crawl
drain ➡ dry, empty
drained ➡ tired
drainpipe ➡ pipe
dram ➡ drink
drama ➡ emotion, play
dramatic ➡ sensational
dramatization ➡ play
dramatize ➡ exaggerate, act
drape ➡ hang

drastic ➡ excessive
drawback ➡ defect
drawing ➡ picture
drawing room ➡ living room
drawl ➡ accent
drawn ➡ tense
draw near ➡ approach
dread ➡ fear
dreadful ➡ awful, scary
dreamer ➡ idealist
dreaming ➡ asleep
drear ➡ bleak
dreary ➡ bleak, dull
drench ➡ wet
drenched ➡ wet

➡ = synonym cross-reference • ⇨ = antonym cross-reference

drink 1. *n* beverage, refreshment, alcohol, liquor, spirits ➡ **soda, liquid**
2. *n* sip, glass, swallow, taste, drop, dram, nip, swig, gulp, draft
3. *vb* swallow, gulp, guzzle, quaff, sip, swig, imbibe, down

drive 1. *vb* steer, maneuver, navigate, pilot, ride, propel, jockey ➡ **operate, control**
2. *vb* ➡ **banish**
3. *n* ➡ **trip**
4. *n* ➡ **ambition, energy**

drop 1. *n* droplet, raindrop, teardrop, tear, bead, drip, glob, trickle, dribble ➡ **ball**
2. *n* ➡ **drink**
3. *n* plunge, reduction, decrease, descent, decline, slump, downturn, dip ➡ **fall**
4. *vb* drip, trickle, leak, seep, ooze ➡ **splash**
5. *vb* ➡ **descend, fall, lose, shed**

drug *n* antibiotic, narcotic, sedative, tranquilizer, painkiller, anesthetic, opiate, hallucinogen, antidepressant ➡ **medicine**

drunk *adj* drunken, intoxicated, inebriated, tipsy, besotted

drunkard *n* alcoholic, drinker, inebriate, sot, souse, tippler, lush *(informal)*, wino *(informal)*

dry 1. *adj* arid, parched, dehydrated, dessicated, dusty, thirsty ➡ **stale** ⇨ *wet*
2. *adj* ➡ **dull**
3. *adj* droll, wry, deadpan, sardonic ➡ **funny**
4. *adj* ➡ **sour**
5. *vb* wipe, drain
6. *vb* evaporate, dehydrate, wilt, wither, shrivel ➡ **harden**

due 1. *adj* unpaid, payable, outstanding, overdue, receivable
2. *adj* expected, scheduled, anticipated
3. *adv* ➡ **precisely**

dull 1. *adj* uninteresting, boring, tedious, dreary, monotonous, tiresome, prosaic, humdrum, shallow, deadly, dry, drab ➡ **insipid** ⇨ *interesting, lively*
2. *adj* slow, stolid, obtuse, dense, unimaginative, square ➡ **stupid**
3. *adj* blunt, unsharpened ⇨ *sharp*
4. *adj* drab, dim, dingy, faded, lackluster, flat ➡ **bleak, dark, dim** ⇨ *bright*

If the word you want is not a main entry above, look below to find it.

dresser ➡ chest, table

dressing ➡ bandage

dressing gown ➡ bathrobe

dribble ➡ drop

drift ➡ blow², fly, wander

drifter ➡ loafer

drill ➡ dig, teach, practice, lesson

drinker ➡ drunkard

drip ➡ drop

dripping ➡ wet

drivel ➡ nonsense

drive out, drive away ➡ banish

driver's seat ➡ wheel

drizzle ➡ rain

drizzly ➡ wet

droll ➡ dry

drone ➡ hum

droop ➡ bend, weaken

droopy ➡ limp

drop by, drop in ➡ visit

drop-kick ➡ kick

droplet ➡ drop

drown ➡ choke, flood

drowsy ➡ listless

drudgery ➡ work

drum ➡ barrel, knock

drunken ➡ drunk

dry cleaning ➡ laundry

dub ➡ name

dubious ➡ doubtful, suspicious

duck ➡ avoid, bend, sink

duct ➡ pipe, blood vessel

duct tape ➡ adhesive

dud ➡ disappointment

due to ➡ because

duel ➡ fight

due process ➡ justice

duffel bag ➡ luggage

dumb *adj* mute, speechless, silent, inarticulate, voiceless, wordless, tongue-tied ➡ **quiet**
For the informal use of **dumb** *meaning "not very smart," see* **stupid**.

dumbfounded *adj* astonished, amazed, bewildered, thunderstruck, flabbergasted, surprised

dump 1. *n* landfill, recycling center, trash heap, junkyard
2. *vb* ➡ **discard, empty**

duplicate 1. *n* double, twin, replica, counterpart, equivalent, analogue, parallel
➡ **copy, model**
2. *vb* ➡ **repeat, reproduce**

during *prep* throughout, through

duty 1. *n* responsibility, obligation, trust, charge
2. *n* ➡ **job**
3. *n* ➡ **tax**

If the word you want is not a main entry above, look below to find it.

dullard ➡ boor
dummy ➡ fake, fool, puppet
dunce ➡ fool
dune ➡ hill
dungeon ➡ jail
dunk ➡ sink
duo ➡ pair

dupe ➡ cheat, tool
duplicity ➡ dishonesty
durable ➡ strong, tough, unbreakable, permanent
duration ➡ period
duress ➡ stress
dusk ➡ dark, evening
dusky ➡ dark, gray

dust ➡ dirt, sweep
dustcloth ➡ cloth
dust jacket ➡ wrapper
dusty ➡ dirty, dry
dutiful ➡ good
duvet ➡ blanket
dwarf ➡ midget

dwell ➡ live¹
dwelling ➡ home
dwindle ➡ decrease
dye ➡ paint
dying ➡ death
dynamic ➡ active
dynamo ➡ engine

➡ = synonym cross-reference • ⇨ = antonym cross-reference

E

eager *adj* enthusiastic, keen, avid, anxious, ardent, passionate, fervent, exuberant, impatient ➡ **ready, ambitious**

early 1. *adj* initial, original, first, earliest, pioneering, pioneer, primary, inaugural, introductory, preliminary, incipient, embryonic, developing, nascent ⇨ *late*
2. *adj* premature, untimely, precocious, hasty, prompt ➡ **sudden** ⇨ *late*
3. *adj* primitive, primeval, prehistoric, primal, archaic, primordial ➡ **old** ⇨ *modern*

earn 1. *vb* make, collect, realize, profit, net, gross, draw, take (in) ➡ **get, receive, win, pay**
2. *vb* ➡ **deserve**

earth 1. *n* world, globe, nature, creation ➡ **planet, space**
2. *n* ➡ **dirt**

earthquake *n* quake, tremor, tremblor, shock, aftershock ➡ **vibration**

easy *adj* effortless, light, simple, moderate, straightforward ➡ **obvious, plain** ⇨ *hard*

eat 1. *vb* consume, devour, dine, feast, feed, graze, browse, gulp, gobble, wolf, gorge, bolt, prey on
2. *vb* ➡ **corrode**
The words breakfast *and* lunch, *but not* dinner *or* supper, *can also be used as verbs meaning "to eat breakfast or lunch."*

economy 1. *n* thrift, thriftiness, frugality, austerity, prudence, conservation
2. *n* ➡ **brevity**

ecstatic *adj* elated, overjoyed, thrilled, blissful, jubilant, exultant, triumphant ➡ **happy**

edge *n* rim, margin, fringe, brink, boundary, verge, brim, lip, hem, periphery ➡ **border, circumference, side, shore**

educated *adj* literate, learned, knowledgeable, informed, studious, scholarly, erudite, lettered, well-read, well-informed, well-versed, schooled, bookish ➡ **smart** ⇨ *ignorant*

education *n* learning, schooling, instruction, teaching, tuition, training, scholarship, erudition ➡ **study, lesson, knowledge**

If the word you want is not a main entry above, look below to find it.

each ➡ **all, any**

eagerness ➡ **enthusiasm, ambition**

earlier ➡ **before, older**

earliest ➡ **early**

earnest ➡ **serious**

earnestly ➡ **sincerely**

earnings ➡ **wage**

earsplitting ➡ **loud**

earthenware ➡ **pottery**

earthworm ➡ **worm**

earthy ➡ **dirty**

ease ➡ **calm, facilitate, relieve, rest, comfort, freedom, leisure**

easygoing ➡ **carefree, tolerant**

eating area ➡ **dining room**

eavesdrop ➡ **listen, spy**

ebb ➡ **retreat, decrease**

ebony ➡ **black, dark**

eccentric ➡ **strange**

eccentricity ➡ **oddity**

ecclesiastical ➡ **religious**

echo ➡ **answer, reflect, repeat**

eclectic ➡ **different**

eclipse ➡ **hide, exceed**

economic ➡ **financial**

economical ➡ **efficient, cheap**

economics ➡ **business**

ecosystem ➡ **habitat**

ecstasy ➡ **pleasure**

Eden ➡ **utopia**

edgy ➡ **nervous**

edibles ➡ **food**

edict ➡ **order**

edifice ➡ **building**

edit ➡ **correct, write**

educate ➡ **teach**

educational ➡ **intellectual**

educator ➡ **teacher**

eerie ➡ **strange**

efface ➡ **erase**

n = noun • *vb* = verb • *adj* = adjective • *adv* = adverb • *prep* = preposition • *conj* = conjunction

effect 1. *n* result, outcome, consequence, upshot, aftermath, issue ➡ **product**
2. *n* impact, impression, influence
3. *vb* ➡ **cause**
Be careful not to confuse the verb **effect** *with the verb* **affect**. *See the note at* **affect**.

efficiency *n* productivity, effectiveness, efficacy, proficiency

efficient *adj* proficient, productive, competent, effective, economical, expedient, cost-effective, practical ➡ **able, useful**

egg 1. *n* ovum, embryo, germ, roe, spawn ➡ **seed**
2. *vb* ➡ **urge**

elapse *vb* pass, lapse, slip by, expire

elegance *n* class, taste, polish, style, grace, splendor, glory, grandeur, sophistication, opulence, luxury ➡ **beauty**

embalm *vb* preserve, mummify ➡ **keep**

embarrass *vb* abash, disconcert, rattle, faze, discomfit, fluster, mortify, chagrin ➡ **shame**

embed *vb* imbed, enclose, insert, inset, wedge, implant, lodge, inlay ➡ **put**

embody *vb* represent, typify, incorporate, exemplify ➡ **contain**

If the word you want is not a main entry above, look below to find it.

effective ➡ efficient, successful
effectively ➡ practically
effectiveness ➡ efficiency
effects ➡ property, luggage
effeminate ➡ feminine
efficacy ➡ efficiency, ability
effigy ➡ statue, god
effort ➡ work, try
effortless ➡ easy
effusive ➡ talkative
eggshell ➡ shell
egg timer ➡ clock
ego ➡ mind, soul
egocentric ➡ proud
egotism ➡ pride
egotistic ➡ proud
Einstein ➡ genius
either ➡ any
eject ➡ exclude, oust
elaborate ➡ complicated, fancy, exaggerate
elaboration ➡ exaggeration

elastic ➡ flexible, rubber band
elastic band ➡ rubber band
elated ➡ ecstatic
elbow ➡ push
elbow grease ➡ work
elbowroom ➡ space
elder ➡ ancestor, older
elderly ➡ old
elect ➡ choose
election ➡ vote, appointment
elective ➡ course
electric ➡ exciting
electricity ➡ energy
electrify ➡ shock
electrifying ➡ exciting
electroplate ➡ plate
elegant ➡ beautiful, grand, fashionable
elegy ➡ dirge
element ➡ matter, part

elemental ➡ basic
elementary ➡ basic
elevate ➡ lift, promote
elevation ➡ height, promotion
elf ➡ fairy
elfin ➡ mischievous
elfish ➡ mischievous
elicit ➡ extract
eligible ➡ able, single
eliminate ➡ abolish, exclude
elite ➡ noble, aristocracy
elocution ➡ delivery
elongate ➡ lengthen
elongated ➡ long
elope ➡ escape
eloquent ➡ articulate
else ➡ different, differently
elsewhere ➡ absent
elucidate ➡ explain
elude ➡ avoid, escape
elusive ➡ inaccessible, sly

elysian fields, Elysium ➡ heaven
emaciated ➡ thin, hungry
e-mail ➡ send
emancipate ➡ free
emancipated ➡ free
emancipation ➡ salvation
embankment ➡ dam
embargo ➡ ban
embark ➡ leave, enter
embarkation ➡ departure
embarrassed ➡ ashamed
embarrassment ➡ shame
embellish ➡ decorate, exaggerate
embellished ➡ fancy
embellishment ➡ decoration, exaggeration
embezzle ➡ steal
embezzlement ➡ theft
embitter ➡ anger
emblem ➡ badge
emboss ➡ print

---

embrace 1. *vb* hug, clasp, cuddle, enfold, envelop, squeeze, hold, grip, grasp, clench
2. *vb* ➡ **adopt**
3. *n* hug, clasp, handshake, caress, squeeze

emergency *n* crisis, exigency, extremity ➡ **disaster, trouble, accident**

emotion *n* sentiment, passion, drama, affect ➡ **feeling**

emotional 1. *adj* moving, poignant, touching, tearful, passionate, impassioned ➡ **pitiful, sad**
2. *adj* sentimental, demonstrative, sensitive, impetuous, overemotional, maudlin ➡ **temperamental, excited, loving**

emperor *n* czar, tzar, tsar (*Russian*), kaiser (*German*), caliph (*Islamic*), pharaoh (*Egyptian*), mikado (*Japanese*) ➡ **ruler, king**

emphasize *vb* highlight, feature, stress, accent, accentuate, underscore, underline

employed *adj* working, occupied, busy, engaged ⇨ *unemployed*

empress *n* czarina, tzarina, tsarina (*Russian*), kaiserin (*German*) ➡ **ruler, queen**

empty 1. *adj* vacant, unoccupied, uninhabited, bare, austere, blank, void, devoid, hollow, open ➡ **abandoned** ⇨ *full*
2. *adj* idle, vain, meaningless, hollow
3. *vb* unload, unpack, unwrap, remove, dump out, pour out, clean out, evacuate, vacate, deflate, drain

enchant *vb* beguile, entrance, charm, bewitch, hypnotize, mesmerize, spellbind, snow ➡ **fascinate, tempt**

enchantment *n* charm, spell, allure ➡ **attraction, magic**

encore *interj* bravo, brava, bravissimo, hurrah ➡ **again**

enemy *n* rival, adversary, antagonist, foe, attacker, assailant ➡ **opponent**

If the word you want is not a main entry above, look below to find it.

embroider ➡ sew, exaggerate

embroidery ➡ exaggeration

embryo ➡ egg

embryonic ➡ early

emcee ➡ host

emend ➡ correct

emendation ➡ correction

emerald ➡ green

emerge ➡ appear

emigrant ➡ exile, foreigner

emigrate ➡ move

emigration ➡ movement

emigré ➡ exile, foreigner

eminence ➡ excellence, fame

eminent ➡ famous

emissary ➡ messenger, diplomat

emit ➡ throw

empathy ➡ pity

emphasis ➡ accent

employ ➡ hire, use

employee ➡ servant, worker

employer ➡ boss

employment ➡ profession, use

emporium ➡ market

empower ➡ let

emulate ➡ imitate

enable ➡ let

enact ➡ act, commit

enactment ➡ approval

encephalogram ➡ X ray

enchanted ➡ magic

enchanter ➡ magician

encircle ➡ ring

enclose ➡ ring, embed

enclosure ➡ booth, pen

encompass ➡ ring, concern

encounter ➡ face, fight, meeting, experience

encourage ➡ urge

encouragement ➡ incentive, support

encroach ➡ intrude

encumber ➡ load

encumbered ➡ disabled

encyclopedia ➡ dictionary

end ➡ abolish, finish, back, destination, fate, point, side

endanger ➡ jeopardize

endeavor ➡ try, work

ended ➡ past

endemic ➡ native

ending ➡ finish

endless ➡ eternal, infinite

endlessly ➡ forever

endorse ➡ approve, prefer, sign

endow ➡ give

endowment ➡ gift, inheritance

endurance ➡ energy, patience

endure ➡ bear, weather, continue, experience

enduring ➡ permanent

n = noun • *vb* = verb • *adj* = adjective • *adv* = adverb • *prep* = preposition • *interj* = interjection

energy 1. *n* vigor, vitality, life, liveliness, pep, stamina, endurance, vim, drive, get-up-and-go, zip, steam ➡ **strength, excitement**
2. *n* power, horsepower, pressure, thrust, propulsion, voltage, current, electricity, heat, fuel

engine *n* motor, machine, generator, turbine, dynamo

enough *adj* ample, sufficient, adequate, abundant, plentiful, plenty, much
> Note that **enough, plenty,** and **much** *cannot be used after an or before a singular noun such as supply, amount, quantity, or number. The other words in this list can be used in this way: "an* **ample** *supply," "a* **sufficient** *amount," "an* **abundant** *quantity," "an* **adequate** *number of items," "a* **plentiful** *supply."*

enter 1. *vb* penetrate, invade, infiltrate ➡ **go, approach, intrude** ⇨ *leave*
2. *vb* board, mount, embark, entrain, enplane ⇨ *leave*
3. *vb* ➡ **join**

entertain 1. *vb* amuse, divert, cheer (up), beguile, regale, enthrall, humor ➡ **please**
2. *vb* host, receive, treat, invite ➡ **welcome**
3. *vb* ➡ **consider**

entertainment *n* diversion, recreation, amusement, divertissement ➡ **pleasure, play, game, program**

enthusiasm *n* passion, zeal, fervor, zest, ardor, eagerness, exuberance, gusto ➡ **pleasure, excitement, ambition**

If the word you want is not a main entry above, look below to find it.

energetic ➡ lively

energize ➡ excite

enfold ➡ embrace

enforce ➡ support

engage ➡ interest, hire

engaged ➡ absorbed, employed, married

engagement ➡ meeting, fight

engaging ➡ interesting

engender ➡ cause

engineer ➡ control, creator

engrave ➡ carve, print

engraving ➡ inscription, print

engross ➡ interest

engrossed ➡ absorbed

engrossing ➡ interesting

engulf ➡ flood, sink

enhance ➡ strengthen, suit

enigma ➡ problem

enigmatic ➡ mysterious, obscure

enjoy ➡ appreciate, like, own

enjoyable ➡ pleasant

enjoyment ➡ pleasure

enlarge ➡ grow, strengthen

enlargement ➡ addition, growth

enlighten ➡ teach

enlightenment ➡ civilization

enlist ➡ join, hire, mobilize

enliven ➡ excite

en masse ➡ together

enmity ➡ opposition

ennui ➡ boredom

enormous ➡ huge

enormously ➡ much

enplane ➡ enter

enrage ➡ anger

enraged ➡ violent

enrich ➡ help

enroll ➡ join, hire

enrollee ➡ member

ensemble ➡ band, choir, suit

enshrine ➡ bury

ensign ➡ flag

enslave ➡ catch

enslavement ➡ slavery

ensnare ➡ catch

ensue ➡ follow, happen

ensuing ➡ consecutive, following

ensure ➡ guarantee, verify

entangle ➡ catch

enterprise ➡ ambition, adventure, business

enterprising ➡ ambitious

entertainer ➡ actor, musician, host

entertaining ➡ interesting

enthrall ➡ fascinate, entertain

enthrone ➡ crown

enthusiast ➡ fan

enthusiastic ➡ eager

entice ➡ tempt, persuade

enticement ➡ attraction

entire ➡ all, complete

entirely ➡ completely

entirety ➡ total

entitle ➡ name, let

entomb ➡ bury

entourage ➡ court, following

entrain ➡ enter

entrance ➡ door, enchant

entranceway ➡ threshold

entrancing ➡ magic

entreat ➡ beg

entrepreneur ➡ tycoon

➡ = synonym cross-reference • ⇨ = antonym cross-reference

entrust *vb* commit, confide, consign, delegate, relegate

envy 1. *vb* desire, covet, resent, grudge, begrudge ➡ **want**
2. *n* jealousy, covetousness, resentment, spite, desire, malice ➡ **greed**

epidemic 1. *n* plague, pestilence, outbreak, eruption, rash, pandemic ➡ **disease**
2. *adj* ➡ **contagious**

equal 1. *adj* ➡ **same, fair**
2. *n* peer, fellow, mate, match, compeer ➡ **duplicate**

equipment *n* machinery, apparatus, paraphernalia, device, implement, fixture, gear, tackle, harness, kit, accoutrement, facilities ➡ **tool**

erase *vb* obliterate, delete, scratch, eradicate, expunge, efface ➡ **abolish**

escape 1. *vb* flee, elude, evade, dodge, break out, bolt, elope ➡ **avoid, leave**
2. *n* flight, getaway, evasion, desertion, deliverance, rescue ➡ **departure**

essence *n* core, heart, substance, quintessence, bottom, marrow, root, gist ➡ **basis, middle, soul**

If the word you want is not a main entry above, look below to find it.

entry ➡ approach, door, contestant

entryway ➡ hall, threshold

enumerate ➡ list

enunciate ➡ pronounce

enunciation ➡ speech, delivery

envelop ➡ embrace, wrap

envelope ➡ wrapper

envious ➡ jealous

environment ➡ habitat, setting, terrain, nature

envisage ➡ imagine

envision ➡ imagine

envoy ➡ messenger, diplomat

eon ➡ period

épée ➡ sword

ephemeral ➡ temporary

epic ➡ myth

epicure ➡ glutton

epilogue ➡ conclusion

episode ➡ division, event

epistle ➡ letter

epitaph ➡ inscription

epithet ➡ name

epoch ➡ period

epoxy ➡ adhesive

equalize ➡ balance

equatorial ➡ tropical

equestrian ➡ rider

equidistant ➡ parallel

equilibrium ➡ balance

equip ➡ supply

equipped ➡ ready

equitable ➡ fair

equity ➡ justice

equivalent ➡ alike, same, duplicate

equivocate ➡ hesitate, lie

equivocator ➡ liar

era ➡ period

eradicate ➡ abolish, erase, kill

erect ➡ build, lift, vertical

erection ➡ assembly

ergo ➡ therefore

erode ➡ corrode, weaken

err ➡ misunderstand, sin

errand ➡ job

erratic ➡ fickle, periodic, variable, zigzag

erroneous ➡ wrong

error ➡ mistake

ersatz ➡ fake

erudite ➡ educated, profound

erudition ➡ education, knowledge

erupt ➡ explode

eruption ➡ epidemic

escalation ➡ growth

escapade ➡ adventure

escape artist ➡ magician

escapee ➡ runaway

escarpment ➡ cliff

eschew ➡ abstain

escort ➡ accompany, bring, guide, patrol

escutcheon ➡ badge

esoteric ➡ secret

especial ➡ special

especially ➡ chiefly

espionage ➡ spying

espousal ➡ marriage

espouse ➡ adopt, marry

espoused ➡ married

essay ➡ report, try

essayist ➡ writer

essential ➡ necessary, important, necessity

essentially ➡ chiefly, practically

establish ➡ base, verify

establishment ➡ business

estate ➡ property

esteem ➡ respect

esthetics ➡ philosophy

estimable ➡ praiseworthy

estimate 1. *vb* calculate, evaluate, approximate, reckon, figure, gauge, assess, judge, appraise
➡ **guess**
2. *n* approximation, evaluation, appraisal, assessment, estimation, bid, quotation, quote, comparison ➡ **budget**

eternal *adj* everlasting, endless, unending, perpetual, interminable, infinite, immortal, deathless, undying ➡ **continual, permanent**

evening *n* nightfall, twilight, dusk, eventide, sundown, sunset ➡ **afternoon, night**
⇨ *morning*

event 1. *n* incident, occurrence, episode, circumstance, occasion, happening, phenomenon, actuality, fact
2. *n* milestone, landmark, breakthrough, achievement, experience, adventure
➡ **ceremony, disaster**
3. *n* ➡ **game**

exaggerate *vb* overstate, overdo, inflate, embellish, embroider, elaborate, gild, magnify, dramatize

exaggeration *n* overstatement, hyperbole, embroidery, embellishment, elaboration

examination 1. *n* exam, test, quiz, final, midterm, take-home, inquest, trial
2. *n* ➡ **study**

examine 1. *vb* investigate, scrutinize, inspect, probe, scan ➡ **study, look**
2. *vb* test, quiz, interrogate ➡ **ask**

example *n* instance, case, illustration, specimen, sample, representation, representative
➡ **model**

exceed *vb* outdo, surpass, pass, top, better, best, transcend, outshine, eclipse, outnumber, overstep ➡ **excel**

excel *vb* dominate, prevail ➡ **exceed**

excellence *n* perfection, faultlessness, superiority, greatness, distinction, eminence, majesty

---

If the word you want is not a main entry above, look below to find it.

estimated ➡ approximate

estimation ➡ estimate, reputation, respect, worth

estuary ➡ bay, river

etch ➡ carve

etching ➡ print

eternally ➡ forever

eternity ➡ future

ethereal ➡ invisible

ethics ➡ philosophy

etiquette ➡ behavior

euphonious ➡ musical

evacuate ➡ empty, leave

evade ➡ avoid, escape

evaluate ➡ estimate, study

evaluation ➡ estimate

evaluator ➡ judge

evaporate ➡ disappear, dry, melt

evasion ➡ escape

even ➡ level, parallel, straight

evenhandedness ➡ justice

eventide ➡ evening

eventuality ➡ possibility

eventually ➡ finally

ever ➡ regularly

evergreen ➡ pine, tree

everlasting ➡ eternal

evermore ➡ forever

every ➡ all, any

everybody ➡ all

everyday ➡ common

everyone ➡ all

every other ➡ alternate

everything ➡ all

everywhere ➡ about

evict ➡ banish

evidence ➡ proof, knowledge

evident ➡ obvious

evidently ➡ apparently

evil ➡ bad, wicked, crime, disaster, immorality

evoke ➡ extract

evolution ➡ change

evolve ➡ grow

ewer ➡ bottle

exact ➡ careful, correct, literal, extract, inflict

exacting ➡ strict

exactitude ➡ accuracy

exactly ➡ precisely

exactness ➡ accuracy

exaggerated ➡ sensational

exalt ➡ bless, worship

exalted ➡ grand

exam ➡ examination

exasperate ➡ anger

exasperated ➡ angry

excavate ➡ dig

excavation ➡ mine

exceeding ➡ above

excellent ➡ good, model, cool

---

excerpt *n* clause, section, provision, passage, portion, quotation, selection, extract

excessive *adj* extreme, drastic, radical, inordinate, immoderate, intemperate, exorbitant, overabundant ➡ **unnecessary**

excite *vb* stimulate, exhilarate, agitate, thrill, energize, arouse, galvanize, enliven ➡ **fan** ⇨ *calm*

excited *adj* thrilled, exhilarated, hysterical, stimulated ➡ **eager, nervous, frantic, angry, emotional**

excitement *n* agitation, tumult, exhilaration, stimulation, thrill, zest, fever, fireworks ➡ **enthusiasm, energy, confusion, hysteria**

exciting *adj* riveting, gripping, breathtaking, sensational, electric, electrifying, rousing, thrilling, exhilarating ➡ **interesting**

exclude *vb* eliminate, suspend, reject, omit, eject, skip, neglect, ignore, overlook, miss, remove, rid ➡ **banish, bar, forbid, forget**

exercise 1. *n* exertion, training, workout, activity, conditioning
2. *n* ➡ **use**
3. *n* ➡ **lesson**
4. *vb* train, work out, condition
5. *vb* ➡ **use**

exhaustion *n* fatigue, weariness, tiredness, listlessness, prostration

exile 1. *n* expulsion, banishment, deportation, transportation, ostracism
2. *n* refugee, fugitive, emigré, emigrant, deportee, expatriate, outcast, pariah ➡ **foreigner**
3. *vb* ➡ **banish**

existence *n* being, reality, substance, materiality

If the word you want is not a main entry above, look below to find it.

excellently ➡ well

except ➡ but

exceptional ➡ special

excess ➡ abundance

exchange ➡ trade, change

exchequer ➡ bank

exclaim ➡ say

excluding ➡ but

exclusive ➡ private

exclusively ➡ only

excursion ➡ trip

excuse ➡ apology, alibi, opportunity, pretense, forgive, relieve

execrate ➡ hate

execute ➡ act, kill, hang

execution ➡ behavior

executioner ➡ killer

executive ➡ official

executor ➡ agent

exemplar ➡ model

exemplary ➡ perfect

exemplify ➡ embody, explain

exempt ➡ free

exert ➡ use

exertion ➡ exercise, work

exhalation ➡ breath

exhale ➡ breathe

exhaust ➡ tire, use

exhausted ➡ tired

exhaustive ➡ complete, comprehensive

exhibit ➡ display, show

exhibition ➡ display

exhibition hall ➡ gallery

exhilarate ➡ excite

exhilarated ➡ excited

exhilarating ➡ exciting

exhilaration ➡ excitement

exhort ➡ preach, warn

exigency ➡ emergency

exist ➡ happen, live[1]

exit ➡ departure, door, leave

exodus ➡ departure

exonerate ➡ forgive

exoneration ➡ forgiveness

exorbitant ➡ excessive

exotic ➡ foreign

expand ➡ grow, spread, swell, strengthen

expanse ➡ distance, space

expansion ➡ addition, growth

expansive ➡ broad

expatriate ➡ banish, exile

expect ➡ anticipate, hope

expectant ➡ optimistic, pregnant

expectation ➡ possibility

expected ➡ due

expecting ➡ pregnant

expedient ➡ efficient

expedite ➡ facilitate

expedition ➡ trip

expeditious ➡ punctual

expeditiously ➡ quickly

expel ➡ banish, oust

expend ➡ pay, use

expenditure ➡ use

expense ➡ price

expenses ➡ budget

expensive *adj* costly, invaluable, precious, dear, high-priced, overpriced, extravagant, upscale
➡ **valuable, rich** ⇨ *cheap*

experience 1. *n* background, training, knowledge, skill, know-how, expertise
➡ **knowledge, wisdom, event**
2. *vb* undergo, encounter, endure, live through
➡ **bear**

experiment 1. *n* trial, test, experimentation, demonstration ➡ **examination, study**
2. *vb* ➡ **try, study**

experimental *adj* test, trial, innovative, developmental, provisional

expert 1. *n* authority, specialist, master, virtuoso, ace, connoisseur
2. *adj* proficient, skilled, masterly, adroit, ace, versed, well-versed ➡ **able, smart**

explain *vb* clarify, interpret, justify, demonstrate, elucidate, illustrate, illuminate, exemplify, expound, show, treat ➡ **solve, describe**

explicit *adj* vivid, realistic, graphic, precise
➡ **straightforward** ⇨ *obscure*

explode *vb* erupt, discharge, detonate, blow up, burst ➡ **break**

extinguish *vb* put out, quench, douse, smother, stifle ➡ **contain, kill**

extract 1. *vb* remove, withdraw, retract, pluck, extricate, leach ➡ **gather, pull**
2. *vb* elicit, evoke, extort, exact, derive ➡ **get, pull**
3. *n* ➡ **excerpt**

extremist *n* zealot, fanatic, maniac, radical ➡ **rebel**

If the word you want is not a main entry above, look below to find it.

experienced ➡ cosmopolitan

experimentation ➡ experiment

expertise ➡ experience, talent

expiate ➡ pay

expiration ➡ death

expire ➡ breathe, die, finish, elapse

explanation ➡ answer, reason, apology

expletive ➡ curse

exploit ➡ adventure, act, use

exploration ➡ hunt, study

explore ➡ hunt, travel

explosion ➡ bang

explosive ➡ dangerous, inflammable

export ➡ send

expose ➡ disprove, reveal, weather

exposed ➡ naked

expound ➡ explain

express ➡ say

expression ➡ face, saying, speech, word, sign

expressionless ➡ blank

expressive ➡ meaningful

expressway ➡ highway

expropriate ➡ take

expulsion ➡ exile, suspension

expunge ➡ erase

exquisite ➡ beautiful, perfect

extemporaneous ➡ spontaneous

extend ➡ lengthen, spread, offer, lend

extended ➡ long

extension ➡ addition

extensive ➡ broad, long, general

extent ➡ depth, distance, range, period

exterior ➡ outside

exterminate ➡ abolish, kill

external ➡ outside

extinct ➡ dead

extol ➡ praise

extort ➡ extract

extortion ➡ theft

extra ➡ more, unnecessary

extraction ➡ ancestry

extraneous ➡ unnecessary

extraordinary ➡ special

extravagant ➡ expensive, wasteful

extreme ➡ excessive, last

extremely ➡ much, very

extremity ➡ emergency, limb, foot

extricate ➡ extract, free

exuberance ➡ enthusiasm

exuberant ➡ eager

exude ➡ sweat

exult ➡ boast

exultant ➡ ecstatic

eye ➡ look

eyeglasses ➡ glasses

eyeless ➡ blind

eyesight ➡ sight

eyewitness ➡ observer

F

face 1. *n* features, visage, countenance, expression, profile ➡ **appearance**
2. *n* ➡ **side**
3. *vb* oppose, confront, defy, brave, challenge, encounter ➡ **bear, compete, fight** ⇨ *retreat*

facilitate *vb* ease, expedite, simplify, foster ➡ **help**

factory *n* plant, shop, workshop, mill, assembly plant ➡ **business**

faculty 1. *n* staff, personnel ➡ **teacher**
2. *adj* ➡ **ability**

fair 1. *adj* just, impartial, equal, unbiased, equitable, objective, unprejudiced, neutral, nonpartisan, detached, impersonal ➡ **right**
2. *adj* satisfactory, acceptable, adequate, mediocre, decent
3. *adj* clear, sunny, bright, pleasant, mild ➡ **bright** ⇨ *cloudy*
4. *adj* blond, blonde, light, white, ivory, creamy, bleached ➡ **pale**
5. *adj* ➡ **pretty**
6. *n* ➡ **carnival**

fairy *n* elf, pixie, sprite, spirit, brownie, leprechaun

faithful 1. *adj* loyal, true, devoted, steadfast, constant, trusty, trustworthy, resolute, staunch, fast, unfailing, unshaken, committed, tenacious ➡ **reliable, religious** ⇨ *unfaithful*
2. *adj* ➡ **correct**

fake 1. *adj* false, artificial, imitation, dummy, ersatz, counterfeit, spurious, phony, bogus, sham, mock ➡ **dishonest** ⇨ *real*
2. *n* phony, counterfeit, forgery, imitation, dummy ➡ **copy**
3. *n* ➡ **cheat**
4. *vb* forge, counterfeit, falsify ➡ **imitate, pretend**

fall 1. *vb* drop, collapse, plunge, topple, tumble, plummet, slump, plump, crumple, subside, slip, lapse, sink, set ➡ **descend, trip, lose**
2. *n* tumble, spill, dive, nosedive ➡ **drop**
3. *n* ➡ **wig**

fame *n* renown, celebrity, glory, eminence, standing, notoriety, popularity, prestige ➡ **reputation, respect**

If the word you want is not a main entry above, look below to find it.

fable ➡ **myth, superstition**

fabled ➡ **legendary**

fabric ➡ **cloth**

fabricate ➡ **build, invent, lie**

fabrication ➡ **pretense, lie, assembly**

fabulous ➡ **legendary, great**

façade ➡ **outside**

facet ➡ **side, part**

facetious ➡ **funny**

facile ➡ **suave**

facilities ➡ **equipment, bathroom**

facility ➡ **talent**

facing ➡ **opposite**

facsimile ➡ **copy**

fact ➡ **knowledge, detail, event, certainty**

faction ➡ **party, movement**

factor ➡ **detail**

factual ➡ **correct**

fad ➡ **fashion**

fade ➡ **disappear, tire, bleach**

faded ➡ **dull**

fail ➡ **lose, disappoint**

failing ➡ **fault**

failure ➡ **defeat, disappointment, inability**

faint ➡ **dim, dizzy**

fainthearted ➡ **cowardly**

fairness ➡ **justice**

fair-skinned ➡ **white**

faith ➡ **belief, religion, hope**

faithfully ➡ **carefully**

faithfulness ➡ **loyalty**

faker ➡ **hypocrite**

fallacious ➡ **illogical**

fallacy ➡ **mistake**

falling-out ➡ **argument**

falling star ➡ **meteor**

false ➡ **fake, wrong, unfaithful**

false-hearted ➡ **unfaithful**

falsehood ➡ **lie**

falsifier ➡ **liar**

falsify ➡ **lie, fake**

falter ➡ **hesitate, limp**

famed ➡ **famous**

n = noun • *vb* = verb • *adj* = adjective • *adv* = adverb • *prep* = preposition • *conj* = conjunction

family 1. *n* relative, relation, kin, people, kindred, lineage, clan, tribe, stock, strain
➡ **ancestry**
2. *adj* familial, domestic, home, homey, household, residential

famous *adj* famed, noted, prominent, renowned, eminent, notorious, celebrated, illustrious, distinguished, well-known, popular, important, great

fan 1. *n* enthusiast, supporter, devotee, aficionado, fanatic, addict, partisan, lover
2. *vb* ventilate, aerate, cool
3. *vb* inflame, incite, excite, stir up, arouse, agitate

fancy 1. *adj* elaborate, ornate, embellished, decorative, ostentatious, flamboyant
➡ **loud, rich**
2. *n* whim, caprice, fantasy, notion, fiction, figment ➡ **illusion, imagination, impulse**
3. *vb* ➡ **imagine**
4. *vb* ➡ **like**

far 1. *adj* distant, remote, faraway, far-flung, removed, outlying, yonder
2. *adv* considerably, incomparably, notably, greatly ➡ **much**
   As adverbs, **far** and its synonyms are used with comparative adjectives: "I'm feeling **far** better today." "This hill is **considerably** steeper than I remembered it!"

farm 1. *n* ranch, homestead, plantation, spread, farmstead
2. *vb* till, harvest, garden ➡ **grow**

farmer *n* planter, grower, breeder, rancher, husbandman, sharecropper, farmhand, peasant, yeoman, serf ➡ **worker**

farming 1. *n* agriculture, cultivation, husbandry, horticulture, sharecropping, homesteading, ranching ➡ **rural**
2. *adj* agricultural, agrarian

fascinate *vb* attract, intrigue, captivate, enthrall, charm, appeal ➡ **interest, enchant**

fashion 1. *n* style, trend, fad, craze, rage, mode, vogue, thing
2. *vb* ➡ **make, form, build**

fashionable *adj* stylish, chic, elegant, dapper, dashing, popular, trendy, hot, contemporary, sharp, with-it, smart, in (*informal*) ➡ **suave, cool**

fast 1. *adj* rapid, quick, speedy, swift, fleet, hasty, hurried, prompt, cursory, perfunctory, snap ➡ **sudden** ⇨ *slow*
2. *adj* ➡ **faithful**
3. *adj* ➡ **tight**
4. *adv* ➡ **quickly**

If the word you want is not a main entry above, look below to find it.

familial ➡ family
familiar ➡ common
familiarize ➡ introduce
family room ➡ den
famine ➡ hunger
famished ➡ hungry
fanatic ➡ fan, extremist
fanciful ➡ imaginary

fanny pack ➡ bag
fantasize ➡ imagine
fantastic ➡ nice
fantasy ➡ fancy
faraway ➡ far
farce ➡ play
farcical ➡ funny

fare ➡ board, food, price, traveler
far-flung ➡ far
farewell ➡ departure, good-bye
farmhand ➡ farmer, field
farmstead ➡ farm
fascinating ➡ interesting, attractive

fascination ➡ attraction, obsession
fascism ➡ tyranny
fascist ➡ dictator, dictatorial
fashion model ➡ model
fasten ➡ join, close, lock, tie
fastener ➡ clasp
fastidious ➡ choosy

➡ = synonym cross-reference • ⇨ = antonym cross-reference

fat 1. *adj* plump, obese, stout, overweight, corpulent, portly, chubby, brawny, husky, heavyset, stocky, pudgy, squat
➡ **big, heavy**
2. *n* oil, lard, shortening, tallow, suet, grease

fate 1. *n* destiny, lot, doom, death, end, ruin, downfall ➡ **future**
2. *n* ➡ **chance**

fatherly *adj* paternal, parental, protective
➡ **masculine** ⇨ *motherly*

faucet *n* spigot, tap, spout, nozzle, valve, petcock

fault *n* failing, weakness, vice ➡ **defect, guilt, mistake**

favorite 1. *adj* preferred, favored, pet, choice, best-liked, popular
2. *n* darling, pet, precious, ideal ➡ **lover**
3. *n* ➡ **preference**

fear 1. *n* alarm, fright, dread, terror, panic, horror, phobia, anxiety, apprehension, foreboding, dismay, consternation, scare
➡ **worry**
2. *vb* flinch, cower, tremble, quail, quake, dread

feast 1. *n* banquet, fiesta, repast, spread (*informal*) ➡ **meal, party**
2. *vb* ➡ **eat**

feeling 1. *n* sense, sensation, perception, feel, touch ➡ **quality**
2. *n* sensitivity, sentimentality, intuition, instinct, heart, soul, warmth
➡ **emotion, impulse**
3. *n* ➡ **belief**

feminine *adj* female, ladylike, womanly, matronly, effeminate, motherly ⇨ *masculine*

fertile 1. *adj* fruitful, productive, prolific, teeming, fecund, gravid ⇨ *sterile*
2. *adj* ➡ **talented**

If the word you want is not a main entry above, look below to find it.

fatal ➡ deadly
fatalistic ➡ pessimistic
fatality ➡ casualty
father ➡ parent
fatherland ➡ country
fathom ➡ know
fatigue ➡ tire, exhaustion
fatigued ➡ tired
fattening ➡ rich
faultless ➡ correct, perfect, infallible, innocent
faultlessness ➡ excellence
faulty ➡ broken
faux pas ➡ mistake
favor ➡ approve, resemble, prefer, gift
favorable ➡ good, successful
favorably ➡ well

favored ➡ favorite
favorite son ➡ candidate
favoritism ➡ prejudice
fawn ➡ flatter, brown
fawning ➡ servile
faze ➡ embarrass
fealty ➡ loyalty
fearful ➡ cowardly, scary, superstitious
fearless ➡ brave
feasible ➡ possible
feasibly ➡ maybe
feat ➡ act
featherbed ➡ blanket
feature ➡ emphasize, detail
features ➡ appearance, face
fecund ➡ fertile
federal ➡ public

federation ➡ union
fee ➡ wage, tax, price
feeble ➡ weak
feed ➡ eat, support, hay
feel ➡ touch, feeling
feign ➡ pretend
feint ➡ tactic
felicity ➡ pleasure
fell ➡ hide
fellow ➡ man, equal, member
fellowship ➡ friendship, award
felon ➡ criminal
felony ➡ crime
female ➡ woman, feminine
fen ➡ swamp
fence ➡ wall

fender-bender ➡ collision
fend off ➡ repel
ferocious ➡ wild
ferret out ➡ discover
fervent ➡ eager
fervor ➡ enthusiasm
festival ➡ carnival, ceremony
festive ➡ happy
festivity ➡ party, mirth
festoon ➡ decorate
fetch ➡ bring
fete ➡ party
fetish ➡ obsession
fetter ➡ bond
feud ➡ fight
fever ➡ disease, excitement
feverish ➡ frantic

few *adj* several, couple, scant, scanty, negligible, sporadic ⇨ **many**
   Note that **few** and **couple** are used with a, but **several** is not.

fickle *adj* changeable, untrustworthy, inconstant, mercurial, irresolute, flighty, erratic ➡ **variable, arbitrary, unreliable, unfaithful**

fidget 1. *vb* squirm, twitch, wiggle, wriggle, writhe, stir
2. *vb* ➡ **tinker**

field 1. *n* meadow, pasture, clearing, glade, plot, hayfield, cornfield, wheatfield, farmland ➡ **pen**
2. *n* playing field, athletic field, diamond, gridiron, arena, track, court, stadium, coliseum ➡ **gymnasium**
3. *n* airfield, airport, battlefield, battleground
4. *n* subject, area, sphere, realm, discipline, province, arena, bailiwick, domain, orbit ➡ **department, profession, specialty**

fight 1. *vb* battle, struggle, wrestle, grapple, combat, clash, conflict, war, brawl, feud, duel, skirmish, scrap, strive, resist ➡ **argue, attack, compete, face**
   All the terms at **fight** 1 are used as nouns as well as verbs, except for **wrestle, grapple, strive,** and **resist.**
2. *n* battle, engagement, struggle, war, action, strife, conflict, hostilities, warfare, combat, skirmish, confrontation, encounter ➡ **violence, competition, game**
3. *n* altercation, clash, scuffle, tussle, scrap, melee, brawl, feud, duel, showdown, fray, rumble ➡ **argument, disturbance**
4. *n* defiance, resistance, opposition, struggle

finally 1. *adv* conclusively, decisively, irrevocably, permanently ➡ **certainly**
2. *adv* eventually, ultimately, lastly

financial *adj* monetary, fiscal, economic, pecuniary, commercial, budgetary ➡ **business**

find *vb* locate, come across, spot, retrieve, stumble across ➡ **discover, recover, learn, notice, get** ⇨ **lose**

If the word you want is not a main entry above, look below to find it.

fewer ➡ less
fiancé ➡ love
fiancée ➡ love
fiasco ➡ disappointment
fib ➡ lie
fibber ➡ liar
fiber ➡ string
fiction ➡ lie, fancy
fictional ➡ imaginary
fictitious ➡ imaginary
fiddle ➡ tinker
fidelity ➡ loyalty
fidgety ➡ nervous

field house ➡ gymnasium
fiend ➡ devil
fiendish ➡ wicked
fierce ➡ wild, sharp, violent, stormy
fiery ➡ burning, wild
fiesta ➡ feast
fighter ➡ soldier
figment ➡ fancy
figure ➡ number, estimate, body, statue
figure out ➡ solve
figurine ➡ doll, statue
filament ➡ string

filch ➡ steal
file ➡ document, row, arrange, walk, sharpen
fill ➡ load, close, occupy
filled ➡ full
filly ➡ horse
film ➡ movie, coat, layer
filter ➡ net, clean, sift
filth ➡ dirt
filthy ➡ dirty
fin ➡ limb
final ➡ last, latter, examination
finale ➡ finish

finalize ➡ finish
finance ➡ back, business
finances ➡ budget
financier ➡ tycoon
finding ➡ decision, discovery
find out ➡ learn
fine ➡ good, punish
finer ➡ better
finery ➡ clothes
finesse ➡ tact
finest ➡ best
finger ➡ play
fingerprint ➡ print
finicky ➡ choosy

➡ = *synonym cross-reference* • ⇨ = *antonym cross-reference*

finish 1. *vb* complete, end, terminate, conclude, attain, expire, wind up, finalize, clinch, use up, dissolve, disband ➡ **stop, use, climax** ⇨ *start*
2. *n* end, conclusion, ending, finale, completion, termination, culmination, death, fulfillment
3. *n* shine, polish, paint, varnish, shellac, lacquer, stain, wax

finite *adj* limited, measurable, restricted
⇨ *infinite*

fire 1. *n* flame, blaze, conflagration, combustion, campfire, bonfire, pyre, inferno, holocaust ➡ **fireplace**
2. *n* gunfire, shooting, firing, shelling, bombardment
3. *vb* ➡ **shoot**
4. *vb* dismiss, discharge, terminate, lay off, let go, sack (*informal*), can (*informal*)
➡ **oust** ⇨ *hire*

fireplace *n* hearth, chimney, fireside, barbecue ➡ **fire**

fireworks *n* pyrotechnics, illuminations
➡ **excitement**

firm 1. *adj* rigid, hard, solid, stiff, inflexible, steady, compact, dense ➡ **tough, hard, thick**
2. *n* ➡ **business**

fit[1] 1. *adj* suitable, proper, appropriate, fitting, apt, applicable, pertinent, apposite
➡ **correct, relevant**
2. *adj* ➡ **healthy, able**
3. *vb* ➡ **suit, belong**

fit[2] 1. *n* seizure, attack, convulsion, spasm, paroxysm, spell ➡ **illness**
2. *n* outburst, tantrum, frenzy, huff, snit, conniption (*informal*) ➡ **hysteria**

fix 1. *vb* repair, mend, patch, restore, renovate, renew, rebuild, overhaul, recondition, service
➡ **adjust, correct, tinker**
2. *vb* ➡ **sterilize**
3. *n* ➡ **trouble**

flag 1. *n* banner, standard, pennant, colors, ensign, jack
2. *vb* ➡ **wave**
3. *vb* ➡ **weaken**
4. *vb* ➡ **cover**

flatter *vb* adulate, fawn, pander, butter up, kowtow to ➡ **praise, suit**

flavor *n* taste, savor, tang, flavoring ➡ **spice**

If the word you want is not a main entry above, look below to find it.

finished ➡ past
fir ➡ pine
firearm ➡ gun
fireside ➡ fireplace
firewood ➡ wood
firing ➡ fire
firn ➡ snow
first ➡ early, best
first-rate ➡ model
fiscal ➡ financial
fish ➡ hunt
fishpond ➡ lake

fissure ➡ hole
fitful ➡ periodic
fitness ➡ health
fitting ➡ fit[1], correct
five o'clock shadow ➡ beard
fixation ➡ obsession
fixed ➡ stationary, tight
fixture ➡ equipment
fizz ➡ foam
fizzle ➡ disappear
flabbergast ➡ surprise
flabbergasted

➡ dumbfounded
flabby ➡ limp
flaccid ➡ limp
flagrant ➡ bald
flair ➡ talent
flake ➡ bit
flamboyant ➡ fancy
flame ➡ fire
flaming ➡ burning
flammable ➡ inflammable
flank ➡ border
flap ➡ wave

flare ➡ burn, light[1]
flash ➡ light[1], moment, blink
flashlight ➡ light[1]
flashy ➡ loud, bright
flask ➡ bottle
flat ➡ level, prone, dull, insipid, stale, room
flatten ➡ level, iron, trample
flattery ➡ praise
flaunt ➡ advertise
flavorful ➡ delicious
flavoring ➡ herb, flavor

n = noun • *vb* = verb • *adj* = adjective • *adv* = adverb • *prep* = preposition • *conj* = conjunction

flexible *adj* bendable, limber, supple, lithe, malleable, elastic, pliable, plastic, soft, resilient, pliant ➡ **limp**

flight 1. *n* flying, gliding, soaring
2. *n* aviation, aeronautics, flying, space flight
3. *n* ➡ **escape**
4. *n* ➡ **floor**

flood 1. *n* deluge, torrent, inundation, cascade ➡ **rain, storm**
2. *n* river, surge, current, rush, flow, stream, tide ➡ **wave, fountain**
3. *n* barrage, hail, volley, spate, deluge, torrent, storm
4. *vb* inundate, overflow, submerge, drown, engulf, swamp, overwhelm ➡ **flow**

floor 1. *n* flooring, ground, deck, bed, bottom ➡ **base**
2. *n* story, flight, stage, tier, level
3. *vb* ➡ **surprise**

flow 1. *vb* pour, cascade, stream, run, spill, gush, spurt, squirt ➡ **flood**
2. *n* ➡ **flood**
3. *n* distribution, circulation, dissemination, dispersal, spread ➡ **delivery**

flower 1. *n* blossom, bloom, bud, floret, cluster, posy
2. *n* wildflower, perennial, annual, bulb, vine, houseplant ➡ **plant**
3. *vb* ➡ **blossom, prosper**

fly 1. *vb* soar, glide, float, drift, wing, hover, sail, flutter
2. *vb* ➡ **hurry**
3. *n* housefly, horsefly, bluebottle, blackfly, fruit fly ➡ **bug**
4. *n* ➡ **tent**

If the word you want is not a main entry above, look below to find it.

flaw ➡ defect

flawless ➡ perfect, correct

flaxen ➡ yellow

flay ➡ peel

flea market ➡ market

fleck ➡ bit

fledgling ➡ bird

flee ➡ escape, leave

fleece ➡ hide, coat

fleecy ➡ fuzzy

fleet ➡ fast, navy

fleeting ➡ temporary, short

fleshly ➡ physical

flex ➡ bend

flick ➡ lick, movie

flicker ➡ blink

flier ➡ advertisement, pilot

flighty ➡ fickle

flimsy ➡ breakable, thin, unreliable, weak

flinch ➡ jump, fear

fling ➡ throw, binge, adventure

flintlock ➡ gun

flip ➡ turn, rude

flipper ➡ limb

flirt ➡ court

float ➡ fly, blow², swim

flock ➡ herd, crowd, church

floe ➡ glacier

flog ➡ whip

flooring ➡ floor

flop ➡ disappointment

floppy ➡ limp

flora ➡ plant

floret ➡ flower

florid ➡ red

flotilla ➡ navy

flotsam ➡ trash

flounce ➡ strut

flounder ➡ fumble

flourish ➡ prosper, swing, decoration

flout ➡ refuse

flowery ➡ pompous

flowing ➡ liquid

fluctuate ➡ alternate, swing

fluent ➡ articulate

fluffy ➡ fuzzy

fluid ➡ liquid

flurry ➡ snow

flush ➡ blush, level

flushed ➡ red

fluster ➡ embarrass

flutter ➡ wave, fly, shake, rustle

flying ➡ flight

flying machine ➡ airplane

➡ = *synonym cross-reference* • ⇨ = *antonym cross-reference*

foam *n* froth, lather, bubbles, suds, head, fizz, spume, scum, spray

fog *n* mist, smog, haze, murk ➡ **cloud, smoke**

fold 1. *n* crease, pleat, tuck, lap, overlap ➡ **wrinkle**
2. *n* ➡ **pen**
3. *vb* crease, pleat, tuck, double, lap, overlap ➡ **wrinkle**

follow 1. *vb* succeed, ensue, supplant, supersede, replace ⇨ *lead, precede*
2. *vb* pursue, chase, trail, track, shadow, hunt, stalk, hound, tail
3. *vb* ➡ **obey**
4. *vb* ➡ **know**

following 1. *adj* succeeding, next, ensuing, subsequent, later, latter ➡ **adjacent**
2. *n* entourage, retinue, coterie, public ➡ **audience, fan**

food *n* nourishment, diet, sustenance, edibles, victuals, refreshment, rations, provisions, cuisine, fare, nutrition, fuel ➡ **board, meal**

fool 1. *n* simpleton, nitwit, idiot, dunce, imbecile, nincompoop, blockhead, moron, oaf, clown, ignoramus, buffoon, dolt, dummy, half-wit, ninny
2. *vb* outsmart, outwit, outfox, delude ➡ **cheat**

foolish *adj* silly, ridiculous, absurd, preposterous, ludicrous, idiotic, crazy, nonsensical, asinine, imbecilic ➡ **funny, stupid** ⇨ *smart*

foot 1. *n* paw, hoof, pad, extremity, claw, talon
2. *n* ➡ **base**
3. *n* ➡ **measure**

forbid *vb* prohibit, ban, disallow, outlaw, censor, gag, boycott, proscribe, sanction ➡ **bar, exclude** ⇨ *let*

force 1. *vb* require, compel, coerce, make, oblige, obligate, impel, constrain, pressure ➡ **insist, order**
2. *n* ➡ **strength**
3. *n* ➡ **army**

foreign *adj* alien, imported, exotic, remote, distant, nonnative, immigrant ➡ **strange**

foreigner *n* alien, immigrant, émigré, emigrant ➡ **stranger, exile**

If the word you want is not a main entry above, look below to find it.

foal ➡ horse

focus ➡ middle, concentrate, clarity

fodder ➡ hay

foe ➡ enemy, opponent

foggy ➡ dim, obscure

foil ➡ sword, prevent, repel

folder ➡ wrapper

foliage ➡ plant

folio ➡ page

folk ➡ people

folklore ➡ myth

folly ➡ nonsense

fond ➡ loving

fondle ➡ pet

fondness ➡ love

font ➡ source

foolhardy ➡ thoughtless

foolishness ➡ nonsense

footfall ➡ step

foothill ➡ hill

footing ➡ balance, base

footlocker ➡ chest

footpath ➡ path

footprint ➡ print, track

footrace ➡ race

footstep ➡ step

footwear ➡ shoe

for ➡ because, therefore

forage ➡ hunt

foray ➡ attack

forbear ➡ abstain

forbearance ➡ abstinence, pity

forbearing ➡ patient

forceful ➡ certain, strong

fore ➡ front

forearm ➡ arm

forebear ➡ ancestor

foreboding ➡ ominous, fear

forecast ➡ prediction, predict

forefather ➡ ancestor

foregoing ➡ past

foregone conclusion ➡ certainty

foreground ➡ front

n = noun • *vb* = verb • *adj* = adjective • *adv* = adverb • *prep* = preposition • *conj* = conjunction

foresight 1. *n* foreknowledge, prescience, vision
2. *n* forethought, prudence, anticipation

forest *n* woods, wood, woodland, rainforest, jungle, timberland, grove, thicket, copse

forever *adv* always, eternally, permanently, perpetually, interminably, endlessly, evermore ➡ **regularly**

forget *vb* neglect, omit, overlook, disregard, misremember ➡ **exclude** ⇨ *remember*

forgive *vb* excuse, pardon, absolve, acquit, exonerate, clear, vindicate, condone ⇨ *blame*

forgiveness *n* absolution, pardon, remission, reprieve, exoneration, amnesty, mercy, clemency ➡ **salvation**

form 1. *vb* shape, mold, fashion, pattern ➡ **build, invent, make**
2. *vb* ➡ **appear**
3. *n* mold, die, cast, frame ➡ **structure**
4. *n* ➡ **body**
5. *n* ➡ **document**

forward 1. *adj* front, advance, foremost, progressive
2. *adj* ➡ **rude**
3. *adv* forwards, forth, ahead, onward, onwards ⇨ *backward*
4. *vb* ➡ **send**

fountain 1. *n* spout, geyser, spray, stream, jet, squirt ➡ **well, flood**
2. *n* ➡ **source**

fragrant *adj* pungent, aromatic, savory, perfumed, scented, redolent ➡ **smelly, spicy**

framework 1. *n* frame, shell, hull, skeleton, chassis
2. *n* ➡ **setting**

If the word you want is not a main entry above, look below to find it.

foreknowledge ➡ foresight
forelimb ➡ arm
foreman ➡ boss
foremost ➡ forward, best, important
forerunner ➡ ancestor
foresee ➡ anticipate, predict
forestall ➡ prevent
foretell ➡ predict
forethought ➡ foresight
forewarn ➡ warn
forewarning ➡ warning
foreword ➡ introduction
forfeit ➡ abandon, surrender
forge ➡ make, fake, furnace
forge ahead ➡ go
forgery ➡ fake
forgetful ➡ absentminded
forgo ➡ abstain

fork ➡ divide, branch
forlorn ➡ sorry, sad
formal ➡ official, dignified, prim
formality ➡ ceremony
formation ➡ order, assembly
former ➡ past
formerly ➡ once, before
formfitting ➡ tight
formidable ➡ strong
formula ➡ recipe
formulate ➡ invent
forsake ➡ leave
forsaken ➡ abandoned
fort ➡ castle
forte ➡ specialty
forth ➡ forward
forthcoming ➡ future
forthright ➡ straightforward, bald

forthwith ➡ soon
fortification ➡ castle
fortify ➡ protect, strengthen
fortitude ➡ courage, strength, patience
fortress ➡ castle
fortuitous ➡ accidental, successful
fortuitously ➡ accidentally
fortunate ➡ lucky, successful
fortune ➡ chance, wealth
fortune-telling ➡ prediction
fortune-teller ➡ prophet
forum ➡ court
forwards ➡ forward
fossil fuel ➡ oil
fossilize ➡ harden
foster ➡ adopt, facilitate, support
foster parent ➡ parent

foul ➡ smelly, dirty
found ➡ base
foundation ➡ base, basis, organization
founder ➡ creator
fount ➡ source
fountain pen ➡ pen
fountainhead ➡ source
four-sided ➡ square
foursquare ➡ square
fowl ➡ bird
foyer ➡ hall
fracas ➡ disturbance
fraction ➡ part, number, share
fracture ➡ break
fractured ➡ broken
fragile ➡ breakable, weak
fragment ➡ part, bit

➡ = synonym cross-reference • ⇨ = antonym cross-reference

frantic 1. *adj* frenzied, distraught, overwrought, frenetic, desperate, delirious, feverish ⇨ *calm*
2. *adj* hectic, chaotic, furious ⇨ *calm*

free 1. *vb* release, liberate, emancipate, deliver, discharge, extricate, exempt, loose, loosen, unloose, unloosen
➡ **forgive, open**
2. *adj* independent, liberated, sovereign, self-governing, autonomous, emancipated, unconfined, unrestrained, unfettered, unshackled, loose, exempt
3. *adj* complimentary, gratis, gratuitous
4. *adj* ➡ **generous**

freedom 1. *n* liberty, independence, autonomy, liberation, sovereignty ⇨ *slavery*
2. *n* license, liberty, immunity, frankness, openness, ease, spontaneity ➡ **right**
3. *n* ➡ **leisure**

frequent 1. *adj* regular, recurrent, habitual, incessant, chronic ➡ **continual, usual, many**
2. *vb* visit, haunt, patronize, attend

friction 1. *n* rubbing, abrasion, scraping, resistance, traction, grating, grinding
2. *n* ➡ **fight, disagreement**

friend *n* girlfriend, boyfriend, companion, associate, partner, acquaintance, ally, comrade, pal, chum, playmate, buddy, *amigo (Spanish)*
⇨ *enemy, opponent*

friendly *adj* sociable, social, cordial, neighborly, amiable, genial, intimate, close, sweet, warm, convivial, hearty, hospitable
➡ **kind, nice, loving, peaceful** ⇨ *unfriendly*

friendship *n* companionship, amity, company, society, camaraderie, comradeship, fellowship, brotherhood, sisterhood, fraternity
➡ **relationship, link, kindness**

frog *n* bullfrog, spring peeper, tadpole, polliwog

front 1. *n* fore, lead, head, van, vanguard, foreground, bow (*of a boat*), prow (*of a boat*), obverse (*of a coin*) ➡ **beginning** ⇨ *back*
2. *adj* ➡ **forward**

If the word you want is not a main entry above, look below to find it.

fragmentary ➡ partial

fragrance ➡ smell

frail ➡ weak, mortal

frame ➡ body, form, framework

framer ➡ creator

franchise ➡ license

frank ➡ straightforward

frankly ➡ sincerely

frankness ➡ freedom, honesty

fraternity ➡ organization, friendship

fraternize ➡ mix

fraud ➡ cheat, rascal, theft, pretense

fraudulence ➡ dishonesty

fray ➡ fight

frayed ➡ ragged

freak ➡ monster

freebooter ➡ pirate

freedom fighter ➡ rebel

freely ➡ voluntary

freethinker ➡ atheist

freeway ➡ highway

freeze ➡ harden, cool

freezer ➡ refrigerator

freezing ➡ cold

freight ➡ load

frenetic ➡ active, frantic

frenzied ➡ frantic

frenzy ➡ fit²

frequently ➡ often

fresh ➡ new, rude, clean, cool

freshman ➡ student

freshness ➡ novelty

fret ➡ worry, grieve

friable ➡ breakable

friar ➡ religious

friary ➡ monastery

fridge ➡ refrigerator

friendless ➡ lonely, unpopular

friendliness ➡ kindness

fright ➡ fear

frighten ➡ scare

frightened ➡ afraid

frightening ➡ scary

frightful ➡ scary

frigid ➡ cold

fringe ➡ edge

frippery ➡ trinket

frisk ➡ play

fritter away ➡ waste

frivolity ➡ nonsense

frivolous ➡ arbitrary, trivial

frock ➡ dress

frolic ➡ play, dance

front ➡ forward

frontier ➡ border, country

frontiersman ➡ pioneer

fronting ➡ opposite

---

n = noun • *vb* = verb • *adj* = adjective • *adv* = adverb • *prep* = preposition • *conj* = conjunction

frown 1. *vb, n* scowl, grimace, glare, pout, glower, lower ⇨ *smile*
2. *vb* ➡ **object**

fruit *n* seed, grain, nut, legume, berry ➡ **plant, vegetable**

full 1. *adj* packed, loaded, laden, filled, crowded, stuffed, replete, sated, brimful, crammed, jammed ⇨ *empty*
2. *adj* ➡ **complete**

fumble *vb* bungle, flounder, stumble, wallow, muddle, muff, botch, goof, louse ➡ **try**

function 1. *n* capacity, office, role, part ➡ **duty, job, object, use**
2. *n* ➡ **party**
3. *n* ➡ **behavior**
4. *n* ➡ **sense**
5. *vb* ➡ **operate, act**

fungus 1. *n* mold, mildew, rot, rust, blight
2. *n* mushroom, toadstool, lichen, truffle

funny 1. *adj* laughable, amusing, humorous, witty, hilarious, comical, comic, ridiculous, whimsical, facetious, antic, farcical, zany, ludicrous ➡ **dry, foolish, strange**
2. *adj* ➡ **sick**

furnace *n* heater, boiler, burner, stove, incinerator, kiln, forge

future 1. *n* hereafter, eternity, futurity, *mañana (Spanish)*, tomorrow, morrow, destiny, fate
2. *adj* imminent, impending, pending, forthcoming, upcoming, approaching, prospective, projected

fuzzy *adj* furry, downy, hairy, woolly, shaggy, fluffy, fleecy, velvety, soft

---

If the word you want is not a main entry above, look below to find it.

front-runner ➡ candidate

frost ➡ ice

frosting ➡ icing

frosty ➡ cold, white

froth ➡ foam

frugal ➡ cheap, plain

frugality ➡ economy

fruitcake ➡ cake

fruit fly ➡ fly

fruitful ➡ fertile

fruitless ➡ useless

frustrate ➡ prevent, disappoint

frustration ➡ disappointment

fry ➡ cook

fuel ➡ light[1], energy, food

fugitive ➡ runaway, exile

fulcrum ➡ axis

fulfill ➡ keep, satisfy

fulfillment ➡ satisfaction, finish

full-grown ➡ adult

fully ➡ completely

fumbling ➡ clumsy

fume ➡ smoke

fumes ➡ smoke

fuming ➡ violent

fun ➡ pleasure

fund ➡ supply, back

fundamental ➡ necessary, basic

fundamentally ➡ chiefly, practically

funeral march ➡ dirge

funnel ➡ pipe, lead

fur ➡ hair, coat

furious ➡ angry, violent, frantic

furlough ➡ vacation

furnish ➡ give, supply, lend

furrow ➡ channel

furry ➡ fuzzy

further ➡ more

furthermore ➡ more, besides

furtive ➡ sly

furtiveness ➡ secrecy

fury ➡ anger

fuse ➡ melt, unify

fusion ➡ union

fuss ➡ argument, complain

fussy ➡ choosy, cross

futile ➡ useless

futon ➡ bed

futurity ➡ future

➡ = *synonym cross-reference* • ⇨ = *antonym cross-reference*

G

gait *n* pace, stride, tread, step, walk, carriage, movement, swagger, strut

gallery 1. *n* art gallery, exhibition hall, salon, showroom, studio, museum
2. *n* ➡ **room, porch**
3. *n* ➡ **audience**

gallows *n* scaffold, gibbet, yardarm

gambling *n* betting, gaming, wagering
➡ **lottery**

game *n* sport, pastime, recreation, contest, match, competition, bout, event, meet, tournament, series ➡ **fight**

garage 1. *n* carport, parking garage
2. *n* service station, gas station, repair shop

gargoyle *n* grotesque, rainspout, waterspout

gasoline *n* gas, petrol (*British*) ➡ **oil**

gather 1. *vb* collect, assemble, accumulate, amass, compile, congregate, convene, meet, rendezvous ➡ **save, pile**
2. *vb* pick, harvest, reap, pluck, garner, glean
3. *vb* ➡ **assume, infer**

general 1. *adj* widespread, extensive, comprehensive ➡ **common, usual, universal**
2. *adj* ➡ **approximate**

generosity *n* liberality, bounty, benevolence, philanthropy, charitableness, charity, unselfishness, munificence, largess
➡ **help** ⇨ *greed*

If the word you want is not a main entry above, look below to find it.

gadget ➡ object, tool

gag ➡ joke, forbid, quiet, vomit

gaggle ➡ herd

gaiety ➡ mirth

gain ➡ get, take, growth

gal ➡ woman

gala ➡ party, dance

gale ➡ wind, storm

gall ➡ audacity

gallant ➡ brave

gallantry ➡ courage

galley ➡ kitchen

gallop ➡ run

galvanize ➡ excite

gambit ➡ tactic

gamble ➡ bet

gambol ➡ play, dance

game farm, game preserve
➡ zoo

gamin ➡ urchin

gaming ➡ gambling

gamma ray ➡ X ray

gamut ➡ assortment

gang ➡ group

gangplank ➡ bridge

gangway ➡ bridge

gap ➡ hole, break, valley, distance

gape ➡ stare, spread

garb ➡ clothes

garbage ➡ trash

garble ➡ disturb

garden ➡ farm

gargantuan ➡ huge

garish ➡ loud

garland ➡ bouquet, crown, prize

garment bag ➡ luggage

garments ➡ clothes

garner ➡ gather

garnish ➡ decorate, decoration

garret ➡ attic

garrison ➡ castle, troop

garrulous ➡ talkative

gas ➡ smoke, gasoline

gash ➡ cut

gasp ➡ breathe

gas station ➡ garage

gate ➡ door

gatekeeper ➡ doorman

gateway ➡ door

gathering ➡ party, meeting

gauche ➡ clumsy

gaudy ➡ loud

gauge ➡ estimate, measure

gaunt ➡ thin

gauntlet ➡ glove

gauze ➡ bandage

gavel ➡ hammer

gawk ➡ stare

gay ➡ happy, bright

gaze ➡ stare, look

gazette ➡ paper

gear ➡ luggage, equipment

gelatinous ➡ thick

geld ➡ sterilize

gelding ➡ horse

gem ➡ jewel

gemstone ➡ jewel

general store ➡ market

generalize ➡ stereotype

generally ➡ chiefly, usually

generate ➡ cause, reproduce

generator ➡ engine

generous 1. *adj* unselfish, charitable, liberal, unsparing, altruistic, kind, free ➡ **noble**
⇨ *selfish*
2. *adj* liberal, handsome, lavish ➡ **abundant, big**

genius 1. *n* prodigy, virtuoso, mastermind, wizard, Einstein (*informal*), wunderkind (*German*), brain (*informal*), whiz (*informal*), rocket scientist (*informal*)
2. *n* ➡ **talent**
3. *n* ➡ **soul**

gentle 1. *adj* light, mild, soft, tender, moderate, temperate ➡ **calm**
2. *adj* ➡ **friendly, kind**
3. *adj* docile, meek, tractable ➡ **tame**

get 1. *vb* obtain, acquire, gain, win, take, procure, earn, score ➡ **catch, receive, seize, find**
2. *vb* ➡ **know**
3. *vb* ➡ **persuade**

ghost *n* spirit, apparition, shade, specter, wraith, spook, phantom ➡ **soul**

giant 1. *n* behemoth, mammoth, titan, leviathan, colossus, Goliath ➡ **monster**
2. *adj* ➡ **big**

gift 1. *n* present, donation, grant, contribution, endowment, offering, alms, sacrifice, favor, surprise, boon ➡ **inheritance, prize**
2. *n* ➡ **talent**

gifted *adj* precocious, advanced, progressive, mature ➡ **talented, smart**

give 1. *vb* present, donate, grant, endow, bestow, impart, award, confer, bequeath, contribute ➡ **supply** ⇨ *receive*
2. *vb* pass, hand, deliver, convey, render, serve, dish out, hand over, hand in, submit, dispense, distribute, inflict ➡ **offer**
3. *vb* have, hold, stage ➡ **act, play**
4. *vb* ➡ **surrender**
5. *vb* yield, bear, produce, furnish ➡ **make**

glacier *n* iceberg, floe, ice floe, icecap

glass 1. *n* cup, mug, tumbler, goblet, beaker ➡ **container, drink**
2. *n* ➡ **mirror**
3. *n* telescope, binocular, spyglass, magnifying glass, lens, microscope

If the word you want is not a main entry above, look below to find it.

genesis ➡ beginning
genetic ➡ natural
genial ➡ friendly
geniality ➡ hospitality
genre ➡ type
gentleman ➡ man
gentlemanly ➡ masculine
gentlewoman ➡ woman
gentry ➡ aristocracy
genuflect ➡ bend
genuine ➡ real, sincere
genuinely ➡ really, sincerely
germ ➡ poison, egg

germane ➡ relevant
germ-free ➡ sterile
germinate ➡ grow
gesture ➡ wave, sign
getaway ➡ escape
get-together ➡ visit
get-up-and-go ➡ ambition, energy
gewgaw ➡ trinket
geyser ➡ fountain
ghastly ➡ awful
ghoul ➡ monster
gibber ➡ chatter
gibberish ➡ talk

gibbet ➡ gallows
gibe ➡ ridicule
giddy ➡ dizzy
gift wrap ➡ wrap
gigantic ➡ huge
giggle ➡ laugh
gild ➡ plate, exaggerate
gimp ➡ limp
gingerly ➡ carefully
gird ➡ ring
girdle ➡ band
girl ➡ woman, child
girlfriend ➡ friend, love

girlhood ➡ childhood
girlish ➡ young
girth ➡ width
gist ➡ subject, essence
give off ➡ throw
giver ➡ patron
glad ➡ happy
gladden ➡ please
glade ➡ field
gladiator ➡ soldier
glamorous ➡ beautiful
glance ➡ look
glare ➡ light[1], frown
glaring ➡ bright, obvious

glasses *n* eyeglasses, spectacles, sunglasses, goggles, bifocals, trifocals, shades, contact lenses, contacts

glove *n* mitten, mitt, gauntlet

glutton *n* gourmand, epicure, pig *(informal)*, hog *(informal)*

go 1. *vb* progress, proceed, pass, head, advance, forge ahead ➡ **leave, move, travel** ⇨ *come*
2. *vb* ➡ **act**
3. *vb* ➡ **belong**
4. *vb* ➡ **happen**
5. *n* ➡ **try**

god *n* goddess, deity, divinity, demigod, immortal, idol, icon, effigy

good 1. *adj* fine, excellent, outstanding, choice, admirable, splendid, rave, favorable, hopeful, positive, suitable, proper, capital, tiptop ➡ **fair, great, nice, cool** ⇨ *bad*
2. *adj* honest, honorable, virtuous, worthy, respectable, reputable, moral, righteous, scrupulous ➡ **kind**
3. *adj* obedient, well-behaved, dutiful, well-mannered, respectful, obliging ➡ **polite** ⇨ *rude*
4. *n* ➡ **welfare**

good-bye *interj* farewell, so long, adieu, *adios (Spanish), au revoir (French), ciao (Italian), arrivederci (Italian), auf Wiedersehen (German), shalom (Hebrew), salaam (Arabic), toodle-oo (informal), cheerio (informal)* ⇨ *hello*

If the word you want is not a main entry above, look below to find it.

glasshouse ➡ greenhouse
glassy ➡ slippery
glaze ➡ icing
gleam ➡ shine, light[1]
gleaming ➡ shiny
glean ➡ gather
glee ➡ pleasure
glee club ➡ choir
gleeful ➡ happy
glen ➡ valley
glib ➡ superficial, suave
glide ➡ fly, slide, dance
gliding ➡ flight
glimmer ➡ light[1], bit
glimpse ➡ view, look, see
glint ➡ light[1]
glisten ➡ shine
glistening ➡ shiny
glitter ➡ light[1]
gloat ➡ boast

glob ➡ drop, lump
global ➡ universal
globe ➡ earth, ball
globular ➡ round
globule ➡ ball
glockenspiel ➡ xylophone
gloom ➡ cloud, dark, sorrow
gloomy ➡ dark, bleak, sad
glorify ➡ worship, bless
glorious ➡ grand
glory ➡ elegance, fame
gloss ➡ light[1]
glossary ➡ dictionary
glossy ➡ shiny
glow ➡ light[1], shine, blush, burn
glower ➡ frown
glowing ➡ bright
glue ➡ adhesive, stick
glut ➡ abundance, load
glutinous ➡ thick

gluttonous ➡ greedy
gluttony ➡ greed
gnarled ➡ bent
gnash ➡ grind
gnaw ➡ bite
go back ➡ return
goad ➡ urge
goal ➡ object, base, plan
goatee ➡ beard
gobble ➡ eat
gobbledygook ➡ nonsense
go-between ➡ agent
goblet ➡ glass
goblin ➡ bogeyman
goddess ➡ god
God-fearing ➡ religious
godly ➡ religious
godsend ➡ luck
goggles ➡ glasses
going ➡ departure

gold ➡ yellow
Goliath ➡ giant
gong ➡ bell
good day ➡ hello
good deal ➡ bargain
good-for-nothing ➡ loafer
good-humored ➡ nice
good-looking ➡ pretty
good looks ➡ beauty
good-natured ➡ nice
goodness ➡ virtue
goods ➡ property, product
goodwill ➡ kindness
goof ➡ fumble
goose egg ➡ zero
gore ➡ stick
gorge ➡ canyon, eat
gorgeous ➡ beautiful
gory ➡ bloody
gossamer ➡ thin
gossip ➡ rumor, chatter

govern *vb* rule, reign, administer, legislate ➡ **control, lead**

government *n* administration, legislature, congress, senate, parliament, assembly, regime ➡ **rule**

grade *n* class, rank, step, score, standing, position, degree, plateau ➡ **level, state, slant**

grand *adj* magnificent, superb, majestic, splendid, stately, glorious, grandiose, august, regal, imposing, sumptuous, elegant, exalted, commanding, awe-inspiring, proud ➡ **great, good, rich, dignified**

grateful *adj* thankful, pleased, appreciative, indebted, obliged, gratified, beholden

gratitude *n* appreciation, thankfulness, thanks, gratefulness, recognition, acknowledgment

grave 1. *n* tomb, sepulcher, mausoleum, crypt, vault, catacomb, barrow, pit ➡ **cemetery, monument**
2. *adj* ➡ **serious**

gray *adj, n* grey, drab, leaden, dusky, slate, smoky

great 1. *adj, interj* wonderful, terrific, superb, remarkable, astounding, incredible, spectacular, tremendous, marvelous, fabulous, super, heavenly ➡ **good, grand, nice**
2. *adj* ➡ **famous**
3. *adj* ➡ **big**

greed *n* greediness, selfishness, avarice, gluttony ➡ **desire, envy** ⇨ *generosity*

greedy *adj* selfish, possessive, covetous, acquisitive, avaricious, stingy, rapacious, grasping, voracious, insatiable, gluttonous ➡ **jealous, predatory**

green 1. *adj, n* emerald, chartreuse, lime, olive, kelly, pea green, verdant, veridian
2. *adj* ➡ **naive, amateur**
3. *n* ➡ **park**
4. *n* ➡ **vegetable**

greenhouse *n* nursery, conservatory, hothouse, glasshouse, arboretum

---

If the word you want is not a main entry above, look below to find it.

gouge ➡ cut
gourmand ➡ glutton
governmental ➡ public
governor ➡ ruler
gown ➡ dress
GP ➡ doctor
grab ➡ seize, catch
grace ➡ beauty, class, elegance
gracious ➡ polite
gradual ➡ slow
graduate ➡ promote
graft ➡ join
grain ➡ seed, fruit

grain elevator ➡ warehouse
granary ➡ warehouse
grandeur ➡ elegance
grandiloquent ➡ pompous
grandiose ➡ pompous, grand
grandstand ➡ seat
grant ➡ gift, license, award, give
graph ➡ table
graphic ➡ visible, explicit
grapnel ➡ anchor
grapple ➡ fight
grasp ➡ catch, know, embrace

grasping ➡ greedy
grass ➡ hay, plant
grassland ➡ plain
grate ➡ cut, grind, squeak
gratefulness ➡ gratitude
gratification ➡ satisfaction
gratified ➡ grateful
gratify ➡ please
gratifying ➡ pleasant
grating ➡ hoarse, friction
gratis ➡ free
gratuitous ➡ free, unnecessary
gratuity ➡ tip
graupel ➡ snow

gravel ➡ dirt, rock
gravelly ➡ hoarse
graveyard ➡ cemetery
gravid ➡ pregnant, fertile
gravitate toward ➡ approach
gravity ➡ importance, depth
graze ➡ eat, rub
grease ➡ fat, oil
grease monkey ➡ mechanic
greater ➡ better
greatest ➡ most
greatly ➡ very, far, much
greatness ➡ excellence
greediness ➡ greed

---

grieve *vb* mourn, lament, fret, rue, languish, bewail, pine ➡ **sadden, mope**

grind 1. *vb* crush, pulverize, crumble, powder, mash
2. *vb* ➡ **sharpen**
3. *vb* grate, grit, gnash ➡ **rub**

group 1. *n* gang, bunch, crew, pack, set, class, band, body, cluster, ring, bloc, clique, syndicate, junta ➡ **troop**
2. *n* ➡ **band**

grow 1. *vb* sprout, germinate, develop, expand, increase, mature, ripen, evolve, enlarge, wax, magnify, amplify, heighten, augment, mushroom, multiply ➡ **prosper, blossom, strengthen**
2. *vb* raise, breed, cultivate, nurture, rear ➡ **plant**

growth 1. *n* development, spread, enlargement, expansion, proliferation, escalation, rise, inflation, gain, hike, increment, increase ➡ **progress**

2. *n* lump, tumor, cancer, swelling, cyst, mole, polyp, sarcoma
3. *n* crop, harvest, yield

gruesome *adj* morbid, gross, sick, sadistic, grisly, macabre, grim ➡ **awful, bad, mean**

grunt *vb, n* groan, snort, oink, croak ➡ **cry**

guarantee 1. *vb* insure, assure, secure, ensure, warrant, certify ➡ **promise**
2. *n* ➡ **promise**

guardian *n* guard, custodian, caretaker, overseer, curator, trustee, keeper, monitor, watchdog ➡ **parent, patrol, guide, boss, savior**

guess *vb* suppose, think, believe, imagine, suspect, reckon, speculate, surmise ➡ **estimate, assume**

guide 1. *n* conductor, escort, leader, usher, shepherd, pilot
2. *n* ➡ **pattern**
3. *vb* ➡ **lead**

If the word you want is not a main entry above, look below to find it.

greet ➡ welcome, receive
greeting ➡ welcome
greetings ➡ hello
grey ➡ gray
gridiron ➡ field
grief ➡ sorrow, misery
grievance ➡ complaint
grievous ➡ awful
grill ➡ cook, ask
grim ➡ bleak, gruesome
grimace ➡ frown
grime ➡ dirt
grimy ➡ dirty
grin ➡ smile

grinding ➡ friction
grip ➡ embrace
gripe ➡ complain
gripping ➡ exciting
grisly ➡ gruesome, ugly
grit ➡ dirt, courage, grind
groan ➡ cry, complain, grunt
grocery ➡ market
groom ➡ spouse, comb, dress
groove ➡ channel
grope ➡ touch
gross ➡ obvious, huge, gruesome, earn
grotesque ➡ ugly, gargoyle

grotto ➡ cave
grouch ➡ complain
grouchy ➡ cross
ground ➡ base, floor, dirt, terrain
groundless ➡ superstitious
grounds ➡ basis, property, reason
grove ➡ forest
grovel ➡ crawl
grower ➡ farmer
growl ➡ bark
grown-up ➡ adult
grub ➡ larva, dig
grubby ➡ dirty

grudge ➡ complaint, envy
grudging ➡ reluctant
gruff ➡ hoarse, abrupt
grumble ➡ complain
grumpy ➡ cross
guard ➡ protect, watch, guardian
guarded ➡ safe, careful
guest ➡ visitor, occupant
guest room ➡ bedroom
guffaw ➡ laugh
guidance ➡ advice, leadership
guideline ➡ rule

n = noun • *vb* = verb • *adj* = adjective • *adv* = adverb • *prep* = preposition • *conj* = conjunction

guilt *n* fault, blame, responsibility, culpability, liability ➡ **shame**

guilty *adj* culpable, blameworthy, responsible, liable, derelict ⇨ *innocent*

gun *n* firearm, weapon, pistol, revolver, sidearm, handgun, rifle, carbine, shotgun, machine gun, musket, flintlock, muzzle loader, blunderbuss, cannon ➡ **arms**

gymnasium *n* gym, sports center, recreation center, field house

gymnastics *n* acrobatics, tumbling, vaulting, aerobatics, aerobics ➡ **exercise**

If the word you want is not a main entry above, look below to find it.

guild ➡ union	gully ➡ canyon	guru ➡ teacher	guy ➡ man, rope
guile ➡ dishonesty	gulp ➡ drink, eat, breathe	gush ➡ flow	guzzle ➡ drink
guiltless ➡ innocent	gum band ➡ rubber band	gust ➡ wind	gym ➡ gymnasium
guise ➡ disguise	gummy ➡ sticky	gusto ➡ enthusiasm	gymnast ➡ acrobat
gulch ➡ canyon	gun down ➡ shoot	gut ➡ stomach	gyp ➡ cheat
gulf ➡ bay, difference	gunfire ➡ fire	guts ➡ courage	gypsy ➡ traveler
gullible ➡ naive	gurney ➡ bed	gutter ➡ channel	gyrate ➡ turn
		guttural ➡ hoarse	

H

habit 1. *n* custom, practice, routine, institution, usage, rule
2. *n* dependency, addiction, instinct, reflex, wont ➡ **tendency**
3. *n* mannerism, affectation, quirk, trait ➡ **oddity**
4. *n* ➡ **clothes**

habitat *n* environment, habitation, ecosystem ➡ **den, house**

hair *n* locks, tresses, mane, fur ➡ **braid, lock, wig, beard, coat**

hall 1. *n* corridor, hallway, passage, passageway, entryway, foyer, vestibule, lobby, lounge, anteroom
2. *n* auditorium, theater, arena, amphitheater ➡ **room, building**

halo *n* nimbus, corona, aurora

hammer 1. *n* clawhammer, mallet, maul, sledgehammer, sledge, ball-peen hammer, gavel ➡ **tool**
2. *vb* ➡ **hit**

handwriting *n* writing, penmanship, script, cursive, longhand, printing, calligraphy ➡ **print**

hang 1. *vb* dangle, drape, suspend, swing, hover ➡ **depend**
2. *vb* lynch, execute ➡ **kill**

happen *vb* occur, transpire, chance, go, befall, ensue, arise, recur, exist

happy *adj* glad, cheerful, joyful, joyous, merry, gay, jolly, delighted, gleeful, proud, jovial, high, festive, bright ➡ **ecstatic, satisfied, lucky** ⇨ *sad*
  *Note that **happy**, **glad**, and **delighted** are often used in statements simply to be polite: "I'm **happy/glad/delighted** to meet you."*

If the word you want is not a main entry above, look below to find it.

habitation ➡ home, habitat

habitual ➡ usual, automatic, frequent

habitually ➡ regularly

hack ➡ taxi, cut

hackneyed ➡ trite

haggard ➡ thin

haggle ➡ negotiate

hail ➡ flood, welcome, snow, ice

hailstorm ➡ storm

hairless ➡ bald

hairpiece ➡ wig

hairpin ➡ pin

hairy ➡ fuzzy

hale ➡ healthy

haleness ➡ health

half-wit ➡ fool

hallow ➡ bless

hallowed ➡ holy

hallucinating ➡ delirious

hallucination ➡ illusion

hallucinatory ➡ imaginary

hallucinogen ➡ drug

hallway ➡ hall

halt ➡ stop, limp

halve ➡ divide

ham ➡ actor

hamlet ➡ town

hamper ➡ delay

hampered ➡ disabled

hand ➡ worker, lift, give

handbag ➡ bag

handbook ➡ book

handcuff ➡ bond

hand down ➡ leave

handgun ➡ gun

handicap ➡ disability, bar

handicapped ➡ disabled

hand in ➡ give

handkerchief ➡ scarf

hand over ➡ give

handle ➡ touch, sell, control

handler ➡ agent

handling ➡ treatment

handshake ➡ embrace

handsome ➡ pretty, generous

handy ➡ useful, available, able

hanging ➡ gallows

hanker ➡ want

haphazard ➡ arbitrary

hapless ➡ unfortunate

happening ➡ event

happenstance ➡ chance

happiness ➡ pleasure

harangue ➡ yell

harass ➡ bother, abuse

n = noun • *vb* = verb • *adj* = adjective • *adv* = adverb • *prep* = preposition • *conj* = conjunction

harbor *n* port, haven, anchorage ➡ **dock, bay, protection**

hard 1. *adj* stony, rocky, adamant ➡ **firm, tough**
2. *adj* difficult, tough, demanding, strenuous, arduous, rigorous, heavy, rough, trying ⇨ *easy*
3. *adj* harsh, severe, bitter, austere, stark, stern

harden *vb* solidify, freeze, petrify, fossilize, set, temper, dry, calcify, toughen, clot, congeal, jell, thicken, coagulate, congeal, cake ➡ **strengthen**

hardship *n* misfortune, adversity, affliction, need, tribulation, want, complaint, injustice ➡ **trouble, misery, poverty**

harm 1. *n* injury, hurt, loss, impairment, detriment, disadvantage ➡ **abuse, damage**
2. *vb* ➡ **hurt, damage**

harmless 1. *adj* innocuous, inoffensive, unobjectionable ➡ **naive, kind**
2. *adj* ➡ **safe**

hat *n* cap, helmet, headgear, chapeau, bonnet

hate 1. *vb* detest, abhor, despise, deplore, loathe, disdain, dislike, abominate, scorn, execrate ⇨ *love*
2. *n* ➡ **hatred**

hatred *n* hate, abhorrence, aversion, revulsion, loathing, contempt, scorn, malice, hostility, dislike, disdain, antipathy, animosity, malevolence ➡ **prejudice** ⇨ *love*

hay *n* fodder, feed, grass, timothy, alfalfa

headline *n* head, heading, leader, title, header, caption, screamer *(informal)*

heal *vb* cure, remedy, mend, knit, treat, medicate, nurse, doctor
In general, **heal** *refers to the making better or getting better of a sore, wound, or injury.* **Cure** *usually refers to getting rid of a disease or illness.*

If the word you want is not a main entry above, look below to find it.

hard of hearing ➡ **deaf**

hardcover ➡ **book**

hardhearted ➡ **insensitive**

hardly ➡ **only, seldom**

hardwood ➡ **tree**

hardworking ➡ **diligent**

hardy ➡ **strong, healthy**

hark ➡ **listen**

harmful ➡ **dangerous, destructive, unhealthy**

harmonious ➡ **musical, compatible, unanimous**

harmonize ➡ **sing, agree**

harmony ➡ **music, peace, unity, balance, agreement**

harness ➡ **equipment, control**

harrow ➡ **dig**

harry ➡ **attack, trouble**

harsh ➡ **sharp, hard, rough**

harvest ➡ **gather, farm, growth**

hash ➡ **assortment, mess**

haste ➡ **hurry**

hasten ➡ **hurry**

hastily ➡ **quickly**

hasty ➡ **fast, early**

hat pin ➡ **pin**

hatch ➡ **reproduce, invent**

hatchet ➡ **ax, axe**

hateful ➡ **awful**

haughtiness ➡ **pride**

haughty ➡ **proud**

haul ➡ **pull, carry**

haunch ➡ **back**

haunt ➡ **frequent**

haut monde ➡ **aristocracy**

have ➡ **keep, own, give, need**

haven ➡ **harbor, protection**

havoc ➡ **damage**

hawk ➡ **sell**

hayfield ➡ **field**

hazard ➡ **danger, dare, jeopardize**

hazardous ➡ **dangerous**

haze ➡ **fog, cloud**

hazy ➡ **cloudy, dim**

head ➡ **front, boss, chairperson, bathroom, foam, headline, go**

headache ➡ **nuisance**

header ➡ **headline**

headgear ➡ **hat**

heading ➡ **headline, name, course**

headland ➡ **cape**

headlong ➡ **quickly**

headmaster ➡ **principal**

head-over-heels ➡ **upside down**

headquarters ➡ **base, office**

headstrong ➡ **stubborn**

headway ➡ **progress**

healing ➡ **cure, medicinal**

➡ = synonym cross-reference • ⇨ = antonym cross-reference

health *n* fitness, condition, shape, vigor, vitality, haleness, wellness, healthfulness ➡ **welfare**

healthy 1. *adj* well, fit, sound, hale, hardy, hearty, vigorous, whole ➡ **better, strong** ⇨ *sick*
2. *adj* healthful, nourishing, nutritious, wholesome

heaven 1. *n* paradise, bliss, nirvana, elysian fields, Elysium, Valhalla ➡ **utopia, pleasure**
2. *n* ➡ **air**

heavenly 1. *adj* divine, sublime, celestial, spiritual ➡ **supernatural**
2. *adj* ➡ **great**

heavy 1. *adj* cumbersome, hefty, ponderous, massive, weighty, bulky ➡ **big** ⇨ *light*
2. *adj* ➡ **serious**
3. *adj* ➡ **hard**

hedge *n* hedgerow, shrubbery, bushes,

height 1. *n* altitude, elevation, stature, loftiness, tallness ⇨ *depth*
2. *n* ➡ **top**

hello *interj* good day, how do you do?, greetings, hi, *hola (Spanish)*, *bonjour (French)*, *ciao (Italian)*, *shalom (Hebrew)*, howdy *(informal)*, yo *(informal)* ⇨ **good-bye**

help 1. *vb* assist, aid, serve, wait on, cooperate, collaborate, team up, succor, benefit, improve, enrich, avail ➡ **relieve, support**
2. *n* aid, assistance, cooperation, relief, service ➡ **support, comfort, generosity, welfare**
3. *n* ➡ **worker**

helper *n* assistant, aide, deputy, lieutenant, subordinate ➡ **partner, worker**

herb *n* seasoning, flavoring ➡ **plant, spice**

herd *n* flock, pack, swarm, hive, colony, bevy, brood, school, gaggle, pod ➡ **group, crowd**

hermit *n* recluse, shut-in, ascetic

hesitate *vb* falter, vacillate, balk, pause, demur, equivocate, waver ➡ **stop, delay, wait**

If the word you want is not a main entry above, look below to find it.

healthful ➡ healthy
healthfulness ➡ health
heap ➡ pile
hear ➡ listen
hearing ➡ tryout, suit
hearing-impaired ➡ deaf
hearken ➡ listen
hearsay ➡ rumor
heart ➡ essence, feeling
heartache ➡ sorrow, misery
heartbreaking ➡ pitiful
hearten ➡ please
heartfelt ➡ sincere
hearth ➡ fireplace

heartily ➡ sincerely
heartless ➡ insensitive
hearty ➡ friendly, healthy
heat ➡ energy
heated ➡ warm
heater ➡ furnace
heath ➡ plain
heathen ➡ atheist
heave ➡ lift, throw, vomit
heavens ➡ space
heaviness ➡ weight
heavyset ➡ fat
hectic ➡ frantic
hedgerow ➡ hedge

heed ➡ obey, notice
heedless ➡ unaware, thoughtless
heft ➡ weight
hefty ➡ heavy
heighten ➡ grow
heinous ➡ wicked
heirloom ➡ antique
helm ➡ wheel
helmet ➡ hat
helmsman ➡ pilot
helpful ➡ useful
helpless ➡ weak
helpmate ➡ spouse

hem ➡ edge
hem and haw ➡ stammer
hence ➡ therefore
herald ➡ welcome, precede
here ➡ present
hereafter ➡ future
hereditary ➡ natural
heresy ➡ disagreement
heritage ➡ inheritance
hero ➡ winner, savior
heroic ➡ brave
heroism ➡ courage
hesitant ➡ reluctant

hide 1. *vb* conceal, disguise, secrete, bury, withhold, hoard, squirrel (away) ⇨ **reveal**
2. *vb* cover (up), camouflage, obscure, eclipse, mask, block, screen, shade, shroud, veil, cloak
➡ **cover**
3. *n* pelt, skin, fleece, fell, rawhide, chamois
➡ **coat**

high 1. *adj* tall, lofty, towering, soaring ➡ **big**
2. *adj* high-pitched, shrill, treble, piping
➡ **loud** ⇨ *low*
3. *adj* ➡ **important**
4. *adj* ➡ **happy**

highway *n* interstate, expressway, freeway, thruway, turnpike, parkway ➡ **road**

hill 1. *n* knoll, mound, hillock, foothill, down, dune, bank, ridge ➡ **pile, mountain, cliff**
⇨ *valley*
2. *n* ➡ **slant**

hire 1. *vb* (*in reference to people*) engage, employ, appoint, enlist, draft, recruit, enroll ⇨ **fire**
2. *vb* (*in reference to things or property*) rent, charter, lease, let, sublet
➡ **lend, borrow**

hit 1. *vb* strike, pound, batter, beat, maul, bash, bump, pelt, smash, smack, swat, hammer, buffet, pat, clobber (*informal*), slug (*informal*), whack (*informal*) ➡ **punch, knock, collide, whip**
2. *n* ➡ **blow**[1]

hoarse *adj* raspy, gruff, grating, throaty, guttural, husky, gravelly ➡ **rough**

hole 1. *n* hollow, cavity, pit, crater, abyss, chasm, crevasse ➡ **cave, den, well**
2. *n* puncture, perforation, opening, aperture, vent, crack, cleft, fissure, crevice, split, gap, rupture, leak, pore

---

If the word you want is not a main entry above, look below to find it.

heterogeneous ➡ **different**
hew ➡ **cut, carve**
hex ➡ **curse**
hi ➡ **hello**
hiatus ➡ **break**
hibernate ➡ **sleep**
hibernating ➡ **asleep**
hidden ➡ **secret, invisible**
hidebound ➡ **provincial**
hideous ➡ **ugly**
hiding ➡ **secrecy**
highborn ➡ **noble**
higher than ➡ **above**
highland ➡ **plateau**
highlight ➡ **emphasize**
highly ➡ **well**
high-pitched ➡ **high**
high-priced ➡ **expensive**

high seas ➡ **ocean**
high society ➡ **aristocracy**
high-strung ➡ **tense, nervous**
hijack ➡ **seize**
hike ➡ **walk, growth**
hiker ➡ **pedestrian**
hilarious ➡ **funny**
hilarity ➡ **laughter**
hillock ➡ **hill**
hinder ➡ **prevent, bar, delay**
hindmost ➡ **last**
hindquarters ➡ **back**
hindrance ➡ **barrier, disability**
hinge ➡ **depend, turn, axis**
hint ➡ **suggest, bit, reminder, tip**
hinterland ➡ **country**

hiss ➡ **yell**
historian ➡ **writer**
historic ➡ **memorable**
history ➡ **past, story**
hitch ➡ **knot, trap, tie**
hitchhiker ➡ **rider**
hive ➡ **herd**
hoard ➡ **save, hide, wealth, supply**
hoarder ➡ **miser**
hoary ➡ **old**
hoax ➡ **trick**
hobble ➡ **limp, prevent**
hobby ➡ **pastime**
hobgoblin ➡ **bogeyman**
hobnob ➡ **mix**
hobo ➡ **beggar**
hock ➡ **pawn**

hocus-pocus ➡ **magic**
hodgepodge ➡ **mess**
hoe ➡ **dig**
hog ➡ **glutton**
hogshead ➡ **barrel**
hogwash ➡ **nonsense**
hoi polloi ➡ **people**
hoist ➡ **lift**
hola ➡ **hello**
hold ➡ **contain, own, support, embrace, believe, give**
holder ➡ **owner**
holding ➡ **supply**
holdings ➡ **property**
holiday ➡ **vacation**
holier-than-thou ➡ **self-righteous**

---

holy *adj* sacred, divine, hallowed, blessed, consecrated, sacramental

home 1. *n* house, apartment, condominium, condo (*informal*), dwelling, residence, abode, domicile, habitation, cabin, cottage, bungalow, chalet, mansion, palace, manor, villa, chateau ➡ **den, shack**
2. *n* ➡ **family**
3. *n* ➡ **base**
4. *n* ➡ **hospital**

homeless *adj* vagrant, vagabond, derelict, outcast, stray, lost, displaced, dispossessed

homonym *n* homograph, homophone

honesty *n* candor, frankness, veracity ➡ **truth, virtue**

hope 1. *vb* wish, expect, anticipate, aspire ➡ **believe, want, intend**
2. *n* desire, faith, longing, aspiration, dream ➡ **ambition**
3. *n* ➡ **virtue**

horizon *n* skyline, limit, range ➡ **border**

horse *n* pony, foal, colt, filly, stallion, mare, steed, mount, gelding

hospital *n* infirmary, clinic, medical center, rehabilitation center, sanatorium, sanitarium, nursing home, home

hospitality *n* geniality, cordiality, warmth, amiability, courtesy, welcome ➡ **generosity, kindness**

host 1. *n* hostess, entertainer, presenter, moderator, master of ceremonies, MC, emcee, chaperon, chaperone
2. *n* hostess, innkeeper, bartender, barkeep, maitre d'
3. *n* ➡ **crowd**
4. *vb* ➡ **entertain**

hot 1. *adj* scalding, boiling, broiling, roasting, sizzling, sweltering, torrid ➡ **warm, burning, tropical** ⇨ **cold**
2. *adj* ➡ **spicy**
3. *adj* ➡ **fashionable**

If the word you want is not a main entry above, look below to find it.

hollow ➡ empty, hole, valley
holm ➡ island
holocaust ➡ fire
homage ➡ respect
home base ➡ base
homecoming ➡ return
homegrown ➡ native
homeland ➡ country
homely ➡ plain
homesick ➡ lonely
homestead ➡ farm
homesteader ➡ pioneer
homesteading ➡ farming
homework ➡ lesson
homey ➡ comfortable, family
homicidal ➡ deadly

homicide ➡ murder
hominid ➡ human being
homogeneity ➡ unity
homograph ➡ homonym
homophone ➡ homonym
hone ➡ sharpen, perfect
honed ➡ sharp
honest ➡ good, sincere
honestly ➡ sincerely
honeyed ➡ rich
honk ➡ blow²
honor ➡ respect, virtue, award, praise, celebrate, keep
honorable ➡ good
hood ➡ top, vandal
hoodlum ➡ vandal

hoodwink ➡ cheat
hoof ➡ foot
hook ➡ lock
hooligan ➡ bully, vandal
hoop ➡ circle, ring
hoot ➡ yell
hop ➡ jump
hopeful ➡ good, optimistic
hopeless ➡ bleak, useless
horde ➡ crowd
horizontal ➡ level, prone
horrible ➡ awful
horrid ➡ ugly
horrify ➡ scare, shock
horrifying ➡ scary
horror ➡ fear

horsefly ➡ fly
horseman ➡ rider
horseplay ➡ play
horsepower ➡ energy
horse race ➡ race
horseshoe ➡ curve
horsewoman ➡ rider
horticulture ➡ farming
hose ➡ pipe
hospitable ➡ friendly
hostage ➡ prisoner
hostel ➡ hotel
hostess ➡ host
hostile ➡ belligerent
hostilities ➡ fight
hostility ➡ opposition, anger, hatred

hotel *n* inn, motel, hostel, lodge, bed-and-breakfast, resort, spa, retreat

house 1. *n* ➡ **home**
2. *vb* accommodate, board, lodge, put up, shelter, quarter, billet

huge *adj* enormous, immense, gigantic, prodigious, colossal, tremendous, mighty, vast, gross, gargantuan, monstrous, jumbo, mammoth, massive, titanic, humongous (*informal*) ➡ **big**

hum *vb* buzz, drone, murmur, whir, purr ➡ **sing**

human being *n* human, person, individual, being, soul, body, mortal, hominid ➡ **humanity, man, woman, people**

humanity 1. *n* humankind, mankind, man, society, human race ➡ **people, human being, man, woman**
2. *n* ➡ **kindness**

Many people object to the words **man** (*when used without the or a*), *and* **mankind** *in the sense of "humanity," because the word* **man** *is more frequently used to mean "an adult male person." Because this more common sense (a man, the*

young man) *refers to males and not to females, they feel that the "humanity" sense of* **man** *and* **mankind** *also excludes women. It may be more thoughtful to use* **humanity, humankind,** *the phrase the* **human race,** *or the plural compound* **human beings** *when you want to refer to humans in general. The "humanity" sense of* **man** *is very common in the writing of earlier periods.*

humble 1. *adj* meek, modest, unassuming, unpretentious, self-deprecating, self-effacing ➡ **shy** ⇨ *proud*
2. *adj* ➡ **common**
3. *vb* ➡ **condescend**

humidity *n* moisture, dampness, mugginess, wetness, dew ➡ **liquid**

humor 1. *n* wit, comedy, levity, amusement, jest, jocularity, whimsicality ➡ **irony**
2. *n* ➡ **mood**
3. *vb* ➡ **entertain, pamper**

hunger 1. *n* starvation, famine ➡ **poverty**
2. *n* ➡ **appetite, desire**

hungry *adj* starving, starved, famished, ravenous, underfed, malnourished, undernourished, emaciated, wasted

---

If the word you want is not a main entry above, look below to find it.

hothouse ➡ greenhouse

Houdini ➡ magician

hound ➡ dog, bother, follow

hourglass ➡ clock

housebroken ➡ tame

housefly ➡ fly

houseguest ➡ visitor

household ➡ family

householder ➡ occupant

houseplant ➡ flower

house-trained ➡ tame

housing estate ➡ development

hovel ➡ shack

hover ➡ hang, fly

how do you do? ➡ hello

howdy ➡ hello

however ➡ but, anyway

howl ➡ cry, bark, laugh

hub ➡ middle

hubbub ➡ noise

hubris ➡ pride

huddle ➡ snuggle

hue ➡ color

huff ➡ breathe, fit²

hug ➡ embrace

hull ➡ framework

hullabaloo ➡ noise

human ➡ human being, mortal

humane ➡ kind

humanistic ➡ liberal

humankind ➡ humanity

human-made ➡ manufactured

human race ➡ humanity

humbug ➡ cheat

humdrum ➡ dull

humid ➡ damp, tropical

humiliate ➡ insult, shame

humiliated ➡ ashamed

humiliation ➡ shame

humongous ➡ huge

humorist ➡ writer, comic

humorous ➡ funny

hump ➡ bulge

humus ➡ dirt

hunch ➡ impulse, belief, bend

hunk ➡ block, lump

➡ = synonym cross-reference • ⇨ = antonym cross-reference

hunt 1. *vb* fish, shoot, poach, track ➡ **follow**
2. *vb* search, seek, look, investigate, scour, forage, probe, ransack, rummage, delve, explore, prospect, comb, sift
3. *n* search, investigation, pursuit, chase, quest, exploration ➡ **study**

hurry 1. *vb* rush, hasten, hustle, speed, race, hurtle, accelerate, quicken, scurry, sally, dash, zip, whiz, zoom, scamper, scuttle, surge, swarm, pour, stampede, storm
2. *n* rush, haste, scramble, stampede ➡ **speed**

hurt 1. *vb* injure, afflict, damage, wound, bruise, tear, wrench, twist, dislocate ➡ **harm, abuse, hit, insult, punish, break, pull**

2. *vb* smart, sting, burn, irritate, ache, throb ➡ **tingle**

hybrid *n* cross, crossbreed, mongrel ➡ **mixture**

hymn *n* carol, anthem, psalm, chant, motet, oratorio, cantata ➡ **song, dirge**

hypocrite *n* deceiver, faker, dissembler, quack, con artist ➡ **cheat**

hypocritical *adj* insincere, two-faced, dissembling ➡ **self-righteous, dishonest, sly**

hysteria *n* delirium, rage, mania, madness, panic, hysterics ➡ **excitement, confusion, fit**

If the word you want is not a main entry above, look below to find it.

hurdle ➡ barrier, jump
hurl ➡ throw
hurrah ➡ encore
hurricane ➡ storm
hurried ➡ abrupt, fast
hurriedly ➡ quickly
hurtful ➡ sore
hurtle ➡ hurry

husband ➡ man, spouse
husbandman ➡ farmer
husbandry ➡ farming
hush ➡ calm, quiet
hushed ➡ quiet
husk ➡ shell, peel
husky ➡ fat, hoarse

hustle ➡ hurry
hut ➡ shack
hygienic ➡ sterile
hype ➡ advertising
hyperactive ➡ active
hyperbole ➡ exaggeration
hypnotize ➡ enchant

hypocrisy ➡ dishonesty
hypothesis ➡ theory
hypothetical ➡ theoretical, imaginary
hysterical ➡ excited, delirious
hysterics ➡ hysteria

I

ice *n* frost, hail, sleet, icicle, ice cube, permafrost

ice cream *n* ice milk, sherbet, sorbet, sundae, spumoni, parfait

icing *n* frosting, glaze, topping, meringue

idea *n* thought, concept, impression, inspiration, notion, inkling ➡ **belief, theory, plan, suggestion**

idealist *n* optimist, romantic, perfectionist, dreamer, visionary

idealistic *adj* utopian, romantic, visionary ➡ **optimistic, impractical**

ignorance *n* illiteracy, innocence, simplicity, inexperience, denseness, stupidity, unawareness

ignorant *adj* illiterate, uneducated, unlearned, unlettered, unschooled, unread ➡ **naive, stupid, unaware** ⇨ *educated*

illegal *adj* unlawful, illegitimate, illicit, criminal, outlawed, wrongful, prohibited, taboo

illegible *adj* indecipherable, unreadable, unintelligible ➡ **dim**

illness *n* sickness, ailment, malady, affliction, disorder, infirmity, complaint ➡ **disease, nausea**

illogical *adj* irrational, unreasonable, absurd, fallacious, inconsistent, incoherent ➡ **wrong**

illusion *n* mirage, hallucination, delusion, apparition ➡ **fancy, trick**

imaginary *adj* unreal, nonexistent, fictional, fictitious, illusory, hypothetical, fanciful, hallucinatory ➡ **legendary** ⇨ *real*

imagination *n* fancy, ingenuity, creativity, originality, vision, inspiration

---

If the word you want is not a main entry above, look below to find it.

ICBM ➡ missile
iceberg ➡ glacier
icebox ➡ refrigerator
icecap ➡ glacier
ice cube ➡ ice
ice floe ➡ glacier
ice milk ➡ ice cream
ice storm ➡ storm
icicle ➡ ice
icon ➡ god
icy ➡ cold, slippery
ideal ➡ perfect, model, favorite
identical ➡ same
identification ➡ discovery
identify ➡ name, distinguish

identity ➡ personality, unity
ideology ➡ philosophy
idiom ➡ dialect
idiosyncrasy ➡ oddity
idiosyncratic ➡ unique
idiot ➡ fool
idiotic ➡ foolish
idle ➡ passive, lazy, unemployed, empty, rest
idleness ➡ laziness
idler ➡ loafer
idol ➡ god, statue
idolize ➡ love
ignite ➡ light[1]
ignoble ➡ shameful

ignoramus ➡ fool
ignore ➡ exclude
ill ➡ sick
ill-advised ➡ imprudent
ill at ease ➡ uncomfortable
ill-behaved ➡ mischievous
illegitimate ➡ illegal
illiberal ➡ conservative
illicit ➡ illegal
illiteracy ➡ ignorance
illiterate ➡ ignorant
ill-natured ➡ cross
ill-tempered ➡ cross
ill-treat ➡ abuse
ill-treatment ➡ abuse

illuminate ➡ light[1], explain
illumination ➡ light[1]
illuminations ➡ fireworks
illumine ➡ light[1]
illusionist ➡ magician
illusory ➡ imaginary
illustrate ➡ draw, explain
illustration ➡ picture, example
illustrative ➡ visible
illustrious ➡ famous
image ➡ picture, statue, photograph
imaginable ➡ possible
imaginative ➡ talented

---

imagine 1. *vb* conceive, picture, see, envision, envisage, visualize, fancy, fantasize ➡ **pretend**
2. *vb* ➡ **guess, think**

imitate *vb* copy, mimic, emulate, simulate, parrot, ape, parody, mock, lampoon, satirize, impersonate, caricature

immoral *adj* unethical, unprincipled, shameless, dissolute, degenerate, depraved, perverted ➡ **bad, wrong**

immorality *n* sin, depravity, wickedness, evil, iniquity, perversion, perversity

impassable *adj* closed, obstructed, trackless, pathless, untrodden, impenetrable ➡ **inaccessible**

importance *n* significance, consequence, import, moment, value, gravity, weight, stature, dignity ➡ **relevance, worth**

important 1. *adj* significant, principal, chief, major, main, essential, primary, critical, key, paramount, prime, cardinal, foremost, high, weighty ➡ **urgent, necessary, valuable, meaningful, memorable, predominant**
2. *adj* influential, prominent, powerful ➡ **famous**

impossible 1. *adj* inconceivable, unattainable, unthinkable, incomprehensible ➡ **useless, illogical, unbelievable**
2. *adj* insoluble, unsolvable, inexplicable, unexplainable, unaccountable
3. *adj* ➡ **intolerable**

If the word you want is not a main entry above, look below to find it.

imbecile ➡ fool

imbecilic ➡ foolish

imbed ➡ embed

imbibe ➡ drink

imbue ➡ instill

imitation ➡ fake, parody

immaculate ➡ perfect, clean

immature ➡ young, childish

immaturity ➡ childhood

immeasurable ➡ infinite

immediate ➡ sudden, near

immediately ➡ now

immense ➡ huge

immensely ➡ very

immerse ➡ sink, wet

immersed ➡ absorbed

immigrant ➡ foreign, foreigner, pioneer

immigrate ➡ move

immigration ➡ movement

imminent ➡ near, future

immobile ➡ stationary

immobilize ➡ paralyze

immoderate ➡ excessive

immortal ➡ eternal, god

immovable ➡ tight

immune ➡ safe

immunity ➡ freedom

immunize ➡ vaccinate

imp ➡ rascal, urchin

impact ➡ collision, blow[1], effect, collide

impair ➡ damage, weaken

impaired ➡ disabled

impairment ➡ disability, harm

impalpable ➡ invisible

impart ➡ give

impartial ➡ fair

impartiality ➡ justice

impassioned ➡ emotional

impassive ➡ blank

impatient ➡ eager

impeach ➡ try

impeccable ➡ perfect, innocent

impede ➡ bar, delay

impediment ➡ barrier, disability

impel ➡ push, force

impending ➡ ominous, future

impenetrable ➡ impassable, thick

imperative ➡ necessary, urgent

imperceptible ➡ invisible

imperfect ➡ partial

imperfection ➡ defect

imperial ➡ noble

imperil ➡ jeopardize

imperious ➡ dignified, dogmatic

impermanent ➡ mortal

impermeable ➡ tight

impersonal ➡ cool, fair

impersonate ➡ act, imitate

impertinence ➡ audacity

impertinent ➡ rude

impetuous ➡ abrupt, emotional

impetus ➡ impulse

impinge ➡ intrude

impish ➡ mischievous

implant ➡ instill, embed, put

implausible ➡ unbelievable

implement ➡ tool, equipment

implicate ➡ blame

implication ➡ meaning

implicit ➡ virtual

implied ➡ virtual

implore ➡ beg

imply ➡ suggest, matter, mean

impolite ➡ rude

import ➡ importance, meaning

importantly ➡ chiefly

imported ➡ foreign

importune ➡ beg

impose ➡ order, inflict, disturb

imposing ➡ grand

imposter ➡ cheat

---

n = noun • *vb* = verb • *adj* = adjective • *adv* = adverb • *prep* = preposition • *conj* = conjunction

impractical *adj* unrealistic, quixotic, unfeasible ➡ **illogical, idealistic** ⇨ *practical*

improper *adj* inappropriate, unseemly, unbecoming, indecent, indelicate, indecorous, unsuitable, unbefitting, impure ➡ **wrong, bad, shameful**

imprudent *adj* ill-advised, inadvisable, unwise, rash, indiscreet, overconfident, unsound

impulse 1. *n* whim, fancy, caprice, whimsy, hunch
2. *n* thrust, surge, pulse, pulsation, impetus, shove, momentum

inability *n* incapability, ineptitude, incompetence, incapacity, inefficacy, impotence, powerlessness, failure

inaccessible *adj* unobtainable, unattainable, unreachable, out-of-the-way, elusive, unavailable ➡ **impassable**

inadequate *adj* lacking, deficient, short, sparse, insufficient ➡ **poor**

incentive *n* motivation, motive, encouragement, inspiration, inducement, stimulus, spur, spark ➡ **reason, support**

incompetent *adj* incapable, inept, ineffectual, unqualified, unfit, inefficient, unable ➡ **amateur, clumsy**

If the word you want is not a main entry above, look below to find it.

impotence ➡ inability
impotent ➡ weak, sterile
impound ➡ jail
impoverish ➡ ruin
impoverished ➡ poor, underdeveloped
impoverishment ➡ poverty
impregnable ➡ safe
impress ➡ affect, print
impression ➡ idea, effect, print, track, dent
impressive ➡ awesome, striking
imprint ➡ print, track, signature
imprison ➡ jail
improbable ➡ unbelievable
impromptu ➡ spontaneous
improve ➡ correct, help
improved ➡ better
improvement ➡ repair, progress
improving ➡ better
improvise ➡ invent
impudence ➡ rudeness

impudent ➡ rude
impulsive ➡ spontaneous, arbitrary
impure ➡ improper, dirty
in ➡ fashionable
inaccuracy ➡ mistake
inaccurate ➡ wrong
inactive ➡ passive, unemployed
inadequacy ➡ mediocrity
inadvertent ➡ accidental
inadvertently ➡ accidentally
inadvisable ➡ imprudent
inane ➡ trite
inanimate ➡ dead, unconscious
inappropriate ➡ improper
inarticulate ➡ dumb
inattentive ➡ absentminded, negligent
inaudible ➡ quiet
inaugural ➡ early
inaugurate ➡ start, crown
inauguration ➡ beginning
inauspicious ➡ ominous

inborn ➡ natural
incapability ➡ inability
incapable ➡ incompetent
incapacitate ➡ weaken
incapacitated ➡ disabled
incapacity ➡ inability
incarcerate ➡ jail
incense ➡ anger, smell
incessant ➡ continual, frequent
inch ➡ crawl
inchworm ➡ worm
incident ➡ event
incidental ➡ accidental, circumstantial
incidentally ➡ accidentally
incinerate ➡ burn
incinerator ➡ furnace
incipient ➡ early
incise ➡ carve
incision ➡ cut
incisive ➡ smart
incite ➡ urge, fan
inclement ➡ wet, stormy

inclination ➡ preference, tendency
incline ➡ slant
inclined ➡ likely
include ➡ contain, add
inclusive ➡ comprehensive
incoherent ➡ illogical, delirious
income ➡ wage
incomparable ➡ unique
incomparably ➡ far
incompetence ➡ inability
incomplete ➡ partial, unresolved
incompletely ➡ partly
incomprehensible ➡ obscure, impossible
inconceivable ➡ impossible
inconclusive ➡ circumstantial
incongruity ➡ contradiction, irony
inconsiderate ➡ thoughtless
inconsistency ➡ contradiction

➡ = synonym cross-reference • ⇨ = antonym cross-reference

inconspicuous *adj* unnoticeable, unobtrusive, unapparent ➡ **invisible** ⇨ *obvious*

inconvenient *adj* awkward, bothersome, troublesome, onerous, irksome, annoying, untimely

indirect *adj* circuitous, roundabout, twisting, meandering, tortuous, rambling, devious ➡ **circumstantial**

indiscriminate *adj* aimless, uncritical,

promiscuous ➡ **thoughtless, carefree, arbitrary**

inexcusable *adj* unforgiveable, unpardonable, unjustifiable, indefensible

infallible *adj* unerring, faultless, irrefutable, authoritative, incontrovertible ➡ **perfect, certain, reliable**

infer *vb* deduce, conclude, gather, judge, reason, ascertain ➡ **assume, mention**

If the word you want is not a main entry above, look below to find it.

inconsistent ➡ illogical, variable

inconstant ➡ fickle

incontrovertible ➡ infallible

inconvenience ➡ nuisance, trouble

incorporate ➡ add, embody

incorrect ➡ wrong

incorrigible ➡ bad

increase ➡ more, growth, strengthen, grow

incredible ➡ great, unbelievable

incredulity ➡ surprise

incredulous ➡ doubtful

increment ➡ growth

inculcate ➡ instill

incur ➡ catch

incurable ➡ deadly

incursion ➡ attack

indebted ➡ grateful

indebtedness ➡ debt

indecent ➡ improper

indecipherable ➡ illegible

indecorous ➡ improper

indeed ➡ certainly, really

indefensible ➡ inexcusable

indefinite ➡ doubtful

indelible ➡ permanent

indelicate ➡ improper

indent ➡ dent

indentation ➡ dent, print

independence ➡ freedom

independent ➡ free

independently ➡ apart

indescribable ➡ unbelievable

indestructible ➡ unbreakable

indeterminate ➡ unresolved

index ➡ sign

indicate ➡ read, mean

indication ➡ sign

indict ➡ try

indictment ➡ complaint

indifference ➡ apathy, neglect

indifferent ➡ apathetic

indigence ➡ poverty

indigenous ➡ native

indigent ➡ poor

indigestion ➡ nausea

indignant ➡ angry

indignation ➡ anger

indignity ➡ insult

indirectly ➡ sideways

indiscernible ➡ invisible

indiscreet ➡ imprudent

indispensable ➡ necessary

indisposed ➡ sick

indistinct ➡ dim

indite ➡ write

individual ➡ human being, private

indivisible ➡ inseparable

indolence ➡ laziness

indolent ➡ lazy

indomitable ➡ invincible

indoor ➡ inside

induce ➡ persuade

inducement ➡ incentive

induct ➡ crown

induction ➡ reason

indulge ➡ pamper

indulgent ➡ tolerant

industrialist ➡ tycoon

industrious ➡ lively, ambitious, diligent

industry ➡ diligence, work, business

inebriate ➡ drunkard

inebriated ➡ drunk

ineffective ➡ useless

ineffectual ➡ incompetent, useless

inefficacy ➡ inability

inefficient ➡ incompetent

inept ➡ clumsy, incompetent

ineptitude ➡ inability

inequality ➡ difference

inert ➡ passive, stationary, dead

inescapable ➡ certain

inestimable ➡ valuable

inevitable ➡ certain

inexact ➡ approximate

inexhaustible ➡ infinite, diligent

inexpensive ➡ cheap

inexperience ➡ ignorance

inexperienced ➡ naive, amateur, unprepared

inexpert ➡ amateur

inexplicable ➡ mysterious, obscure, impossible

infamous ➡ bad

infancy ➡ childhood, beginning

infant ➡ baby

infantile ➡ childish

infatuation ➡ love, desire

infect ➡ dirty

infection ➡ disease, poison

infectious ➡ contagious

n = noun • *vb* = verb • *adj* = adjective • *adv* = adverb • *prep* = preposition • *conj* = conjunction

infest *vb* overrun, plague, swarm, beset

infinite *adj* boundless, unbounded, endless, limitless, unlimited, interminable, countless, immeasurable, inexhaustible ➡ **eternal, big** ⇨ *finite*

inflammable *adj* flammable, combustible, burnable, volatile, explosive

inflict *vb* impose, exact, dispense, wreak, mete out ➡ **give**

inheritance *n* bequest, legacy, heritage, patrimony, endowment, trust ➡ **gift, acquisition**

innocent 1. *adj* blameless, guiltless, faultless, sinless, pure, chaste, angelic, impeccable ⇨ *guilty*
2. *adj* ➡ **naive**

insane *adj* crazy, mad, crazed, lunatic, psychotic, maniacal, demented, deranged, berserk, paranoid, unbalanced, unhinged, mental (*informal*) ⇨ *sane*

If the word you want is not a main entry above, look below to find it.

inference ➡ conclusion

inferential ➡ circumstantial

inferior ➡ cheap, poor, subordinate

inferiority ➡ mediocrity

inferior to ➡ under

inferno ➡ fire

infertile ➡ sterile

infidel ➡ atheist

infiltrate ➡ enter

infinity ➡ space

infirm ➡ weak, sick

infirmary ➡ hospital

infirmity ➡ illness

inflame ➡ fan

inflamed ➡ sore, burning

inflammation ➡ sore

inflate ➡ swell, exaggerate

inflation ➡ growth

inflection ➡ accent

inflexible ➡ firm

influence ➡ affect, effect, persuade

influential ➡ important

inform ➡ tell, introduce, teach

informal ➡ carefree

information ➡ knowledge

informed ➡ educated

inform on ➡ betray

infraction ➡ crime

infrequent ➡ rare

infrequently ➡ seldom

infringe ➡ intrude

infuriate ➡ anger

infuriated ➡ angry

infuse ➡ instill

ingenious ➡ talented

ingenuity ➡ ability, imagination

ingenuous ➡ naive, straightforward

ingest ➡ take

ingredient ➡ part

inhabit ➡ live[1]

inhabitant ➡ citizen, occupant

inhalation ➡ breath

inhale ➡ breathe, smoke

inherent ➡ natural

inherit ➡ receive

inherited ➡ natural

inhibit ➡ prevent

inhospitable ➡ unfriendly

inhuman ➡ mean

iniquity ➡ immorality

initial ➡ early, sign

initialism ➡ abbreviation

initiate ➡ start

initiation ➡ beginning, introduction

initiative ➡ ambition

inject ➡ instill

injection ➡ medicine

injunction ➡ ban

injure ➡ hurt

injurious ➡ destructive, unhealthy

injury ➡ cut, damage, scar, harm, abuse, casualty

injustice ➡ hardship

inkling ➡ idea

inky ➡ black

inlay ➡ embed

inlet ➡ bay

inmate ➡ prisoner

inn ➡ hotel, restaurant

innate ➡ natural

inner ➡ inside, middle

innermost ➡ inside

innkeeper ➡ host

innocence ➡ virtue, ignorance

innocuous ➡ harmless

innovate ➡ start, change

innovation ➡ invention

innovative ➡ experimental

innovator ➡ creator

innumerable ➡ many

inoculate ➡ vaccinate

inoffensive ➡ harmless

inordinate ➡ excessive

inpatient ➡ patient

inquest ➡ examination

inquire ➡ ask

inquiring ➡ curious

inquiry ➡ question, study

inquisitive ➡ curious

inquisitiveness ➡ interest

---

inscription *n* engraving, dedication, epitaph, legend, lettering ➡ **signature**

insensitive *adj* unfeeling, uncaring, tactless, heartless, hardhearted, coldhearted, callous, unsympathetic, cold-blooded ➡ **thoughtless, apathetic, stubborn** ⇨ *thoughtful*

inseparable *adj* indivisible, unified, united, integrated, integral, joined

inside 1. *adj* interior, internal, inner, indoor, innermost ➡ **middle**
2. *n* ➡ **middle**
Note that **inside** and **interior** are often used as nouns: "The **inside** of the house is as beautiful as the outside." "We grew up in the **interior** of the country." **Inside** may also be used as a preposition ("I put your things **inside** the suitcase") or an adverb ("Greg went **inside** when it started raining").

insipid 1. *adj* bland, tasteless, flat, mild
2. *adj* ➡ **trite, dull**

insist *vb* demand, require, assert ➡ **argue, order, force**

instead *adv* rather, alternatively, alternately, preferably

instill *vb* infuse, suffuse, imbue, inject, interject, implant, inculcate ➡ **teach, give, put**

insult 1. *vb* offend, humiliate, slander, defame, malign, smear, slight, snub, outrage, tease, taunt, scorn ➡ **abuse, hurt, ridicule**
2. *n* affront, offense, indignity, outrage, slander, libel, smear, jeer, put-down (*informal*)

intellectual *adj* scholarly, scholastic, educational, academic, cerebral, mental ➡ **profound, thoughtful**

If the word you want is not a main entry above, look below to find it.

insatiable ➡ greedy

inscribe ➡ write, print, carve, sign

inscrutable ➡ obscure

insect ➡ bug

insecure ➡ anxious, unsteady

insensate ➡ unconscious

insensible ➡ unconscious

insert ➡ put, embed

inset ➡ embed

insight ➡ depth

insightful ➡ smart

insignia ➡ badge, label

insignificant ➡ trivial

insincere ➡ hypocritical

insinuate ➡ suggest

insolence ➡ audacity, rudeness

insolent ➡ rude

insoluble ➡ impossible

inspect ➡ examine, patrol

inspection ➡ look

inspiration ➡ imagination, idea, incentive

inspire ➡ cause, urge

install ➡ put, crown

installation ➡ appointment

instance ➡ example

instant ➡ moment

instantaneous ➡ sudden

instantaneously ➡ quickly

instantly ➡ now

instigate ➡ urge

instinct ➡ habit, feeling, belief

instinctive ➡ automatic, natural

institute ➡ school, college

institution ➡ organization, college, habit

institutionalize ➡ jail

instruct ➡ teach, order

instruction ➡ education

instructions ➡ recipe

instructor ➡ teacher

instrument ➡ tool

instrumentalist ➡ musician

insubordinate ➡ rebellious

insubordination ➡ disobedience

insubstantial ➡ light^2, thin

insufferable ➡ intolerable

insufficient ➡ inadequate

insular ➡ private, provincial

insulate ➡ separate

insure ➡ guarantee

insurgence ➡ revolution

insurgent ➡ rebel

insurrection ➡ revolution

intact ➡ complete

intake ➡ wage

integer ➡ number

integral ➡ inseparable

integrate ➡ unify, add

integrated ➡ inseparable

integrity ➡ virtue, unity

intellect ➡ mind, wisdom

intelligence ➡ mind, wisdom, spying

intelligent ➡ smart

intelligible ➡ articulate

intemperate ➡ excessive

n = noun • *vb* = verb • *adj* = adjective • *adv* = adverb • *prep* = preposition • *conj* = conjunction

intend *vb* mean, propose, plan, aim, design, purpose ➡ **hope, prepare**

interest 1. *n* curiosity, concern, inquisitiveness ➡ **attention**
2. *n* claim, stake, investment ➡ **share**
3. *n* ➡ **pastime**
4. *vb* engage, absorb, preoccupy, engross ➡ **appeal, entertain**

interesting *adj* fascinating, intriguing, stimulating, engrossing, absorbing, engaging, entertaining, provocative, stirring, compelling ➡ **exciting** ⇨ *dull*

interference *n* intervention, intrusion, interruption, prying, meddling

intolerable *adj* unbearable, insufferable, difficult, impossible

introduce 1. *vb* present, acquaint, familiarize, inform, apprise ➡ **broach**
2. *vb* preface ➡ **precede, start**

introduction 1. *n* meeting, presentation, debut, initiation, acquaintance ➡ **beginning**
2. *n* preface, foreword, prologue, preamble, prelude, overture, intro *(informal)* ⇨ *conclusion*

intrude *vb* trespass, encroach, infringe, invade, impinge ➡ **enter, meddle, disturb**

invent 1. *vb* devise, design, develop, conceive, formulate, originate, contrive, hatch, improvise, ad-lib ➡ **build, discover, form, make, start**
2. *vb* fabricate, concoct, make up, counterfeit ➡ **lie**

If the word you want is not a main entry above, look below to find it.

intense ➡ bright, strong

intensify ➡ strengthen, concentrate

intensity ➡ strength

intent ➡ absorbed, plan, object

intention ➡ object

intentional ➡ voluntary

intentionally ➡ purposely

inter ➡ bury

intercede ➡ negotiate

intercept ➡ seize

interchange ➡ change, trade

intercourse ➡ speech

interfere ➡ meddle, disturb

interfering ➡ meddlesome

interim ➡ temporary

interior ➡ inside, middle

interject ➡ instill

interlace ➡ weave

interlock ➡ join

interlude ➡ break

intermediary ➡ agent

intermediate ➡ middle

interminable ➡ infinite, eternal

interminably ➡ forever

intermingle ➡ mix

intermission ➡ break

intermittent ➡ periodic

intern ➡ page

internal ➡ inside

international ➡ universal

internee ➡ prisoner

interpret ➡ translate, explain

interpretation ➡ translation

interrogate ➡ ask, examine

interrogation ➡ question

interrogative ➡ question

interrupt ➡ disturb

interruption ➡ break, interference

intersection ➡ corner

interstate ➡ highway

intertwine ➡ weave

interval ➡ period, distance

intervene ➡ meddle

intervention ➡ interference

interview ➡ ask, meeting

intimate ➡ friendly, private, near, suggest

intimidate ➡ threaten, discourage

intolerance ➡ prejudice

intolerant ➡ prejudiced, mean, provincial

intoxicated ➡ drunk

intractable ➡ stubborn

intrepid ➡ brave

intricate ➡ complicated

intrigue ➡ fascinate, secret

intriguing ➡ interesting, attractive

intrinsic ➡ natural

intro ➡ introduction

introductory ➡ basic, early

intrusion ➡ interference

intrusive ➡ meddlesome

intuition ➡ feeling

inundate ➡ flood

inundation ➡ flood

invade ➡ attack, enter, intrude

invalid ➡ weak, patient, wrong

invalidate ➡ disprove

invaluable ➡ expensive

invariable ➡ continual

invariably ➡ regularly

invasion ➡ attack

➡ = synonym cross-reference • ⇨ = antonym cross-reference

invention 1. *n* creation, contrivance, innovation, development, breakthrough
➡ **discovery, novelty**
2. *n* ➡ **lie**

invincible *adj* unbeatable, unconquerable, invulnerable, indomitable, unmanageable
➡ **strong, safe**

invisible *adj* imperceptible, indiscernible, undetectable, concealed, hidden, unseen, microscopic, impalpable, ethereal
➡ **supernatural, inconspicuous**

invitation *n* request, bidding, offer, summons
➡ **appeal, suggestion**

iron *vb* press, steam, mangle, flatten

irony *n* sarcasm, satire, incongruity
➡ **parody, humor**

island *n* isle, islet, atoll, key, cay, archipelago, holm

If the word you want is not a main entry above, look below to find it.

inventive ➡ talented
inventor ➡ creator
inventory ➡ supply, list
inverse ➡ opposite
invert ➡ upset, change
inverted ➡ upside down
invest ➡ bank, crown
investigate ➡ examine, hunt
investigation ➡ study, hunt
investiture ➡ appointment
investment ➡ interest
invigorate ➡ renew
invigorating ➡ brisk
invite ➡ call, entertain
inviting ➡ attractive

invoice ➡ bill, charge
invoke ➡ appeal
involuntary ➡ automatic
involve ➡ concern
involved ➡ absorbed, complicated
invulnerable ➡ invincible, safe
iota ➡ bit
irate ➡ angry
ire ➡ anger
irk ➡ bother
irksome ➡ inconvenient
ironic ➡ sarcastic
ironical ➡ sarcastic

irrational ➡ illogical
irrationality ➡ nonsense
irrefutable ➡ infallible
irregular ➡ rough, different, strange, periodic
irregularity ➡ oddity, difference, departure
irrelevant ➡ unnecessary
irresolute ➡ fickle
irresponsible ➡ unreliable, negligent
irreverent ➡ rude
irrevocably ➡ finally
irritable ➡ cross
irritate ➡ hurt, bother

irritated ➡ angry, sore
irritation ➡ nuisance
isle ➡ island
islet ➡ island
isolate ➡ separate
isolated ➡ alone, private
isolation ➡ privacy
issue ➡ subject, effect, descend, print
itch ➡ tingle, desire, want
item ➡ object
itemize ➡ list
itinerant ➡ traveler
itinerary ➡ course
ivory ➡ white, fair

J

jail 1. *n* prison, penitentiary, correctional facility, jailhouse, reformatory, cell, dungeon, brig, stockade, pen (*informal*), slammer (*informal*), clink (*informal*), stir (*informal*), big house (*informal*)
2. *vb* imprison, confine, detain, incarcerate, impound, remand, institutionalize, commit

jealous *adj* envious, resentful, possessive, begrudging ➡ **suspicious, greedy**

jelly *n* jam, preserve, marmalade

jeopardize *vb* risk, endanger, imperil, hazard, threaten

jetty *n* breakwater, dike, sea wall, pier, bulwark ➡ **dam**

jewel *n* gem, gemstone, brilliant, ornament, precious stone, stone, rock ➡ **trinket**

job *n* task, chore, work, duty, errand, assignment, project, mission, labor, living ➡ **profession, function**

join 1. *vb* connect, associate, attach, link, fasten, unite, couple, interlock, anchor, bridge, buckle, clasp, clinch, knit, pair, graft, weld, solder, cement, pin ➡ **tie, unify, marry**
2. *vb* enter, enroll, enlist, register, participate

joke 1. *n* prank, practical joke, gag, caper, antic ➡ **trick**
2. *n* jest, wisecrack, pun, witticism, quip, one-liner, bon mot ➡ **story**
3. *vb* jest, quip, banter, spar, kid, tease, josh

If the word you want is not a main entry above, look below to find it.

jab ➡ stick, blow[1]

jabber ➡ chatter

jack ➡ flag

jacket ➡ coat, wrapper

jackknife ➡ knife

jaded ➡ bored

jagged ➡ zigzag, rough

jailbird ➡ prisoner

jailhouse ➡ jail

jam ➡ jelly, trouble, push

jammed ➡ full

jangle ➡ ring

jar ➡ container, shake, disturb

jargon ➡ dialect

jaunt ➡ trip

jaunty ➡ lively

javelin ➡ missile

jealousy ➡ envy

jeer ➡ insult, ridicule, yell

jell ➡ harden

jeopardy ➡ danger

jerk ➡ pull, jump

jest ➡ joke, humor

jet ➡ fountain, black

jet set ➡ aristocracy

jettison ➡ discard

jibe ➡ agree

jiffy ➡ moment

jingle ➡ ring

jinx ➡ curse

jittery ➡ nervous

jobholder ➡ worker

jobless ➡ unemployed

jock ➡ athlete

jockey ➡ drive, rider

jocularity ➡ humor

jog ➡ run

John Hancock ➡ signature

joined ➡ inseparable

joining ➡ junction

joint ➡ link, common

jointly ➡ together

joist ➡ beam, board

joker ➡ comic

jolly ➡ happy

jolt ➡ shock, blow[1], jump

josh ➡ joke

jostle ➡ push

jot ➡ write, bit

jounce ➡ jump

journal ➡ paper, diary

journalist ➡ reporter

journey ➡ trip, travel

jovial ➡ happy

joviality ➡ mirth

---

judge 1. *n* justice, magistrate, jurist
2. *n* referee, umpire, official, evaluator, reviewer, critic, arbiter
3. *vb* ➡ **decide**
4. *vb* ➡ **estimate, infer**

jump 1. *vb, n* leap, spring, bound, vault, hop, pounce, bounce, jounce, jolt, pop, skip, hurdle, dive, plunge, lunge ➡ **dance**
2. *vb, n* start, flinch, wince, recoil, twitch, jerk, cringe, cower

junction *n* juncture, meeting, convergence, connection, joining ➡ **link, corner**

justice 1. *n* fairness, impartiality, equity, due process, evenhandedness ➡ **honesty, truth, virtue**
2. *n* ➡ **judge**

justification *n* vindication, defense, validation ➡ **basis, reason**

If the word you want is not a main entry above, look below to find it.

joy ➡ pleasure

joyful ➡ happy

joyous ➡ happy

jubilant ➡ ecstatic

jubilee ➡ party

judgment ➡ wisdom, tact, decision

judiciary ➡ court

judicious ➡ careful

jug ➡ bottle

juggle ➡ tinker

juice ➡ liquid

jumble ➡ mess, mix

jumbo ➡ huge

jumper ➡ dress

jumpy ➡ nervous

juncture ➡ junction, corner

jungle ➡ forest, maze

junior ➡ subordinate, student

junior college ➡ college

junk ➡ trash, discard

junkyard ➡ dump

junta ➡ group, party

jurisdiction ➡ rule

jurist ➡ judge

just ➡ fair, only, recently

justify ➡ explain, deserve

jut ➡ swell

juvenile ➡ young, childish, teenager, child

juxtapose ➡ compare

n = noun • *vb* = verb • *adj* = adjective • *adv* = adverb • *prep* = preposition • *conj* = conjunction

K

keep 1. *vb* have, possess, maintain, retain, preserve, sustain ➡ **own**
2. *vb* ➡ **save**
3. *vb* fulfill, honor, respect ➡ **celebrate**
4. *n* ➡ **board**
5. *n* ➡ **castle, tower**

kick 1. *vb* boot, punt, drop-kick, placekick ➡ **hit**
2. *n* ➡ **blow**[1]

kill *vb* murder, slay, assassinate, dispatch, massacre, butcher, execute, slaughter, exterminate, annihilate, eradicate, martyr, sacrifice ➡ **destroy, extinguish, choke**

killer *n* murderer, assassin, slayer, executioner

kind 1. *adj* compassionate, considerate, benevolent, well-meaning, charitable, merciful, kindhearted, tenderhearted, warmhearted, decent, kindly, benign, humane ➡ **friendly, generous, loving, nice, tolerant**
2. *n* ➡ **type**

kindness *n* mercy, charity, compassion, consideration, decency, goodwill, humanity, tenderness, courtesy, thoughtfulness, friendliness ➡ **love, pity**

king *n* monarch, sovereign, maharajah (*India*), rajah (*India*), sultan (*Muslim*), shah (*Iran*), pasha (*Turkey, N. Africa*), khan (*central Asia, China*), sachem (*Native American*) ➡ **ruler, emperor**

kiss *n, vb* peck, buss, smooch, smack

kitchen *n* kitchenette, galley, cookhouse, scullery, pantry, larder ➡ **room**

knife *n* blade, jackknife, penknife, dagger, stiletto, scalpel, razor, cleaver ➡ **sword**

knock 1. *vb* tap, rap, drum, thump, whack ➡ **bang, hit**
2. *n* tap, rap, thump, patter, pitter-patter ➡ **bang, blow**[1]

knot 1. *n* tangle, snarl, snag, hitch, splice
2. *vb* ➡ **tie**

If the word you want is not a main entry above, look below to find it.

kaiser ➡ emperor

kaiserin ➡ empress

keen ➡ sharp, eager, smart

keeper ➡ guardian

keepsake ➡ reminder

keg ➡ barrel

kelly ➡ green

kennel ➡ pen

kernel ➡ seed

kerosene ➡ oil

kettle ➡ pot

key ➡ answer, important, island

khaki ➡ brown

khan ➡ king

kid ➡ joke, child

kidnap ➡ seize

kiln ➡ furnace

kin ➡ family

kindhearted ➡ kind

kindle ➡ light[1]

kindling ➡ wood

kindly ➡ kind, well

kindred ➡ family

kingdom ➡ country

kingly ➡ noble

kink ➡ bend

kinship ➡ relationship

kiosk ➡ booth

kit ➡ equipment

kitchenette ➡ kitchen

knack ➡ talent

knapsack ➡ bag

knave ➡ rascal

knead ➡ rub, mix

kneel ➡ bend

knell ➡ ring

knickknack ➡ novelty

knife-edged ➡ sharp

knit ➡ weave, join, heal

knob ➡ bulge

knock out ➡ paralyze

knoll ➡ hill

---

know *vb* understand, realize, recognize, apprehend, comprehend, see, fathom, grasp, follow, get, penetrate ➡ **remember**

knowledge *n* fact, information, learning, data, evidence, education, awareness, erudition ➡ **experience, wisdom, education**

If the word you want is not a main entry above, look below to find it.

know-how ➡ experience   knowledgeable ➡ educated   kudos ➡ praise

knowingly ➡ purposely   kowtow to ➡ flatter

n = noun • *vb* = verb • *adj* = adjective • *adv* = adverb • *prep* = preposition • *conj* = conjunction

L

label 1. *n* tag, sticker, ticket, tab, marker, insignia, trademark, logo, service mark, brand ➡ **name**
2. *vb* mark, ticket ➡ **name**
3. *vb* ➡ **stereotype**

lag *vb* dawdle, straggle, saunter, plod, trail ➡ **delay, wait**

lake *n* pond, pool, fishpond, lagoon, loch, reservoir

lame 1. *adj* crippled, limping
2. *adj* ➡ **poor**

language *n* tongue, lingua franca ➡ **accent, dialect, speech**

larva *n* grub, maggot, caterpillar ➡ **worm**

last 1. *adj* latest, final, ultimate, extreme, concluding, closing, terminal, hindmost, outermost ➡ **latter**
2. *vb* ➡ **continue**

late 1. *adj* overdue, tardy, belated, delayed, delinquent ⇨ *early, punctual*
2. *adj* ➡ **new**
3. *adj* ➡ **dead**
4. *adv* behind, behindhand, belatedly, tardily

latent *adj* potential, dormant, undeveloped, unrealized, underlying

latter *adj* second, final ➡ **last, following**

If the word you want is not a main entry above, look below to find it.

labor ➡ work, job
laborer ➡ worker
labyrinth ➡ maze
lace ➡ string, tie
lacerate ➡ cut
laceration ➡ cut
lack ➡ need, want, absence
lackadaisical ➡ slow
lacking ➡ inadequate
lackluster ➡ dull
laconic ➡ short
lacquer ➡ finish
lad ➡ man
laden ➡ full
ladle ➡ spoon
lady ➡ woman, noble
ladylike ➡ feminine
lagoon ➡ bay, lake

laid-back ➡ carefree
lair ➡ den
lamasery ➡ monastery
lameness ➡ limp
lament ➡ grieve, regret, complaint, dirge
lamentable ➡ unfortunate
laminate ➡ plate
lamp ➡ light[1]
lampoon ➡ imitate
lance ➡ stick, missile
land ➡ property, country, dirt, terrain, descend, leave, dock
landfill ➡ dump
landing ➡ dock
landlady ➡ owner
landlord ➡ owner
landmark ➡ event

landowner ➡ owner
landscape ➡ country, nature, terrain, background
landslide ➡ avalanche
lane ➡ road, path
languid ➡ listless
languish ➡ grieve
languor ➡ laziness
languorous ➡ listless
lank ➡ thin
lanky ➡ thin
lantern ➡ light[1]
lap ➡ fold, lick
lapse ➡ relapse, fall, elapse
larceny ➡ theft
lard ➡ fat
larder ➡ closet, kitchen
large ➡ big

largess ➡ generosity
lariat ➡ rope
lark ➡ adventure
lash ➡ tie, whip
lass ➡ woman
lassitude ➡ laziness
lasso ➡ rope
lasting ➡ permanent
lastly ➡ finally
latch ➡ lock
lately ➡ recently
later ➡ following
latest ➡ last, new
lather ➡ foam
latrine ➡ bathroom
latter-day ➡ modern
latterly ➡ recently

➡ = synonym cross-reference • ⇨ = antonym cross-reference

laugh *vb, n* giggle, chuckle, snicker, roar, guffaw, snigger, titter, cackle, howl, shriek ➡ **smile**

laughter *n* hilarity, merriment, levity ➡ **laugh, ridicule, mirth**

laundry *n* wash, washing, cleaning, dry cleaning

layer *n* stratum, tier, sheet, level, film, membrane ➡ **coat**

laziness *n* indolence, sloth, lethargy, listlessness, idleness, torpor, languor, lassitude

lazy *adj* indolent, idle, shiftless, slothful, apathetic ➡ **listless** ➾ *ambitious*

lead 1. *vb* guide, direct, conduct, usher, steer, take, send, show, funnel ➡ **bring** ➾ *follow*
2. *vb* direct, manage, supervise, administer, run, preside, oversee, chair, officiate ➡ **control, govern, command** ➾ *follow*
3. *n* ➡ **front**

leadership *n* supervision, management, guidance, administration, direction ➡ **rule**

learn 1. *vb* ascertain, realize, discover, determine, see, find, find out
2. *vb* memorize, absorb, assimilate, master, digest ➡ **study, remember, practice**

least *adj* smallest, tiniest, minutest, slightest, minimal, minimum, merest ➾ *best*

leave 1. *vb* depart, exit, embark, withdraw, desert, abandon, vacate, evacuate, forsake, quit, maroon, strand, set out, set off, flee, defect ➡ **go, move** ➾ *enter, wait*
2. *vb* disembark, detrain, deplane, land ➡ **descend** ➾ *enter*
3. *vb* will, bequeath, bestow, hand down ➡ **give**
4. *n* ➡ **vacation**

legal *adj* lawful, legitimate, permissible, statutory, prescribed, allowable, licit, constitutional, sanctioned, valid ➡ **official** ➾ *illegal*

legendary *adj* mythical, mythological, fabulous, fabled, apocryphal, traditional, proverbial ➡ **imaginary**

If the word you want is not a main entry above, look below to find it.

laud ➡ praise, worship
laudable ➡ praiseworthy
laughable ➡ funny
launch ➡ shoot, throw, start
launder ➡ clean
laurel ➡ prize
lavatory ➡ bathroom, sink
lavender ➡ purple
lavish ➡ generous, rich, wasteful
law ➡ rule, act
lawbreaker ➡ criminal
law court ➡ court
lawful ➡ legal

lawlessness ➡ confusion
lawsuit ➡ suit
lawyer ➡ adviser
lax ➡ negligent
lay ➡ put
layabout ➡ loafer
layer cake ➡ cake
lay off ➡ fire
layout ➡ order
lay to rest ➡ bury
laze ➡ rest
lazybones ➡ loafer
leach ➡ extract
leaden ➡ gray

leader ➡ boss, ruler, official, guide, headline
leading ➡ best
leaf ➡ page
leaflet ➡ pamphlet
league ➡ union, party
leak ➡ drop, hole
lean ➡ slant, thin
leaning ➡ tendency
leap ➡ jump
learned ➡ smart, educated
learner ➡ student
learning ➡ knowledge, education
lease ➡ agreement, hire

leash ➡ rope, prevent
leaving ➡ departure
lecher ➡ rascal
lecture ➡ speech, teach
lecturer ➡ speaker, teacher
ledge ➡ shelf
leery ➡ suspicious
leftover ➡ unnecessary
left-wing ➡ liberal
leg ➡ limb
legacy ➡ inheritance
legal pad ➡ notepad
legalize ➡ approve
legend ➡ myth, inscription

n = noun • *vb* = verb • *adj* = adjective • *adv* = adverb • *prep* = preposition • *conj* = conjunction

legible *adj* readable, decipherable, distinct, clear, neat

leisure *n* freedom, relaxation, recreation, repose, ease ➡ **vacation**

lend *vb* loan, advance, furnish, extend ➡ **give, hire**

lengthen *vb* stretch, extend, prolong, elongate, protract, distend, amplify ⇨ *shrink, condense*

less 1. *adj* fewer, smaller, diminished, reduced, lower ⇨ *more*
2. *prep* ➡ **minus**

lesson *n* class, teaching, drill, exercise, homework, assignment ➡ **education**

let 1. *vb* allow, permit, authorize, license, tolerate, enable, entitle, qualify, empower ➡ **agree** ⇨ *prevent*
2. *vb* ➡ **hire**

letter *n* message, card, postcard, note, epistle, missive, memorandum, memo, reminder, dispatch ➡ **mail**

letter carrier *n* mail carrier, mailman, postman, postmaster, postmistress ➡ **messenger**

level 1. *adj* flat, smooth, even, flush, parallel, trim ➡ **straight**
2. *adj* plane, horizontal, flat ➡ **low**
3. *n* ➡ **grade, layer, floor**
4. *vb* ➡ **destroy**
5. *vb* even, smooth, flatten, grade, plane ➡ **straighten**

liar *n* fibber, storyteller, deceiver, prevaricator, perjurer, falsifier, equivocator ➡ **cheat**

liberal 1. *adj* ➡ **generous**
2. *adj* progressive, broadminded, radical, left-wing, reformist, humanistic ➡ **tolerant** ⇨ *conservative*

license 1. *n* permit, registration, copyright, franchise, charter, patent, grant ➡ **document**
2. *n* ➡ **permission, freedom, right**
3. *vb* ➡ **let**

lick 1. *vb* lap, tongue, flick
2. *n* ➡ **blow**[1]
3. *n* ➡ **bit**

If the word you want is not a main entry above, look below to find it.

legion ➡ crowd, army
legislate ➡ govern
legislation ➡ act
legislature ➡ government
legitimate ➡ legal, official, real
legume ➡ fruit
leisurely ➡ slow
leitmotif ➡ chorus
lemon ➡ yellow
length ➡ distance
lengthy ➡ long
lenient ➡ tolerant

lens ➡ glass
leprechaun ➡ fairy
lessen ➡ decrease, relieve
less than ➡ under
let down ➡ disappoint
letdown ➡ disappointment
let go ➡ fire
lethal ➡ deadly
lethargic ➡ listless
lethargy ➡ laziness
lettered ➡ educated
lettering ➡ inscription

letters ➡ literature
levee ➡ dam
lever ➡ lift
leviathan ➡ giant
levity ➡ humor, laughter
levy ➡ tax
lewd ➡ dirty
lexicon ➡ dictionary
liability ➡ guilt, debt
liable ➡ likely, guilty
liaison ➡ agent
libel ➡ insult

liberality ➡ generosity
liberate ➡ free
liberated ➡ free
liberation ➡ freedom, salvation
libertine ➡ rascal
liberty ➡ freedom
library ➡ den
libretto ➡ book
licensed ➡ official
lichen ➡ fungus
licit ➡ legal
lid ➡ top

➡ = synonym cross-reference • ⇨ = antonym cross-reference

lie 1. *n* falsehood, fib, untruth, fiction, story, tale, fabrication, invention, deception, disinformation, misrepresentation, concoction, canard ➡ **pretense, dishonesty** ⇨ *truth*
2. *vb* deceive, fib, prevaricate, falsify, mislead, dissemble, misstate, equivocate, fabricate ➡ **invent, pretend**
3. *vb* rest, recline, repose, sprawl, loll

life 1. *n* being, animation, vitality, breath, sentience, consciousness, living ➡ **existence**
2. *n* lifetime, longevity, span, career
3. *n* ➡ **energy**

lift 1. *vb* raise, elevate, hoist, boost, heave, uplift, rear, erect, pry, lever
2. *vb* ➡ **stop**
3. *vb* ➡ **disappear**
4. *n* boost, hand

light¹ 1. *n* radiance, illumination, luminosity, brilliance, brightness, glare, glow, sheen, glimmer, shine, gleam, luster, gloss, glitter, twinkle, sparkle, glint
2. *n* ➡ **day**
3. *n* lamp, lightbulb, bulb, streetlight, lantern, chandelier, flashlight, torch
4. *n* ray, beam, beacon, flash, flare, signal, spark
5. *adj* ➡ **bright**
6. *adj* ➡ **fair**

7. *vb* illuminate, light up, illumine, brighten, lighten
8. *vb* ignite, kindle, strike, fuel ➡ **burn**

light² 1. *adj* lightweight, underweight, slight, slender, scant, sparse, buoyant, weightless, insubstantial ⇨ *heavy*
2. *adj* ➡ **gentle**
3. *adj* ➡ **easy**
4. *vb* ➡ **descend**

like 1. *vb* enjoy, be fond of, care for, relish, fancy, delight in ➡ **love, appreciate**
2. *adj* ➡ **alike, same**

likely 1. *adj* liable, prone, apt, inclined, disposed
2. *adj* probable, apparent ➡ **possible**

limb 1. *n* bough, offshoot ➡ **branch, stick**
2. *n* member, appendage, extremity, arm, leg, wing, pinion, flipper, fin

limp 1. *vb* shuffle, stagger, hobble, totter, dodder, falter ➡ **walk**
2. *n* falter, halt, lameness, shuffle, gimp
3. *adj* flaccid, droopy, floppy, flabby, limber, slack ➡ **flexible**

link 1. *n* connection, association, contact, bond, correlation, attachment, tie, joint, affinity, affiliation, bridge, junction ➡ **union**
2. *vb* ➡ **join**

If the word you want is not a main entry above, look below to find it.

lieutenant ➡ helper
lifeless ➡ dead, passive
lifesaver ➡ savior
lifetime ➡ life
lightbulb ➡ light¹
lighten ➡ light¹, relieve, bleach
light-headed ➡ dizzy
lighthearted ➡ carefree

lightweight ➡ light²
likelihood ➡ possibility
liken ➡ compare
likeness ➡ similarity, photograph, copy, statue
likewise ➡ alike
lilac ➡ purple
Lilliputian ➡ small

limber ➡ flexible, agile, limp
lime ➡ green
limit ➡ contain, horizon
limitation ➡ term
limited ➡ finite
limitless ➡ infinite, universal
limo ➡ taxi
limousine ➡ taxi
limpid ➡ transparent

limping ➡ lame
line ➡ rope, string, row
lineage ➡ ancestry, family
linear ➡ straight
lineup ➡ ballot
linger ➡ wait
lingo ➡ dialect
lingua franca ➡ language
lip ➡ edge

n = noun • *vb* = verb • *adj* = adjective • *adv* = adverb • *prep* = preposition • *conj* = conjunction

liquid 1. *n* fluid, juice, sap, water, liquor
➡ **humidity**
2. *adj* fluid, flowing, molten, aqueous, watery ➡ **wet, damp**

list 1. *n* catalog, program, schedule, agenda, outline, menu, roster, inventory ➡ **table**
2. *vb* itemize, record, catalogue, inventory, register, tabulate, enumerate ➡ **specify**
3. *vb* ➡ **slant**

listen *vb* hear, hearken, hark, overhear, eavesdrop, attend

listless *adj* lethargic, sluggish, drowsy, languid, languorous ➡ **tired, lazy, passive, dull, slow** ➪ *active*

literal 1. *adj* word-for-word, verbatim, exact ➡ **correct**
2. *adj* ➡ **real**

literature *n* letters, writing, belles lettres

live¹ 1. *vb* exist, be, thrive, subsist, breathe ➡ **experience**
2. *vb* survive, outlive, outlast, persevere, persist ➡ **continue** ➪ *die*
3. *vb* reside, dwell, stay, abide, inhabit, lodge, room, sojourn ➡ **occupy**

live² *adj* ➡ **lively, alive, active**

lively *adj* vital, energetic, vivacious, vigorous, industrious, spry, zestful, playful, spirited, sprightly, jaunty, brisk, zippy ➡ **active, alive** ➪ *dull*

livestock *n* cattle, animals

living room *n* sitting room, drawing room, parlor, salon, lounge ➡ **room**

load 1. *n* burden, cargo, freight, shipment ➡ **weight**
2. *n* ➡ **abundance**
3. *vb* fill, pack, encumber, burden, stuff, cram, glut, stock, stow

loafer 1. *n* idler, layabout, slacker, sluggard, lazybones (*informal*), malingerer, ne'er-do-well, good-for-nothing (*informal*), drifter, deadbeat
2. *n* ➡ **shoe**

loan 1. *n* credit, advance, mortgage, rental, accommodation, allowance
2. *vb* ➡ **lend**

lock 1. *vb* fasten, latch, bolt, bar, secure ➡ **close**
2. *n* latch, catch, hook, bolt, padlock ➡ **clasp**
3. *n* tuft, ringlet, curl, tress, shock ➡ **braid, hair**

If the word you want is not a main entry above, look below to find it.

liquefy ➡ melt
liquor ➡ drink, liquid
listeners ➡ audience
listlessness ➡ exhaustion, laziness
literally ➡ really
literate ➡ educated
lithe ➡ flexible
lithograph ➡ print
litigant ➡ party
litigation ➡ suit
litter ➡ trash, mess, bed

little ➡ small
liturgical ➡ religious
livelihood ➡ support, profession
liveliness ➡ energy, activity
live through ➡ experience
livid ➡ angry, sore
living ➡ alive, life, job
lizard ➡ reptile
loaded ➡ full
loaf ➡ bread, rest
loam ➡ dirt

loath ➡ reluctant
loathe ➡ hate
loathing ➡ hatred, disgust
loathsome ➡ ugly
lobby ➡ hall, party
local ➡ native, near
locale ➡ place
locality ➡ place
locate ➡ find, base, place
location ➡ place
loch ➡ lake

locker ➡ closet, cupboard, chest
locks ➡ hair
locomotion ➡ movement
locution ➡ speech, word
lodge ➡ house, hotel, live¹, embed
lodging ➡ room
loft ➡ attic
loftiness ➡ height
lofty ➡ high, dignified
log ➡ wood

➡ = *synonym cross-reference* • ➪ = *antonym cross-reference*

lonely *adj* lonesome, homesick, solitary, friendless, outcast ➠ **alone, sad**

long 1. *adj* lengthy, tall, extended, elongated, outstretched, extensive ➠ **big** ⇨ *short*
2. *adj* lengthy, protracted, unending, long-winded, sustained
3. *vb* ➠ **want**

look 1. *vb* watch, glance, observe, witness, view, regard, spy, sight, eye, survey, peek ➠ **see, stare, examine**
2. *vb* seem, appear ➠ **resemble**
3. *vb* ➠ **hunt**
4. *n* glance, peek, view, gaze, glimpse, scrutiny, inspection
5. *n* ➠ **appearance**

lose 1. *vb* misplace, mislay, drop, miss ➠ **forget** ⇨ *find*
2. *vb* succumb, fall, fail ➠ **surrender** ⇨ *win*

lost 1. *adj* missing, mislaid, misplaced ➠ **absent**
2. *adj* ➠ **homeless**

lottery *n* raffle, pool, sweepstakes, wager ➠ **gambling**

loud 1. *adj* noisy, resounding, deafening, thunderous, earsplitting, piercing, resonant, strident, shrill ➠ **audible, high** ⇨ *quiet*
2. *adj* boisterous, rowdy, rambunctious, raucous, vociferous, clamorous, obstreperous, stentorian, cacophonous, uproarious ➠ **rude**
3. *adj* garish, flashy, gaudy, showy, ostentatious, tacky ➠ **bright, fancy**

love 1. *vb* adore, cherish, admire, worship, idolize, dote on, revere ➠ **like, court** ⇨ *hate*
2. *n* affection, devotion, fondness, passion, tenderness, adoration, attachment, infatuation ➠ **kindness, desire, virtue** ⇨ *hate*
3. *n* ➠ lover, beloved, darling, dear, sweetheart, girlfriend, boyfriend, fiancé, fiancée
4. *n* ➠ **zero** (*in tennis*)

loving *adj* affectionate, caring, devoted, tender, attentive, demonstrative, amorous, romantic, passionate, adoring, ardent, fond ➠ **friendly, eager**

If the word you want is not a main entry above, look below to find it.

logic ➠ reason

logical ➠ valid

logician ➠ philosopher

logo ➠ label

loiter ➠ wait

loll ➠ lie

lone ➠ alone, only

lonesome ➠ lonely

longevity ➠ life

longhand ➠ handwriting

longing ➠ hope, desire

long-suffering ➠ patient

long-winded ➠ long, talkative

look forward to ➠ anticipate

looking glass ➠ mirror

look like ➠ resemble

lookout ➠ patrol, watch

looks ➠ appearance

loom ➠ approach, tower

loop ➠ round, circle, ring

loose ➠ free

loosen ➠ free

loot ➠ booty, pillage

looting ➠ theft

lope ➠ run

loquacious ➠ talkative

lord ➠ ruler, noble

lore ➠ myth, superstition

loss ➠ defeat, death, harm

lot ➠ chance, number, property, abundance, fate

lotion ➠ medicine

lounge ➠ bar, hall, living room, rest

louse ➠ fumble

lousy ➠ bad

lout ➠ boor

loveliness ➠ beauty

lovely ➠ pretty

lover ➠ love

n = noun • *vb* = verb • *adj* = adjective • *adv* = adverb • *prep* = preposition • *conj* = conjunction

low 1. *adj* squat, level, low-lying, low-hanging ➡ **short**
2. *adj* low-pitched, bass, baritone
3. *adj* ➡ **quiet**
4. *adj* ➡ **mean**
5. *adj* ➡ **sad**

loyalty *n* allegiance, fidelity, faithfulness, devotion, fealty, dependability, dedication, patriotism

luck *n* windfall, godsend, opportunity, break, success ➡ **chance**

lucky *adj* fortunate, auspicious, serendipitous, providential ➡ **accidental, magic**

luggage *n* baggage, suitcase, trunk, duffel bag, overnight bag, garment bag, valise, gear, effects ➡ **bag**

lump *n* mass, glob, clot, clump, chunk, hunk, blob, tuft ➡ **bulge, growth, pile**

If the word you want is not a main entry above, look below to find it.

lower ➡ less, subordinate, decrease, frown

lowering ➡ cloudy

lower than ➡ under

lowest ➡ worst

low-hanging ➡ low

lowland ➡ valley

low-lying ➡ low

lowness ➡ depth

low-pitched ➡ low

low-priced ➡ cheap

loyal ➡ faithful, patriotic

LPN ➡ nurse

lube ➡ oil

lubricate ➡ oil

lucid ➡ articulate, sane, transparent

lucidity ➡ reason, clarity

ludicrous ➡ foolish, funny, strange

lug ➡ carry

lukewarm ➡ warm

lull ➡ break, calm

lullaby ➡ song

lumber ➡ board, wood, walk

luminary ➡ celebrity

luminosity ➡ light[1]

luminous ➡ bright

lummox ➡ boor

lunacy ➡ nonsense

lunatic ➡ insane

luncheonette ➡ restaurant

lunchtime ➡ afternoon

lunge ➡ jump

lurch ➡ trip, swing

lure ➡ tempt, attraction

lurid ➡ sensational

lurk ➡ sneak

luscious ➡ delicious, rich

lush ➡ rich, tropical, drunkard

lust ➡ desire

luster ➡ light[1]

lustrous ➡ shiny

luxurious ➡ rich

luxury ➡ wealth, elegance

lying ➡ dishonest

lying (down) ➡ prone

lyric ➡ song, poem

lyrical ➡ musical

M

magic 1. *adj* enchanted, charmed, magical, mystical, occult, bewitching, entrancing, spellbinding ➡ **lucky, mysterious**
2. *n* sorcery, witchcraft, wizardry, enchantment, hocus-pocus, voodoo

magician 1. *n* conjurer, enchanter, sorcerer, wizard, witch, warlock, shaman, medicine man ➡ **prophet**
2. *n* illusionist, prestidigitator, escape artist, Houdini

mail 1. *n* post, correspondence, communication ➡ **letter, package**

2. *vb* ➡ **send**

make 1. *vb* create, make up, manufacture, produce, fashion, model, compose, constitute, forge, strike ➡ **build, form, invent**
2. *vb* ➡ **force**
3. *vb* ➡ **earn**
4. *n* brand, model, brand name ➡ **type**

man *n* gentleman, boy, guy, fellow, husband, male, chap, lad ➡ **human being, humanity, adult**

If the word you want is not a main entry above, look below to find it.

macabre ➡ gruesome

machine ➡ tool, engine

machine gun ➡ gun

machine-made ➡ manufactured

machinery ➡ equipment

machinist ➡ mechanic

macho ➡ masculine

mad ➡ angry, insane

madden ➡ anger

made ➡ manufactured

madness ➡ hysteria, nonsense

madrigal ➡ song

magazine ➡ paper, warehouse

magenta ➡ purple

maggot ➡ larva

magical ➡ magic

magistrate ➡ judge

magnanimous ➡ noble

magnate ➡ tycoon

magnetic ➡ attractive

magnetism ➡ personality

magnificent ➡ grand, beautiful

magnify ➡ strengthen, grow, exaggerate

magnifying glass ➡ glass

magnitude ➡ size

magnum opus ➡ masterpiece

maharajah ➡ king

maharani ➡ queen

maiden ➡ woman

mail carrier ➡ letter carrier

mailman ➡ letter carrier

maim ➡ mutilate

main ➡ important

mainly ➡ chiefly

mainstay ➡ anchor, support

maintain ➡ keep, save, own, support, argue

maintenance ➡ support

maitre d' ➡ host

majestic ➡ grand

majesty ➡ excellence

major ➡ important, course

majority ➡ most, maturity

makeshift ➡ temporary

makeup ➡ disguise

malady ➡ illness

male ➡ man, masculine

malefactor ➡ criminal

malevolence ➡ hatred

malevolent ➡ wicked, ominous

malfunctioning ➡ broken

malice ➡ hatred, envy

malicious ➡ mean

malign ➡ insult

malignant ➡ mean, deadly

malingerer ➡ loafer

mall ➡ market

malleable ➡ flexible

mallet ➡ hammer, bat

malnourished ➡ hungry

maltreat ➡ abuse

mammoth ➡ giant, huge

manacle ➡ bond

manage ➡ control, afford, lead

manageable ➡ tame

management ➡ leadership

manager ➡ boss

mañana ➡ future

mandarin orange ➡ orange

mandate ➡ order

mandatory ➡ necessary

mane ➡ hair

maneuver ➡ movement, tactic, drive

mangle ➡ mutilate, iron

mangy ➡ shabby

manhood ➡ maturity

mania ➡ obsession, hysteria

manufactured *vb* made, machine-made, manmade, mass-produced, synthetic, artificial, human-made

many 1. *adj* numerous, various, countless, manifold, diverse, multiple, innumerable, sundry, myriad ➡ **different** ⇨ *few*
2. *n* ➡ **abundance**

market 1. *n* supermarket, store, shop, grocery, mall, shopping mall, marketplace, mart, general store, bazaar, emporium, flea market
2. *vb* ➡ **sell**

marriage 1. *n* wedding, nuptials, espousal
➡ **union**

2. *n* matrimony, wedlock

married *adj* wed, wedded, espoused, attached, betrothed, engaged ⇨ *single*

marry *vb* wed, espouse ➡ **join**

masculine *adj* male, manly, virile, macho, gentlemanly, fatherly ➡ **feminine**

masterpiece *n* masterwork, showpiece, classic, magnum opus (*Latin*), *pièce de résistance* (*French*), monument

mathematics *n* computation, calculation, math ➡ **science**

If the word you want is not a main entry above, look below to find it.

maniac ➡ extremist

maniacal ➡ insane

manifest ➡ show

manifestation ➡ sign

manifold ➡ many

manikin ➡ midget

manipulate ➡ touch, tinker

mankind ➡ humanity

manly ➡ masculine

manmade ➡ manufactured

mannequin ➡ model, doll, puppet

manner ➡ method, type, bearing

mannerism ➡ habit

manners ➡ behavior

manor ➡ home

mansion ➡ home

manslaughter ➡ murder

mantel ➡ shelf

mantelpiece ➡ shelf

mantle ➡ wrap, coat

manual ➡ book

manufacture ➡ make, assembly

manufacturing ➡ business

manuscript ➡ book, document

map ➡ plan

mar ➡ damage

marathon ➡ race

marauder ➡ pirate

march ➡ walk, parade, movement, border

mare ➡ horse

margin ➡ edge

marimba ➡ xylophone

marine ➡ nautical

mariner ➡ sailor

marionette ➡ puppet

maritime ➡ nautical

mark ➡ spot, signature, tick, label, scar

marked ➡ obvious

marker ➡ pen, monument, label

marketing ➡ sale

marketplace ➡ market

marmalade ➡ jelly

maroon ➡ red, leave

marrow ➡ essence

marsh ➡ swamp

marshal ➡ police officer, mobilize, deploy

marshland ➡ swamp

mart ➡ market

martial ➡ military

martyr ➡ kill

marvel ➡ miracle

marvelous ➡ great

mash ➡ grind

mask ➡ disguise, hide

masking tape ➡ adhesive

masquerade ➡ disguise

mass ➡ size, density, weight, measure, lump, pile

massacre ➡ kill, murder

massage ➡ rub

massive ➡ heavy, huge

mass media ➡ media

mass-produced ➡ manufactured

master ➡ learn, expert, principal, owner

masterly ➡ expert

mastermind ➡ genius

master of ceremonies ➡ host

masterwork ➡ masterpiece

mastery ➡ victory, rule

mat ➡ cushion, rug

match ➡ game, agree, resemble, compare, equal

matching ➡ same

matchless ➡ unique

mate ➡ equal, spouse

material ➡ cloth, matter, real

materiality ➡ existence

materialize ➡ appear

matériel ➡ arms, ammunition

maternal ➡ motherly

math ➡ mathematics

matriarch ➡ ancestor

---

matter 1. *n* substance, material, body, element, constituent, stuff
2. *n* ➡ **subject**
3. *n* ➡ **business**
4. *n* ➡ **trouble**
5. *vb* count, signify, imply ➡ **mean**

maturity *n* adulthood, majority, womanhood, manhood

maybe *adv* perhaps, possibly, conceivably, feasibly, perchance ➡ **probably**
All of these words express uncertainty about something. **Maybe** *and* **perhaps** *are very close synonyms and it usually makes no difference which one you use.* **Possibly** *stresses the uncertainty more than* **maybe. Conceivably** *and* **feasibly** *suggest even greater uncertainty.* **Perchance** *is a more formal and less common synonym.*

maze *n* labyrinth, network, morass, jungle, tangle ➡ **net, mess, confusion**

meal *n* refreshment, repast, bite, snack, picnic, banquet, dish ➡ **feast, food, board**

mean 1. *adj* cruel, vicious, malicious, merciless, savage, malignant, ruthless, brutal, low, cold-blooded, inhuman, relentless, pitiless, unkind ➡ **violent, revengeful**

2. *adj* small-minded, petty, selfish, intolerant ➡ **prejudiced, greedy** ⇨ *tolerant*
3. *adj* ➡ **middle**
4. *n* ➡ **average**
5. *vb* signify, indicate, symbolize, connote, denote, imply, spell ➡ **matter, intend, suggest**

meaning *n* sense, denotation, connotation, definition, significance, implication, import

meaningful *adj* significant, telling, pregnant, expressive ➡ **important**

measure 1. *n* dimension, distance, capacity, weight, volume, mass, amount ➡ **number, size, speed**
2. *n* rule, gauge, scale, standard, criterion, benchmark, yardstick, touchstone
3. *n* ➡ **rhythm**
4. *vb* weigh, gauge, rule, time

mechanic *n* repairman, machinist, technician, grease monkey (*informal*)

meddle *vb* interfere, intervene, intrude, pry, snoop, tamper

meddlesome *adj* intrusive, obtrusive, interfering, meddling, pushy ➡ **curious**

media *n, pl* mass media, communications

If the word you want is not a main entry above, look below to find it.

matrimony ➡ marriage
matron ➡ woman
matronly ➡ feminine
matter-of-fact ➡ practical
mattress ➡ bed
mature ➡ adult, old, gifted, grow
maudlin ➡ emotional
maul ➡ hit, hammer
mausoleum ➡ grave, monument

mauve ➡ purple
maxim ➡ saying
maximum ➡ most
mayhem ➡ confusion, mess, damage
MC ➡ host
M.D. ➡ doctor
meadow ➡ field
meager ➡ small, trivial
mealy-mouthed ➡ servile
meander ➡ wander, bend

meandering ➡ zigzag, indirect
meanest ➡ worst
meaningless ➡ empty
means ➡ tool, wealth
measurable ➡ finite
mechanical ➡ automatic
mechanism ➡ tool
mechanized ➡ automatic
medal ➡ award
medalist ➡ winner

medallion ➡ badge
meddling ➡ meddlesome, interference
median ➡ average, middle
mediate ➡ negotiate, decide
medic ➡ nurse
medical ➡ medicinal
medical center ➡ hospital
medicate ➡ heal
medication ➡ medicine

n = noun • *vb* = verb • *adj* = adjective • *adv* = adverb • *prep* = preposition • *pl* = plural

medicinal *adj* medical, therapeutic, healing, curative, remedial, pharmaceutical

medicine 1. *n* medication, prescription, pill, tablet, capsule, ointment, lotion, injection, shot, vaccine ➡ **cure, drug**
2. *n* medical science, medical profession, healing ➡ **science**

mediocrity *n* inferiority, inadequacy, ordinariness

meditate *vb* ponder, contemplate, muse, reflect, speculate ➡ **think, consider**

meeting 1. *n* appointment, engagement, date, rendezvous, tryst, encounter, confrontation, run-in, brush
2. *n* conference, assembly, gathering, reunion, convention, council, interview, session ➡ **talk**
3. *n* ➡ **introduction**
4. *n* ➡ **junction**

melt *vb* dissolve, thaw, liquefy, fuse, evaporate, soften ➡ **disappear**

member 1. *n* affiliate, constituent, fellow, enrollee, colleague, participant ➡ **partner**
2. *n* ➡ **limb**

memorable *adj* unforgettable, momentous, historic, notable, monumental ➡ **important**

memory *n* recollection, reminiscence, recall, remembrance, déjà vu

mention 1. *vb* refer to, touch on, infer, allude, state, name, specify ➡ **say, suggest, broach**
2. *n* ➡ **remark**

mess 1. *n* jumble, tangle, litter, clutter, mayhem, hodgepodge, muddle, hash ➡ **confusion**
2. *vb* ➡ **disturb, dirty**
3. *vb* ➡ **tinker**

messenger *n* courier, carrier, runner, envoy, ambassador, emissary

messy *adj* untidy, disorderly, sloppy, slovenly, disheveled, bedraggled, unkempt ➡ **dirty** ⇨ *neat*

If the word you want is not a main entry above, look below to find it.

medicine man ➡ magician

mediocre ➡ cheap, average, fair

meditative ➡ thoughtful

medium ➡ average, setting, tool, prophet

medley ➡ assortment

meek ➡ humble, shy, gentle

meet ➡ touch, gather, obey, game

megalopolis ➡ town

melancholy ➡ sad, sorrow

melee ➡ fight

mellow ➡ carefree

melodious ➡ musical

melodrama ➡ play

melodramatic ➡ sensational

melody ➡ song, music

membrane ➡ layer

memento ➡ reminder

memo ➡ letter

memoir ➡ diary

memo pad ➡ notepad

memorandum ➡ letter

memorial ➡ reminder, monument

memorial park ➡ cemetery

memorialize ➡ remember

memorize ➡ learn

menace ➡ danger, threaten

menacing ➡ ominous

menagerie ➡ zoo

mend ➡ fix, repair, heal, sew

men's room ➡ bathroom

mental ➡ insane, intellectual

mental health ➡ reason

mentor ➡ teacher

menu ➡ list

mercenary ➡ soldier

merchandise ➡ product

merchant ➡ seller

merciful ➡ kind

merciless ➡ mean

mercurial ➡ fickle

mercy ➡ kindness, pity, forgiveness

mere ➡ trivial

merely ➡ only

merest ➡ least

merge ➡ mix, unify

merger ➡ union

meringue ➡ icing

merit ➡ worth, deserve

meritorious ➡ praiseworthy

merriment ➡ mirth, laughter

merry ➡ happy

merrymaking ➡ party

mesa ➡ mountain, plateau

mesh ➡ net

mesmerize ➡ enchant

message ➡ announcement, letter

metamorphosis ➡ change

metaphysics ➡ philosophy

➡ = *synonym cross-reference* • ⇨ = *antonym cross-reference*

meteor *n* meteorite, shooting star, falling star, comet, asteroid

method *n* approach, procedure, process, technique, system, routine, manner, way
➡ **plan**

middle 1. *n* center, core, midpoint, hub, nucleus, focus, midst, interior, inside, soul, depth ➡ **essence**
2. *adj* central, inner, interior, median, mean, midmost, intermediate ➡ **inside, average**

midget *n* dwarf, pygmy, manikin

military 1. *adj* armed, militant, combative, warlike, martial, militaristic, bellicose, soldierly
2. *n* ➡ **army**

mind 1. *n* brain, intellect, intelligence, psyche, consciousness, subconscious, ego
➡ **soul, wisdom**
2. *n* ➡ **belief**

3. *vb* ➡ **protect**
4. *vb* ➡ **obey**

mine 1. *n* quarry, pit, excavation, tunnel
➡ **hole**
2. *n* ➡ **supply**

minister 1. *n* preacher, pastor, rector, chaplain, clergyman, clergywoman, clergy, cleric ➡ **priest, religious**
2. *n* ➡ **diplomat**

minus 1. *prep* less, without, diminished by
2. *n* ➡ **defect**

miracle *n* wonder, marvel, phenomenon, rarity, oddity, portent

mirror 1. *n* looking glass, glass, reflector
2. *vb* ➡ **reflect**

mirth *n* merriment, joviality, festivity, gaiety
➡ **humor, pleasure, laughter**

If the word you want is not a main entry above, look below to find it.

meteoric ➡ sudden

meteorite ➡ meteor

mete out ➡ inflict, share

meter ➡ rhythm

meticulous ➡ careful

meticulously ➡ carefully

métier ➡ specialty

metropolis ➡ town

metropolitan ➡ urban

mettle ➡ courage

microscope ➡ glass

microscopic ➡ invisible

microwave ➡ cook

midday ➡ day, afternoon

middleman ➡ agent

midmost ➡ middle

midnight ➡ night

midpoint ➡ middle, average

midriff ➡ stomach

midsection ➡ stomach

midshipman ➡ sailor

midst ➡ middle

midterm ➡ examination

mien ➡ bearing, appearance

might ➡ strength

mighty ➡ strong, huge

migrant ➡ traveler

migrate ➡ move

migration ➡ movement

mikado ➡ emperor

mild ➡ gentle, fair, insipid, warm

mildew ➡ fungus

mild-tempered ➡ patient

milestone ➡ event

milieu ➡ setting

militant ➡ belligerent, military

militaristic ➡ military

militia ➡ army

milky ➡ white

mill ➡ factory

millionaire ➡ tycoon

mimic ➡ imitate

minaret ➡ tower

mince ➡ cut

mindfully ➡ carefully

mingle ➡ mix

miniature ➡ small, model

minimal ➡ least

minimum ➡ least

minion ➡ servant

minor ➡ trivial, child, course

minority ➡ childhood

minstrel ➡ musician

minstrelsy ➡ music

minute ➡ small, trivial, moment

minutest ➡ least

miraculous ➡ awesome

mirage ➡ illusion

mire ➡ swamp, dirt, catch

misanthrope ➡ miser, skeptic

misapprehension ➡ misunderstanding

misbehave ➡ disobey

misbehavior ➡ mischief

miscalculation ➡ mistake

miscellaneous ➡ different

miscellany ➡ assortment, mixture

mischief *n* misconduct, misbehavior, devilment, tomfoolery, rascality, shenanigans (*informal*) ➡ **trouble**

mischievous *adj* naughty, disobedient, unruly, wayward, spoiled, ill-behaved, impish, elfish, elfin ➡ **rude, rebellious, bad** ⇨ *good*

miser *n* skinflint, penny-pincher, scrooge, niggard, cheapskate, tightwad, hoarder, misanthrope

misery *n* suffering, agony, anguish, distress, grief, pain, torment, torture, heartache ➡ **hardship, sorrow**

missile 1. *n* projectile, arrow, dart, lance, spear, javelin, bullet, shell, bolt, slug
2. *n* rocket, torpedo, ICBM

mistake 1. *n* error, slip, blunder, oversight, faux pas, inaccuracy, fallacy, miscalculation, blooper (*informal*), boo-boo (*informal*) ➡ **fault, defect, misunderstanding**
2. *vb* ➡ **misunderstand**

misunderstand *vb* misinterpret, misjudge, misconstrue, mistake, err

misunderstanding 1. *n* misapprehension, misconception, confusion ➡ **mistake**
2. *n* ➡ **argument**

mix 1. *vb* combine, blend, merge, mingle, compound, consolidate, stir, whip, beat, knead, roll, churn, jumble, scramble, shuffle ➡ **join**
2. *vb* associate, mingle, intermingle, socialize, fraternize, consort, hobnob (*informal*) ➡ **join**
3. *n* ➡ **assortment**

mixture *n* combination, blend, composite, compound, solution, amalgam, amalgamation, potpourri, miscellany, concoction ➡ **mess, hybrid**

mobilize *vb* muster, enlist, marshal, summon, rally ➡ **gather**

If the word you want is not a main entry above, look below to find it.

misconception ➡ **misunderstanding**

misconduct ➡ **mischief**

misconstrue ➡ **misunderstand, distort**

misdeed ➡ **crime**

misdemeanor ➡ **crime**

miserable ➡ **sad, bad**

miserly ➡ **cheap**

misfortune ➡ **hardship, disaster**

misgiving ➡ **doubt**

mishap ➡ **accident**

misinterpret ➡ **misunderstand**

misjudge ➡ **misunderstand**

mislaid ➡ **lost**

mislay ➡ **lose**

mislead ➡ **lie**

misleading ➡ **unreliable**

mispend ➡ **waste**

misplace ➡ **lose**

misplaced ➡ **lost**

misremember ➡ **forget**

misrepresent ➡ **distort**

misrepresentation ➡ **lie, pretense**

miss ➡ **lose, exclude**

misshapen ➡ **bent**

missing ➡ **absent, lost**

mission ➡ **job, committee, church**

missive ➡ **letter**

misstate ➡ **lie**

mist ➡ **fog, cloud**

mistaken ➡ **wrong**

mistreat ➡ **abuse**

mistreatment ➡ **abuse**

mistress ➡ **owner**

mistrust ➡ **doubt**

misty ➡ **wet**

misuse ➡ **abuse, waste**

mitigate ➡ **relieve**

mitt ➡ **glove**

mitten ➡ **glove**

mixer ➡ **dance**

moan ➡ **cry, complain**

moat ➡ **channel**

mob ➡ **crowd**

mobile ➡ **portable**

mobility ➡ **movement**

mock ➡ **imitate, ridicule, fake**

mockery ➡ **ridicule**

mock-up ➡ **model**

mode ➡ **fashion**

➡ = *synonym cross-reference* • ⇨ = *antonym cross-reference*

model 1. *n* paragon, ideal, archetype, exemplar, paradigm, nonpareil, standard, prototype, original ➡ **example**
2. *n* miniature, representation, reduction, mock-up ➡ **copy, duplicate**
3. *n* ➡ **make, pattern**
4. *n* subject, sitter, fashion model, poser, mannequin
5. *vb* ➡ **make**
6. *vb* pose, sit ➡ **show**
7. *adj* classic, outstanding, first-rate, excellent, authoritative, typical, archetypal, definitive ➡ **perfect**

modern 1. *adj* contemporary, current, up-to-date, stylish, recent, modernistic, newfangled, space-age, state-of-the-art, latter-day ➡ **new**
2. Modern *adj* ➡ **art**

moment 1. *n* instant, point, minute, second, twinkling, wink, jiffy, flash, trice, time ➡ **period**
2. *n* ➡ **importance**

monastery *n* abbey, convent, nunnery, cloister, priory, friary, lamasery, ashram

money *n* cash, currency, coin, revenue, capital, specie ➡ **wealth, property**

monopoly *n* trust, syndicate, cartel, corner, consortium, ownership

monster *n* beast, ogre, ghoul, brute, savage, freak, monstrosity ➡ **animal**

monument 1. *n* marker, shrine, mausoleum, memorial, tribute ➡ **reminder, statue**
2. *n* ➡ **masterpiece**

mood *n* humor, morale, temper, temperament, disposition, spirits, vein ➡ **state, setting**

mope *vb* sulk, pout, brood ➡ **worry, grieve**

more 1. *adj* additional, extra, added, further, supplementary, another, new ⇨ *less*
2. *adv* additionally, furthermore, still, yet, better, preferably, sooner, rather
3. *n* increase, supplement, extra, surplus

If the word you want is not a main entry above, look below to find it.

moderate ➡ easy, gentle, slow, conservative, negotiate

moderation ➡ abstinence

moderator ➡ host

modernistic ➡ modern

modernity ➡ novelty

modest ➡ humble, average

modesty ➡ virtue

modicum ➡ bit

modification ➡ change

modify ➡ change, adjust, soften

moist ➡ damp

moisten ➡ wet

moisture ➡ humidity

mold ➡ form, fungus

molder ➡ decay

moldy ➡ stale, bad

mole ➡ growth

molecule ➡ atom

molest ➡ abuse

mollify ➡ pacify

molt ➡ shed

molten ➡ liquid

momentarily ➡ soon

momentary ➡ temporary

momentous ➡ memorable

momentum ➡ progress, impulse

monarch ➡ king, queen

monetary ➡ financial

moneyed ➡ rich

mongrel ➡ dog, hybrid

monitor ➡ guardian

monk ➡ religious

monogram ➡ signature

monotonous ➡ dull

monotony ➡ boredom

monsoon ➡ storm

monstrosity ➡ monster

monstrous ➡ huge

monumental ➡ memorable

mooch ➡ borrow

moody ➡ temperamental, sad

moor ➡ dock, plain

mooring ➡ anchor

mop ➡ sweep

moral ➡ good

morale ➡ mood

morality ➡ virtue

moralize ➡ preach

morass ➡ maze

morbid ➡ gruesome

moreover ➡ besides

more than ➡ above

n = noun • *vb* = verb • *adj* = adjective • *adv* = adverb • *prep* = preposition • *conj* = conjunction

morning *n* a.m., daybreak, dawn, sunrise, sunup, morn ➡ **day** ⇨ *evening*

mortal 1. *adj* human, transient, frail, impermanent, perishable ➡ **temporary** ⇨ *eternal*
2. *adj* ➡ **deadly**
3. *n* ➡ **human being**

most 1. *adj* maximum, utmost, greatest
2. *n* majority, maximum, bulk, preponderance
3. *adv* ➡ **very, best**

motherly *adj* maternal, parental, protective ➡ **feminine** ⇨ *fatherly*

mountain *n* mount, peak, ridge, summit, butte, mesa ➡ **hill, cliff** ⇨ *valley*

move 1. *vb* shift, remove, budge, dislodge ➡ **carry, push**
2. *vb* transfer, relocate, migrate, emigrate, immigrate ➡ **leave, go, travel**
3. *vb* ➡ **affect**
4. *vb* ➡ **suggest**

movement 1. *n* locomotion, motion, progress, shift, mobility, play, maneuver ➡ **activity, speed**
2. *n* campaign, crusade, march, faction, demonstration ➡ **cause**
3. *n* migration, immigration, emigration, transition, displacement, removal, transfer, transmission, conveyance
4. *n* ➡ **gait**

movie *n* film, picture, show, video, flick (*informal*) ➡ **play**

movies *n* pictures, cinema, silver screen

much 1. *adv* greatly, enormously, extremely, dearly ➡ **very, far**
2. *adj* ➡ **enough, abundant**
3. *n* ➡ **abundance**

mumble *vb* murmur, mutter, whisper, breathe, sigh ➡ **complain, say, talk, stammer**

If the word you want is not a main entry above, look below to find it.

morn ➡ morning
moron ➡ fool
morose ➡ pessimistic
morrow ➡ future
morsel ➡ bite
mortgage ➡ loan, pawn
mortified ➡ ashamed
mortify ➡ embarrass
mosque ➡ church
mostly ➡ chiefly
motel ➡ hotel
motet ➡ hymn
mother ➡ parent
motherland ➡ country
motif ➡ pattern, chorus

motion ➡ movement, activity, wave
motionless ➡ stationary, passive, dead
motivate ➡ cause
motivation ➡ incentive
motive ➡ reason, incentive
motley ➡ different
motor ➡ engine
motorcade ➡ parade
motorcyclist ➡ rider
motorized ➡ automatic
mottled ➡ speckled
motto ➡ saying
mound ➡ pile, hill
mount ➡ ascend, enter, mountain, horse

mourn ➡ grieve
mournful ➡ pitiful
mouth ➡ door
mouthful ➡ bite
mouth-watering ➡ delicious
movable ➡ portable
moving ➡ emotional
mow ➡ cut
mucilage ➡ adhesive
muck ➡ dirt
mud ➡ dirt
muddle ➡ fumble, mess
muddy ➡ dirty
mudslide ➡ avalanche
muff ➡ fumble

muffle ➡ quiet
muffler ➡ wrap
mug ➡ glass, attack
mugginess ➡ humidity
muggy ➡ damp, tropical
mulish ➡ stubborn
multiple ➡ many
multiply ➡ reproduce, grow
multitude ➡ crowd
mum ➡ quiet
mummify ➡ embalm, bury
munch ➡ bite
municipal ➡ public, urban
municipality ➡ town
munificence ➡ generosity
munitions ➡ ammunition

➡ = synonym cross-reference • ⇨ = antonym cross-reference

murder 1. *n* homicide, manslaughter, assassination, bloodshed, massacre, slaughter, slaying, carnage, annihilation ➡ **crime**
2. *vb* ➡ **kill**

music *n* harmony, melody, minstrelsy ➡ **song**

musical 1. *adj* harmonious, melodious, tuneful, lyrical, symphonic, rhythmical, euphonious, assonant
2. *adj* ➡ **talented**
3. *n* ➡ **play**

musician *n* composer, player, instrumentalist, performer, entertainer, minstrel, troubadour, bard ➡ **singer, artist**

mutilate *vb* maim, disfigure, dismember, mangle, disable ➡ **hurt, destroy**

mysterious *adj* puzzling, enigmatic, perplexing, baffling, inexplicable, uncanny, mystic, mystical ➡ **magic, strange, obscure**

myth *n* legend, fable, epic, lore, folklore, tradition, mythology ➡ **story, superstition**

If the word you want is not a main entry above, look below to find it.

murderer ➡ killer

murderous ➡ deadly

murk ➡ fog

murky ➡ dark, dim

murmur ➡ mumble, hum, rustle

muscle ➡ strength

muscular ➡ strong

muse ➡ meditate

museum ➡ gallery

mushroom ➡ fungus, grow

musket ➡ gun

muss ➡ disturb

must ➡ need, necessity

muster ➡ mobilize

musty ➡ stale, trite

mutable ➡ variable

mutate ➡ change

mutation ➡ change

mute ➡ dumb, quiet

mutineer ➡ rebel

mutinous ➡ rebellious

mutiny ➡ treason, rebel

mutt ➡ dog

mutter ➡ mumble

mutual ➡ common

mutually ➡ together

muumuu ➡ dress

muzzle ➡ quiet

muzzle loader ➡ gun

myriad ➡ many

mystery ➡ secret, problem, play

mystic ➡ mysterious

mystical ➡ magic, mysterious, supernatural

mystify ➡ confuse

mythical ➡ legendary

mythological ➡ legendary

mythology ➡ myth, religion

n = noun • *vb* = verb • *adj* = adjective • *adv* = adverb • *prep* = preposition • *conj* = conjunction

N

nail 1. *n* spike, brad, stud, tack, bolt, rivet, screw, peg, dowel ➡ **pin**
2. *vb* pin, tack, screw, bolt, rivet ➡ **join**

naive *adj* unsophisticated, inexperienced, simple, innocent, artless, ingenuous, trusting, green, gullible, credulous ➡ **unaware, amateur, harmless**

naked *adj* undressed, nude, exposed, unclothed, unclad, bare, stripped, bald
Some people consider **nude** *to be a more polite word than* **naked** *when referring to the unclothed human body.* **Nude** *is the term regularly used in reference to works of art showing unclothed figures.*

name 1. *n* appellation, proper name, surname, designation, nickname, epithet, title, heading ➡ **label**
2. *n* ➡ **reputation**
3. *n* ➡ **celebrity**
4. *vb* christen, nickname, call, dub, designate, entitle, title, label, identify
5. *vb* ➡ **mention**
6. *vb* appoint, delegate, nominate, assign ➡ **choose**

narrow *adj* snug, thin, slender, constricted, close, slim ➡ **small** ⇨ *broad*

native 1. *adj* indigenous, aboriginal, endemic, original, domestic, local, homegrown ➡ **natural**
2. *n* ➡ **citizen**

natural 1. *adj* organic, pure, unprocessed, raw, uncooked ➡ **plain, normal**
2. *adj* inborn, inherent, instinctive, innate, hereditary, inherited, congenital, genetic, intrinsic ➡ **native**

nature 1. *n* environment, outdoors, out-of-doors, landscape ➡ **earth**
2. *n* ➡ **type**
3. *n* ➡ **personality**

nausea *n* indigestion, queasiness, vomiting, sickness, qualm ➡ **illness**

nautical *adj* maritime, marine, naval, sailing, boating, yachting, seagoing

navy 1. *n* fleet, flotilla, armada, naval forces ➡ **army**
2. *adj* ➡ **blue**

If the word you want is not a main entry above, look below to find it.

nab ➡ arrest
nag ➡ bother, complain
nah ➡ no
nameless ➡ anonymous
nap ➡ sleep
napping ➡ asleep, unprepared
narcissism ➡ pride

narcotic ➡ drug
narrate ➡ tell
narration ➡ story
narrative ➡ story
narrow-minded ➡ provincial
nascent ➡ early
nasty ➡ bad
nation ➡ country

national ➡ citizen
national park ➡ park
nationalistic ➡ patriotic
nativity ➡ birth
naturally ➡ regularly
naught ➡ zero
naughty ➡ bad, mischievous
nauseate ➡ disgust
nauseated ➡ sick

nauseating ➡ bad
nauseous ➡ sick
naval ➡ nautical
naval forces ➡ navy
navel orange ➡ orange
navigate ➡ drive, pilot
navigator ➡ pilot
nay ➡ no

---

near 1. *adj* close, nearby, immediate, intimate, imminent, local ➡ **adjacent, about, approximate**
2. *adj* ➡ **future**
3. *prep* ➡ **beside**
4. *vb* ➡ **approach**

neat *adj* tidy, trim, orderly, organized, shipshape, precise, spruce ➡ **clean, prim, legible** ⇨ *messy*

necessary *adj* essential, indispensable, basic, required, requisite, fundamental, mandatory, compulsory, obligatory, imperative ➡ **important**

necessity *n* requirement, essential, staple, requisite, prerequisite, qualification, must, need ➡ **reason**

need 1. *vb* require, lack ➡ **want**
2. *vb* must, should, ought, have
3. *n* ➡ **necessity, reason**
4. *n* ➡ **hardship, poverty**

neglect 1. *n* indifference, disregard, disrespect
2. *vb* ➡ **forget, exclude**

negligent *adj* neglectful, inattentive, lax, remiss, derelict, delinquent, slack, dilatory, irresponsible ➡ **thoughtless, absent-minded**

negotiate *vb* mediate, moderate, bargain, referee, confer, transact, haggle, parley, intercede, arbitrate ➡ **decide**

neighborhood *n* community, block, vicinity, quarter, precinct, ward, borough ➡ **place, zone**

nervous *adj* restless, fidgety, shaky, edgy, uptight, skittish, self-conscious, jittery, jumpy, high-strung ➡ **afraid, anxious, cowardly**

net 1. *n* screen, mesh, web, webbing, network, sieve, filter, sifter
2. *vb* ➡ **earn**

new 1. *adj* fresh, original, recent, late, latest, novel, brand-new, trendy, up-to-date, unused, unspoiled, pristine, virgin, untouched ➡ **modern** ⇨ *old*
2. *adj* ➡ **more**

If the word you want is not a main entry above, look below to find it.

nearby ➡ near, about

nearly ➡ about, practically

nearness ➡ presence

nebulous ➡ obscure

neck ➡ cape

necktie ➡ tie

needle ➡ bother

needless ➡ unnecessary

needy ➡ poor

ne'er-do-well ➡ loafer

nefarious ➡ bad

negative ➡ no, pessimistic

neglected ➡ abandoned

neglectful ➡ negligent

negligee ➡ bathrobe

negligible ➡ trivial, few

neighbor ➡ border

neighboring ➡ adjacent

neighborly ➡ friendly

neophyte ➡ amateur

nerve ➡ audacity, courage

nervousness ➡ confusion

nest ➡ den

nestle ➡ snuggle

network ➡ net, maze

neuter ➡ sterilize

neutral ➡ fair

neutralize ➡ balance

névé ➡ snow

nevertheless ➡ anyway, but

newborn ➡ baby

newcomer ➡ stranger

newfangled ➡ modern

newly ➡ recently

newness ➡ novelty

news ➡ announcement

newscaster ➡ reporter

newsman ➡ reporter

newspaper ➡ paper

newspaperman ➡ reporter

newspaperwoman ➡ reporter

newsprint ➡ paper

newswoman ➡ reporter

next ➡ adjacent, following

next door ➡ adjacent

next to ➡ beside

nib ➡ pen

nibble ➡ bite

---

nice 1. *adj* agreeable, delightful, fantastic
➡ **good, great, pleasant**
2. *adj* good-natured, charming, pleasant, agreeable, affable, good-humored
➡ **thoughtful, polite, friendly, kind**
3. *adj* ➡ **careful**
Nice *is a very general word to describe someone or something you like, but it is not very specific. Be careful not to overuse it. Often a stronger or more specific synonym is better.*

night *n* nighttime, p.m., bedtime, midnight, dark ➡ **evening** ⇨ *day*

no *interj* nay, negative, nope (*informal*), nah (*informal*) ⇨ **yes**

noble 1. *adj* royal, aristocratic, highborn, patrician, titled, blue-blooded, princely, kingly, regal, imperial, elite
2. *adj* worthy, generous, magnanimous, courtly, chivalrous, chivalric ➡ **grand, good**

3. *n* nobleman, noblewoman, aristocrat, peer, lord, lady

noise *n* sound, din, uproar, clamor, racket, hubbub, tumult, commotion, pandemonium, hullabaloo, peal ➡ **bang, cry, peep**

nonsense 1. *n* foolishness, stupidity, absurdity, irrationality, madness, lunacy, senselessness, silliness, folly, frivolity
2. *n* poppycock, balderdash, twaddle, gobbledygook, drivel, buncombe, bunk, claptrap, baloney, hogwash

normal *adj* typical, average, natural, standard, conventional ➡ **common, usual**

nose *n* nostril, snout, proboscis, beak, bill, trunk

notepad *n* pad, memo pad, tablet, notebook, steno pad, legal pad ➡ **paper**

If the word you want is not a main entry above, look below to find it.

niche ➡ bay
nick ➡ cut, dent
nickname ➡ name, pseudonym
niggard ➡ miser
niggardly ➡ cheap
nightclub ➡ bar
nightcrawler ➡ worm
nightfall ➡ evening
nighttime ➡ night
nil ➡ zero
nimble ➡ agile
nimbleness ➡ agility
nimbus ➡ halo
nincompoop ➡ fool
ninny ➡ fool
nip ➡ squeeze, drink, bite

nippy ➡ cool
nirvana ➡ heaven
nitwit ➡ fool
nobility ➡ aristocracy
nobleman ➡ noble
noblewoman ➡ noble
nod ➡ sleep
noiseless ➡ quiet
noisy ➡ loud
nomad ➡ traveler
nom de plume ➡ pseudonym
nominate ➡ name
nomination ➡ appointment
nominee ➡ candidate
nonattendance ➡ absence

nonbeliever ➡ skeptic, atheist
nonchalance ➡ apathy
nonchalant ➡ carefree, apathetic
none ➡ zero
nonetheless ➡ anyway
nonexistent ➡ imaginary
nonnative ➡ foreign
nonpareil ➡ model
nonpartisan ➡ fair
nonprofessional ➡ amateur
nonsensical ➡ foolish
nonstop ➡ continual
nonviolent ➡ peaceful
nook ➡ bay
nope ➡ no

nor'easter ➡ storm
norm ➡ average
normally ➡ usually
nosedive ➡ fall
nosegay ➡ bouquet
nostalgia ➡ desire
nostril ➡ nose
nosy ➡ curious
notable ➡ memorable, celebrity
notably ➡ chiefly, far
notch ➡ cut, dent
note ➡ notice, letter
notebook ➡ notepad
noted ➡ famous
notepaper ➡ paper

➡ = synonym cross-reference • ⇨ = antonym cross-reference

notice 1. *vb* observe, note, perceive ➡ **discover, look, see**
2. *n* attention, observation, regard, heed, note, publicity ➡ **warning**
3. *n* ➡ **advertisement, announcement, reminder**

novelty 1. *n* newness, originality, freshness, uniqueness, modernity ➡ **invention**
2. *n* oddity, curiosity, knickknack, curio ➡ **trinket**

now *adv* immediately, straightaway, directly, right away, instantly ➡ **quickly, soon**

nuisance *n* annoyance, inconvenience, irritation, bother, pain, pest, headache, vexation ➡ **trouble**

number 1. *n* numeral, figure, digit, cipher, integer, fraction
2. *n* amount, quantity, batch, lot, bunch, bundle ➡ **group, assortment**
3. *n* ➡ **act**
Number and **batch** *usually refer to plural nouns:* "a **number** of mistakes," "a **batch** of cookies." **Amount** *is usually used with nouns that are not plural:* "a small **amount** of sunshine," "a tiny **amount** of water."

nurse 1. *n* RN, LPN, medic, orderly
2. *vb* ➡ **heal**

If the word you want is not a main entry above, look below to find it.

noteworthy ➡ special

nothing ➡ zero

noticeable ➡ obvious

notification ➡ announcement

notify ➡ tell

notion ➡ belief, idea, fancy

notoriety ➡ fame

notorious ➡ famous

notwithstanding ➡ anyway

nought ➡ zero

nourish ➡ support

nourishing ➡ healthy

nourishment ➡ food

novel ➡ new

novelist ➡ writer

novice ➡ amateur

noxious ➡ deadly, unhealthy

nozzle ➡ faucet

nuance ➡ difference

nucleus ➡ middle

nude ➡ naked

nudge ➡ push

nugget ➡ pile

nullify ➡ abolish

numb ➡ paralyze

numeral ➡ number

numerical ➡ consecutive

numerous ➡ many

nun ➡ religious

nunnery ➡ monastery

nuptials ➡ marriage

nursery ➡ bedroom, greenhouse

nursing home ➡ hospital

nurture ➡ grow, support

nut ➡ seed, fruit

nutrition ➡ food

nutritious ➡ healthy

nuzzle ➡ snuggle

n = noun • *vb* = verb • *adj* = adjective • *adv* = adverb • *prep* = preposition • *conj* = conjunction

O

obey *vb* comply, mind, follow, heed, behave, adhere, observe, meet ⇨ **disobey**

object 1. *vb* protest, disagree, dissent, oppose, dispute, disapprove, frown ➡ **argue, complain, contradict** ⇨ **agree**
2. *n* thing, article, item, gadget, device
3. *n* objective, purpose, aim, goal, sake, target, intention, intent, ambition

obscure 1. *adj* ➡ **dim, dark**
2. *adj* ambiguous, cryptic, enigmatic, inscrutable, unclear, inexplicable, abstruse, vague, incomprehensible, foggy, cloudy, nebulous ➡ **mysterious** ⇨ **obvious, explicit**
3. *vb* ➡ **hide**

observer *n* spectator, witness, eyewitness, viewer, onlooker, bystander

obsession *n* fixation, fascination, preoccupation, compulsion, mania, fetish ➡ **desire**

obvious *adj* clear, evident, apparent, transparent, noticeable, overt, glaring, blatant, gross, conspicuous, prominent, palpable, pronounced, marked, distinct, patent ➡ **bald, easy, plain** ⇨ **obscure**

occupant *n* resident, tenant, renter, householder, inhabitant, guest

occupy *vb* fill, pervade, take up ➡ **live, own, seize**

ocean *n* sea, deep, high seas, seven seas

oddity *n* peculiarity, abnormality, irregularity, idiosyncrasy, eccentricity, aberration, anomaly ➡ **novelty, miracle**

If the word you want is not a main entry above, look below to find it.

oaf ➡ fool, boor
oar ➡ paddle
oath ➡ promise, curse
obdurate ➡ stubborn
obedient ➡ good
obelisk ➡ tower
obese ➡ fat
objection ➡ complaint
objectionable ➡ bad
objective ➡ object, fair, real
obligate ➡ force
obligation ➡ duty, debt
obligatory ➡ necessary
oblige ➡ force
obliged ➡ grateful

obliging ➡ good
oblique ➡ zigzag
obliquely ➡ sideways
obliterate ➡ erase, abolish
oblivious ➡ unaware, absentminded
obnoxious ➡ bad
obscene ➡ dirty
obsequious ➡ servile
observable ➡ visible
observation ➡ remark, notice
observe ➡ look, see, notice, celebrate, obey
obsolete ➡ old
obstacle ➡ barrier

obstinate ➡ stubborn, wild
obstreperous ➡ loud
obstruct ➡ bar, close
obstructed ➡ impassable
obstruction ➡ barrier
obtain ➡ get
obtrusive ➡ meddlesome
obtuse ➡ unaware, dull
obverse ➡ front
obviously ➡ apparently
occasion ➡ opportunity, event, party
occasional ➡ periodic, rare
occasionally ➡ seldom
occult ➡ magic, supernatural

occupation ➡ profession
occupied ➡ employed
occur ➡ happen
occurrence ➡ event, presence
odd ➡ strange
odious ➡ awful
odor ➡ smell
odorous ➡ smelly
odyssey ➡ trip
offend ➡ insult, disgust, sin
offender ➡ criminal
offense ➡ crime, insult, attack
offensive ➡ bad, attack

➡ = synonym cross-reference • ⇨ = antonym cross-reference

offer 1. *vb* propose, present, tender, bid, proffer, extend, suggest, quote ➡ **give, sell**
2. *n* ➡ **suggestion, invitation**

office 1. *n* workplace, headquarters ➡ **den**
2. *n* ➡ **function**

official 1. *adj* authentic, authorized, legitimate, approved, licensed, valid, formal ➡ **real, correct**
2. *n* leader, administrator, executive, bureaucrat, civil servant, public servant ➡ **boss, judge**

often *adv* frequently, repeatedly, oftentimes, recurrently ➡ **regularly, usually** ⇨ *seldom*

oil 1. *n* petroleum, kerosene, crude oil, fossil fuel ➡ **gasoline**
2. *n* ➡ **fat**
3. *vb* grease, lubricate, lube (*informal*)

old 1. *adj* elderly, aged, venerable, mature, senior, hoary, seasoned ⇨ *young*
2. *adj* ancient, old-fashioned, antique, archaic, antiquated, obsolete, outdated ⇨ *new*
3. *adj* worn, used, rundown, worn-out, secondhand, decrepit ➡ **shabby, ragged**

older *adj* elder, senior, prior, earlier

ominous *adj* foreboding, threatening, baleful, menacing, malevolent, sinister, impending, inauspicious, unfavorable ➡ **bad**

once *adv* previously, formerly ➡ **before**

only 1. *adv* just, barely, hardly, scarcely, merely, simply, exclusively
2. *adj* single, sole, solitary, unique, one, lone

open 1. *adj* ajar, uncovered, unfastened, unlocked, accessible, unobstructed, unsealed
2. *adj* spacious, deserted, clear ➡ **empty**
3. *vb* unfasten, undo, unbolt, untie, free, clear ➡ **separate**
4. *vb* ➡ **start**

operate *vb* function, perform, run ➡ **drive, act, work, use**

opponent *n* rival, competitor, opposition, challenger, antagonist, adversary, foe, competition ➡ **contestant, enemy** ⇨ *friend*

opportunity *n* chance, occasion, excuse, opening, situation ➡ **luck**

If the word you want is not a main entry above, look below to find it.

offering ➡ gift

officer ➡ police, soldier

office-seeker ➡ candidate

officiate ➡ lead

offset ➡ balance

offshoot ➡ branch, limb, product

offspring ➡ child

oftentimes ➡ often

ogle ➡ stare

ogre ➡ monster

oink ➡ grunt

ointment ➡ medicine

OK ➡ yes

okay ➡ yes

okey-dokey ➡ yes

old-fashioned ➡ old

old wives' tale ➡ superstition

olive ➡ green

omen ➡ warning, sign

omit ➡ forget, exclude

on ➡ above

on account of ➡ because

once more ➡ again

one ➡ only

one-liner ➡ joke

onerous ➡ inconvenient

one-sided ➡ prejudiced

on hand ➡ present

ongoing ➡ continual

onlooker ➡ observer, audience

onset ➡ beginning, attack

onslaught ➡ attack

onward ➡ forward

onwards ➡ forward

ooze ➡ dirt, drop

opaque ➡ dark

open fire ➡ shoot

opening ➡ hole, break, opportunity, door

openness ➡ freedom, truth

operation ➡ behavior, use, attack

opiate ➡ drug

opinion ➡ belief

opinionated ➡ stubborn, dogmatic

oppose ➡ object, face

opposed ➡ opposite

opposing ➡ opposite

n = noun • *vb* = verb • *adj* = adjective • *adv* = adverb • *prep* = preposition • *conj* = conjunction

opposite 1. *adj* opposing, contradictory, contrary, conflicting, inverse, converse, reverse, contrasting, antithetical, counter ➡ **different**
2. *adj* facing, opposed, fronting, confronting
3. *n* reverse, contrary, converse, antithesis, inverse
4. *prep* facing, across from, against, opposed to, versus

opposition 1. *n* disapproval, dislike, aversion, antagonism, hostility, antipathy, enmity ➡ **disagreement, fight** ⇨ *support*
2. *n* ➡ **opponent**

optimistic *adj* hopeful, confident, cheerful, sanguine, expectant, bullish ➡ **idealistic, certain** ⇨ *pessimistic*

orange 1. *adj, n* tangerine, apricot, peach, coral, salmon
2. *n* navel orange, Seville orange, mandarin orange, tangerine, clementine, tangelo ➡ **fruit, tree**

order 1. *vb* command, direct, instruct, decree, bid, dictate, impose, prescribe, ordain, mandate ➡ **ask, tell, insist, force**
2. *vb* ➡ **arrange, straighten**
3. *n* arrangement, formation, organization, layout, disposition, alignment, placement, sequence, succession, system ➡ **plan**
4. *n* decree, command, commandment, demand, ultimatum, direction, directive, charge, mandate, edict, behest, writ
5. *n* ➡ **religion**

organization 1. *n* association, corporation, institution, foundation, society, club, fraternity, sorority ➡ **business, union, group**
2. *n* ➡ **order**

If the word you want is not a main entry above, look below to find it.

oppress ➡ abuse, sadden
oppression ➡ tyranny
oppressive ➡ bleak, sharp
opt ➡ choose
optical ➡ visible
optimist ➡ idealist
optimum ➡ best
option ➡ choice
optional ➡ voluntary, unnecessary
opulence ➡ wealth, elegance
opulent ➡ rich
opus ➡ work
oracle ➡ prophet
oral ➡ spoken

oration ➡ speech
orator ➡ speaker
oratorio ➡ hymn
orb ➡ ball
orbit ➡ circle, field
orchestra ➡ band
orchestration ➡ score
ordain ➡ order, bless
ordeal ➡ shock, trouble
orderly ➡ neat, nurse
ordinance ➡ act
ordinarily ➡ usually
ordinariness ➡ mediocrity
ordinary ➡ common, usual
ordination ➡ appointment

ordnance ➡ arms
organic ➡ natural, alive
organism ➡ animal, plant
organize ➡ arrange
organized ➡ neat
orient ➡ arrange, adjust
orientate ➡ arrange
orientation ➡ perspective
origin ➡ beginning, cause, source
original ➡ new, early, model, native
originality ➡ novelty, imagination
originate ➡ start, invent
originator ➡ creator

ornament ➡ jewel, decoration, decorate
ornamentation ➡ decoration
ornate ➡ rich, fancy
ornery ➡ stubborn
orthodox ➡ religious, conservative
orthodoxy ➡ religion
oscillate ➡ alternate, swing
oscillation ➡ vibration
ostentatious ➡ loud, fancy
ostracism ➡ exile
ostracize ➡ banish
other ➡ different
otherwise ➡ differently
ought ➡ need

➡ = synonym cross-reference • ⇨ = antonym cross-reference

oust *vb* eject, remove, expel, depose, dethrone, unseat ➡ **fire, banish**

outside 1. *n* exterior, surface, façade
2. *adj* exterior, external, outer, outermost, outward, outdoor, alfresco
3. *adv* outdoors, out-of-doors, out, alfresco

own 1. *vb* possess, hold, have, retain, maintain, enjoy, occupy ➡ **keep**
2. *vb* ➡ **admit**
3. *adj* ➡ **private**

owner *n* proprietor, buyer, possessor, holder, master, mistress, landowner, landlord, landlady

---

If the word you want is not a main entry above, look below to find it.

out ➡ outside

outbreak ➡ epidemic

outburst ➡ fit²

outcast ➡ exile, lonely, homeless

out cold ➡ unconscious

outcome ➡ effect, score

outcry ➡ complaint

outdated ➡ old

outdo ➡ exceed

outdoor ➡ outside

outdoors ➡ outside, nature

outer ➡ outside

outer space ➡ space

outermost ➡ outside, last

outfit ➡ dress, suit, business, supply

outfox ➡ fool

outgrowth ➡ shoot, product

outing ➡ trip

outlandish ➡ strange

outlast ➡ live¹

outlaw ➡ criminal, forbid

outlawed ➡ illegal

outlay ➡ price

outlet ➡ door

outline ➡ circumference, summary, list, plan

outlive ➡ live¹

outlook ➡ view

outlying ➡ far

outmoded ➡ unpopular

outnumber ➡ exceed

out-of-doors ➡ outside, nature

out of order ➡ broken

out-of-the-way ➡ inaccessible

out-of-towner ➡ stranger

out-of-work ➡ unemployed

outpatient ➡ patient

output ➡ productivity

outrage ➡ insult, anger

outrageous ➡ awful

outright ➡ bald, perfect, unconditional

outrun ➡ catch

outset ➡ beginning

outshine ➡ exceed

outsider ➡ stranger

outsmart ➡ fool

outspoken ➡ straightforward

outstanding ➡ good, special, model, due

outstretched ➡ long

outstrip ➡ catch

outward ➡ outside

outwit ➡ fool

oval ➡ round

over ➡ above, again, past

overabundant ➡ excessive

overbearing ➡ dogmatic

overcast ➡ dark, cloudy

overcoat ➡ coat

overcome ➡ defeat, win, weather

overconfident ➡ imprudent

overdo ➡ exaggerate

overdue ➡ late, due

overemotional ➡ emotional

overflow ➡ flood

overgrown ➡ wild

overhaul ➡ fix

overhead ➡ above

overhear ➡ listen

overjoyed ➡ ecstatic

overlap ➡ fold

overlay ➡ plate

overlook ➡ forget, exclude, tower

overlooked ➡ unnoticed

overnight bag ➡ luggage

overpass ➡ bridge

overpower ➡ defeat

overpriced ➡ expensive

overrule ➡ abolish

overrun ➡ wild, infest

overseas ➡ abroad

oversee ➡ lead

overseer ➡ guardian

oversight ➡ mistake

overspread ➡ cover

overstate ➡ exaggerate

overstatement ➡ exaggeration

overstep ➡ exceed

overt ➡ obvious

overtake ➡ catch

overthrow ➡ victory, defeat

overture ➡ introduction

overturn ➡ upset

overused ➡ trite

overweight ➡ fat

overwhelm ➡ flood, shock

overwrought ➡ frantic

ovum ➡ egg

ownership ➡ possession, monopoly

oxbow ➡ curve

oxidize ➡ corrode

oxygen ➡ air

oxymoron ➡ contradiction

---

n = noun • *vb* = verb • *adj* = adjective • *adv* = adverb • *prep* = preposition • *conj* = conjunction

P

pacify *vb* appease, placate, soothe, mollify ➡ **calm, satisfy**

package 1. *n* parcel, packet, bundle, pack ➡ **container, mail**
2. *vb* ➡ **wrap**

paddle 1. *n* oar, scull, sweep
2. *vb* row, scull, pole
3. *vb* ➡ **punish, hit, whip**
4. *vb* ➡ **swim**

page 1. *n* sheet, leaf, folio
2. *n* intern ➡ **servant**
3. *vb* ➡ **call**

pain 1. *n* suffering, discomfort, ache, pang, soreness, twinge, stitch, spasm, cramp, sting
2. *n* ➡ **misery**
3. *n* ➡ **nuisance**

paint 1. *n* pigment, dye, stain, tint ➡ **color, finish**
2. *vb* ➡ **draw**

pair 1. *n* couple, duo, twosome, twins, brace (*of animals*), yoke (*of oxen*), span (*of horses*) ➡ **team**
2. *vb* ➡ **join**

pale 1. *adj* pallid, pasty, wan, sallow, ashen, chalky ➡ **white, fair**
2. *vb* ➡ **bleach**

pamper *vb* coddle, spoil, indulge, dote on, humor, baby, patronize ➡ **please**

pamphlet *n* booklet, brochure, leaflet, tract ➡ **book**

paper 1. *n* stationery, notepaper, writing paper, newsprint, crepe paper, tissue, wax paper, tar paper, parchment, vellum
2. *n* ➡ **document, report**
3. *n* newspaper, magazine, journal, periodical, tabloid, gazette, daily, weekly

parade 1. *n* procession, march, demonstration, cavalcade, motorcade
2. *vb* ➡ **walk, strut**
3. *vb* ➡ **advertise**

If the word you want is not a main entry above, look below to find it.

pace ➡ speed, step, gait

pacific ➡ peaceful

pacifist ➡ peaceful

pack ➡ bag, package, load, group, herd, carry

packed ➡ full, thick

packet ➡ package

pact ➡ agreement

pad ➡ cushion, notepad, foot, protect

padding ➡ cushion

paddock ➡ pen

padlock ➡ lock

pageant ➡ play

pail ➡ container

painful ➡ sore, uncomfortable

painkiller ➡ drug

pains ➡ work

painstaking ➡ careful

painter ➡ artist, rope

painting ➡ picture

pal ➡ friend

palace ➡ castle, home

palisade ➡ cliff, wall, barrier

pall ➡ cloud

pallet ➡ cushion

palliate ➡ soften

pallid ➡ pale

palpable ➡ real, obvious

paltry ➡ poor, small, trivial

pan ➡ pot

panache ➡ class

pandemic ➡ epidemic

pandemonium ➡ noise

pander ➡ flatter

panel ➡ committee

pang ➡ pain

panhandler ➡ beggar

panic ➡ fear, hysteria

panorama ➡ view

pant ➡ breathe

pantry ➡ kitchen, closet

paparazzo, paparazzi ➡ photographer

paperback ➡ book

par ➡ average

paradigm ➡ model

---

parallel 1. *adj* equidistant, collateral, aligned, even, alongside, abreast ➡ **level**
2. *adj* ➡ **alike**
3. *n* ➡ **duplicate, similarity**
4. *vb* ➡ **compare**

paralyze *vb* disable, cripple, immobilize, numb, stun, knock out

parent *n* father, mother, foster parent, stepparent ➡ **ancestor, guardian**

park 1. *n* green, common, square, playground, recreational area
2. *n* national park, state park, reserve, preserve, reservation, refuge ➡ **zoo**
3. *vb* ➡ **put**

parody 1. *n* imitation, satire, caricature, burlesque ➡ **irony**
2. *vb* ➡ **imitate**

part 1. *n* piece, section, portion, segment, fragment, fraction, share, element, facet, aspect, component, ingredient, content ➡ **bit, block, division** ⇨ *total*

2. *vb* ➡ **divide, separate**
3. *n* ➡ **role, function**

partial 1. *adj* incomplete, unfinished, fragmentary, deficient, imperfect ⇨ *complete*
2. *adj* ➡ **prejudiced**

partly *adv* partially, partway, somewhat, incompletely, slightly

partner 1. *n* associate, co-worker, confederate, accomplice, accessory, sidekick ➡ **helper**
2. *n* ➡ **friend**
3. *n* ➡ **love, spouse**

party 1. *n* celebration, festivity, gathering, reception, soiree, fete, occasion, gala, function, revelry, jubilee, merrymaking ➡ **feast**
2. *n* faction, bloc, league, lobby, junta, cabal ➡ **organization, group**
3. *n* participant, litigant, principal ➡ **member, contestant**
4. *vb* ➡ **celebrate**

If the word you want is not a main entry above, look below to find it.

paradise ➡ heaven, utopia

paradox ➡ contradiction

paragon ➡ model

paragraph ➡ division

paramount ➡ important

paranoid ➡ suspicious, insane

paranormal ➡ supernatural

parapet ➡ wall

paraphernalia ➡ equipment

paraphrase ➡ summary, translation, quote, translate

parboil ➡ boil

parcel ➡ package

parched ➡ dry

parchment ➡ paper

pardon ➡ forgive, forgiveness

pare ➡ peel

parental ➡ motherly, fatherly

parfait ➡ ice cream

pariah ➡ exile

parish ➡ church

parishioners ➡ church

parka ➡ coat

parking garage ➡ garage

parkway ➡ highway

parley ➡ negotiate, talk

parliament ➡ government

parlor ➡ living room

parochial ➡ provincial

paroxysm ➡ fit[2]

parrot ➡ imitate, quote

parry ➡ repel

partiality ➡ preference, prejudice

partially ➡ partly

participant ➡ contestant, member, party

participate ➡ join

particle ➡ bit

particular ➡ special, careful, choosy, detail

particularize ➡ specify

particularly ➡ chiefly

partisan ➡ fan, prejudiced

partition ➡ wall, division, divider, divide

partnership ➡ business, union

partway ➡ partly

pasha ➡ king

pass ➡ exceed, go, throw, give, catch, elapse, ticket

passage ➡ hall, door, approval, excerpt, division, trip, travel

passageway ➡ hall

pass away ➡ die

passenger ➡ rider

passerby ➡ pedestrian

passing ➡ death

passion ➡ love, desire, enthusiasm, emotion

passionate ➡ emotional, loving, eager

pass on ➡ die

passive 1. *adj* idle, inactive, inert, lifeless, motionless, sedentary ➡ **listless, lazy, slow** ⟹ *active*
2. *adj* resigned, submissive, docile, deferential, compliant, yielding ➡ **patient**

past 1. *adj* former, preceding, foregoing, prior, previous, antecedent ➡ **old**
2. *adj* finished, over, ended, through, done
3. *n* history, antiquity, yesterday, yesteryear, yore
4. *prep* beyond, through, behind, over, after

pastime *n* activity, pursuit, interest, hobby, avocation, venture ➡ **game**

pastry *n* baked goods, delicacy, Danish, pie, tart, shortbread, cookie ➡ **cake, bread**

path *n* pathway, footpath, trail, track, lane, walk, walkway, runway, shortcut ➡ **road, course**

patience *n* tolerance, understanding, fortitude, stoicism, endurance, perserverance, persistence

patient 1. *adj* understanding, forbearing, mild-tempered, long-suffering ➡ **tolerant, calm, passive**
2. *adj* persistent, perservering, steadfast, assiduous ➡ **diligent**

3. *n* subject, victim, sufferer, convalescent, invalid, outpatient, inpatient

patriotic *adj* loyal, zealous, nationalistic, chauvinistic ➡ **faithful**

patrol 1. *n* scout, lookout, sentinel, sentry, escort, vanguard, picket, watch ➡ **guardian**
2. *vb* police, inspect, cruise, reconnoiter, scout ➡ **protect**

patron 1. *n* sponsor, benefactor, philanthropist, supporter, contributor, donor, subscriber, giver
2. *n* client, customer, buyer, shopper, regular ➡ **audience**

pattern 1. *n* design, motif, configuration ➡ **structure, plan**
2. *n* model, blueprint, template, diagram, guide, sketch
3. *vb* ➡ **form**

pawn 1. *vb* hock, pledge, mortgage ➡ **sell**
2. *n* ➡ **tool**

pay 1. *vb* compensate, recompense, spend, reward, tip, remunerate, settle, disburse, expend, atone, expiate ➡ **give, earn, refund**
2. *n* ➡ **wage**

If the word you want is not a main entry above, look below to find it.

passport ➡ document, ticket
paste ➡ stick, adhesive
pastor ➡ minister
pastoral ➡ rural
pastry chef ➡ cook
pasture ➡ field
pasty ➡ pale
pat ➡ pet, hit
patch ➡ fix, repair

patent ➡ license, obvious
patently ➡ apparently
paternal ➡ fatherly
pathetic ➡ pitiful
pathless ➡ impassable
pathway ➡ path
patio ➡ porch, court
patois ➡ dialect
patriarch ➡ ancestor

patrician ➡ noble
patrimony ➡ inheritance
patriotism ➡ loyalty
patrolman ➡ police officer
patrolwoman ➡ police officer
patronize ➡ frequent, condescend, pamper
patrons ➡ audience
patter ➡ talk, knock, rustle

paucity ➡ want
paunch ➡ stomach
pauper ➡ beggar
pause ➡ stop, hesitate, break
pave ➡ cover
pavilion ➡ tent
paw ➡ foot, touch
payable ➡ due
pay for ➡ afford, buy
payment ➡ price

➡ = synonym cross-reference • ⟹ = antonym cross-reference

peace *n* harmony, concord, repose, amity, reconciliation ➡ **agreement, calm, truce**

peaceful 1. *adj* ➡ **calm**
2. *adj* peaceable, pacific, amicable, nonviolent, pacifist, conciliatory ➡ **friendly**

pedestrian 1. *n* walker, hiker, passerby, rover, stroller, straggler
2. *adj* ➡ **common, poor**

peel 1. *vb* skin, pare, strip, scale, husk, shuck, flay ➡ **cut**
2. *n* skin, rind, bark ➡ **shell**

peep *n* squeak, chirp, cheep, squawk, clink, tinkle, click, ping, pop, plink, plunk ➡ **noise, bang**

pen 1. *n* corral, fold, pound, paddock, enclosure, coop, cage, sty, stall, kennel ➡ **barn, field, jail**

2. *n* ballpoint, marker, fountain pen, quill, nib
3. *vb* ➡ **write**

pension *n* benefit, support, annuity, Social Security ➡ **wage**

people 1. *n* citizenry, populace, public, population, society, civilization, community, folk, hoi polloi (*Greek*), bourgeoisie (*French*) ➡ **human being, humanity, citizen**
2. *n* ➡ **family**

perfect 1. *adj* ideal, flawless, faultless, impeccable, unblemished, immaculate, exquisite, exemplary, model ➡ **correct, infallible**
2. *adj* pure, sheer, outright ➡ **complete**
3. *vb* polish, hone, amend ➡ **fix, correct**

If the word you want is not a main entry above, look below to find it.

peaceable ➡ **peaceful**

peacefulness ➡ **calm**

peach ➡ **orange**

pea green ➡ **green**

peak ➡ **top, mountain, climax, bill**

peal ➡ **ring, noise**

pearl ➡ **ball**

peasant ➡ **farmer**

pebble ➡ **rock**

peck ➡ **abundance, stick, kiss**

peculiar ➡ **strange, special**

peculiarity ➡ **oddity, detail**

pecuniary ➡ **financial**

peddle ➡ **sell**

peddler ➡ **seller**

pedestal ➡ **post**

peek ➡ **look**

peer ➡ **stare, equal, noble**

peerless ➡ **unique**

peevish ➡ **cross**

peg ➡ **nail**

peignoir ➡ **bathrobe**

pellet ➡ **ball**

pelt ➡ **hit, hide**

penalize ➡ **punish**

penalty ➡ **punishment**

penance ➡ **punishment**

penchant ➡ **tendency**

pending ➡ **future, unresolved**

penetrate ➡ **enter, stick, know**

penetrating ➡ **profound**

peninsula ➡ **cape**

penitent ➡ **sorry**

penitentiary ➡ **jail**

penknife ➡ **knife**

penmanship ➡ **handwriting**

pen name ➡ **pseudonym**

pennant ➡ **flag**

penniless ➡ **poor**

penny-pinching ➡ **cheap**

penny-pincher ➡ **miser**

pensive ➡ **thoughtful**

penurious ➡ **cheap**

penury ➡ **poverty**

pep ➡ **energy**

peppery ➡ **spicy**

perceivable ➡ **visible**

perceive ➡ **see, notice, read**

percent ➡ **share**

percentage ➡ **share**

perceptible ➡ **audible, visible**

perception ➡ **sight, wisdom, feeling**

perceptive ➡ **smart**

perch ➡ **descend, seat**

perchance ➡ **maybe**

perennial ➡ **flower, permanent**

perfection ➡ **excellence**

perfectionist ➡ **idealist**

perfectly ➡ **certainly**

perfidious ➡ **unfaithful**

perforate ➡ **stick**

perforation ➡ **hole**

perform ➡ **act, operate, play**

performance ➡ **act, behavior, delivery, program**

performer ➡ **actor, musician**

perfume ➡ **smell**

perfumed ➡ **fragrant**

perfunctory ➡ **fast, superficial**

perhaps ➡ **maybe**

peril ➡ **danger**

perilous ➡ **dangerous**

perimeter ➡ **circumference, circle**

period 1. *n* interval, term, span, spell, duration, extent, stretch, streak, cycle, bout, season, phase, stage, time, shift, watch, tour, stint ➡ **round, moment**
2. *n* age, eon, era, epoch, date

periodic *adj* intermittent, cyclic, cyclical, recurrent, spasmodic, sporadic, fitful, erratic, irregular, occasional ➡ **alternate, frequent**

permanent *adj* durable, lasting, enduring, abiding, perennial, persistent, indelible ➡ **continual, eternal, stationary** ⇨ *temporary*

permission *n* consent, authorization, authority, approval, license, sanction ➡ **support**

personality 1. *n* character, disposition, temperament, temper, nature, identity

2. *n* charisma, charm, presence, allure, magnetism ➡ **bearing, attraction**
3. *n* ➡ **celebrity**

perspective *n* point of view, viewpoint, standpoint, orientation, direction, angle, position, attitude, side ➡ **view**

persuade *vb* convince, satisfy, influence, induce, dispose, coax, sway, get, wheedle, cajole, entice, prevail, snow ➡ **urge, tempt** ⇨ *discourage*

pessimistic *adj* cynical, negative, glum, sullen, morose, fatalistic ➡ **bleak, sad** ⇨ *optimistic*

pet 1. *vb* pat, caress, fondle, stroke, tickle ➡ **rub**
2. *adj, n* ➡ **favorite**

If the word you want is not a main entry above, look below to find it.

periodical ➡ paper

periphery ➡ edge, circumference, circle

perish ➡ die

perishable ➡ mortal

periwig ➡ wig

perjurer ➡ liar

perk ➡ tip

permafrost ➡ ice

permanently ➡ forever, finally

permissible ➡ legal

permissive ➡ tolerant

permit ➡ let, ticket, license

perpendicular ➡ vertical, steep

perpetrate ➡ commit

perpetrator ➡ criminal

perpetual ➡ eternal

perpetually ➡ forever

perplex ➡ confuse

perplexed ➡ doubtful

perplexing ➡ mysterious

perplexity ➡ confusion

perquisite ➡ tip

persecute ➡ abuse

perseverance ➡ diligence, patience

persevering ➡ patient

persevere ➡ continue, live[1]

persist ➡ continue, live[1]

persistence ➡ diligence, patience

persistent ➡ patient, continual, permanent

person ➡ human being

personage ➡ celebrity

personal ➡ private

personnel ➡ faculty

perspiration ➡ sweat

perspire ➡ sweat

pert ➡ rude

pertain ➡ belong, concern

pertinaceous ➡ stubborn

pertinence ➡ relevance

pertinent ➡ relevant, fit[1]

perturb ➡ disturb, scare

peruse ➡ read

pervade ➡ occupy

perverse ➡ stubborn

perversion ➡ immorality

perversity ➡ immorality

pervert ➡ debase, distort

perverted ➡ immoral

pessimist ➡ skeptic

pest ➡ nuisance, bug

pester ➡ bother

pestilence ➡ epidemic

petcock ➡ faucet

petition ➡ appeal, ask

petrified ➡ afraid

petrify ➡ scare, harden

petrol ➡ gasoline

petroleum ➡ oil

petty ➡ trivial, mean

petulant ➡ temperamental, cross

pew ➡ seat

phantom ➡ ghost

pharaoh ➡ emperor

pharmaceutical ➡ medicinal

phase ➡ state, period

Ph.D. ➡ doctor

phenomenal ➡ special

phenomenon ➡ event, miracle

philanthropist ➡ patron

philanthropy ➡ generosity

➡ = synonym cross-reference • ⇨ = antonym cross-reference

philosopher *n* thinker, sage, logician, scholar

philosophy *n* metaphysics, theory, thought, ideology, esthetics, ethics ➡ **knowledge, wisdom, belief**

photograph *n* photo, snapshot, image, slide, print, likeness ➡ **picture, X ray**

photographer *n* camerman, cinematographer, paparazzo (*Italian; plural:* paparazzi), shutterbug (*informal*) ➡ **artist**

physical *adj* bodily, corporal, corporeal, fleshly ➡ **real**

picture 1. *n* portrait, image, drawing, painting, illustration, representation, diagram, sketch, cartoon, poster, work, plate, print ➡ **description, photograph, X ray**
2. *n* ➡ **movie**
3. *vb* ➡ **imagine**
4. *vb* ➡ **draw**

pile 1. *n* heap, stack, mound, hill, lump, wad, clump, mass, nugget ➡ **bulk, assortment**
2. *vb* heap, stack ➡ **gather**
3. *n* ➡ **post**

pillage 1. *vb* plunder, ransack, sack, loot ➡ **steal, attack**
2. *n* ➡ **theft, booty**

pilot 1. *n* aviator, flier, airman, aeronaut
2. *n* helmsman, navigator, coxswain, steersman
3. *vb* sail, navigate ➡ **lead, guide, drive**

pin 1. *n* safety pin, straight pin, bobby pin, hairpin, hat pin, cotter pin, brooch, tiepin, clip ➡ **nail**
2. *vb* attach ➡ **join, nail**

pine 1. *n* fir, evergreen ➡ **tree**
2. *vb* ➡ **grieve**
3. *vb* ➡ **want**

pioneer 1. *n* settler, homesteader, backwoodsman, frontiersman, immigrant, colonist, colonizer
2. *n* ➡ **creator**
3. *adj* ➡ **early**

pipe *n* tube, drainpipe, waterpipe, duct, conduit, pipeline, tubing, hose, funnel ➡ **channel**

If the word you want is not a main entry above, look below to find it.

Philistine ➡ boor

philosophical ➡ theoretical, profound

phobia ➡ fear

phone ➡ call

phony ➡ fake

photo ➡ photograph

photocopy ➡ reproduce, print, copy

phrase ➡ saying, say

physically challenged ➡ disabled

physician ➡ doctor

physics ➡ science

physique ➡ body

piazza ➡ court, porch

pick ➡ choose, gather, choice

pickax ➡ ax, axe

picket ➡ post, patrol, protest

pickle ➡ trouble

pick up ➡ continue

picky ➡ choosy

picnic ➡ meal

pictorial ➡ scenic

pictures ➡ movies

picturesque ➡ scenic

piddling ➡ trivial

pidgin ➡ dialect

pie ➡ pastry

piebald ➡ speckled

piece ➡ part, bit, block

pièce de résistance ➡ masterpiece

pier ➡ dock, jetty, post

pierce ➡ stick

piercing ➡ loud

pig ➡ glutton

pigeonhole ➡ stereotype

pigheaded ➡ stubborn

pigment ➡ paint

pigtail ➡ braid

pilfer ➡ steal

pilgrim ➡ traveler

pilgrimage ➡ trip

pill ➡ medicine

pillar ➡ post, support

pillow ➡ cushion

pinafore ➡ dress

pinch ➡ squeeze, steal, trouble, bit

ping ➡ peep

pinion ➡ limb

pink ➡ red

pinnacle ➡ top, tower

pioneering ➡ early

pious ➡ religious

pip ➡ seed

pipeline ➡ pipe

piping ➡ high

piquant ➡ spicy

---

n = noun • *vb* = verb • *adj* = adjective • *adv* = adverb • *prep* = preposition • *conj* = conjunction

pirate 1. *n* buccaneer, privateer, freebooter, corsair, plunderer, marauder ➡ **criminal, vandal**
2. *vb* ➡ **steal**

pitiful *adj* pathetic, piteous, pitiable, mournful, woeful, distressing, heartbreaking ➡ **sad, sorry, poor, unfortunate, emotional**

pity 1. *n* sympathy, compassion, empathy, mercy, forbearance, ruth, clemency, condolence, commiseration ➡ **kindness, comfort**
2. *vb* sympathize, commiserate, comfort
3. *n* ➡ **disaster**

place 1. *n* location, position, situation, locale, site, spot, locality, region, vicinity ➡ **space, zone**
2. *vb* locate, situate, assign, store ➡ **put**
3. *vb* ➡ **arrange**
4. *n* ➡ **house**
5. *n* ➡ **profession**

plain 1. *adj* simple, uncomplicated, unadorned, unvarnished, frugal, severe, austere, stark ➡ **common, humble, natural, naked** ⇨ *complicated*
2. *adj* unattractive, homely, drab, unlovely ➡ **ugly** ⇨ *pretty*
3. *adj* ➡ **obvious, straightforward**
4. *n* prairie, range, grassland, savanna, heath, moor, tundra, downs ➡ **field, plateau**

plan 1. *n* design, project, plot, schematic, outline, map ➡ **table**
2. *n* aim, intent, goal, purpose, strategy, scheme, plot, conspiracy, program, policy, platform, plank, provision ➡ **method, recipe**
3. *vb* plot, scheme, conspire, contrive, connive, chart, map, outline ➡ **arrange, prepare, intend**

planet *n* heavenly body, celestial body, satellite ➡ **earth, space**

plant 1. *n* shrub, weed, grass, bush, shrub, vegetation, flora, foliage, organism ➡ **flower, tree, herb, vegetable, fruit**
2. *n* ➡ **factory**
3. *vb* seed, sow, pot, transplant, propagate, set, broadcast, scatter ➡ **grow**
4. *vb* ➡ **put**

plate 1. *n* dish, platter, saucer, dinnerware, china ➡ **bowl, tray**
2. *n* ➡ **picture**
3. *n* ➡ **base**
4. *vb* laminate, overlay, gild, electroplate ➡ **cover**

plateau 1. *n* tableland, table, mesa, steppe, upland, highland ➡ **plain**
2. *n* ➡ **grade**

platform 1. *n* stage, dais, pulpit, rostrum, stand, riser
2. *n* ➡ **plan**

If the word you want is not a main entry above, look below to find it.

pirouette ➡ dance

pistol ➡ gun

pit ➡ dent, hole, grave, mine, seed

pitch ➡ throw, advertise, swing, slant, advertisement

pitch-black ➡ black, dark

pitcher ➡ bottle

piteous ➡ pitiful

pitfall ➡ trap

pitiable ➡ pitiful

pitiless ➡ mean

pitter-patter ➡ knock

pivot ➡ axis, turn

pixie ➡ fairy

pizzeria ➡ restaurant

placate ➡ pacify

place-kick ➡ kick

placement ➡ order

placid ➡ calm

plagiarize ➡ steal

plague ➡ epidemic, infest, bother

plainly ➡ apparently

plait ➡ braid, weave

plane ➡ airplane, level, side

plank ➡ board, wood, plan

plantation ➡ farm

planter ➡ farmer

plastic ➡ flexible

platitude ➡ cliché

platter ➡ plate, tray

➡ = synonym cross-reference • ⇨ = antonym cross-reference

play 1. *vb* frisk, sport, disport, romp, frolic, gambol, recreate
2. *vb* ➡ **compete**
3. *vb* perform, finger, bow, strum ➡ **practice, blow²**
4. *vb* ➡ **act**
5. *vb* run, show, present, air, broadcast
6. *n* recreation, horseplay, clowning ➡ **pleasure, entertainment**
7. *n* drama, dramatization, skit, pageant, tragedy, melodrama, comedy, farce, musical, mystery ➡ **program, movie**
8. *n* ➡ **movement**

pleasant 1. *adj* pleasurable, gratifying, agreeable, pleasing, enjoyable, congenial, satisfying, appealing, desirable, delightful, sweet ➡ **happy**
2. *adj* ➡ **nice, friendly**
3. *adj* ➡ **fair**

please *vb* delight, gratify, gladden, content, hearten ➡ **satisfy, entertain, pamper**

pleasure *n* amusement, joy, happiness, fun, delight, glee, enjoyment, pride, ecstasy, bliss, rapture, content, felicity ➡ **satisfaction, entertainment, play** ⇨ *pain*

pocket 1. *n* pouch, sac ➡ **bag**
2. *vb* ➡ **steal**

poem *n* verse, poetry, lyric, rhyme ➡ **stanza, song, work**

point 1. *n* end, tip, spike, tine ➡ **top, thorn**
2. *n* ➡ **cape**
3. *n* ➡ **subject**
4. *n* ➡ **detail**
5. *n* ➡ **moment**

poison 1. *n* venom, toxin, bane, infection, virus, germ
2. *vb* ➡ **kill**

If the word you want is not a main entry above, look below to find it.

plausibility ➡ possibility
plausible ➡ possible
plausibly ➡ probably
player ➡ actor, musician, athlete, contestant
playful ➡ lively
playground ➡ park
playing field ➡ field
playmate ➡ friend
playroom ➡ den
plaything ➡ toy
playwright ➡ writer
plaza ➡ court
plea ➡ appeal
plead ➡ argue, beg
pleased ➡ grateful
pleasing ➡ pleasant
pleasurable ➡ pleasant

pleat ➡ fold
plebeian ➡ common
pledge ➡ promise, dedicate, pawn
plenteous ➡ abundant
plentiful ➡ abundant, enough
plenty ➡ abundance, enough
plethora ➡ abundance
pliable ➡ flexible
pliant ➡ flexible
plight ➡ trouble
plink ➡ peep
plod ➡ walk, lag
plot ➡ plan, property, field, story
plow ➡ dig
ploy ➡ trick

pluck ➡ pull, gather, extract
plucky ➡ brave
plug ➡ close, repair, advertise, advertisement, top
plum ➡ purple
plumb ➡ vertical
plummet ➡ fall
plump ➡ fat, fall
plunder ➡ booty, pillage
plunderer ➡ pirate
plunge ➡ fall, drop, jump, stick, swim
plunk ➡ peep
plus ➡ besides, advantage
ply ➡ act
p.m. ➡ night, afternoon
poach ➡ boil, hunt, steal
pocketbook ➡ bag, wallet

pod ➡ shell, herd
poet ➡ writer
poetry ➡ poem
poignant ➡ emotional
pointed ➡ sharp
pointer ➡ tip
pointless ➡ unnecessary
point of view ➡ perspective
pointy ➡ sharp
poise ➡ balance, tact
poised ➡ calm
poisonous ➡ deadly
poke ➡ push, stick, blow¹
poker-faced ➡ blank
polar ➡ cold
pole ➡ bar, bat, paddle
poleax ➡ ax, axe

---

n = noun • *vb* = verb • *adj* = adjective • *adv* = adverb • *prep* = preposition • *conj* = conjunction

police 1. *n* authorities, officer ➡ **police officer**
2. *vb* ➡ **patrol**

police officer *n* policeman, policewoman, cop (*informal*), patrolman, patrolwoman, constable, sheriff, marshal, detective

polite *adj* courteous, well-mannered, civil, chivalrous, gracious ➡ **friendly, thoughtful, nice, prim** ⇨ *rude*

pompous *adj* grandiloquent, flowery, grandiose, bombastic, pretentious, turgid, condescending ➡ **proud**

poor 1. *adj* needy, penniless, destitute, broke, impoverished, deprived, indigent, poverty-stricken ⇨ *rich*
2. *adj* pitiful, sorry, paltry, inferior, shoddy, deficient, pedestrian, tawdry, unsatisfactory, inadequate, worthless, wretched, abject, lame

porch *n* veranda, stoop, piazza, patio, breezeway, portico, gallery

portable *adj* movable, transportable, mobile ⇨ *stationary*

porter *n* redcap, skycap, bellboy, bellhop, baggage carrier ➡ **doorman**

possession 1. *n* ownership, custody, title, proprietorship, receipt ➡ **control, rule**
2. *n* ➡ **property, acquisition**
3. *n* ➡ **colony**

possibility *n* probability, likelihood, chance, plausibility, prospect, expectation, eventuality, potential, potentiality

possible *adj* plausible, conceivable, believable, credible, feasible, potential, reasonable, imaginable, practicable, viable ➡ **likely**

post 1. *n* pillar, column, pedestal, stud, upright, picket, stanchion, pier, pile
2. *n* ➡ **profession**
3. *n* ➡ **mail**
4. *n* ➡ **base**
5. *vb* ➡ **send**

If the word you want is not a main entry above, look below to find it.

policeman ➡ police officer

policewoman ➡ police officer

policy ➡ plan

polish ➡ shine, finish, perfect, class, elegance, civilization

politic ➡ careful

poll ➡ vote, study

polliwog ➡ frog

pollute ➡ dirty, debase

polluted ➡ dirty

polyp ➡ growth

pomp ➡ ceremony

pond ➡ lake

ponder ➡ meditate

ponderous ➡ heavy

pontiff ➡ priest

pony ➡ horse

pool ➡ lake, lottery

pop ➡ bang, peep, soda, jump

pope ➡ priest

poppycock ➡ nonsense

populace ➡ people

popular ➡ common, fashionable, famous, favorite

popularity ➡ fame

population ➡ people

porcelain ➡ pottery

pore ➡ hole

pore over ➡ study

pornographic ➡ dirty

port ➡ harbor

portal ➡ door

portend ➡ predict

portent ➡ miracle

portico ➡ porch

portion ➡ part, excerpt, divide

portly ➡ fat

portrait ➡ picture, description

portray ➡ act, draw

portrayal ➡ description, role

pose ➡ posture, model, act

poser ➡ model

posh ➡ rich

position ➡ place, put, deploy, grade, profession, reputation, perspective

positive ➡ certain, good

positively ➡ certainly

possess ➡ own, keep

possessive ➡ greedy, jealous

possessor ➡ owner

possibly ➡ maybe

postcard ➡ letter

poster ➡ picture, advertisement

posterior ➡ back

postlude ➡ conclusion

➡ = synonym cross-reference • ⇨ = antonym cross-reference

posture *n* pose, stance, carriage, bearing, attitude

pot 1. *n* pan, saucepan, kettle, teakettle, teapot, coffeepot, vat, cauldron ➡ **bowl, container**
2. *vb* ➡ **plant**

pottery *n* ceramics, porcelain, china, earthenware, stoneware, terra cotta

poverty *n* destitution, want, need, penury, indigence, privation, impoverishment ➡ **hardship**

practical 1. *adj* matter-of-fact, down-to-earth, realistic, reasonable, rational, sensible, unsentimental ➡ **able** ⇨ *impractical*
2. *adj* ➡ **useful, efficient**
3. *adj* ➡ **virtual**

practically *adv* virtually, effectively, essentially, fundamentally, nearly, basically, principally ➡ **about**

practice 1. *vb* rehearse, drill, train ➡ **study, learn**
2. *vb* ➡ **use**
3. *n* rehearsal, repetition, preparation ➡ **discipline**
4. *n* ➡ **habit**

praise 1. *n* applause, acclaim, compliment, approval, adulation, acclamation, kudos, congratulations, flattery ➡ **respect**
2. *vb* commend, extol, acclaim, laud, compliment, honor, decorate, congratulate, toast, rave ➡ **celebrate, clap, flatter, worship**

praiseworthy *adj* commendable, laudable, deserving, creditable, estimable, worthy, meritorious

preach *vb* exhort, sermonize, moralize, proclaim ➡ **teach**

precede *vb* preface, herald, antedate, introduce ⇨ *follow*

precisely *adv* exactly, directly, right, due ➡ **correctly, carefully**

If the word you want is not a main entry above, look below to find it.

postman ➡ **letter carrier**

postmaster ➡ **letter carrier**

postmistress ➡ **letter carrier**

postpone ➡ **delay**

postscript ➡ **conclusion**

postulate ➡ **assume**

posy ➡ **bouquet, flower**

potency ➡ **strength**

potent ➡ **strong**

potentate ➡ **ruler**

potential ➡ **possible, latent, possibility**

potentiality ➡ **possibility**

potpourri ➡ **mixture, assortment**

potter ➡ **tinker**

pouch ➡ **bag, pocket**

pounce ➡ **jump**

pound ➡ **hit, pen**

pour ➡ **flow, rain, hurry**

pour out ➡ **empty**

pout ➡ **frown, mope**

poverty-stricken ➡ **poor**

powder ➡ **grind, snow**

powder blue ➡ **blue**

power ➡ **strength, energy, ability, right**

powerful ➡ **strong, important**

powerless ➡ **weak**

powerlessness ➡ **inability**

practicable ➡ **possible**

practical joke ➡ **joke**

pragmatic ➡ **useful**

prairie ➡ **plain**

prank ➡ **joke**

prate ➡ **chatter**

prattle ➡ **chatter, talk**

pray ➡ **appeal**

prayer ➡ **worship**

preacher ➡ **minister, speaker**

preamble ➡ **introduction**

precarious ➡ **unsteady, dangerous**

precaution ➡ **protection**

preceding ➡ **before, past**

precept ➡ **rule**

precinct ➡ **neighborhood**

precious ➡ **valuable, expensive, favorite**

precious stone ➡ **jewel**

precipice ➡ **cliff**

precipitate ➡ **sudden, rain**

precipitation ➡ **rain**

precipitous ➡ **steep**

précis ➡ **summary**

precise ➡ **correct, careful, neat, punctual, explicit**

precision ➡ **accuracy**

precocious ➡ **gifted, early**

n = noun • *vb* = verb • *adj* = adjective • *adv* = adverb • *prep* = preposition • *conj* = conjunction

predatory *adj* voracious, rapacious, ravenous, bloodthirsty, carnivorous ➡ **greedy**

predict *vb* forecast, foretell, prophesy, prognosticate, project, divine, tell, foresee, augur, portend, presage ➡ **anticipate**

prediction 1. *n* forecast, prognostication 2. *n* prophecy, divination, fortune-telling, augury

predominant *adj* dominant, preeminent, prevalent, prevailing ➡ **important**

prefer *vb* favor, endorse, advocate ➡ **choose, like, want**

preference *n* favorite, partiality, predilection, inclination, proclivity ➡ **choice, tendency**

pregnant 1. *adj* expecting, expectant, with child, gravid 2. *adj* ➡ **meaningful**

prejudice *n* intolerance, bigotry, bias, partiality, predisposition, predilection, favoritism, discrimination, racism, sexism, chauvinism, ageism ➡ **hatred**

prejudiced *adj* biased, unfair, unjust, partial, one-sided, partisan, predisposed, bigoted, intolerant, discriminatory

prepare *vb* develop, provide, ready, plan, adapt, prime, process, refine ➡ **arrange, cook, make, invent**

presence 1. *n* proximity, nearness, closeness ⇨ *absence* 2. *n* attendance, occurrence ➡ **existence** ⇨ *absence* 3. *n* ➡ **bearing, personality**

present 1. *adj* here, on hand ➡ **near** ⇨ *absent* 2. *vb* ➡ **give, offer** 3. *vb* ➡ **introduce** 4. *vb* ➡ **play, show** 5. *n* ➡ **gift**

If the word you want is not a main entry above, look below to find it.

predecessor ➡ ancestor

predicament ➡ trouble

predicate ➡ base

predilection ➡ prejudice, preference

predisposed ➡ prejudiced, ready

predisposition ➡ prejudice

predominantly ➡ chiefly

preeminent ➡ best, predominant

preface ➡ introduction, introduce, precede

preferable ➡ better

preferably ➡ more, instead

preferment ➡ promotion

preferred ➡ favorite

prehistoric ➡ early

preliminary ➡ early

prelude ➡ introduction

premature ➡ early

premier ➡ ruler

premise ➡ theory

premises ➡ property

premium ➡ best, prize

premonition ➡ warning

preoccupation ➡ obsession

preoccupied ➡ absorbed, absentminded

preoccupy ➡ interest

preparation ➡ practice

preparatory school ➡ school

prepared ➡ ready

preponderance ➡ most

preposterous ➡ foolish

prerequisite ➡ necessity

prerogative ➡ right

presage ➡ predict

prescience ➡ foresight

prescribe ➡ order, suggest

prescribed ➡ legal

prescription ➡ medicine, recipe

presentation ➡ display, introduction, program, delivery

presenter ➡ host

presently ➡ soon

preservation ➡ salvation

preserve ➡ save, keep, embalm, park, jelly

preside ➡ lead

president ➡ ruler

press ➡ push, squeeze, iron, urge

pressing ➡ urgent

pressure ➡ weight, energy, stress, force

prestidigitator ➡ magician

prestige ➡ fame, respect

presumably ➡ apparently, probably

presume ➡ assume, dare

presumption ➡ theory

presumptuous ➡ rude

presuppose ➡ assume

---

pretend *vb* feign, affect, simulate, profess ➡ **act, assume, imagine, lie, fake**

pretense 1. *n* affectation, deceit, deception, fabrication, trickery, misrepresentation, fraud ➡ **act, lie, disguise, dishonesty**
2. *n* excuse, pretext, subterfuge ➡ **trick**

pretty *adj* lovely, handsome, attractive, good-looking, fair, becoming, comely, striking ➡ **beautiful, cute** ⇨ *ugly*

prevent *vb* avert, hinder, forestall, check, restrain, thwart, foil, frustrate, deter, inhibit, stunt, hobble, leash ➡ **stop, block, discourage, contain** ⇨ *let*

prey 1. *n* quarry, victim, target
2. *vb* ➡ **eat**
3. *vb* ➡ **cheat**

price *n* charge, expense, cost, fare, payment, amount, fee, consideration, outlay ➡ **worth, bill**

pride 1. *n* self-respect, self-esteem, dignity, self-confidence ➡ **respect**
2. *n* vanity, conceit, arrogance, vainglory, egotism, hubris, narcissism, haughtiness
3. *n* ➡ **pleasure**

priest *n* vicar, bishop, cardinal, pope, pontiff, rabbi ➡ **minister, religious**

prim *adj* proper, formal, stiff, wooden, stilted, decorous ➡ **correct, neat, polite**

primitive 1. *adj* ➡ **basic**
2. *adj* ➡ **early**
3. *adj* uncivilized, simple, crude, rough, rustic, unsophisticated, untamed, aboriginal, pristine

principal 1. *adj* ➡ **important**
2. *n* headmaster, master, administrator, superintendent, dean ➡ **boss**
3. *n* ➡ **party**

print 1. *vb* publish, issue, reprint ➡ **write**
2. *vb* imprint, impress, engrave, stamp, emboss, inscribe
3. *n* etching, engraving, woodcut, lithograph, photocopy ➡ **photograph, picture**
4. *n* impression, imprint, indentation, fingerprint, footprint ➡ **track**
5. *n* text, printing, type, typescript, writing

prisoner *n* captive, inmate, detainee, internee, slave, hostage, jailbird (*informal*)

privacy *n* solitude, seclusion, isolation, retirement, withdrawal, confinement, quarantine, segregation ➡ **secrecy**

If the word you want is not a main entry above, look below to find it.

pretentious ➡ **pompous, proud**

preternatural ➡ **supernatural**

pretext ➡ **pretense**

prettiness ➡ **beauty**

prevail ➡ **win, excel, persuade**

prevailing ➡ **predominant**

prevalent ➡ **predominant, common**

prevaricate ➡ **lie**

prevaricator ➡ **liar**

previous ➡ **past**

previously ➡ **once, before**

priceless ➡ **valuable**

prick ➡ **stick**

prickle ➡ **tingle**

primal ➡ **early**

primarily ➡ **chiefly**

primary ➡ **basic, important, early**

prime ➡ **best, important, top, prepare**

prime minister ➡ **ruler**

primeval ➡ **early**

primordial ➡ **early**

prince ➡ **ruler**

princely ➡ **noble**

principally ➡ **chiefly, practically**

principle ➡ **rule, belief, cause, virtue**

printing ➡ **print, handwriting**

prior ➡ **past, older, religious**

prior to ➡ **before**

prioress ➡ **religious**

priory ➡ **monastery**

prison ➡ **jail**

pristine ➡ **clean, new, primitive**

---

n = noun • *vb* = verb • *adj* = adjective • *adv* = adverb • *prep* = preposition • *conj* = conjunction

private 1. *adj* secluded, isolated, remote, withdrawn, insular, quarantined
2. *adj* personal, individual, intimate, own
⇨ **public**
3. *adj* exclusive, restricted, reserved, special
⇨ **public**
4. *adj* ➡ **secret**

prize 1. *n* reward, premium, bonus, trophy, garland, laurel, winnings, purse ➡ **award, gift, booty**
2. *vb* ➡ **appreciate, respect**

probably *adv* presumably, apparently, plausibly, seemingly ➡ **maybe**
Note that **probably** *and its synonyms also express a degree of uncertainty about something, but not as much as* **maybe** *and its synonyms.*

problem 1. *n* mystery, puzzle, riddle, dilemma, enigma, ambiguity, conundrum ➡ **contradiction, question**
2. *n* ➡ **trouble**

product 1. *n* merchandise, commodity, goods, wares
2. *n* by product, outgrowth, derivative, derivation, offshoot, spin off ➡ **answer, effect**

productivity *n* turnout, output, production, volume ➡ **growth, efficiency**

profession *n* occupation, employment, appointment, vocation, avocation, calling, career, livelihood, post, position, situation, place, craft, trade ➡ **job, field, business, specialty**

profound *adj* deep, sage, sagacious, intellectual, philosophical, penetrating, discerning, erudite, cerebral ➡ **smart, thoughtful, serious**

program 1. *n* performance, concert, recital, show, production, broadcast, telecast, presentation, series ➡ **play, movie, entertainment**
2. *n* ➡ **list**
3. *n* ➡ **plan, course**

If the word you want is not a main entry above, look below to find it.

privateer ➡ pirate

privation ➡ poverty

privilege ➡ right

prized ➡ valuable

prizewinner ➡ winner

probability ➡ possibility

probable ➡ likely

probe ➡ stick, hunt, study, examine

proboscis ➡ nose

procedure ➡ method

proceed ➡ go, continue

process ➡ method, prepare

procession ➡ parade

proclaim ➡ advertise, preach

proclamation ➡ announcement

proclivity ➡ tendency, preference

procrastinate ➡ delay

procreate ➡ reproduce

procure ➡ get

procurement ➡ acquisition

prod ➡ push, urge

prodigal ➡ wasteful, abundant

prodigious ➡ huge

prodigy ➡ genius

produce ➡ make, cause, give, show, vegetable

production ➡ program, assembly, productivity

productive ➡ successful, efficient, fertile

profanity ➡ curse

profess ➡ pretend, tell

professor ➡ teacher, doctor

proffer ➡ offer

proficiency ➡ ability, efficiency

proficient ➡ able, expert, efficient

profile ➡ face, description

profit ➡ advantage, wage, earn

profitable ➡ useful

profligate ➡ wasteful

profoundness ➡ depth

profundity ➡ depth

profuse ➡ abundant, thick, rich

profusion ➡ abundance

progenitor ➡ ancestor

progeny ➡ child

prognosticate ➡ predict

prognostication ➡ prediction

progression ➡ progress

progressive ➡ forward, gifted, consecutive, liberal

prohibit ➡ forbid

prohibited ➡ illegal

prohibition ➡ ban

---

progress 1. *n* improvement, progression, headway, advance, advancement, momentum ➡ **movement, growth, success**
2. *vb* ➡ **go**

promise 1. *n* oath, vow, word, pledge, assurance, commitment, covenant, guarantee
2. *vb* swear, pledge, vow, assure, warrant ➡ **guarantee**

promote 1. *vb* raise, advance, elevate, graduate, upgrade
2. *vb* ➡ **back, support**
3. *vb* ➡ **advertise**

promotion 1. *n* advancement, preferment, elevation, raise
2. *n* ➡ **advertisement, advertising**

prone 1. *adj* ➡ **likely**
2. *adj* prostrate, flat, supine, recumbent, lying (down), reclining, horizontal
3. *adj* ➡ **vulnerable**

pronounce *vb* enunciate, articulate, utter, vocalize ➡ **say, tell**

proof *n* evidence, testimony, verification, certification, documentation, data, corroboration, confirmation, substantiation, authentication

property 1. *n* possessions, belongings, effects, goods, assets, holdings, capital, things, stuff ➡ **wealth, acquisition**
2. *n* land, lot, estate, yard, grounds, premises, plot, tract
3. *n* ➡ **quality**

prophet *n* seer, soothsayer, oracle, clairvoyant, medium, fortune teller, astrologer, diviner ➡ **magician**

prosper *vb* flourish, thrive, succeed, benefit, flower ➡ **blossom, grow, excel**

protect 1. *vb* defend, guard, shield, safeguard, fortify, watch, mind, tend ➡ **save, patrol** ⇨ *attack*
2. *vb* shelter, cover, cushion, pad

If the word you want is not a main entry above, look below to find it.

project ➡ plan, job, development, shoot, throw, swell, predict

projected ➡ future

projectile ➡ missile

projection ➡ branch

proliferate ➡ reproduce

proliferation ➡ growth

prolific ➡ fertile

prologue ➡ introduction

prolong ➡ lengthen

prom ➡ dance

prominence ➡ accent

prominent ➡ famous, obvious, important

promiscuous ➡ indiscriminate

promised land ➡ utopia

promontory ➡ cape, cliff

prompt ➡ early, fast, punctual, reminder, cause, urge

promptly ➡ quickly

pronounced ➡ obvious

pronouncement ➡ announcement

pronunciation ➡ accent, delivery

prop ➡ support

propaganda ➡ advertising

propagate ➡ reproduce, plant

propel ➡ shoot, throw, drive

propensity ➡ tendency

proper ➡ fit¹, correct, prim, good, special

properly ➡ well, correctly

proper name ➡ name

prophecy ➡ prediction

prophesy ➡ predict

proportion ➡ balance, size, share

proposal ➡ suggestion

propose ➡ offer, suggest, intend

proposition ➡ suggestion

proprietor ➡ owner

proprietorship ➡ possession

propulsion ➡ energy

prosaic ➡ dull

proscribe ➡ forbid

proscription ➡ ban

prosecute ➡ try

prospect ➡ view, possibility, hunt

prospective ➡ future

prosperity ➡ wealth, welfare, success

prosperous ➡ rich

prostrate ➡ prone

prostration ➡ exhaustion

protected ➡ safe

protective ➡ motherly, fatherly

protection 1. *n* security, safety, defense, caution, precaution, care, safeguard
➡ **support**
2. *n* shelter, refuge, cover, retreat, harbor, haven, sanctuary, asylum, shield, buffer

protest 1. *n* demonstration, strike, sit-in, teach-in, rally ➡ **complaint**
2. *vb* demonstrate, picket, strike, walk out
➡ **complain, object**
3. *vb* ➡ **complain, object, argue**

proud 1. *adj* egotistic, conceited, vain, arrogant, egocentric, haughty, smug, superior, pretentious ➡ **pompous**
⇨ *humble*
2. *adj* ➡ **grand**
3. *adj* ➡ **happy**

provincial 1. *adj* ➡ **rural**
2. *adj* narrow-minded, unsophisticated, parochial, unpolished, intolerant, insular, hidebound ➡ **naive, primitive, mean**

pseudonym *n* pen name, alias, stage name, nom de plume, nickname, sobriquet

public 1. *adj* civic, civil, governmental, communal, municipal, federal, social
➡ **common** ⇨ *private*
2. *n* ➡ **people**
3. *n* ➡ **following**

pull 1. *vb* tow, drag, haul, draw, tug, yank, jerk, pluck, attract, bring, tighten, strain
➡ **extract** ⇨ *push*
2. *vb* sprain, strain ➡ **hurt**
3. *n* tug, yank, drag, jerk, wrench
➡ **attraction**

punch 1. *vb* slap, belt, pummel, box ➡ **hit**
2. *n* ➡ **blow**[1]

punctual *adj* timely, prompt, precise, expeditious, punctilious ⇨ *late*

punish *vb* discipline, penalize, sentence, correct, fine ➡ **abuse, hurt, hit, scold, whip**

If the word you want is not a main entry above, look below to find it.

protector ➡ savior

protocol ➡ ceremony

prototype ➡ model

protract ➡ lengthen

protracted ➡ long

protrude ➡ swell

protrusion ➡ bulge

protuberance ➡ bulge

prove ➡ verify

proverb ➡ saying

proverbial ➡ legendary

provide ➡ supply, prepare

providential ➡ lucky

province ➡ state, field

provision ➡ plan, supply, excerpt

provisional ➡ temporary, experimental

provisions ➡ food

provocative ➡ interesting

provoke ➡ anger, dare, urge

prow ➡ front

prowess ➡ talent

prowl ➡ sneak

proximity ➡ presence

prudence ➡ foresight, economy

prudent ➡ careful, cheap

prudently ➡ carefully

prune ➡ cut, condense

pry ➡ lift, meddle, spy

prying ➡ curious, interference

psalm ➡ hymn

pseudonymous ➡ anonymous

psyche ➡ mind, soul

psychic ➡ supernatural

psychology ➡ science

psychotic ➡ insane

pub ➡ bar

puberty ➡ childhood

public assistance ➡ welfare

publication ➡ book

publicity ➡ advertising, notice

publicize ➡ advertise

public servant ➡ official

publish ➡ print, write

pucker ➡ wrinkle

pudgy ➡ fat

puerile ➡ childish

puff ➡ wind, smoke, breathe

puff up ➡ swell

pugnacious ➡ belligerent

puke ➡ vomit

pulchritude ➡ beauty

pull out ➡ retreat

pulpit ➡ platform

pulsar ➡ star

pulsate ➡ shake

pulsation ➡ impulse

pulse ➡ rhythm, impulse

pulverize ➡ grind

pummel ➡ punch

pun ➡ joke

punctilious ➡ punctual

puncture ➡ hole, stick

pungent ➡ fragrant, spicy

---

punishment *n* penalty, sentence, penance, deserts, retribution, consequence, discipline ➡ **abuse**

puppet 1. *n* marionette, dummy, mannequin ➡ **doll**
2. *n* ➡ **tool**

purple *adj, n* violet, magenta, lilac, mauve, plum, lavender

purposely *adv* deliberately, purposefully, intentionally, consciously, knowingly, willfully ⇨ *accidentally*

push 1. *vb* press, shove, impel, thrust, jostle, nudge, elbow, shoulder, shove, slide, thrust, prod, poke, ram, jam, wedge ➡ **move, force** ⇨ *pull*
2. *vb* ➡ **urge**
3. *n* ➡ **blow, impulse**

put *vb* set, lay, park, deposit, plant, position, implant, install, insert ➡ **place**

If the word you want is not a main entry above, look below to find it.

punk ➡ vandal

punt ➡ kick

puny ➡ weak

pupil ➡ student

puppy ➡ dog

purchase ➡ acquisition, sale, buy

pure ➡ innocent, perfect, natural, real

purify ➡ clean

purity ➡ virtue

purloin ➡ steal

purpose ➡ reason, object, plan, use, intend

purposefully ➡ purposely

purr ➡ hum

purse ➡ bag, wallet, prize

pursue ➡ follow

pursuit ➡ pastime, hunt

pushy ➡ meddlesome

put-down ➡ insult

put off ➡ delay

put out ➡ extinguish

putrefy ➡ decay

putrid ➡ smelly, bad

putter ➡ tinker

put up ➡ house

puzzle ➡ problem, confuse

puzzlement ➡ confusion

puzzle out ➡ solve

puzzling ➡ mysterious

pygmy ➡ midget

pyre ➡ fire

pyrotechnics ➡ fireworks

n = noun • *vb* = verb • *adj* = adjective • *adv* = adverb • *prep* = preposition • *conj* = conjunction

quality *n* property, characteristic, character, trait, attribute, air, atmosphere, texture, tone ➡ **class, feeling**

queen *n* monarch, sovereign, maharani (*India*), rani (*India*), sultana (*Muslim*) ➡ **ruler, empress**

question 1. *n* query, inquiry, interrogation, interrogative ➡ **problem** ⇨ *answer*
2. *n* ➡ **doubt**
3. *n* ➡ **subject**
4. *vb* ➡ **ask**

quickly *adv* speedily, hastily, hurriedly, fast, rapidly, expeditiously, instantaneously, promptly, headlong ➡ **now, soon**

quiet 1. *adj* silent, still, hushed, noiseless, soundless, inaudible, mute, mum, speechless ➡ **low** ⇨ *loud*
2. *n* ➡ **calm**
3. *vb* hush, silence, soften, mute, muffle, stifle, muzzle, gag

quote 1. *vb* cite, repeat, parrot, paraphrase, recite, declaim, render ➡ **mention, say, tell**
2. *n* ➡ **estimate**

If the word you want is not a main entry above, look below to find it.

quack ➡ cheat, hypocrite

quad ➡ court

quadrangle ➡ square, court

quadrilateral ➡ square

quaff ➡ drink

quagmire ➡ swamp

quail ➡ fear, retreat

quaint ➡ strange, cute

quake ➡ shake, fear, vibration, earthquake

qualification ➡ necessity, term

qualified ➡ able, ready

qualify ➡ let, soften

qualm ➡ doubt, nausea

quandary ➡ trouble

quantity ➡ number, size

quarantine ➡ privacy, separate

quarantined ➡ private

quarrel ➡ argue, argument

quarrelsome ➡ unfriendly

quarry ➡ prey, mine

quarter ➡ term, zone, neighborhood, divide, house

quash ➡ subdue, contain

quaver ➡ vibration, shake

quay ➡ dock

queasiness ➡ nausea

queasy ➡ sick

queer ➡ strange, suspicious

quell ➡ contain

quench ➡ extinguish, contain, satisfy

query ➡ question, ask

quest ➡ hunt

questionable ➡ doubtful

queue ➡ braid, row

quibble ➡ argue

quick ➡ fast, agile, smart, alive

quicken ➡ hurry

quill ➡ pen

quilt ➡ blanket

quintessence ➡ essence

quip ➡ joke

quirk ➡ habit

quit ➡ abandon, leave, surrender

quite ➡ completely, very

quiver ➡ shake, vibration

quixotic ➡ impractical

quiz ➡ examination, examine, ask

quota ➡ share

quotation ➡ excerpt, estimate

➡ = synonym cross-reference • ⇨ = antonym cross-reference

R

race 1. *n* run, dash, sprint, relay, marathon, footrace, horse race, steeplechase, derby ➡ **game**
2. *vb* ➡ **run, hurry**
3. *n* ➡ **type**
4. *n* ➡ **humanity**

ragged *adj* tattered, frayed, threadbare, torn, rent ➡ **old, shabby**

rain 1. *n* precipitation, shower, downpour, drizzle, cloudburst, torrent ➡ **storm**
2. *vb* pour, drizzle, sprinkle, shower, teem, precipitate

range 1. *n* extent, scope, spread, reach, compass, sweep, spectrum ➡ **assortment, space, horizon**
2. *n* ➡ **plain**
3. *vb* ➡ **wander**
4. *vb* ➡ **spread**

rare *adj* uncommon, scarce, infrequent, occasional ➡ **special, valuable**

rascal *n* scoundrel, villain, knave, wretch, scamp, imp, sneak, charlatan, fraud, swindler, rogue, rake, libertine, lecher ➡ **bully, criminal**

If the word you want is not a main entry above, look below to find it.

rabbi ➡ priest

racetrack ➡ course

rack ➡ shelf

racket ➡ noise

racy ➡ dirty

radiance ➡ light[1]

radiant ➡ bright

radiate ➡ shine, throw

radiation ➡ X ray

radical ➡ excessive, liberal, extremist

radiograph ➡ X ray

raffle ➡ lottery

rafter ➡ beam, board

rag ➡ cloth

ragamuffin ➡ urchin

rage ➡ anger, hysteria, fashion

raging ➡ rough, wild

raid ➡ attack

rail ➡ bar

raincoat ➡ coat

raindrop ➡ drop

rainforest ➡ forest

rainspout ➡ gargoyle

rainstorm ➡ storm

rainy ➡ wet, stormy

raise ➡ lift, grow, adopt, build, broach, promote, promotion

raison d'être ➡ basis

rajah ➡ king

rake ➡ dig, rascal

rally ➡ mobilize, protest

ram ➡ push

ramble ➡ wander, chatter

rambling ➡ indirect

rambunctious ➡ loud

ramp ➡ channel

rampage ➡ disturbance

rampant ➡ wild

rampart ➡ wall

ranch ➡ farm

rancher ➡ farmer

ranching ➡ farming

rancid ➡ sour, smelly, bad

random ➡ arbitrary

R & R ➡ vacation

range ➡ plain

rani ➡ queen

rank ➡ grade, row, arrange, smelly

rankle ➡ bother

ransack ➡ pillage, hunt

ransom ➡ recover

rant ➡ yell

rap ➡ knock, talk

rapacious ➡ greedy, predatory

rapid ➡ fast, sharp

rapidity ➡ speed

rapidly ➡ quickly

rapier ➡ sword

rapport ➡ relationship

rapture ➡ pleasure

rarely ➡ seldom

rarity ➡ miracle

rascality ➡ mischief

rash ➡ thoughtless, imprudent, epidemic

rasp ➡ squeak

raspy ➡ hoarse

rate ➡ speed, deserve

rather ➡ very, more, instead

ratification ➡ approval

ratify ➡ approve

ratio ➡ share

ration ➡ share, budget

rational ➡ practical, sane

rationale ➡ reason

rations ➡ food

rattle ➡ embarrass, bang

raucous ➡ loud

ravage ➡ destroy, attack

rave ➡ yell, praise, good

raven ➡ black

ravenous ➡ hungry, predatory

ravine ➡ canyon

ravishing ➡ beautiful

raw ➡ natural, cold, sore

rawhide ➡ hide

ray ➡ light[1]

n = noun • *vb* = verb • *adj* = adjective • *adv* = adverb • *prep* = preposition • *conj* = conjunction

read 1. *vb* peruse, skim, scan, browse
➡ **study**
2. *vb* comprehend, decipher, decode, perceive
3. *vb* indicate, register, record ➡ **show**

ready 1. *adj* prepared, set, qualified, ripe, equipped ➡ **available**
2. *adj* willing, disposed, predisposed
➡ **eager, likely**
3. *vb* ➡ **prepare**

real 1. *adj* actual, material, tangible, substantive, concrete, objective, solid, true, palpable ➡ **physical** ⇨ *imaginary*
2. *adj* actual, genuine, authentic, bona fide, veritable, literal, legitimate, pure ➡ **natural** ⇨ *fake*

really 1. *adv* actually, genuinely, literally, indeed, veritably ➡ **certainly**
2. *adv* ➡ **very**

reason 1. *n* purpose, cause, motive, explanation, call, grounds, need, rationale ➡ **necessity, incentive, justification**
2. *n* logic, reasoning, thinking, induction, deduction, analysis ➡ **wisdom**
3. *vb* ➡ **think, infer**
4. *n* sanity, mental health, lucidity, saneness

rebel 1. *vb* revolt, mutiny, resist, defy
➡ **face, dare**
2. *n* revolutionary, insurgent, mutineer, subversive, dissident, freedom fighter, traitor, turncoat ➡ **extremist**

rebellious *adj* disobedient, mutinous, defiant, insubordinate, seditious

receive 1. *vb* accept, admit, take, inherit, greet
➡ **get** ⇨ *give, refuse*
2. *vb* ➡ **welcome, entertain**

recently *adv* lately, newly, just, latterly

recipe *n* formula, directions, instructions, prescription ➡ **plan**

If the word you want is not a main entry above, look below to find it.

raze ➡ destroy

razor ➡ knife

reach ➡ come, touch, range

react ➡ answer

reaction ➡ answer

reactionary ➡ conservative

readable ➡ legible

readers ➡ audience

reading ➡ tryout

realign ➡ straighten

realistic ➡ practical, explicit

reality ➡ existence, certainty

realize ➡ learn, know, earn

realm ➡ country, field

reap ➡ cut, gather

reappear ➡ return

reappearance ➡ return

rear ➡ back, adopt, grow, lift, tower

rearend ➡ back, collide

rearward ➡ backward

reasonable ➡ practical, sane, possible, cheap

reasoning ➡ reason

reassure ➡ comfort

reawaken ➡ renew

reawakening ➡ revival

rebate ➡ refund

rebellion ➡ revolution, disobedience

rebirth ➡ revival

rebound ➡ reflect, return

rebuff ➡ rejection, refuse

rebuild ➡ fix

rebuke ➡ scold

rebut ➡ disprove

recall ➡ remember, memory

recapitulate ➡ repeat

recede ➡ retreat

receipt ➡ ticket, possession

receivable ➡ due

recent ➡ new, modern

receptacle ➡ container

reception ➡ welcome, party, treatment

recess ➡ break, vacation, bay

recession ➡ depression

reciprocate ➡ alternate, answer

reciprocation ➡ answer

recital ➡ program

recite ➡ quote, tell

reckless ➡ thoughtless, wasteful

reckon ➡ guess, estimate

reckoning ➡ score, addition

reclaim ➡ recover

recline ➡ lie

reclining ➡ prone

recluse ➡ hermit

recognition ➡ gratitude

recognize ➡ remember, distinguish, know

recoil ➡ retreat, jump

recollect ➡ remember

recollection ➡ memory

recommence ➡ continue

recommend ➡ suggest, approve

recommendation ➡ advice, suggestion

---

recover *vb* regain, retrieve, recoup, reclaim, redeem, ransom ➡ **find, save**

red 1. *adj, n* pink, scarlet, crimson, maroon, vermilion, carmine, ruby, rose
2. *adj* ruddy, rosy, flushed, florid, blushing

reflect 1. *vb* echo, mirror, ricochet, rebound, bounce
2. *vb* ➡ **consider, meditate**

refrigerator *n* icebox, fridge, freezer, cooler

refund 1. *vb* reimburse, repay, remit, compensate ➡ **pay**

2. *n* reimbursement, repayment, compensation, rebate

refuse 1. *vb* deny, reject, decline, dismiss, disapprove, spurn, repudiate, rebuff, snub, scorn, flout ➡ **deprive, repel**
2. *n* ➡ **trash**

regret 1. *vb* repent, apologize, bewail, bemoan, lament, deplore, rue ➡ **grieve**
2. *n* compunction, repentance
➡ **disappointment, sorrow, shame**

If the word you want is not a main entry above, look below to find it.

recompense ➡ pay

reconcile ➡ correct, decide

reconciliation ➡ peace

recondition ➡ fix

reconnoiter ➡ patrol

record ➡ document, list, write, read

recount ➡ describe, repeat

recoup ➡ recover

recourse ➡ choice

recovery ➡ return, cure

recreate ➡ play

recreation ➡ game, leisure, entertainment, play

recreational area ➡ park

recreation center ➡ gymnasium

recreation room ➡ den

rec room ➡ den

recruit ➡ soldier, hire

rectangle ➡ square

rectangular ➡ square

rectification ➡ correction

rectify ➡ correct

rectilinear ➡ square

rector ➡ minister

recumbent ➡ prone

recuperate ➡ rest

recuperation ➡ cure

recur ➡ repeat, return, happen

recurrence ➡ return, relapse

recurrent ➡ frequent, periodic

recurrently ➡ often

recycling center ➡ dump

redcap ➡ porter

redden ➡ blush

redecorate ➡ decorate

redecoration ➡ decoration

redeem ➡ balance, recover

redeemer ➡ savior

redemption ➡ salvation

redirect ➡ detour

redo ➡ repeat

redolent ➡ fragrant

redress ➡ correct

reduce ➡ decrease

reduced ➡ less

reduction ➡ subtraction, drop, bargain, model

redundant ➡ unnecessary, talkative

reduplicate ➡ repeat

reek ➡ smell

reel ➡ swing

reestablish ➡ renew

referee ➡ judge, negotiate

referendum ➡ vote

refer to ➡ mention, concern, use

refill ➡ renew

refine ➡ prepare

refinement ➡ class, civilization

reflective ➡ thoughtful

reflector ➡ mirror

reflex ➡ automatic, habit

reform ➡ correct

reformatory ➡ jail

reformist ➡ liberal

refrain ➡ abstain, chorus, stanza

refresh ➡ renew

refreshment ➡ meal, food, drink

refrigerate ➡ cool

refuge ➡ protection, park

refugee ➡ exile

refurbish ➡ decorate

refusal ➡ rejection

refute ➡ contradict, disprove

regain ➡ recover

regal ➡ noble, grand

regale ➡ entertain

regard ➡ look, notice, respect, concern

regarding ➡ about

regardless ➡ anyway

regime ➡ government

regimen ➡ discipline

regimentation ➡ discipline

region ➡ zone, place

register ➡ read, join, list, table, cash register

registration ➡ license

regress ➡ relapse

regression ➡ relapse

regressive ➡ backward

regressively ➡ backward

regrets ➡ apology

regrettable ➡ unfortunate

regular ➡ usual, frequent, straight, patron

regularly *adv* constantly, invariably, always, ever, continually, habitually, routinely, religiously, naturally, typically ➡ **often, usually, forever**

rejection *n* refusal, rebuff, denial, dismissal, renunciation, repudiation, veto

relapse 1. *vb* regress, backslide, revert, deteriorate, lapse, retrogress, worsen
2. *n* regression, reversion, recurrence, reverse, setback

relationship *n* relation, kinship, affinity, rapport, compatibility ➡ **link, friendship**

relevance *n* connection, bearing, significance, pertinence ➡ **importance**

relevant *adj* pertinent, germane, apposite, applicable, apropos, related, relative ➡ **fit**

reliable *adj* dependable, trustworthy, responsible, reputable, unimpeachable, solid, conscientious, sure, surefire ➡ **faithful, able, indisputable**

relieve 1. *vb* alleviate, ease, soothe, lessen, lighten, mitigate, allay ➡ **help, please**

2. *vb* dismiss, replace, discharge, substitute, excuse ➡ **free**

religion 1. *n* faith, mythology, theology, religiosity, spirituality, orthodoxy ➡ **belief, philosophy**
2. *n* denomination, sect, order, cult

religious 1. *adj* devout, pious, spiritual, orthodox, godly, reverent, God-fearing, reverential, churchgoing ➡ **faithful**
2. *adj* sacred, divine, ecclesiastical, clerical, liturgical, theological ➡ **holy**
3. *n* monk, friar, brother, abbot, prior, nun, sister, abbess, prioress ➡ **priest, minister**

reluctant *adj* hesitant, unwilling, grudging, disinclined, loath, averse, diffident, squeamish

remainder *n* remains, rest, remnant, residue, balance, surplus

remark 1. *n* comment, statement, mention, observation, commentary, utterance ➡ **saying**
2. *vb* ➡ **say**
3. *vb* ➡ **see**

If the word you want is not a main entry above, look below to find it.

regulate ➡ adjust, control
regulation ➡ rule
regurgitate ➡ vomit
rehabilitation ➡ cure
rehabilitation center ➡ hospital
rehash ➡ repeat
rehearsal ➡ practice
rehearse ➡ practice, repeat
reign ➡ govern
reimburse ➡ refund
reimbursement ➡ refund, return
rein ➡ rope
reinforce ➡ strengthen

reinforcement ➡ support
reins ➡ wheel
reiterate ➡ repeat
reject ➡ refuse, exclude, discard
rejected ➡ abandoned
rejoice ➡ celebrate
rejoinder ➡ answer
rejuvenate ➡ renew
rejuvenation ➡ revival
rekindle ➡ renew
relate ➡ tell, belong
related ➡ relevant
relating to ➡ about

relation ➡ family, relationship
relative ➡ family, relevant
relax ➡ calm, rest
relaxation ➡ comfort, leisure, rest
relaxed ➡ calm
relay ➡ race, broadcast
release ➡ free
relegate ➡ entrust
relent ➡ surrender
relentless ➡ continual, mean
relic ➡ antique
relief ➡ help

religiosity ➡ religion
religiously ➡ regularly
relinquish ➡ surrender
relish ➡ like, appreciate, spice
relocate ➡ move
rely ➡ depend
remain ➡ wait, continue
remains ➡ remainder, body
remand ➡ jail
remarkable ➡ great, special
remedial ➡ medicinal
remedy ➡ cure, correction, heal, correct

remember *vb* recall, recollect, reminisce, remind, recognize, commemorate, memorialize ➡ **know, learn** ⇨ *forget*

reminder 1. *n* hint, cue, notice, prompt ➡ **warning, letter**
2. *n* souvenir, memento, token, remembrance, keepsake, memorial

renew 1. *vb* restore, revive, rejuvenate, refresh, reawaken, invigorate, reestablish, rekindle, update ➡ **continue**
2. *vb* refill, replenish, replace, restock
3. *vb* ➡ **fix**

repair 1. *n* adjustment, improvement, renovation, restoration, patch, plug, mend, service, servicing ➡ **correction**
2. *vb* ➡ **fix**

repeat 1. *vb* redo, replicate, duplicate, reduplicate ➡ **reproduce**
2. *vb* recur, reoccur
3. *vb* reiterate, restate, recapitulate, echo, rehearse, rehash, recount ➡ **quote**

repel 1. *vb* repulse, foil, ward off, stave off, fend off, withstand, parry ➡ **refuse**
2. *vb* ➡ **disgust**

report 1. *n* essay, paper, composition, theme, treatise, thesis, dissertation, article ➡ **announcement, speech, story, study**
2. *n* ➡ **bang**
3. *vb* ➡ **tell**

reporter *n* journalist, correspondent, newspaperman, newspaperwoman, newsman, newswoman, newscaster, anchor ➡ **writer**
Note that **reporters** *and other newspeople are referred to as a group as* the press, the media, *and* the fourth estate.

If the word you want is not a main entry above, look below to find it.

remembrance ➡ reminder, memory

remind ➡ remember

reminisce ➡ remember

reminiscence ➡ memory

remiss ➡ negligent

remission ➡ forgiveness

remit ➡ refund

remnant ➡ remainder, cloth

remorse ➡ shame

remorseful ➡ sorry

remote ➡ far, foreign, private, cool

removal ➡ suspension, movement

remove ➡ move, subtract, exclude, oust, empty, extract, shed

removed ➡ far

remunerate ➡ pay

renaissance ➡ revival

rend ➡ rip

render ➡ quote, translate, give, act, do

rendezvous ➡ meeting, gather

rendition ➡ translation

renegade ➡ runaway

renewal ➡ revival

renounce ➡ abstain, abandon

renovate ➡ fix

renovation ➡ repair

renown ➡ fame

renowned ➡ famous

rent ➡ hire, borrow, ragged, rip

rental ➡ loan

renter ➡ occupant

renunciation ➡ rejection, surrender

reoccur ➡ repeat, return

reoccurrence ➡ return

repairman ➡ mechanic

repair shop ➡ garage

reparation ➡ correction

repast ➡ meal, feast

repay ➡ refund, revenge

repayment ➡ refund, return, revenge

repeal ➡ abolish

repeatedly ➡ often

repellent ➡ ugly

repent ➡ regret

repentance ➡ regret

repentant ➡ sorry

repetition ➡ practice

repetitious ➡ talkative

replace ➡ renew, change, relieve, follow

replacement ➡ alternate

replenish ➡ renew

replete ➡ full

replica ➡ duplicate

replicate ➡ repeat

reply ➡ answer

repose ➡ peace, sleep, leisure, rest, comfort, lie

repository ➡ bank

represent ➡ describe, embody

representation ➡ picture, model, example

representative ➡ example, agent

repress ➡ abuse, contain

repression ➡ tyranny

reprieve ➡ forgiveness

reprimand ➡ scold

reprint ➡ print

reproach ➡ scold, complaint

n = noun • *vb* = verb • *adj* = adjective • *adv* = adverb • *prep* = preposition • *conj* = conjunction

reproduce 1. *vb* copy, duplicate, photocopy, clone ➡ **imitate**
2. *vb* procreate, breed, propagate, multiply, proliferate, generate, beget, spawn, hatch

reptile *n* reptilian, amphibian, lizard ➡ **snake, animal**

reputation *n* status, position, repute, estimation, character, name

resemble *vb* look like, take after, match, approximate, favor, correspond

resolute *adj* strong-minded, determined, resolved, steadfast, unwavering, staunch, unyielding, adamant, uncompromising, assured, decisive ➡ **brave, faithful, stubborn**

respect 1. *n* admiration, honor, reverence, dignity, homage, esteem, regard, estimation, deference, courtesy, awe, wonder, prestige ➡ **pride**
2. *vb* esteem, admire, revere, value, prize, cherish ➡ **appreciate**
3. *vb* ➡ **keep**

rest 1. *vb* relax, repose, unwind, recuperate, lounge, loaf, laze, idle, vegetate (*informal*) ➡ **sleep, lie**
2. *vb* ➡ **depend**
3. *n* relaxation, repose, ease ➡ **sleep, break, vacation**
4. *n* ➡ **remainder**

restaurant *n* café, inn, deli, diner, cafeteria, tavern, luncheonette, bistro, pizzeria, canteen, tearoom, coffeehouse

---

If the word you want is not a main entry above, look below to find it.

reproduction ➡ copy
reprove ➡ scold
reptilian ➡ reptile
republic ➡ country
repudiate ➡ refuse
repudiation ➡ rejection
repugnance ➡ disgust
repugnant ➡ ugly
repulse ➡ repel
repulsive ➡ ugly, bad
reputable ➡ good, reliable
repute ➡ reputation
reputedly ➡ apparently
request ➡ ask, appeal, invitation
requiem ➡ dirge
require ➡ force, need, insist
required ➡ necessary

requirement ➡ necessity
requisite ➡ necessary, necessity
requite ➡ revenge
rescind ➡ abolish
rescue ➡ save, escape
rescuer ➡ savior
research ➡ study
resemblance ➡ similarity
resent ➡ envy
resentful ➡ jealous
resentment ➡ envy
reservation ➡ park, doubt, term
reserve ➡ park, supply
reserved ➡ shy, private, cool
reservoir ➡ well, lake, supply
reside ➡ live[1]

residence ➡ home
resident ➡ citizen, occupant
residential ➡ family
residue ➡ remainder
resign ➡ surrender, abandon
resignation ➡ surrender
resigned ➡ passive
resilient ➡ tough, flexible
resist ➡ rebel, fight
resistance ➡ fight, friction
resistant ➡ unbreakable
resolution ➡ will, answer, decision, clarity
resolve ➡ decide, solve, will
resolved ➡ resolute
resonant ➡ loud
resort ➡ hotel
resort to ➡ use

resound ➡ ring
resounding ➡ loud
resource ➡ support
resourceful ➡ ambitious
resources ➡ budget
respectable ➡ correct, good
respectful ➡ good
respective ➡ special
respiration ➡ breath
respire ➡ breathe
respite ➡ break, vacation
resplendent ➡ rich
respond ➡ answer
response ➡ answer
responsibility ➡ duty, guilt
responsible ➡ reliable, guilty
restate ➡ repeat

---

retreat 1. *vb* withdraw, retire, recede, ebb, back out, back down, recoil, shrink, quail, pull out ➡ **abandon, leave**
2. *n* ➡ **protection**
3. *n* ➡ **hotel**

return 1. *vb* come back, go back, revisit, recur, reoccur, resurface, reappear, rebound ➡ **renew**
2. *n* arrival, homecoming, reappearance, recurrence, reoccurrence, resurgence
3. *n* recovery, restoration, restitution, reimbursement, repayment
4. *n* ➡ **wage**

reveal 1. *vb* disclose, divulge, confess, bare, betray ➡ **discover** ⇨ *hide*
2. *vb* expose, uncover, unveil, unearth ➡ **show**

revenge 1. *n* vengeance, retaliation, repayment, compensation, satisfaction, vindication
2. *vb* avenge, retaliate, repay, requite, vindicate

revengeful *adj* vindictive, vengeful, avenging, retaliatory, spiteful ➡ **mean**

revival *n* rebirth, renaissance, resurrection, renewal, reawakening, rejuvenation, revitalization

revolution 1. *n* rebellion, revolt, insurrection, uprising, coup, coup d'état, insurgence ➡ **treason, disturbance**
2. *n* ➡ **change**
3. *n* ➡ **circle**

rhythm *n* beat, cadence, meter, tempo, time, measure, swing, pulse

---

If the word you want is not a main entry above, look below to find it.

restful ➡ comfortable
resting ➡ asleep
restitution ➡ return
restless ➡ nervous
restock ➡ renew
restoration ➡ repair, return
restore ➡ fix, renew
restrain ➡ prevent, contain
restraint ➡ bond
restrict ➡ bar
restricted ➡ finite, private
restriction ➡ ban, term
restroom ➡ bathroom
result ➡ effect, answer
resume ➡ continue
resurface ➡ return
resurgence ➡ return
resurrection ➡ revival
retail ➡ sell
retain ➡ keep, own

retainer ➡ servant
retaliate ➡ revenge
retaliation ➡ revenge
retaliatory ➡ revengeful
retard ➡ delay
retch ➡ vomit
retinue ➡ court, following
retire ➡ retreat
retirement ➡ privacy
retiring ➡ shy
retort ➡ answer
retract ➡ extract
retribution ➡ punishment
retrieve ➡ recover, find
retrograde ➡ backward
retrogress ➡ relapse
reunion ➡ meeting
revel ➡ celebrate
revelation ➡ announcement

revelry ➡ party
revenue ➡ money, wage
revere ➡ respect, love, worship
reverence ➡ respect, worship
reverent ➡ religious
reverential ➡ religious
reverie ➡ dream
reverse ➡ back, opposite, relapse, change
reversed ➡ backward, upside down
reversion ➡ relapse
revert ➡ relapse
review ➡ study
reviewer ➡ judge
revile ➡ curse
revise ➡ correct
revision ➡ correction
revisit ➡ return

revitalization ➡ revival
revive ➡ renew
revoke ➡ abolish
revolt ➡ revolution, rebel, disgust
revolting ➡ ugly
revolutionary ➡ rebel
revolve ➡ turn
revolver ➡ gun
revulsion ➡ hatred, disgust
reward ➡ prize, pay, tip
rhetorical ➡ theoretical
rhetorician ➡ speaker
rhyme ➡ poem
rhythmical ➡ musical
rib ➡ bar
ribald ➡ dirty
ribbon ➡ band, award
ribcage ➡ chest
ribs ➡ chest

n = noun • *vb* = verb • *adj* = adjective • *adv* = adverb • *prep* = preposition • *conj* = conjunction

rich 1. *adj* wealthy, affluent, prosperous, well-to-do, moneyed, well-off, comfortable, posh ➡ **successful** ⇨ *poor*
2. *adj* opulent, resplendent, ornate, lavish, lush, luxurious, profuse ➡ **grand, fashionable, expensive, fancy**
3. *adj* sweet, sugary, creamy, buttery, fattening, luscious, succulent, cloying, saccharine, honeyed ➡ **delicious**
4. *n* ➡ **aristocracy**

rider 1. *n* passenger, hitchhiker, cyclist, bicyclist, motorcyclist
2. *n* jockey, equestrian, horseman, horsewoman
3. *n* ➡ **addition**

ridicule 1. *n* derision, mockery, scorn, disdain ➡ **laughter**
2. *vb* jeer, belittle, deprecate, disparage, mock, deride, scoff, gibe ➡ **insult**

right 1. *n* power, privilege, prerogative, authority, license ➡ **freedom**
2. *adj* ➡ **correct, fit, fair** ⇨ *wrong*
3. *adv* ➡ **correctly**

4. *adv* ➡ **soon**
5. *adv* ➡ **precisely**

ring 1. *n* hoop, circlet ➡ **band, circle**
2. *n* chime, knell, toll, peal, clang, jingle, jangle, tinkle, clang, tintinnabulation ➡ **noise**
3. *n* ➡ **group**
4. *vb* circle, encircle, encompass, surround, enclose, loop, gird
5. *vb* resound, peal, knell, chime, toll, jingle, jangle, clang, bong, ding, sound, tinkle
6. *vb* ➡ **call**

rip 1. *vb* tear, rend, shred ➡ **cut, separate**
2. *n* tear, rent ➡ **hole, cut**

river 1. *n* stream, creek, brook, rivulet, tributary, estuary
2. *n* ➡ **flood**
Both **creek** *and* **brook** *are widely used terms for a small stream. Both words often refer to streams of the same size, but some people use* **brook** *to refer to a stream smaller than one they would call a* **creek**.

If the word you want is not a main entry above, look below to find it.

riches ➡ wealth
rickety ➡ weak
ricochet ➡ reflect
rid ➡ exclude
riddle ➡ problem, stick
ride ➡ drive
ridge ➡ mountain, hill
ridiculous ➡ foolish, funny
rifle ➡ steal, gun
rift ➡ break

rig ➡ supply, tinker
right away ➡ now
righteous ➡ good
right-wing ➡ conservative
rigid ➡ firm
rigorous ➡ hard, strict
rile ➡ anger
rim ➡ edge
rind ➡ peel
ringlet ➡ lock

rinse ➡ clean, wet, cleaning
riot ➡ disturbance
ripe ➡ ready, adult
ripen ➡ grow
riposte ➡ answer
ripple ➡ wave, rustle
rise ➡ ascend, climb, appear, tower, slant, growth
riser ➡ platform
risk ➡ danger, bet, dare, jeopardize

risky ➡ dangerous
risqué ➡ dirty
rite ➡ ceremony
ritual ➡ ceremony
rival ➡ enemy, opponent, competitive, compete
rivalry ➡ competition
rivet ➡ nail
riveting ➡ exciting

---

road *n* street, avenue, boulevard, thoroughfare, artery, roadway, lane, alley ➡ **highway, path**

rock 1. *n* stone, pebble, boulder, gravel, cobblestone ➡ **jewel**
2. *vb* ➡ **swing**

role *n* character, part, portrayal, bit ➡ **function**

room 1. *n* chamber, apartment, salon, suite, lodging, flat, gallery ➡ **living room, kitchen, bedroom, dining room, bathroom, den, basement, hall, attic**
2. *n* ➡ **space**
3. *vb* ➡ **live**[1]

rope *n* line, lasso, lariat, cable, wire, guy, painter, tether, leash, rein, strap ➡ **string**

rough 1. *adj* coarse, uneven, rugged, irregular, bumpy, jagged, crumpled, rumpled, harsh, scratchy ➡ **hoarse**
2. *adj* choppy, raging, ruffled, wild ➡ **stormy**
3. *adj* ➡ **rude, primitive**
4. *adj* ➡ **hard**
5. *adj* ➡ **approximate**

round 1. *adj* circular, spherical, cylindrical, oval, globular, rotund
2. *adv* ➡ **about**
3. *n* circuit, cycle, loop, beat, turn ➡ **period**

row 1. *n* line, string, file, rank, column, chain, queue, series, sequence
2. *n* ➡ **argument**
3. *vb* ➡ **paddle**

rub 1. *vb* scrape, chafe, graze, skim, brush, abrade, scuff, scratch ➡ **grind**
2. *vb* knead, massage, smooth, stroke ➡ **touch, pet**
3. *vb* daub, smear, spread, slather, anoint, dab, swab

rubber band *n* elastic, elastic band, gum band

rude *adj* impolite, insolent, discourteous, ungracious, impertinent, impudent, fresh, uncouth, crude, coarse, crass, bold, brash, presumptuous, audacious, sassy, forward, surly, pert, flip, disrespectful, irreverent, cheeky ➡ **abrupt, cross, thoughtless** ⇨ *polite*

If the word you want is not a main entry above, look below to find it.

rivulet ➡ river
RN ➡ nurse
roadblock ➡ barrier
roadway ➡ road
roam ➡ wander, travel
roar ➡ laugh, cry
roast ➡ cook
roasting ➡ hot
rob ➡ steal, deprive
robber ➡ criminal
robbery ➡ theft
robe ➡ bathrobe, dress
robust ➡ strong
rocket ➡ missile
rocket scientist ➡ genius

rockslide ➡ avalanche
rocky ➡ hard
rod ➡ bar
roe ➡ egg
Roentgen ray ➡ X ray
rogue ➡ rascal
roll ➡ bread, swing, mix
roller ➡ wheel, wave
romance ➡ court
romantic ➡ loving, idealistic, idealist
romp ➡ play, dance
roomy ➡ comfortable
roost ➡ seat
root ➡ base, essence, clap

rose ➡ red
roster ➡ list
rostrum ➡ platform
rosy ➡ red
rot ➡ decay, corrode, fungus
rotate ➡ turn
rotten ➡ bad
rotund ➡ round
roughly ➡ about
roundabout ➡ indirect
rouse ➡ wake
rousing ➡ exciting
rout ➡ defeat
route ➡ course

routine ➡ habit, method, act, average
routinely ➡ regularly
rove ➡ wander
rover ➡ pedestrian
rowdy ➡ loud, bully
royal ➡ noble
royal blue ➡ blue
royal household ➡ court
rubbing ➡ friction
rubbish ➡ trash
rubble ➡ trash
ruby ➡ red
ruddy ➡ red

n = noun • *vb* = verb • *adj* = adjective • *adv* = adverb • *prep* = preposition • *conj* = conjunction

rudeness *n* discourtesy, insolence, vulgarity, impudence, disrespect, crudity, crudeness, coarseness, boorishness

rug 1. *n* carpet, mat, carpeting, runner
2. *n* ➡ **wig**

ruin 1. *vb* ➡ **destroy**
2. *vb* impoverish, bankrupt, beggar
3. *n* ➡ **damage**
4. *n* ➡ **fate**

rule 1. *n* law, regulation, custom, principle, axiom, guideline, code, precept, canon, ultimatum ➡ **act, habit**
2. *n* command, control, authority, mastery, sway, sovereignty, charge, government, jurisdiction, dominion ➡ **leadership**
3. *n* ➡ **measure**
4. *vb* ➡ **govern**
5. *vb* ➡ **decide**

ruler *n* potentate, prince, lord, governor, leader, president, premier, prime minister ➡ **king, queen, emperor, empress, dictator**

rumor *n* gossip, hearsay, scandal, talk

run 1. *vb* jog, trot, dash, sprint, bolt, dart, streak, gallop, lope, canter ➡ **hurry, race**
2. *vb* ➡ **escape, leave**
3. *vb* ➡ **lead**
4. *vb* ➡ **operate**
5. *vb* ➡ **play**
6. *vb* ➡ **flow**
7. *n* ➡ **race**

runaway *n* fugitive, deserter, escapee, renegade, defector, truant, absentee

rural *adj* rustic, pastoral, provincial, backwoods ➡ **farming** ⇨ *urban*

rustle 1. *n* whisper, swish, ripple, crackle, patter, stir
2. *vb* whisper, swish, crackle, sigh, murmur, shuffle, flutter

rusty *adj* corroded, decayed ➡ **old**

If the word you want is not a main entry above, look below to find it.

rudiment ➡ basis
rudimentary ➡ basic
rue ➡ grieve, regret
ruffian ➡ bully
ruffle ➡ disturb
ruffled ➡ rough
rugged ➡ rough, tough, unbreakable

ruinous ➡ destructive
ruling ➡ decision
rumble ➡ bang, fight
rummage ➡ hunt
rump ➡ back
rumple ➡ wrinkle, disturb
rumpled ➡ rough

rundown ➡ old, summary
rung ➡ step
run-in ➡ meeting
runner ➡ messenger, shoot, rug
runway ➡ path
rupture ➡ break, hole

ruse ➡ trick
rush ➡ hurry, flood
rust ➡ corrode, fungus
rustic ➡ rural, primitive
rut ➡ channel
ruth ➡ pity
ruthless ➡ mean

➡ = synonym cross-reference • ⇨ = antonym cross-reference

S

sad *adj* unhappy, miserable, depressed, gloomy, dismal, melancholy, blue, downhearted, downcast, dejected, despondent, doleful, forlorn, moody, down, low, bad, glum ➡ **lonely, pitiful, sorry, thoughtful, pessimistic** ⇨ *happy*

sadden *vb* dishearten, disappoint, grieve, sorrow, oppress, depress, desolate

safe 1. *adj* secure, protected, harmless, snug, guarded, impregnable, invulnerable, immune ➡ **invincible** ⇨ *dangerous*
2. *n* vault, strongbox, chest, coffer, treasury, safe-deposit box ➡ **cash register**

sailor *n* seaman, mariner, seafarer, boatman, yachtsman, midshipman ➡ **soldier**

sale 1. *n* deal, transaction, purchase, marketing, auction ➡ **trade**
2. *n* bargain, deal, clearance, closeout, discount

salty 1. *adj* briny, brackish, saline
2. *adj* ➡ **dirty**

salvation *n* redemption, deliverance, preservation, liberation, emancipation, delivery ➡ **forgiveness, escape**

same *adj* identical, equal, equivalent, corresponding, matching, uniform, consistent, like ➡ **alike** ⇨ *different*

sane *adj* rational, sensible, reasonable, lucid, balanced, sound ⇨ *insane*

If the word you want is not a main entry above, look below to find it.

sabbatical ➡ vacation

saber ➡ sword

sable ➡ black, dark

sabotage ➡ damage, weaken

sac ➡ pocket

saccharine ➡ rich

sachem ➡ king

sack ➡ bag, base, pillage, attack, fire

sacramental ➡ holy

sacred ➡ holy, religious

sacrifice ➡ surrender, kill, gift

sadistic ➡ gruesome

sadness ➡ sorrow

safe-deposit box ➡ safe

safeguard ➡ protect, protection

safety ➡ protection

safety pin ➡ pin

saffron ➡ yellow

sag ➡ slant, weaken

saga ➡ story

sagacious ➡ profound

sagacity ➡ wisdom

sage ➡ philosopher, herb, profound

sail ➡ blow², fly, travel, pilot

sailing ➡ nautical

sake ➡ object

salaam ➡ good-bye

salary ➡ wage

salesman ➡ seller

salesperson ➡ seller

sales slip ➡ ticket

saleswoman ➡ seller

saline ➡ salty

sallow ➡ pale

sally ➡ attack, hurry

salmon ➡ orange

salon ➡ gallery, living room, room

saloon ➡ bar

salutation ➡ welcome

salute ➡ wave, welcome

salvage ➡ save

salver ➡ tray

sameness ➡ unity

sample ➡ example, try

sampling ➡ study

sanatorium ➡ hospital

sanctify ➡ bless, worship

sanctimonious ➡ self-righteous

sanction ➡ approve, forbid, permission, ban

sanctioned ➡ legal

sanctuary ➡ protection

sand ➡ dirt

sandy ➡ yellow

saneness ➡ reason

sanguine ➡ optimistic

sanitarium ➡ hospital

sanitary ➡ sterile

sanity ➡ reason

sap ➡ liquid, tire

sapling ➡ tree

sarcasm ➡ irony

n = noun • *vb* = verb • *adj* = adjective • *adv* = adverb • *prep* = preposition • *conj* = conjunction

sarcastic *adj* scornful, snide, ironic, ironical, satiric, satirical, sardonic, caustic, derisive

satisfaction 1. *n* gratification, fulfillment, contentment ➡ **pleasure**
2. *n* ➡ **revenge**

satisfied *adj* content, contented, self-satisfied, complacent ➡ **happy**

satisfy 1. *vb* appease, slake, quench, sate, satiate ➡ **please, relieve, pacify**
2. *vb* ➡ **persuade**
3. *vb* suffice, serve, do, fulfill, answer

save 1. *vb* keep, preserve, conserve, maintain, hoard, stockpile, stash ➡ **gather** ⇨ *discard, abolish, waste*
2. *vb* rescue, deliver, salvage, spare ➡ **free, protect**
3. *vb* ➡ **bank**
4. *prep* ➡ **but**

savior *n* rescuer, deliverer, protector, hero, champion, redeemer, lifesaver ➡ **guardian**

say *vb* state, speak, remark, exclaim, phrase, verbalize, express, signify, air, vent, dictate
➡ **talk, tell, pronounce, reveal**

saying *n* expression, motto, proverb, maxim, adage, aphorism, axiom, slogan, byword, saw, phrase ➡ **remark, cliché**

scar 1. *n* blemish, cicatrix, injury, disfigurement, mark, discoloration
2. *vb* ➡ **damage**

scare 1. *vb* frighten, alarm, startle, terrify, petrify, shock, horrify, perturb, unnerve, cow
➡ **threaten**
2. *n* ➡ **fear**

scarf *n* sash, bandanna, veil, ascot, handkerchief, do-rag ➡ **wrap**

scary *adj* frightening, frightful, dreadful, terrifying, terrible, horrifying, unnerving, appalling, fearful, awesome

scenic *adj* picturesque, pictorial, spectacular, striking ➡ **pretty**

If the word you want is not a main entry above, look below to find it.

sarcoma ➡ growth

sardonic ➡ sarcastic, dry

sari ➡ dress

sarong ➡ dress

sash ➡ band, scarf

sashay ➡ strut

sassy ➡ rude

satchel ➡ bag

sate ➡ satisfy

sated ➡ full

satellite ➡ colony, planet

satiate ➡ satisfy

satiny ➡ shiny

satire ➡ irony, parody

satiric ➡ sarcastic

satirical ➡ sarcastic

satirize ➡ imitate

satisfactorily ➡ well, correctly

satisfactory ➡ fair

satisfying ➡ pleasant

saturate ➡ wet

saturated ➡ wet

saucepan ➡ pot

saucer ➡ plate

saunter ➡ wander, lag

sauté ➡ cook

savage ➡ wild, mean, violent, monster, vandal

savagery ➡ violence

savanna ➡ plain

savings and loan ➡ bank

savings bank ➡ bank

savoir faire ➡ tact

savor ➡ spice, flavor, appreciate

savory ➡ delicious, fragrant

saw ➡ saying

scaffold ➡ gallows

scalding ➡ hot

scale ➡ climb, measure, peel, coat

scalpel ➡ knife

scamp ➡ rascal

scamper ➡ dance, hurry

scan ➡ read, examine

scandal ➡ rumor

scandalous ➡ sensational, shameful

scant ➡ few, light[2]

scanty ➡ small, few

scarce ➡ rare

scarcely ➡ only, seldom

scarcity ➡ want

scared ➡ afraid

scarlet ➡ red

scatter ➡ spread, plant

scatterbrained ➡ absentminded

scenario ➡ story

scene ➡ view, division

scenery ➡ view, setting

scent ➡ smell

scented ➡ fragrant

schedule ➡ list, table, arrange

scheduled ➡ due

schematic ➡ plan

scheme ➡ plan

➡ = synonym cross-reference • ⇨ = antonym cross-reference

school 1. *n* academy, institute ➡ **college**
2. *vb* ➡ **teach**
3. *n* ➡ **herd**

science *n* discipline, technique ➡ **education, knowledge**

scold *vb* rebuke, admonish, reprimand, chastise, chide, castigate, berate, reproach, upbraid, reprove ➡ **punish, blame** ⇨ *praise*

score 1. *n* count, tally, reckoning, outcome ➡ **grade**
2. *n* transcription, arrangement, composition, orchestration *vb* ➡ **get, add, win**

seat *n* chair, bench, sofa, couch, settee, stool, pew, bleachers, grandstand, stands, perch, roost

secrecy *n* stealth, hiding, confidence, subterfuge, furtiveness ➡ **privacy**

secret 1. *adj* hidden, arcane, cryptic, esoteric ➡ **mysterious, anonymous**
2. *adj* clandestine, confidential, classified, top secret, private, covert, undercover, surreptitious, underground ➡ **sly**
3. *n* mystery, confidence, intrigue ➡ **problem**

If the word you want is not a main entry above, look below to find it.

scheming ➡ sly

schism ➡ break

scholar ➡ student, teacher, philosopher

scholarly ➡ intellectual, educated

scholarship ➡ education, award

scholastic ➡ intellectual

schoolboy ➡ student

schoolchild ➡ student

schooled ➡ educated

schoolgirl ➡ student

schooling ➡ education

schoolmaster ➡ teacher

schoolmistress ➡ teacher

scimitar ➡ sword

scoff ➡ ridicule

scoop ➡ spoon, dig, catch

scope ➡ space, range

scorch ➡ burn

scorn ➡ hatred, hate, ridicule, refuse, insult

scornful ➡ sarcastic

Scotch® tape ➡ adhesive

scoundrel ➡ rascal

scour ➡ clean, shine, hunt

scourge ➡ whip

scout ➡ patrol

scowl ➡ frown

scramble ➡ mix, hurry, climb

scrap ➡ fight, bite, bit, discard

scrape ➡ clean, rub, cut, damage

scraping ➡ friction

scratch ➡ cut, rub, damage, erase

scratchy ➡ rough

scrawl ➡ write

scrawny ➡ thin

scream ➡ yell, cry

screamer ➡ headline

screech ➡ yell, cry, squeak

screen ➡ divider, net, hide, sift

screening ➡ tryout

screenwriter ➡ writer

screw ➡ nail, turn

scribble ➡ write

script ➡ handwriting, book

scriptwriter ➡ writer

scrooge ➡ miser

scrounge ➡ borrow

scrub ➡ clean, brush, cleaning

scruffy ➡ shabby

scrumptious ➡ delicious

scrupulous ➡ careful, good

scrutinize ➡ examine

scrutiny ➡ look

scuff ➡ rub

scuffle ➡ fight

scull ➡ paddle

scullery ➡ kitchen

sculpt ➡ carve

sculptor ➡ artist

sculpture ➡ statue, carve

scum ➡ foam

scurry ➡ hurry

scuttle ➡ hurry, abandon

sea ➡ ocean

seafarer ➡ sailor

seagoing ➡ nautical

seagull ➡ bird

seal ➡ close, signature

sealed ➡ tight

seam ➡ band

seaman ➡ sailor

sear ➡ burn

search ➡ hunt

seashore ➡ shore

seaside ➡ shore

season ➡ period, weather

seasoned ➡ old

seasoning ➡ spice, herb

sea wall ➡ jetty

seclude ➡ separate

secluded ➡ private

seclusion ➡ privacy

second ➡ moment, latter

secondary ➡ subordinate

secondhand ➡ old

second-rate ➡ cheap

secret agent ➡ spy

secrete ➡ hide, sweat

secretive ➡ sly

sect ➡ religion

section ➡ part, excerpt, division, department

secure ➡ safe, guarantee, lock, tie

security ➡ protection

sedate ➡ serious

sedative ➡ drug

n = noun • *vb* = verb • *adj* = adjective • *adv* = adverb • *prep* = preposition • *conj* = conjunction

see 1. *vb* behold, discern, observe, perceive, notice, glimpse, spot, remark ➡ **look**
2. *vb* ➡ **know, learn**
3. *vb* ➡ **imagine**

seed 1. *n* kernel, grain, pit, pip, nut, bulb ➡ **egg, fruit**
2. *vb* ➡ **plant**

seize *vb* take, grab, snatch, clutch, wrest, abduct, kidnap, hijack, skyjack, carjack, occupy, intercept, tackle ➡ **catch, get**

seldom *adv* rarely, occasionally, infrequently, sometimes, scarcely, hardly, barely ⇨ *often*

self-righteous *adj* sanctimonious, holier-than-thou, unctuous ➡ **hypocritical**

sell *vb* carry, stock, retail, handle, trade (in), market, peddle, vend, barter, hawk ➡ **offer**

seller *n* salesperson, salesman, saleswoman, dealer, merchant, vendor, tradesman, shopkeeper, peddler, trader, supplier, wholesaler ➡ **agent**

send 1. *vb* dispatch, transmit, mail, post, e-mail, forward, convey, ship, transfer, export ➡ **spread, broadcast**
2. *vb* ➡ **lead**
3. *vb* ➡ **throw**

sensational 1. *adj* scandalous, shocking, lurid, dramatic, melodramatic, vulgar, exaggerated
2. *adj* ➡ **exciting, awesome**

sense 1. *n* sensation, function, capability ➡ **feeling, ability**
2. *n* ➡ **wisdom**
3. *n* ➡ **meaning**

separate 1. *vb* part, sever, undo, detach, cleave, sunder ➡ **divide, rip, share, open**
2. *vb* isolate, insulate, segregate, discriminate, sequester, quarantine, seclude ➡ **distinguish**
3. *vb* divorce, split up, break up
4. *adj* ➡ **different**

If the word you want is not a main entry above, look below to find it.

sedentary ➡ **passive**

sedition ➡ **treason**

seditious ➡ **rebellious**

seduce ➡ **tempt**

seduction ➡ **attraction**

seedling ➡ **tree**

seedy ➡ **shabby**

seek ➡ **hunt**

seem ➡ **act, look**

seemingly ➡ **apparently, probably**

seemly ➡ **correct**

seep ➡ **drop**

seer ➡ **prophet**

seethe ➡ **boil**

see-through ➡ **transparent**

segment ➡ **part, divide**

segregate ➡ **separate**

segregation ➡ **privacy**

seizure ➡ **arrest, fit²**

select ➡ **choose, special**

selection ➡ **choice, assortment, excerpt, appointment**

self-acting ➡ **automatic**

self-confidence ➡ **pride, certainty**

self-confident ➡ **certain**

self-conscious ➡ **nervous**

self-control ➡ **discipline**

self-denial ➡ **abstinence**

self-deprecating ➡ **humble**

self-effacing ➡ **humble**

self-esteem ➡ **pride**

self-governing ➡ **free**

selfish ➡ **greedy, mean**

selfishness ➡ **greed**

self-possessed ➡ **calm**

self-respect ➡ **pride**

self-restraint ➡ **abstinence, discipline**

self-satisfied ➡ **satisfied**

self-starting ➡ **automatic**

semester ➡ **term**

seminar ➡ **course**

senate ➡ **government**

senior ➡ **old, older, student**

sensation ➡ **feeling, sense**

senseless ➡ **unconscious**

senselessness ➡ **nonsense**

sensible ➡ **practical, sane**

sensitive ➡ **sore, thoughtful, delicate, emotional, temperamental**

sensitivity ➡ **feeling**

sentence ➡ **punish, punishment, decision**

sentience ➡ **life**

sentiment ➡ **emotion, belief**

sentimental ➡ **emotional**

sentimentality ➡ **feeling**

sentinel ➡ **patrol**

sentry ➡ **patrol**

separately ➡ **apart, differently**

separation ➡ **division**

sepulcher ➡ **grave, cemetery**

sequence ➡ **order, row**

sequential ➡ **consecutive**

sequester ➡ **separate**

seraph ➡ **angel**

serendipitous ➡ **lucky**

serendipity ➡ **chance**

---

serious 1. *adj* solemn, grave, somber, earnest, sedate, sober, heavy ➡ **important, profound, dignified**
2. *adj* ➡ **sincere**

servant *n* retainer, domestic, employee, minion, attendant, subordinate ➡ **helper**

servile *adj* obsequious, submissive, subservient, slavish, fawning, sycophantic, spineless, mealy-mouthed, abject ➡ **passive, humble**

setting *n* environment, surroundings, framework, background, context, backdrop, scenery, climate, ambiance, mood, medium, milieu

sew *vb* stitch, mend, embroider, baste, tailor ➡ **weave**

shabby *adj* dilapidated, deteriorated, broken-down, decayed, scruffy, seedy, mangy ➡ **old, ragged, sorry**

shack *n* cabin, hut, shanty, hovel, shed ➡ **house**

shake 1. *vb* vibrate, tremble, shudder, shiver, quiver, quake, quaver, flutter, wobble, wag, waggle, pulsate, throb, jar ➡ **tingle**
2. *vb* ➡ **spread**
3. *n* ➡ **vibration**

shame 1. *n* disgrace, dishonor, discredit, humiliation, remorse, regret, contrition, embarrassment, chagrin ➡ **guilt**
2. *vb* humiliate, dishonor, disgrace, debase, abase, demean, discredit ➡ **embarrass**

shameful *adj* disgraceful, contemptible, scandalous, shocking, disreputable, dishonorable, ignoble, deplorable ➡ **improper, bad**

share 1. *n* division, percentage, allowance, allotment, stake, quota, ration, proportion, fraction, percent, ratio ➡ **part, interest**
2. *vb* distribute, apportion, split (up), deal out, ration, mete out ➡ **divide, budget**

If the word you want is not a main entry above, look below to find it.

serene ➡ calm

serenity ➡ calm

serf ➡ farmer

serfdom ➡ slavery

serial ➡ consecutive

series ➡ row, assortment, program, game

sermon ➡ speech

sermonize ➡ preach

serpent ➡ snake

serve ➡ help, satisfy, act, give

service ➡ ceremony, army, tray, help, repair, fix

serviceman ➡ soldier

service mark ➡ label

service station ➡ garage

servicewoman ➡ soldier

servicing ➡ repair

servitude ➡ slavery

session ➡ meeting

set ➡ put, group, harden, plant, fall, ready, usual

set apart ➡ dedicate

setback ➡ relapse, accident

set off ➡ leave

set out ➡ leave

settee ➡ seat

settle ➡ decide, pay, descend

settlement ➡ town, colony

settler ➡ pioneer

set up ➡ arrange

seven seas ➡ ocean

sever ➡ separate

several ➡ few

severance ➡ division

severe ➡ sharp, hard, plain, strict

severity ➡ strength

Seville orange ➡ orange

shackle ➡ bond

shade ➡ dark, color, bit, ghost, hide

shades ➡ glasses

shadow ➡ dark, cloud, follow

shadowy ➡ dim

shady ➡ dark, suspicious

shaft ➡ bar, well, channel

shaggy ➡ fuzzy

shah ➡ king

shaky ➡ unsteady, nervous

shallow ➡ superficial, dull

shalom ➡ good-bye, hello

sham ➡ fake

shaman ➡ magician

shamed ➡ ashamed

shameless ➡ immoral

Shangri-la ➡ utopia

shanty ➡ shack

shape ➡ form, structure, health

sharecropper ➡ farmer

sharecropping ➡ farming

shared ➡ common

n = noun • *vb* = verb • *adj* = adjective • *adv* = adverb • *prep* = preposition • *conj* = conjunction

sharp 1. *adj* keen, acute, honed, pointed, pointy, sharp-edged, knife-edged
2. *adj* ➡ **smart**
3. *adj* acute, abrupt, rapid ➡ **sudden**
4. *adj* ➡ **steep**
5. *adj* severe, biting, caustic, bitter, harsh, cutting, fierce, brutal, oppressive
6. *adj* ➡ **spicy, sour**
7. *adj* ➡ **smelly**
8. *adj* ➡ **fashionable**

sharpen *vb* whet, hone, file, grind, strop

shed 1. *n* ➡ **shack, barn, building**
2. *vb* remove, take off, cast off, drop, molt, slough ➡ **discard**

shelf *n* rack, counter, stand, ledge, mantel, mantelpiece

shell 1. *n* husk, pod, casing, sheath, carapace, eggshell ➡ **peel**
2. *n* ➡ **framework**
3. *n* ➡ **missile**
4. *vb* ➡ **shoot**

shine 1. *vb* radiate, beam, sparkle, gleam, glow, shimmer, glisten, twinkle
2. *vb* polish, burnish, buff, wax, scour ➡ **clean, finish**
3. *n* ➡ **light**[1]

shiny *adj* lustrous, gleaming, glossy, sleek, glistening, sparkling, silky, satiny ➡ **bright**

shock 1. *vb* astound, appall, dismay, devastate, overwhelm, stun, electrify, stagger, awe, horrify ➡ **surprise, scare**
2. *n* ➡ **blow**[1]**, vibration**
3. *n* ➡ **earthquake**
4. *n* blow, upset, jolt, ordeal, trauma ➡ **surprise**
5. *n* ➡ **lock**

shoe *n* boot, footwear

shoot 1. *vb* fire, discharge, open fire, blast, gun down, shell, propel, launch, project
2. *vb* ➡ **hunt, kill**
3. *n* sprout, bud, runner, twig, outgrowth ➡ **stick**

If the word you want is not a main entry above, look below to find it.

sharp-edged ➡ sharp

sharpness ➡ clarity

shatter ➡ break

shattered ➡ broken

shave ➡ cut

shawl ➡ wrap

shear ➡ cut

sheath ➡ dress, shell

sheathe ➡ wrap

sheen ➡ light[1]

sheer ➡ steep, perfect, thin, transparent

sheet ➡ layer, page, blanket

shellac ➡ finish

shelling ➡ fire

shells ➡ ammunition

shelter ➡ protect, protection, house, building

shenanigans ➡ mischief

shepherd ➡ guide

sherbet ➡ ice cream

sheriff ➡ police officer

shield ➡ protect, protection, badge

shift ➡ move, change, swerve, movement, period, dress

shiftless ➡ lazy

shifty ➡ sly

shimmer ➡ shine

ship ➡ boat, send

shipment ➡ load, delivery

shipshape ➡ neat

shirk ➡ avoid

shirtwaist ➡ dress

shiver ➡ shake

shock absorber ➡ cushion

shocking ➡ sensational, shameful

shoddy ➡ cheap, poor

shooting ➡ fire

shooting star ➡ meteor

shop ➡ market, factory, buy

shopkeeper ➡ seller

shoplift ➡ steal

shoplifting ➡ theft

shopper ➡ patron

shopping mall ➡ market

➡ = synonym cross-reference • ▷ = antonym cross-reference

shore *n* beach, coast, seashore, seaside, strand, bank ➡ **edge**

short 1. *adj* slight, low, undersized, skimpy, brief ➡ **small** ⇨ *long*
2. *adj* brief, concise, compact, succinct, abbreviated, terse, laconic, abridged, fleeting, transient, short-lived ➡ **fast, temporary**
3. *adj* ➡ **abrupt**
4. *adj* ➡ **inadequate**

show 1. *vb* display, exhibit, present, manifest, produce ➡ **reveal, advertise, model**
2. *vb* ➡ **lead**
3. *vb* ➡ **explain, verify**
4. *n* spectacle, display ➡ **play, movie, program**

shrink 1. *vb* contract, shrivel, deflate, constrict ➡ **condense, decrease** ⇨ *grow, lengthen*
2. *vb* ➡ **retreat**

shy *adj* bashful, timid, meek, retiring, diffident, reserved, demure, deferential, timorous, tentative ➡ **humble**

sick 1. *adj* ill, ailing, sickly, unwell, unhealthy, nauseous, nauseated, queasy, infirm, indisposed, funny ➡ **weak** ⇨ *healthy*
2. *adj* ➡ **gruesome**

side 1. *n* surface, face, end, facet, plane ➡ **edge**
2. *n* ➡ **perspective**
3. *n* ➡ **team**

sideways *adv* broadside, obliquely, askance, indirectly

sift 1. *vb* strain, filter, screen, winnow, sort
2. *vb* ➡ **hunt**

sight 1. *n* vision, eyesight, perception ➡ **sense**
2. *n* ➡ **view**
3. *vb* ➡ **look**

sign 1. *n* symbol, signal, token, omen, clue, index, indication, manifestation, symptom, gesture, expression ➡ **track, warning**
2. *vb* autograph, inscribe, endorse, countersign, initial ➡ **write**

If the word you want is not a main entry above, look below to find it.

shortage ➡ want
shortbread ➡ pastry
shortcoming ➡ defect
shortcut ➡ path
shorten ➡ condense
shortening ➡ abbreviation, fat
short-lived ➡ short
shortly ➡ soon
shot ➡ medicine, try
shotgun ➡ gun
should ➡ need
shoulder ➡ push, bear
shout ➡ yell, cry
shove ➡ push, impulse

shovel ➡ dig
showdown ➡ fight
shower ➡ rain, cleaning
showery ➡ wet
show off ➡ boast
showpiece ➡ masterpiece
showroom ➡ gallery
show up ➡ appear
showy ➡ loud
shred ➡ cut, rip, bit
shrewd ➡ sly, smart
shriek ➡ yell, cry, laugh
shrill ➡ loud, high
shrine ➡ monument
shrivel ➡ shrink, decrease, dry

shroud ➡ blanket, wrap, hide
shrub ➡ plant
shrubbery ➡ hedge, brush
shuck ➡ peel
shudder ➡ shake
shuffle ➡ limp, rustle, mix
shun ➡ avoid, abstain
shut ➡ close
shut-eye ➡ sleep
shut-in ➡ hermit
shutterbug ➡ photographer
shyster ➡ cheat
sicken ➡ disgust
sickening ➡ bad
sickly ➡ sick

sickness ➡ illness, nausea
sidearm ➡ gun
sideboard ➡ cupboard
sideburns ➡ beard
sidekick ➡ partner
sidestep ➡ avoid
sideswipe ➡ collide
sidetrack ➡ distract
siesta ➡ sleep
sieve ➡ net
sifter ➡ net
sigh ➡ mumble, rustle
sighting ➡ discovery
sightless ➡ blind
signal ➡ sign, warning, wave, bell, light[1]

n = noun • *vb* = verb • *adj* = adjective • *adv* = adverb • *prep* = preposition • *conj* = conjunction

signature *n* autograph, John Hancock, seal, monogram, mark, stamp, imprint

similarity *n* likeness, resemblance, correspondence, parallel, similitude, affinity, congruity, analogy, comparison

simultaneous *adj* concurrent, coincident, coinciding, synchronized, synchronous, contemporary, contemporaneous

sin 1. *vb* err, offend, transgress, trespass ➡ **disobey**
2. *n* ➡ **crime, immorality**

sincere *adj* genuine, honest, heartfelt, wholehearted, true, trustworthy, serious, straight ➡ **straightforward**

sincerely *adv* truly, honestly, earnestly, genuinely, heartily, frankly

sing *vb* chant, harmonize, vocalize, croon, warble, chirp ➡ **hum**

singer *n* vocalist, chorister, soloist, songster, cantor ➡ **choir, musician**

single 1. *adj* ➡ **only**
2. *adj* alone, unmarried, unwed, unattached, eligible, divorced ⇨ *married*

sink 1. *vb* submerge, submerse, swamp, engulf, immerse, duck, dunk, dip ➡ **descend, fall, flood**
2. *n* washbasin, basin, lavatory, washstand ➡ **bowl**

size *n* magnitude, mass, volume, bulk, quantity, proportion, capacity

skeptic *n* cynic, pessimist, doubter, doubting Thomas

If the word you want is not a main entry above, look below to find it.

significance ➡ importance, meaning, relevance

significant ➡ important, meaningful

signify ➡ mean, matter, say

silence ➡ quiet, calm

silent ➡ dumb, quiet

silhouette ➡ circumference

silky ➡ shiny

sill ➡ threshold

silliness ➡ nonsense

silly ➡ foolish

silo ➡ warehouse

silver screen ➡ movies

silvery ➡ white

similar ➡ alike, compatible

similarly ➡ alike

similitude ➡ similarity

simmer ➡ boil

simple ➡ plain, easy, naive, primitive

simple-minded ➡ stupid

simpleton ➡ fool

simplicity ➡ clarity, ignorance

simplify ➡ facilitate

simply ➡ only

simulate ➡ imitate, pretend

simultaneously ➡ together

since ➡ because

sincerity ➡ truth

sinful ➡ bad

singe ➡ burn

single-handed ➡ alone

singular ➡ unique

sinister ➡ ominous

sinless ➡ innocent

sip ➡ drink

sister ➡ religious

sisterhood ➡ friendship

sit ➡ model

site ➡ place

sit-in ➡ protest

sitter ➡ model

sitting room ➡ living room

situate ➡ place, base

situation ➡ place, state, opportunity, profession

sizzling ➡ hot

skate ➡ slide

skeleton ➡ framework, body

skeptical ➡ doubtful

skepticism ➡ doubt

sketch ➡ picture, pattern, act, draw

skid ➡ slide

skill ➡ talent, art, experience

skilled ➡ expert

skillful ➡ able

skim ➡ read, slide, rub

skimpy ➡ small, short

skin ➡ peel, hide

skin-deep ➡ superficial

skinflint ➡ miser

skinny ➡ thin

skintight ➡ tight

skip ➡ exclude, jump

skipper ➡ boss

skirmish ➡ fight

skirt ➡ dress, border, detour

skit ➡ act, play

skittish ➡ nervous

skulk ➡ sneak

sky ➡ air

sky blue ➡ blue

skycap ➡ porter

skyjack ➡ seize

skyline ➡ horizon

skyscraper ➡ tower

slab ➡ block

slack ➡ limp, negligent

slacker ➡ loafer

slake ➡ satisfy

---

slant 1. *vb* tilt, lean, list, incline, slope, bank, sag, pitch, cant ➡ **bend**
2. *n* slope, incline, climb, ascent, rise, descent, declivity, grade, hill

slavery *n* bondage, servitude, enslavement, serfdom, subjugation, vassalage ⇨ *freedom*

sleep 1. *vb* slumber, doze, snooze, nod, nap, hibernate ➡ **rest**
2. *n* slumber, doze, rest, repose, siesta, nap, catnap, shut-eye (*informal*)

slide 1. *vb* glide, skim, coast, skid, slip, skate ➡ **push**
2. *n* ➡ **channel**
3. *n* ➡ **photograph**
4. *n* ➡ **avalanche**

slippery *adj* smooth, slick, glassy, icy, waxy, soapy

slow 1. *adj* leisurely, gradual, sluggish, deliberate, moderate, torpid ⇨ *fast*
2. *adj* dilatory, lackadaisical ➡ **passive, lazy, listless**
3. *adj* ➡ **dull, stupid**

sly 1. *adj* devious, crafty, cunning, shrewd, subtle, tricky, sneaky, wily, slick, shifty, artful, scheming, underhanded ➡ **dishonest**
2. *adj* secretive, furtive, sneaky, surreptitious, stealthy, elusive ➡ **private**

small 1. *adj* little, tiny, miniature, minute, diminutive, Lilliputian, compact ➡ **trivial** ⇨ *big*
2. *adj* scanty, meager, slight, spare, skimpy, stingy, paltry ➡ **inadequate**

smart 1. *adj* intelligent, clever, bright, wise, learned, brilliant, keen, acute, quick, alert, apt, astute, perceptive, insightful, discerning, incisive, canny, shrewd ➡ **precocious, educated, profound** ⇨ *foolish, stupid*
2. *adj* ➡ **fashionable**
3. *vb* ➡ **hurt**

In general, **smart**, **clever**, *and* **bright**, *which all suggest quickness in learning, are more often applied to young people than are* **intelligent**, **wise**, *and* **learned**, *which suggest the wisdom that comes from experience, education, and age.*

If the word you want is not a main entry above, look below to find it.

slam ➡ close

slammer ➡ jail

slander ➡ insult

slang ➡ dialect

slap ➡ punch, blow[1]

slash ➡ cut, decrease

slat ➡ board

slate ➡ gray, ballot

slather ➡ rub

slaughter ➡ kill, murder

slave ➡ servant, prisoner, work

slavish ➡ servile

slay ➡ kill

slayer ➡ killer

slaying ➡ murder

sled ➡ vehicle

sledge ➡ hammer

sledgehammer ➡ hammer

sleek ➡ shiny

sleeping ➡ asleep

sleepless ➡ awake

sleepy ➡ tired

sleet ➡ ice

slender ➡ thin, narrow, light[2]

slew ➡ abundance

slice ➡ cut, block

slick ➡ slippery, sly

slight ➡ small, thin, short, light[2], insult

slightest ➡ least

slightly ➡ partly

slim ➡ thin, narrow

slime ➡ dirt

sling ➡ throw

slink ➡ sneak

slip ➡ mistake, trip, dock, ticket, slide, fall

slip by ➡ elapse

slit ➡ cut

slither ➡ crawl

slogan ➡ saying

slop ➡ dirt

slope ➡ slant

sloppy ➡ messy

slosh ➡ splash

sloth ➡ laziness

slothful ➡ lazy

slouch ➡ bend

slough ➡ shed

slovenly ➡ messy

sludge ➡ dirt

slug ➡ hit, missile

sluggard ➡ loafer

sluggish ➡ slow, listless

sluice ➡ channel

slumber ➡ sleep

slumbering ➡ asleep

slump ➡ depression, fall, drop, bend

slush ➡ snow

slushy ➡ wet

smack ➡ hit, kiss, blow[1]

smaller ➡ less

smallest ➡ least

small-minded ➡ mean

smash ➡ break, hit, collide

smear ➡ rub, insult

smell 1. *n* scent, odor, aroma, fragrance, perfume, incense, bouquet, stench
2. *vb, n* sniff, whiff, scent ➡ **sense**
3. *vb, n* stink, reek

smelly *adj* odorous, rancid, rank, foul, putrid, acrid, sharp, strong ➡ **fragrant**

smile *vb, n* beam, grin, smirk, sneer ➡ **laugh**
⇨ *frown*

smoke 1. *n* vapor, fumes, gas, steam ➡ **fog**
2. *vb* smolder, fume ➡ **burn**
3. *vb* inhale, puff

snake *n* serpent, viper ➡ **reptile**

sneak 1. *vb* creep, slink, prowl, skulk, steal, tiptoe, lurk
2. *n* ➡ **rascal**

snow 1. *n* snowfall, snowstorm, blizzard, flurry ➡ **storm**
2. *n* snowflake, powder, slush, hail, graupel, névé, firn
3. *vb* ➡ **enchant, persuade**

snuggle *vb* cuddle, nuzzle, nestle, huddle

soda *n* pop, soda pop, soft drink, cola, Coke (*trademark*), tonic ➡ **drink**

soften 1. *vb* ➡ **melt**
2. *vb* modify, assuage, temper, qualify, appease, palliate ➡ **change, quiet**

soldier *n* fighter, warrior, volunteer, conscript, draftee, recruit, cadet, veteran, officer, serviceman, servicewoman, combatant, mercenary, soldier of fortune, gladiator ➡ **army, troop**

If the word you want is not a main entry above, look below to find it.

smirk ➡ smile
smock ➡ dress
smog ➡ fog
smoky ➡ gray
smolder ➡ smoke
smoldering ➡ burning
smooch ➡ kiss
smooth ➡ level, slippery, suave, rub
smother ➡ extinguish, choke
smudge ➡ spot, dirty
smug ➡ proud
snack ➡ meal
snag ➡ knot, catch
snap ➡ break, bite, clasp, fast
snapshot ➡ photograph
snare ➡ trap, catch
snarl ➡ bark, knot
snatch ➡ seize, steal, bit
sneaky ➡ sly
sneer ➡ smile
snicker ➡ laugh

snide ➡ sarcastic
sniff ➡ smell
snigger ➡ laugh
snip ➡ cut
snippet ➡ bit
snit ➡ fit²
snoop ➡ meddle, spy
snooze ➡ sleep
snort ➡ grunt
snout ➡ nose
snowfall ➡ snow
snowflake ➡ snow
snowstorm ➡ snow, storm
snow-white ➡ white
snowy ➡ white, wet
snub ➡ refuse, insult
snug ➡ safe, comfortable, warm, narrow, tight
so ➡ therefore
soak ➡ wet, cleaning, absorb
soaked ➡ wet
soapy ➡ slippery

soar ➡ fly
soaring ➡ high, flight
sob ➡ cry
sober ➡ serious
sobriquet ➡ pseudonym
sociable ➡ friendly
social ➡ friendly, public, dance
socialize ➡ mix
Social Security ➡ pension
society ➡ humanity, people, friendship, organization, aristocracy
sociology ➡ science
soda pop ➡ soda
sodden ➡ wet
sofa ➡ seat
soft ➡ gentle, flexible, fuzzy
soft drink ➡ soda
soggy ➡ wet
soil ➡ dirt, dirty
soiled ➡ dirty

soiree ➡ party
sojourn ➡ live¹, visit
solace ➡ comfort
solder ➡ join
soldier of fortune ➡ soldier
soldierly ➡ military
sole ➡ only
solemn ➡ serious, dignified
solemnity ➡ ceremony
solemnize ➡ celebrate
solicit ➡ beg
solicitous ➡ thoughtful
solid ➡ firm, strong, reliable, real
solidify ➡ harden
solitary ➡ alone, only, lonely
solitude ➡ privacy
solo ➡ alone
soloist ➡ singer
so long ➡ good-bye
solution ➡ answer, mixture

➡ = synonym cross-reference • ⇨ = antonym cross-reference

solve *vb* figure out, puzzle out, resolve, decode, decipher, answer, do, work (out), unravel, unscramble ➡ **explain**

song *n* tune, melody, lyric, theme, ballad, lullaby, ditty, madrigal ➡ **hymn, poem, music**

soon *adv* presently, shortly, forthwith, momentarily, anon ➡ **quickly, now**

sore 1. *adj* painful, sensitive, tender, raw, hurtful, irritated, inflamed, bruised, livid
2. *adj* ➡ **angry**
3. *n* boil, abscess, ulcer, inflammation, welt, swelling ➡ **cut, pain**

sorrow 1. *n* grief, sadness, regret, anguish, melancholy, distress, gloom, woe, heartache ➡ **misery, depression**
2. *vb* ➡ **sadden**

sorry 1. *adj* sorrowful, repentant, apologetic, contrite, penitent, remorseful ➡ **sad**
2. *adj* forlorn, wretched, depressing ➡ **sad, pitiful**
3. *adj* ➡ **poor**

soul 1. *n* spirit, psyche, essence, genius, ego ➡ **mind, ghost**
2. *n* ➡ **human being**
3. *n* ➡ **feeling**
4. *n* ➡ **middle**

sour *adj* tart, bitter, rancid, acidic, sharp, acid, tangy, dry ⇨ **sweet**

source 1. *n* origin, derivation, birthplace, cradle, fountain, fountainhead, font, fount, well, wellspring
2. *n* ➡ **beginning, cause**

space 1. *n* universe, cosmos, heavens, outer space, infinity, void ➡ **air**
2. *n* room, area, scope, range, expanse, territory, elbowroom

speaker *n* lecturer, orator, speechmaker, rhetorician, preacher, talker

special 1. *adj* distinct, particular, specific, especial, distinctive, respective, proper, certain ➡ **unique**
2. *adj* select, choice, extraordinary, exceptional, unusual, peculiar, remarkable, noteworthy, phenomenal, outstanding ➡ **rare, striking, strange**

If the word you want is not a main entry above, look below to find it.

somber ➡ serious, bleak, dark

some ➡ any

sometimes ➡ seldom

somewhat ➡ partly

somnolent ➡ asleep

son ➡ child

songbird ➡ bird

songster ➡ singer

sooner ➡ more

soothe ➡ relieve, pacify, calm

soothsayer ➡ prophet

sophisticated ➡ cosmopolitan, complicated

sophistication ➡ elegance

sophomore ➡ student

sophomoric ➡ childish

sop up ➡ absorb

sorbet ➡ ice cream

sorcerer ➡ magician

sorcery ➡ magic

soreness ➡ pain

sorority ➡ organization

sorrowful ➡ sorry

sort ➡ type, arrange, sift

sortie ➡ attack

sot ➡ drunkard

sound ➡ noise, valid, healthy, sane, strong, blow^2, ring

soundless ➡ quiet

sous-chef ➡ cook

souse ➡ drunkard

souvenir ➡ reminder

sovereign ➡ king, queen, free

sovereignty ➡ freedom, rule

sow ➡ plant

spa ➡ hotel

space-age ➡ modern

space flight ➡ flight

spacey ➡ absentminded

spacious ➡ open, comfortable

span ➡ period, life, bridge, width, pair, team

spank ➡ whip

spar ➡ joke

spare ➡ save, small, thin

spark ➡ light^1, incentive, start

sparkle ➡ shine, light^1

sparkling ➡ shiny

sparse ➡ light^2, inadequate

spasm ➡ pain, fit^2

spasmodic ➡ periodic

spat ➡ argument

spate ➡ flood

spatter ➡ splash

spawn ➡ reproduce, egg

spay ➡ sterilize

speak ➡ say, talk

speak to ➡ approach

spear ➡ stick, missile

---

n = noun • *vb* = verb • *adj* = adjective • *adv* = adverb • *prep* = preposition • *conj* = conjunction

specialty *n* speciality, forte, métier, specialization ➡ **talent, field, profession**

specify *vb* stipulate, define, particularize, detail ➡ **name, mention, list**

speckled *adj* spotted, mottled, variegated, dappled, piebald

speech 1. *n* voice, communication, discourse, intercourse, utterance, articulation, diction, locution, enunciation, expression ➡ **talk, language, remark, accent, dialect**
2. *n* lecture, talk, sermon, address, report, oration

speed 1. *n* velocity, acceleration, swiftness, pace, rate, tempo, rapidity, celerity, dispatch ➡ **hurry**
2. *vb* ➡ **hurry**

spice 1. *n* seasoning, zest, savor, relish ➡ **herb**
2. *n* ➡ **excitement**

spicy *adj* zesty, piquant, tangy, tart, sharp, hot, pungent, peppery

splash *vb, n* splatter, sprinkle, squirt, spray, spatter, slosh ➡ **drop, wet**

spoken *adj* verbal, oral, voiced, stated, unwritten, vocal

spontaneous *adj* impromptu, impulsive, unplanned, extemporaneous, casual ➡ **automatic, voluntary**

spoon *n* ladle, scoop, dipper, tablespoon, teaspoon

spot 1. *n* speck, dot, mark, taint, stain, blot, blemish, blotch, smudge
2. *n* ➡ **place**
3. *n* ➡ **trouble**
4. *vb* ➡ **find, see**

If the word you want is not a main entry above, look below to find it.

specialist ➡ expert
speciality ➡ specialty
specialization ➡ specialty
specie ➡ money
species ➡ type
specific ➡ special, detail
specimen ➡ example
speck ➡ spot
spectacle ➡ show, view
spectacles ➡ glasses
spectacular ➡ great, scenic
spectator ➡ observer
spectators ➡ audience
specter ➡ ghost
spectrum ➡ range
speculate ➡ guess, meditate
speculation ➡ theory
speculative ➡ theoretical
speechless ➡ dumb, quiet

speechmaker ➡ speaker
speedily ➡ quickly
speedy ➡ fast
spell ➡ period, curse, enchantment, dream, fit², mean
spellbind ➡ enchant
spellbinding ➡ magic
spend ➡ pay
spendthrift ➡ wasteful
sphere ➡ ball, field
spherical ➡ round
spider ➡ bug
spigot ➡ faucet
spike ➡ nail, point
spill ➡ flow, fall
spin ➡ turn, trip
spine ➡ thorn
spineless ➡ servile

spinoff ➡ product
spire ➡ tower
spirit ➡ courage, soul, angel, ghost, fairy
spirited ➡ active, lively
spirits ➡ mood, drink
spiritual ➡ religious, heavenly
spirituality ➡ religion
spit ➡ cape
spite ➡ envy
spiteful ➡ revengeful
splatter ➡ splash
splendid ➡ grand, good
splendidly ➡ well
splendor ➡ elegance
splice ➡ knot
splinter ➡ break
split ➡ hole, divide, break

split up ➡ separate, share
spoil ➡ decay, destroy, pamper
spoilage ➡ decay
spoiled ➡ stale, mischievous, bad
spoils ➡ booty
spokesperson ➡ agent
sponsor ➡ patron, back
spontaneity ➡ freedom
spook ➡ ghost, spy
spoor ➡ track
sporadic ➡ few, periodic
sport ➡ game, play
sport coat ➡ coat
sport jacket ➡ coat
sports center ➡ gymnasium
sportsman ➡ athlete
sportswoman ➡ athlete

➡ = synonym cross-reference • ⇨ = antonym cross-reference

spouse *n* mate, partner, husband, wife, bride, groom, consort, helpmate

spread 1. *vb* distribute, disseminate, disperse, circulate, strew, shake, sprinkle, scatter
➡ **send, broadcast**
2. *vb* extend, stretch, range, unfold, expand, widen, gape, yawn
3. *vb* ➡ **cover**
4. *vb* ➡ **rub**
5. *n* ➡ **growth**
6. *n* ➡ **range**
7. *n* ➡ **farm**
8. *n* ➡ **feast**
9. *n* ➡ **flow**

spy 1. *n* agent, counterspy, secret agent, double agent, spook (*informal*)
2. *vb* eavesdrop, pry, snoop
3. *vb* ➡ **look**

spying *n* espionage, surveillance, intelligence, counterespionage, counterintelligence

square 1. *adj* foursquare, four-sided, quadrilateral
2. *adj* ➡ **dull**
3. *n* box, rectangle, quadrilateral, quadrangle
4. *n* ➡ **court, park**

squeak 1. *vb* creak, screech, squeal, rasp, grate
2. *n* ➡ **peep**

squeeze 1. *vb* pinch, clasp ➡ **embrace**
2. *vb* compress, wring, press ➡ **tighten**
3. *n* pinch, nip, tweak ➡ **embrace**

stage 1. *n* ➡ **platform, floor**
2. *n* theater, boards
3. *n* ➡ **state, period**
4. *vb* ➡ **act, give**

stale 1. *adj* moldy, spoiled, wilted, flat, musty
➡ **dry, bad**
2. *adj* ➡ **trite**

stammer 1. *n* stutter, stammering
2. *vb* stutter, hem and haw, sputter
➡ **mumble**

If the word you want is not a main entry above, look below to find it.

spotless ➡ clean

spotted ➡ speckled

spout ➡ fountain, faucet

sprain ➡ pull

sprawl ➡ lie, trip

spray ➡ foam, bouquet, fountain, splash

spreadable ➡ contagious

spreadsheet ➡ table

spree ➡ binge, adventure

sprightly ➡ lively, agile

spring ➡ jump, descend, well

spring peeper ➡ frog

sprinkle ➡ wet, rain, splash, spread

sprint ➡ run, race

sprite ➡ angel, fairy

sprout ➡ grow, shoot

spruce ➡ neat

spry ➡ lively, agile

spryness ➡ agility

spume ➡ foam

spumoni ➡ ice cream

spur ➡ urge, incentive

spurious ➡ fake

spurn ➡ refuse

spurt ➡ flow

sputter ➡ stammer

spyglass ➡ glass

squabble ➡ argue, argument

squad ➡ troop, team

squalid ➡ dirty

squall ➡ storm, yell

squander ➡ waste

squash ➡ trample, break

squat ➡ low, fat, bend

squawk ➡ peep, cry, complain

squeal ➡ cry, squeak

squeamish ➡ reluctant

squirm ➡ crawl, fidget

squirrel (away) ➡ hide

squirt ➡ flow, splash, fountain

squish ➡ trample

stab ➡ stick, blow[1], try

stability ➡ balance

stabilize ➡ balance

stable ➡ stationary, barn

stack ➡ pile

stadium ➡ field

staff ➡ stick, faculty

stage name ➡ pseudonym

stagecoach ➡ wagon

stagger ➡ limp, shock

stagnant ➡ stationary, stuffy, dead

stain ➡ spot, dirty, finish, paint

stair ➡ step

stake ➡ bar, share, bet, interest

stalement ➡ tie

stalk ➡ stick, follow

stall ➡ booth, pen, barn, delay

stallion ➡ horse

stalwart ➡ brave, strong

stamina ➡ energy

stammering ➡ stammer

stamp ➡ print, signature, trample

stanza *n* verse, canto, strophe, stave, refrain, strain ➡ **poem**

star 1. *n* sun
2. *n* ➡ **celebrity, actor**

stare *vb* gaze, peer, gape, ogle, gawk ➡ **look**

start 1. *vb* begin, commence, initiate, cause, activate, launch, originate, stem, inaugurate, introduce, innovate, open, trigger, touch off, spark ➡ **continue** ⇨ *finish, stop*
2. *n* ➡ **beginning**
3. *vb* ➡ **jump**

state 1. *n* condition, circumstance, situation, status, stage, phase ➡ **grade**
2. *n* territory, province, dominion, commonwealth ➡ **country, colony, zone**
3. *vb* ➡ **mention, say, tell**

stationary *adj* fixed, immobile, permanent, motionless, steady, stable, still, stock-still, inert, stagnant ⇨ *portable*

statue *n* sculpture, statuette, figure, figurine, bust, bronze, likeness, image, effigy, idol, statuary ➡ **monument**

steal 1. *vb* rob, swipe, snatch, shoplift, purloin, embezzle, burglarize, rifle, poach, pinch, pilfer, pocket, plagiarize, pirate, filch ➡ **take, seize, pillage**
2. *vb* ➡ **sneak**
3. *n* ➡ **bargain**

steep 1. *adj* sheer, abrupt, precipitous, sharp, perpendicular, vertical, uphill
2. *vb* ➡ **wet**

step 1. *n* footstep, stride, pace, tread, footfall
2. *n* ➡ **gait**
3. *n* ➡ **act**
4. *n* rung, tread, stair ➡ **grade**
5. *vb* ➡ **walk, dance**

stereotype 1. *n* convention, generalization, categorization, characterization ➡ **cliché**
2. *vb* categorize, pigeonhole, characterize, label, generalize

If the word you want is not a main entry above, look below to find it.

stampede ➡ hurry
stance ➡ posture
stanchion ➡ post
stand ➡ bear, booth, platform, shelf, table
standdown ➡ truce
standard ➡ normal, average, model, measure, flag
standing ➡ fame, grade
standoff ➡ tie
standpoint ➡ perspective
stands ➡ seat
staple ➡ necessity, basic
stark ➡ plain, hard, completely
startle ➡ surprise, scare

starvation ➡ hunger
starve ➡ die
starved ➡ hungry
starving ➡ hungry
stash ➡ save
stated ➡ spoken
state-of-the-art ➡ modern
stately ➡ grand, dignified
statement ➡ remark, announcement, bill
state park ➡ park
statesman ➡ diplomat
station ➡ base, destination
stationery ➡ paper
statuary ➡ statue

statuette ➡ statue
stature ➡ height, importance
status ➡ reputation, state
statute ➡ act
statutory ➡ legal
staunch ➡ resolute, faithful
stave ➡ stick, stanza
stave off ➡ repel
stay ➡ live¹, wait, anchor, visit, support
stay with ➡ visit
steadfast ➡ faithful, resolute, patient
steady ➡ balance, firm, stationary, continual
stealing ➡ theft

stealth ➡ secrecy
stealthy ➡ sly
steam ➡ cook, iron, smoke, energy
steed ➡ horse
steeple ➡ tower
steeplechase ➡ race
steer ➡ lead, drive
steering wheel ➡ wheel
steersman ➡ pilot
stem ➡ stick, start, stop
stench ➡ smell
steno pad ➡ notepad
stentorian ➡ loud
stepparent ➡ parent
steppe ➡ plateau

➡ = synonym cross-reference • ⇨ = antonym cross-reference

sterile 1. *adj* antiseptic, sterilized, disinfected, sanitary, hygienic, germ-free ➡ **clean**
2. *adj* infertile, childless, barren, impotent ⇨ *fertile*
3. *adj* waste, desert, arid, barren ➡ **abandoned, empty**

sterilize 1. *vb* ➡ **clean**
2. *vb* spay, neuter, fix, geld, castrate

stick 1. *vb* poke, jab, probe, stab, plunge, pierce, prick, spear, puncture, lance, gore, peck, penetrate, perforate, riddle ➡ **hit**
2. *vb* adhere, cohere, glue, paste, tape, cling, cleave ➡ **join**
3. *n* branch, limb, twig, stem, stalk, staff, stave, wand, cane, club, baton ➡ **bar, bat**

sticky 1. *adj* adhesive, gummy, tacky, viscid, viscous
2. *adj* ➡ **damp**
3. *adj* ➡ **delicate**

stomach 1. *n* abdomen, midsection, paunch, belly, tummy, gut, midriff
2. *vb* ➡ **bear**
3. *n* ➡ **courage**

stop 1. *vb* halt, pause, cease, terminate, brake, arrest, check, stem, discontinue, lift ➡ **finish** ⇨ *start*
2. *vb* ➡ **prevent, bar**
3. *vb* ➡ **close**

storm 1. *n* tempest, gale, rainstorm, snowstorm, blizzard, hailstorm, ice storm, hurricane, typhoon, cyclone, monsoon, tornado, nor'easter, squall ➡ **rain, wind, snow**
2. *n* ➡ **flood**
3. *vb* ➡ **attack**
4. *vb* ➡ **hurry**

stormy *adj* rainy, blustery, inclement, tempestuous, turbulent, tumultuous, wild, fierce, violent ➡ **wet, windy**

story 1. *n* narrative, account, history, saga, chronicle, tale, narration, anecdote, yarn, plot, scenario, version ➡ **report, myth, joke, description**
2. *n* ➡ **lie**
3. *n* ➡ **floor**

If the word you want is not a main entry above, look below to find it.

sterilized ➡ sterile

stern ➡ strict, hard, back

stew ➡ cook, boil, worry

sticker ➡ label

sticks ➡ country

stiff ➡ firm, thick, prim

stiffen ➡ tighten

stifle ➡ choke, extinguish, quiet

stifling ➡ stuffy

stiletto ➡ knife

still ➡ quiet, more, dead, stationary, anyway

stillness ➡ calm

stilted ➡ prim

stimulate ➡ excite

stimulated ➡ excited

stimulating ➡ interesting

stimulation ➡ excitement

stimulus ➡ cause, incentive

sting ➡ hurt, pain

stingy ➡ cheap, greedy, small

stink ➡ smell

stint ➡ period

stipend ➡ wage

stipulate ➡ specify

stipulation ➡ term

stir ➡ mix, fidget, rustle, jail

stir up ➡ fan

stirring ➡ interesting

stitch ➡ sew, pain

stock ➡ sell, supply, load, family, trite

stockade ➡ wall, jail

stockpile ➡ supply, save

stockroom ➡ warehouse

stock-still ➡ stationary

stocky ➡ big, fat

stodgy ➡ stuffy

stoicism ➡ patience

stole ➡ wrap

stolid ➡ dull

stomp ➡ trample

stone ➡ rock, jewel

stoneware ➡ pottery

stony ➡ hard

stooge ➡ tool

stool ➡ seat

stoop ➡ descend, bend, condescend, porch

stopgap ➡ temporary

stopper ➡ top

stopwatch ➡ clock

store ➡ market, place, supply

storehouse ➡ warehouse

storeroom ➡ closet

storm cellar ➡ basement

storyteller ➡ liar

stout ➡ big, tough, fat

stove ➡ furnace

n = noun • *vb* = verb • *adj* = adjective • *adv* = adverb • *prep* = preposition • *conj* = conjunction

straight 1. *adj* direct, undeviating, even, unbent, regular, linear, true ➡ **level, vertical** ⇨ *bent, zigzag*
2. *adj* ➡ **sincere**

straighten 1. *vb* unbend, untwist, order, arrange, align, realign ➡ **level** ⇨ *bend*
2. *vb* ➡ **comb**

straightforward 1. *adj* frank, outspoken, plain, candid, forthright, ingenuous, blunt, vocal ➡ **sincere, explicit**
2. *adj* ➡ **easy**

strange 1. *adj* unfamiliar, unusual, unknown, unaccustomed, outlandish ➡ **foreign, new** ⇨ *common*
2. *adj* odd, peculiar, curious, abnormal, eccentric, quaint, queer, weird, eerie, bizarre, unnatural, ludicrous, different, irregular ➡ **mysterious, funny**

stranger *n* newcomer, outsider, out-of-towner ➡ **foreigner**

strength *n* power, force, might, potency, muscle, fortitude, intensity, vehemence, violence, severity ➡ **ability, energy**

strengthen 1. *vb* intensify, magnify, amplify, increase, expand, enhance, enlarge, boost, augment, swell ➡ **grow**
2. *vb* fortify, brace, buttress, reinforce ➡ **harden, support**

stress 1. *n* pressure, tension, strain, duress ➡ **worry**
2. *n* ➡ **accent**
3. *vb* ➡ **emphasize**

strict *adj* stern, stringent, austere, severe, rigorous, exacting, unyielding, uncompromising

striking *adj* conspicuous, impressive, dazzling, stunning, unusual ➡ **obvious, special, attractive, pretty, scenic**

string 1. *n* cord, line, twine, thread, lace, strap, yarn, fiber, filament, strand, tendril ➡ **rope**
2. *n* ➡ **row**
3. *n* ➡ **team**

strong 1. *adj* powerful, mighty, almighty, hardy, stalwart, robust, muscular, vigorous, athletic, virile, burly ➡ **tough, invincible, healthy** ⇨ *weak*
2. *adj* solid, sturdy, durable, sound, substantial ➡ **tough**
3. *adj* potent, powerful, formidable, violent, forceful, intense
4. *adj* ➡ **smelly**

If the word you want is not a main entry above, look below to find it.

stow ➡ load

straggle ➡ lag

straggler ➡ pedestrian

straightaway ➡ now

straight pin ➡ pin

strain ➡ hurt, pull, work, sift, stress, chorus, stanza, type, family

strait ➡ trouble

strand ➡ leave, string, shore

strangle ➡ choke

strap ➡ string, rope, tie

stratagem ➡ trick, tactic

strategy ➡ plan

stratosphere ➡ air

stratum ➡ layer

stray ➡ wander, homeless, arbitrary

streak ➡ band, period, tendency, run

stream ➡ river, fountain, flow, flood

street ➡ road

streetlight ➡ light[1]

strenuous ➡ active, hard

stretch ➡ distance, period, spread, lengthen, distort

stretched ➡ tense

stretcher ➡ bed

strew ➡ spread

stride ➡ step, gait, walk

strident ➡ loud

strife ➡ fight, disagreement

strike ➡ hit, blow[1], attack, protest, discover, light[1], make

stringent ➡ strict

strip ➡ bar, band, peel, undress

stripe ➡ bar, band

stripped ➡ naked

strive ➡ fight, try, work

stroke ➡ blow[1], pet, rub

stroll ➡ walk

stroller ➡ pedestrian

strongbox ➡ safe

stronghold ➡ castle

strong-minded ➡ resolute

➡ = synonym cross-reference • ⇨ = antonym cross-reference

structure 1. *n* composition, arrangement, shape, form ➡ **pattern**
2. *n* ➡ **building**
3. *vb* ➡ **arrange**

strut 1. *vb* parade, swagger, sashay, flounce ➡ **walk**
2. *n* ➡ **gait**

stubborn *adj* obstinate, headstrong, pertinaceous, dogged, opinionated, obdurate, tenacious, pigheaded, unrelenting, unruly, intractable, difficult, perverse, unmanageable, mulish, ornery ➡ **resolute, dogmatic, wild**

student *n* pupil, learner, scholar, disciple, schoolchild, schoolgirl, schoolboy, freshman, sophomore, junior, senior, undergraduate, trainee, apprentice

study 1. *vb* analyze, evaluate, think through, pore over, review, research, criticize, survey, poll, canvass ➡ **examine, consider, learn, read**
2. *n* examination, analysis, investigation, inquiry, exploration, survey, poll, census, sampling, probe
3. *n* ➡ **report**
4. *n* ➡ **den**
5. *n* ➡ **dream**

stuffy 1. *adj* close, stifling, airless, suffocating, claustrophic, stagnant
2. *adj* congested, clogged
3. *adj* stodgy, conservative, conventional ➡ **dull**

stupid *adj* ignorant, unintelligent, dumb (*informal*), vacuous ➡ **foolish, dull, thoughtless** ⇨ *smart*
Some people consider it rude to use **dumb** *in reference to people. When you are writing, it might be better to use one of the other more specific synonyms.*

suave *adj* urbane, debonair, diplomatic, cultured, charming, smooth, glib, facile ➡ **fashionable**

subdue *vb* subjugate, suppress, quash ➡ **defeat, contain**

subject 1. *n* theme, topic, question, substance, matter, thesis, gist, point, text, issue ➡ **field**
2. *n* ➡ **course**
3. *n* ➡ **model, patient**
4. *n* ➡ **citizen**
5. *vb* ➡ **control**

subordinate 1. *adj* inferior, secondary, auxiliary, junior, lower ➡ **under**
2. *n* ➡ **helper, servant**

If the word you want is not a main entry above, look below to find it.

strop ➡ sharpen
strophe ➡ stanza
struggle ➡ fight, try, work
strum ➡ play
stubble ➡ beard
stud ➡ nail, beam, post
studio ➡ gallery
studious ➡ careful, educated
stuff ➡ matter, property, load
stuffed ➡ full
stumble ➡ trip, fumble

stumble across ➡ find
stump ➡ confuse
stun ➡ shock, paralyze
stunned ➡ unconscious
stunning ➡ beautiful, striking
stunt ➡ trick, prevent
stupidity ➡ ignorance, nonsense
stupor ➡ dream
sturdy ➡ tough, strong
stutter ➡ stammer
sty ➡ pen

style ➡ type, class, fashion, elegance
stylish ➡ fashionable, modern
stymie ➡ confuse
stymied ➡ disabled
subcommittee ➡ committee
subconscious ➡ mind
subdivide ➡ divide
subdivision ➡ division, development
subject to ➡ under

subjective ➡ arbitrary
subjugate ➡ subdue
subjugation ➡ slavery, victory
sublet ➡ hire
sublime ➡ heavenly
submerge ➡ flood, sink
submerse ➡ sink
submission ➡ surrender
submissive ➡ passive, servile
submit ➡ surrender, give, suggest
subordinate to ➡ under

---

n = noun • *vb* = verb • *adj* = adjective • *adv* = adverb • *prep* = preposition • *conj* = conjunction

subtract *vb* deduct, remove, withhold, diminish ➡ **decrease** ⇨ *add*

subtraction *n* deduction, reduction, diminution, discount ⇨ *addition*

success *n* accomplishment, achievement, attainment, progress, prosperity ➡ **victory, luck**

successful 1. *adj* fortunate, accomplished ➡ **rich, famous**
2. *adj* effective, fortuitous, favorable, productive, victorious, triumphant, auspicious

sudden *adj* immediate, abrupt, swift, meteoric, precipitate, instantaneous, unexpected, unforeseen ➡ **sudden, sharp, early**

suggest 1. *vb* recommend, urge, propose, advise, counsel, move, submit, prescribe ➡ **offer**

2. *vb* imply, hint, intimate, insinuate

suggestion 1. *n* proposal, proposition, offer, recommendation ➡ **advice, idea, tip**
2. *n* ➡ **bit**

suit 1. *vb* fit, become, befit, enhance, flatter, agree with, complement
2. *n* outfit, ensemble, uniform, costume ➡ **clothes**
3. *n* lawsuit, litigation, action, hearing, case

summary *n* outline, synopsis, abstract, paraphrase, condensation, abridgment, digest, précis, rundown ➡ **essence**

superficial *adj* cursory, perfunctory, shallow, surface, skin-deep, cosmetic, uncritical, glib ➡ **trivial, trite**

If the word you want is not a main entry above, look below to find it.

subscriber ➡ patron

subsequent ➡ following

subservient ➡ servile

subside ➡ decrease, fall

subsidiary ➡ department

subsist ➡ live[1]

substance ➡ matter, essence, existence, density, weight, subject, support

substantial ➡ big, strong

substantially ➡ chiefly

substantiate ➡ verify

substantiation ➡ proof

substantive ➡ real

substitute ➡ change, trade, relieve, alternate

substitution ➡ trade

subterfuge ➡ pretense, trick, secrecy

subterranean ➡ underground

subtle ➡ sly, complicated, smart

suburb ➡ town

subversive ➡ rebel

subvert ➡ weaken

succeed ➡ prosper, win, follow

succeeding ➡ following

succession ➡ order

successive ➡ consecutive

succinct ➡ short

succinctness ➡ brevity

succor ➡ support, comfort, help

succulent ➡ rich

succumb ➡ surrender, lose, die

suck up ➡ absorb

suds ➡ foam

sue ➡ appeal, try

suet ➡ fat

suffer ➡ bear

sufferer ➡ patient

suffering ➡ pain, misery

suffice ➡ satisfy

sufficient ➡ enough

suffocate ➡ choke

suffocating ➡ stuffy

suffuse ➡ instill

sugary ➡ rich

suitable ➡ fit[1], able, good

suitcase ➡ luggage

suite ➡ room

sulk ➡ mope

sulky ➡ temperamental

sullen ➡ pessimistic, cross

sully ➡ dirty

sultan ➡ king

sultana ➡ queen

sultry ➡ damp, tropical

sum ➡ total, add, all

summation ➡ addition

summit ➡ top, mountain

summon ➡ call, mobilize

summons ➡ invitation

sumptuous ➡ grand

sun ➡ star

sundae ➡ ice cream

sunder ➡ separate

sundial ➡ clock

sundown ➡ evening

sundry ➡ many

sunglasses ➡ glasses

sunken ➡ underground

sunny ➡ bright, fair

sunrise ➡ morning

sunset ➡ evening

sunup ➡ morning

super ➡ great

superb ➡ grand, great

superfluous ➡ unnecessary

➡ = synonym cross-reference • ⇨ = antonym cross-reference

supernatural *adj* preternatural, superhuman, paranormal, unearthly, occult, mystical, psychic ➡ **invisible, heavenly**

superstition *n* old wives' tale, fable, lore ➡ **myth, belief**

superstitious 1. *adj* credulous, fearful
2. *adj* unfounded, groundless

supply 1. *n* stock, store, stockpile, inventory, reserve, hoard, cache, mine, holding, account, fund, reservoir
2. *vb* provide, equip, outfit, furnish, provision, rig ➡ **give, sell**

support 1. *vb* bear, hold (up), bolster (up), brace, sustain, prop (up), buttress, carry, nourish, nurture, feed, promote, foster
➡ **strengthen**
2. *vb* uphold, sustain, maintain, champion, enforce ➡ **back, help, approve**
3. *vb* ➡ **afford**
4. *n* backing, encouragement, assistance, succor, maintenance, livelihood, subsistence, upkeep, resource ➡ **help, protection, approval, permission, incentive, pension**
⇨ *opposition*

5. *n* mainstay, pillar, backer, champion
➡ **patron, fan**
6. *n* brace, prop, buttress, stay, bolster, truss, reinforcement ➡ **base, basis**

surprise 1. *vb* startle, amaze, astonish, daze, dazzle, bedazzle, flabbergast, throw, floor
➡ **shock**
2. *n* amazement, astonishment, wonder, incredulity ➡ **shock**
3. *n* ➡ **gift**

surrender 1. *vb* yield, concede, submit, resign, relinquish, sacrifice, acquiesce, capitulate, quit, give (in), bow, accede, defer, succumb, relent
➡ **lose, abandon**
2. *n* submission, capitulation, resignation, acquiescence, concession, abdication, renunciation, forfeit, sacrifice

suspense *n* uncertainty, apprehension, anticipation ➡ **doubt, fear**

suspension 1. *n* ➡ **break**
2. *n* expulsion, banishment, discharge, removal ➡ **exile**

If the word you want is not a main entry above, look below to find it.

superhuman ➡ supernatural

superintendent ➡ principal

supersede ➡ follow

superior ➡ better, proud, boss

superiority ➡ excellence, advantage

superlative ➡ best

supermarket ➡ market

superstar ➡ celebrity

supervise ➡ lead

supervision ➡ leadership

supervisor ➡ boss

supine ➡ prone

supplant ➡ follow

supple ➡ flexible, agile

supplement ➡ add, more, addition

supplementary ➡ more

supplicate ➡ appeal

supplier ➡ seller

supporter ➡ fan, patron

suppose ➡ guess

supposedly ➡ apparently

supposition ➡ theory

suppress ➡ subdue, contain, abuse

supreme ➡ best

sure ➡ certain, reliable

surefire ➡ reliable

surely ➡ certainly

sure thing ➡ certainty

surf ➡ wave

surface ➡ outside, top, side, appear, cover, superficial

surge ➡ wave, flood, impulse, hurry

surly ➡ rude, cross

surmise ➡ assume, guess, theory

surmount ➡ defeat, tower

surname ➡ name

surpass ➡ exceed

surplus ➡ remainder, abundance, more, unnecessary

surprised ➡ dumbfounded

surreptitious ➡ sly, secret

surrogate ➡ alternate

surround ➡ ring

surroundings ➡ setting

surveillance ➡ watch, spying

survey ➡ look, study, tower

survive ➡ live[1]

susceptible ➡ vulnerable

suspect ➡ guess, doubt, suspicious, defendant

suspend ➡ hang, exclude

suspicious 1. *adj* distrustful, wary, leery, paranoid, apprehensive ➥ **jealous**
2. *adj* suspect, queer, shady, dubious ➥ **doubtful, strange**

swamp 1. *n* marsh, bog, marshland, bottomland, bayou, fen, quagmire, mire
2. *vb* ➥ **flood, sink**

sweat 1. *vb* perspire, swelter, secrete, exude
2. *n* perspiration, body odor, B.O.

sweep 1. *vb* wipe, whisk, brush, swish, dust, mop, vacuum ➥ **clean**
2. *n* ➥ **range**
3. *n* ➥ **paddle**

swell 1. *vb* bulge, distend, protrude, project, jut, balloon, dilate, expand, inflate, puff up

2. *vb* ➥ **strengthen**
3. *n* ➥ **wave**

swerve *vb* veer, shift, diverge, deviate, dodge ➥ **turn**

swim 1. *vb* float, paddle, bathe
2. *n* dip, plunge, swimming, bathing

swing 1. *vb* sway, rock, oscillate, vibrate, fluctuate, undulate, wave, roll, wobble, pitch, lurch, reel, waddle ➥ **turn**
2. *vb* wave, brandish, flourish, wield, whirl, twirl
3. *vb* ➥ **hang**
4. *n* ➥ **rhythm, music**

sword *n* rapier, cutlass, foil, épée, saber, broadsword, scimitar ➥ **knife**

If the word you want is not a main entry above, look below to find it.

suspicion ➥ doubt, belief

sustain ➥ support, keep

sustained ➥ long

sustenance ➥ food

swab ➥ rub

swaddle ➥ wrap

swagger ➥ boast, gait, strut

swallow ➥ drink, take, contain

swap ➥ trade, change

swarm ➥ herd, crowd, hurry, infest

swarthy ➥ dark

swat ➥ hit, blow[1]

swathe ➥ wrap, bandage

sway ➥ swing, wave, affect, persuade, rule

swear ➥ promise, testify, curse

sweepstakes ➥ lottery

sweet ➥ rich, pleasant, friendly

sweetheart ➥ love

swelling ➥ bulge, growth, sore

swelter ➥ sweat

sweltering ➥ hot

swift ➥ fast, sudden

swiftness ➥ speed

swig ➥ drink

swimming ➥ swim

swindle ➥ cheat

swindler ➥ cheat, rascal

swipe ➥ steal

swirl ➥ turn

swish ➥ rustle, sweep

switch ➥ trade, change, alternate, whip

swivel ➥ turn, axis

swoon ➥ dream

swoop ➥ descend

sycophantic ➥ servile

syllable ➥ word

symbol ➥ sign

symbolize ➥ mean

symmetry ➥ balance

sympathetic ➥ thoughtful

sympathize ➥ pity

sympathy ➥ pity, agreement

symphonic ➥ musical

symptom ➥ sign

synagogue ➥ church

synchronized ➥ simultaneous

synchronous ➥ simultaneous

syndicate ➥ group, monopoly

syndrome ➥ disease

synopsis ➥ summary

synthetic ➥ manufactured

syrupy ➥ thick

system ➥ method, order

systematize ➥ arrange

T

table 1. *n* desk, stand, counter, bar, dresser
2. *n* chart, graph, spreadsheet, timetable, schedule, table of contents, catalog, register, appendix ➡ **plan**
3. *n* ➡ **plateau**

tact *n* judgment, poise, diplomacy, savoir faire, discretion, delicacy, circumspection, finesse

tactic *n* strategem, maneuver, gambit, feint
➡ **plan, trick**

take 1. *vb* convey, deliver, transport
➡ **carry, bring, lead**
2. *vb* ➡ **get, receive**
3. *vb* confiscate, appropriate, expropriate, commandeer, usurp, gain ➡ **seize, catch**
4. *vb* ingest, swallow ➡ **eat, drink**
5. *vb* ➡ **bear**
6. *vb* ➡ **choose**
7. *vb* take in ➡ **earn**

talent *n* gift, aptitude, genius, skill, expertise, flair, knack, prowess, adroitness, facility
➡ **ability, agility, specialty, art**

talented *adj* gifted, artistic, musical, creative, inventive, versatile, imaginative, ingenious, fertile ➡ **able**

talk 1. *vb* speak, converse, discuss, chat, communicate, confer, consult, parley, rap
➡ **argue, chatter, say, tell**
2. *n* conversation, discussion, dialogue, consultation, word, chat, chitchat, patter, prattle, gibberish ➡ **speech, rumor, meeting**

talkative *adj* voluble, loquacious, verbose, garrulous, long-winded, effusive, chatty

tame 1. *adj* housebroken, house-trained, trained, manageable, domestic, domesticated, docile, broken ➡ **gentle**
2. *vb* ➡ **control**

If the word you want is not a main entry above, look below to find it.

tab ➡ bill, label
tableland ➡ plateau
tablespoon ➡ spoon
tablet ➡ medicine, notepad
tabloid ➡ paper
taboo ➡ illegal
tabulate ➡ list
tabulating ➡ addition
tack ➡ nail
tackle ➡ equipment, try, seize
tacky ➡ sticky, loud
tactful ➡ thoughtful
tactless ➡ insensitive
tadpole ➡ frog

tag ➡ label
tail ➡ follow, back
tailor ➡ adjust, sew
taint ➡ dirty, spot
take after ➡ resemble
take-home ➡ examination
take in ➡ adopt, take
take off ➡ shed
take on ➡ try
takeover ➡ acquisition
take prisoner ➡ arrest
take up ➡ occupy
tale ➡ story, lie
talker ➡ speaker
tall ➡ high, long

tallness ➡ height
tallow ➡ fat
tally ➡ add, bill, score, vote
talon ➡ foot
tamper ➡ tinker, meddle
tan ➡ brown, dark
tandem ➡ team
tang ➡ flavor, bit
tangelo ➡ orange
tangent ➡ adjacent
tangerine ➡ orange
tangible ➡ real
tangle ➡ knot, mess, maze, bend
tangy ➡ spicy, sour

tank ➡ container
tantalize ➡ tempt
tantrum ➡ fit^2
tap ➡ knock, faucet
tape ➡ adhesive, band, stick
taper ➡ decrease
tardily ➡ late
tardy ➡ late
target ➡ object, prey, destination
tariff ➡ tax
tarnish ➡ corrode, dirty
tarp ➡ tent
tar paper ➡ paper
tarpaulin ➡ tent

n = noun • *vb* = verb • *adj* = adjective • *adv* = adverb • *prep* = preposition • *conj* = conjunction

tax 1. *n* duty, tariff, toll, levy, fee, assessment, tribute
2. *vb* ➡ **tire**

taxi *n* cab, taxicab, limousine, limo, hack ➡ **vehicle**

teach *vb* instruct, educate, train, school, tutor, coach, lecture, inform, drill, enlighten ➡ **explain, preach**

teacher *n* instructor, educator, schoolmaster, schoolmistress, scholar, tutor, mentor, guru, professor, lecturer, academic, don, coach ➡ **adviser, faculty**

team 1. *n* squad, company, unit, crew, side ➡ **group**
2. *n* (*in reference to horses, mules, or oxen*) pair, span, yoke, string, tandem

teenager *n* adolescent, teen, youth, juvenile ➡ **child**

tell *vb* report, narrate, relate, recite, declare, inform, announce, disclose, communicate, convey, notify, state, profess, pronounce, tattle ➡ **say, talk, order, warn, testify, predict**

temperamental *adj* moody, touchy, volatile, sensitive, testy, petulant, sulky ➡ **fickle, emotional**

temporary *adj* transitory, fleeting, momentary, ephemeral, provisional, stopgap, makeshift, interim, acting ➡ **short** ⇨ *permanent*

tempt *vb* entice, tantalize, lure, seduce, decoy, bait ➡ **persuade**

tendency *n* disposition, propensity, trend, proclivity, penchant, streak, inclination, leaning, bias ➡ **habit, preference**

tense 1. *adj* taut, stretched, drawn ➡ **firm, tight**
2. *adj* high-strung, agitated ➡ **anxious, nervous**
3. *vb* ➡ **tighten**

If the word you want is not a main entry above, look below to find it.

tarry ➡ wait

tart ➡ sour, spicy, pastry

task ➡ job

taste ➡ bite, drink, flavor, elegance, try

tasteless ➡ insipid

tasty ➡ delicious

tattered ➡ ragged

tattle ➡ tell, chatter

taunt ➡ insult

taupe ➡ brown

taut ➡ tense

tavern ➡ bar, restaurant

tawdry ➡ poor

tawny ➡ brown

taxicab ➡ taxi

teach-in ➡ protest

teaching ➡ education, lesson

teakettle ➡ pot

team up ➡ help

teapot ➡ pot

tear ➡ drop, hurt, rip

teardrop ➡ drop

tearful ➡ emotional

tearoom ➡ restaurant

tease ➡ bother, insult, joke, comb

teaspoon ➡ spoon

teaspoonful ➡ dose

teatime ➡ afternoon

technician ➡ mechanic

technique ➡ art, method

tedious ➡ dull

tedium ➡ boredom

teem ➡ rain

teeming ➡ fertile

teen ➡ teenager

telecast ➡ broadcast, program

telephone ➡ call

telescope ➡ glass, condense

televise ➡ broadcast

tell on ➡ betray

telling ➡ meaningful, valid

temerity ➡ audacity

temper ➡ personality, anger, mood, harden, soften

temperament ➡ personality, mood

temperance ➡ abstinence

temperate ➡ gentle

tempest ➡ wind, storm

tempestuous ➡ stormy

template ➡ pattern

temple ➡ church

tempo ➡ speed, rhythm

temptation ➡ attraction

tenacious ➡ stubborn, faithful

tenant ➡ occupant

tend ➡ protect

tender ➡ gentle, offer, loving, sore

tenderhearted ➡ kind

tenderness ➡ love, kindness

tendril ➡ string

tent *n* pavilion, canopy, tarp, tarpaulin, fly ➡ **protection**

term 1. *n* ➡ **word**
2. *n* semester, trimester, quarter, tenure ➡ **period**
3. *n* qualification, limitation, condition, restriction, stipulation, reservation, clause

terrain *n* ground, land, territory, landscape, environment, topography

testify *vb* affirm, swear, certify, vouch, attest ➡ **tell**

thankless 1. *adj* ➡ **thoughtless**
2. *adj* unappreciated, unrewarded, unrewarding, disagreeable, distasteful ➡ **useless**

theft *n* robbery, burglary, stealing, larceny, thievery, fraud, extortion, shoplifting, looting, pillage, embezzlement ➡ **crime**

theoretical *adj* hypothetical, academic, abstract, philosophical, rhetorical, speculative, conjectural

theory *n* hypothesis, conjecture, speculation, supposition, premise, presumption, assumption, surmise ➡ **idea, reason, philosophy**

therefore *adv* consequently, hence, accordingly, thus, ergo, wherefore, for, so

thick 1. *adj* dense, compact, close, condensed, packed, impenetrable, profuse ⇨ **thin**
2. *adj* stiff, firm, viscous, syrupy, gelatinous, glutinous, viscid
3. *adj* ➡ **broad**

thin 1. *adj* flimsy, slim, slender, sheer, delicate, diaphanous, insubstantial, gossamer ➡ **weak** ⇨ **thick, heavy**
2. *adj* ➡ **narrow**
3. *adj* slender, slim, lean, slight, skinny, scrawny, lanky, lank, wiry, spare, gaunt, haggard, emaciated ⇨ **big, tough**
4. *vb* ➡ **weaken, disappear**

think 1. *vb* reason, deliberate, cogitate ➡ **consider, meditate, believe**
2. *vb* ➡ **guess**

If the word you want is not a main entry above, look below to find it.

tension ➡ stress

tentative ➡ doubtful, shy

tenure ➡ term

tepid ➡ warm

terminal ➡ base, destination, deadly, last

terminally ➡ deadly

terminate ➡ finish, stop, fire

termination ➡ finish

terminus ➡ destination

terra cotta ➡ pottery

terrarium ➡ zoo

terrible ➡ awful, scary

terribly ➡ very

terrific ➡ great, awesome

terrified ➡ afraid

terrify ➡ scare

terrifying ➡ scary

territory ➡ space, terrain, state

terror ➡ fear

terrorize ➡ threaten

terse ➡ short

terseness ➡ brevity

test ➡ examination, experiment, try, examine, experimental

testament ➡ will

testimony ➡ proof

testy ➡ temperamental, cross

tether ➡ tie, rope

text ➡ book, print, subject

textile ➡ cloth

texture ➡ quality

thank ➡ appreciate

thankful ➡ grateful

thankfulness ➡ gratitude

thanks ➡ gratitude

thaw ➡ melt

theater ➡ stage, hall

theme ➡ subject, report, song, chorus

theme park ➡ carnival

theological ➡ religious

theology ➡ religion

therapeutic ➡ medicinal

therapy ➡ cure

thesaurus ➡ dictionary

thesis ➡ report, subject

thespian ➡ actor

thicken ➡ concentrate, harden

thicket ➡ brush, forest

thief ➡ criminal

thievery ➡ theft

thing ➡ object, fashion

things ➡ property

think through ➡ study

thinker ➡ philosopher

thinking ➡ reason

thirst ➡ appetite

n = noun • *vb* = verb • *adj* = adjective • *adv* = adverb • *prep* = preposition • *conj* = conjunction

thorn *n* briar, brier, bramble, barb, spine
➡ **point**

thoughtful 1. *adj* considerate, sympathetic, tactful, solicitous, sensitive ➡ **friendly, polite, kind, nice** ⇨ *thoughtless*
2. *adj* meditative, contemplative, pensive, reflective, wistful ➡ **sad, absorbed, intellectual**

thoughtless *adj* inconsiderate, careless, reckless, wanton, heedless, rash, foolhardy, ungrateful, thankless, unappreciative ➡ **rude, abrupt, indiscriminate, negligent**
⇨ *thoughtful*

threaten 1. *vb* intimidate, menace, torment, bully, terrorize ➡ **scare**
2. *vb* ➡ **jeopardize**

threshold 1. *n* sill, doorsill, doorstep, entryway, entranceway ➡ **door, porch**
2. *n* ➡ **beginning**

through 1. *prep* among, around, between
➡ **past**
2. *prep* ➡ **during**
3. *adj* ➡ **past**

throw 1. *vb* pitch, toss, hurl, fling, cast, pass, heave, chuck, sling
2. *vb* project, propel, launch, catapult, emit, radiate, send, give off ➡ **shoot**
3. *vb* ➡ **confuse, surprise**
4. *vb* ➡ **defeat**
5. *n* toss, pitch, pass, cast

tick 1. *n* ticktock, beat, click, clack
2. *n* check, check mark, mark, x, cross

ticket 1. *n* pass, admission, voucher, permit, visa, passport, receipt, sales slip, slip
2. *n* ➡ **ballot**
3. *n, vb* ➡ **label**

tie 1. *vb* fasten, secure, knot, bind, lash, tether, hitch, lace, strap ➡ **join, link**
2. *n* necktie, bow tie, cravat, ascot
3. *n* draw, deadlock, stalemate, standoff

tight 1. *adj* fast, unyielding, immovable, fixed
➡ **tense, firm, stationary**
2. *adj* sealed, airtight, watertight, impermeable
3. *adj* snug, close-fitting, skintight, formfitting, constricting
4. *adj* ➡ **cheap**

If the word you want is not a main entry above, look below to find it.

thirsty ➡ dry

thorax ➡ chest

thorough ➡ complete, comprehensive, careful

thoroughfare ➡ road

thoroughly ➡ completely, well, carefully

thoroughness ➡ diligence

though ➡ but

thought ➡ idea, philosophy, attention

thoughtfulness ➡ kindness

thrash ➡ whip

thrashing ➡ defeat

thread ➡ string, bend

threadbare ➡ ragged

threat ➡ danger, warning

threatening ➡ ominous

threnody ➡ dirge

thrift ➡ economy

thriftiness ➡ economy

thrifty ➡ cheap

thrill ➡ excitement, excite

thrilled ➡ ecstatic, excited

thrilling ➡ exciting

thrive ➡ prosper, live[1]

throaty ➡ hoarse

throb ➡ shake, hurt

throng ➡ crowd

throughout ➡ during

throw away ➡ discard

throw up ➡ vomit

thrust ➡ impulse, energy, push

thruway ➡ highway

thud ➡ bang

thug ➡ vandal

thump ➡ knock

thunder ➡ bang, yell

thunderous ➡ loud

thunderstruck ➡ dumbfounded

thus ➡ therefore

thwack ➡ blow[1]

thwart ➡ prevent, bar

thwarted ➡ disabled

tiara ➡ crown

tickle ➡ pet

ticklish ➡ delicate

ticktock ➡ tick

tidal wave ➡ wave

tide ➡ flood

tidings ➡ announcement

tidy ➡ neat, clean

tiepin ➡ pin

tier ➡ layer, floor

tiff ➡ argument

➡ = synonym cross-reference • ⇨ = antonym cross-reference

tighten *vb* stiffen, tense, clench, contract, squeeze ➡ **pull**

tingle *vb* prickle, itch, creep ➡ **hurt, shake**

tinker 1. *vb* putter, fiddle, dabble, mess, potter, twiddle, fidget, toy ➡ **fix**
2. *vb* tamper, juggle, rig, manipulate, fiddle ➡ **change**

tip 1. *n* ➡ **top, point**
2. *n* pointer, suggestion, hint ➡ **advice**
3. *n* gratuity, bonus, perk, perquisite, reward ➡ **wage**
4. *vb* ➡ **pay**
5. *vb* ➡ **upset**
6. *vb* ➡ **warn**

tire 1. *vb* exhaust, fatigue, tax, sap, fade, weary, bore ➡ **weaken**
2. *n* ➡ **wheel**

tired 1. *adj* exhausted, weary, worn out, sleepy, fatigued, listless, drained, dead
2. *adj* ➡ **trite**

together 1. *adv* jointly, mutually, collectively, en masse, cooperatively ⇨ *apart*
2. *adv* simultaneously, concurrently, contemporaneously

tolerant *adj* permissive, lenient, indulgent, easygoing ➡ **liberal, kind, patient**

tool 1. *n* instrument, utensil, machine, appliance, gadget, implement, device, mechanism, apparatus, means, vehicle, medium ➡ **equipment, hammer**
2. *n* instrument, pawn, puppet, stooge, dupe, victim

top 1. *n* peak, summit, pinnacle, apex, apogee, zenith, crest, tip, surface, climax, acme, prime, ultimate ⇨ *base*
2. *n* cover, lid, cap, hood, stopper, cork, plug, bung
3. *adj* ➡ **best**
4. *vb* ➡ **defeat, exceed**

If the word you want is not a main entry above, look below to find it.

tight-fisted ➡ cheap

tightwad ➡ miser

till ➡ until, farm, cash register

tiller ➡ wheel

tilt ➡ slant

timber ➡ wood, board, beam

timberland ➡ forest

time ➡ moment, period, rhythm, measure

timely ➡ punctual

timepiece ➡ clock

timer ➡ clock

timetable ➡ table

timid ➡ shy, cowardly

timorous ➡ shy, cowardly, afraid

timothy ➡ hay

tine ➡ point

tinge ➡ color

tiniest ➡ least

tinkle ➡ ring, peep

tint ➡ color, paint

tintinnabulation ➡ ring

tiny ➡ small

tippler ➡ drunkard

tipsy ➡ drunk, dizzy

tiptoe ➡ sneak

tiptop ➡ good

tiredness ➡ exhaustion

tireless ➡ diligent

tiresome ➡ dull

tissue ➡ paper

titan ➡ giant

titanic ➡ huge

title ➡ name, possession, headline

titled ➡ noble

titter ➡ laugh

to ➡ until

toadstool ➡ fungus

toast ➡ praise

toddler ➡ baby

toil ➡ work

toilet ➡ bathroom

token ➡ sign, reminder

tolerance ➡ patience

tolerate ➡ bear, let

toll ➡ tax, ring

tomahawk ➡ ax, axe

tomb ➡ grave

tome ➡ book

tomfoolery ➡ mischief

tomorrow ➡ future

ton ➡ abundance

tone ➡ color, quality

tongue ➡ language, lick

tongue-tied ➡ dumb

tonic ➡ soda

too ➡ besides, very

toodle-oo ➡ good-bye

toot ➡ blow²

topic ➡ subject

topography ➡ terrain

topping ➡ icing

topple ➡ fall, upset

n = noun • *vb* = verb • *adj* = adjective • *adv* = adverb • *prep* = preposition • *conj* = conjunction

total 1. *n* sum, whole, aggregate, amount, totality, entirety ➡ **all** ⇨ *part*
2. *adj* ➡ **all, complete**
3. *vb* ➡ **add**

touch 1. *vb* feel, handle, caress, manipulate, paw, clutch, grope ➡ **rub**
2. *vb* contact, meet, reach ➡ **border**
3. *vb* ➡ **concern**
4. *n* ➡ **feeling, sense**
5. *n* ➡ **bit**

tough 1. *adj* sturdy, durable, stout, unbreakable, rugged, resilient, firm ➡ **strong**
2. *adj* ➡ **hard**
3. *n* ➡ **bully, vandal**

tower 1. *n* spire, steeple, turret, belfry, campanile, keep, minaret, pinnacle, obelisk, skyscraper
2. *vb* overlook, survey, loom, rise, rear, surmount

town *n* city, village, municipality, township, hamlet, community, borough, suburb, metropolis, megalopolis, settlement ➡ **neighborhood**

toy 1. *n* plaything, amusement ➡ **trinket, pastime, game**
2. *vb* ➡ **tinker**

track 1. *n* ➡ **path, course, field**
2. *n* trail, footprint, print, impression, imprint, spoor, sign, trace
3. *vb* ➡ **follow, hunt**

trade 1. *vb* exchange, swap, barter, switch, substitute, interchange, traffic, trade in ➡ **sell, change**
2. *n* exchange, swap, switch, substitution ➡ **sale**
3. *n* ➡ **business, profession**

If the word you want is not a main entry above, look below to find it.

top secret ➡ secret
topsoil ➡ dirt
topsy-turvy ➡ upside down
torch ➡ light[1]
torment ➡ abuse, threaten, misery
tormentor ➡ bully
torn ➡ ragged
tornado ➡ storm
torpedo ➡ missile
torpid ➡ slow
torpor ➡ laziness
torrent ➡ rain, flood
torrid ➡ hot, tropical
torso ➡ body
torte ➡ cake
tortilla ➡ bread
tortuous ➡ indirect

torture ➡ misery, abuse
toss ➡ throw
tot ➡ baby
totalitarian ➡ dictator, dictatorial
totalitarianism ➡ tyranny
totality ➡ all, total
totally ➡ completely
tote ➡ bag, carry
tote bag ➡ bag
totter ➡ limp
touching ➡ about, emotional
touch off ➡ start
touch on ➡ mention
touchstone ➡ measure
touchy ➡ temperamental, delicate

toughen ➡ harden
toupee ➡ wig
tour ➡ trip, travel, period
touring ➡ abroad
tourist ➡ traveler, visitor
tournament ➡ game
tow ➡ pull
towering ➡ high
township ➡ town
toxic ➡ deadly, unhealthy
toxin ➡ poison
trace ➡ bit, draw, track
trackless ➡ impassable
tract ➡ property, pamphlet
tractable ➡ gentle
traction ➡ friction
trademark ➡ label
trader ➡ seller

tradesman ➡ seller
tradition ➡ myth, ceremony
traditional ➡ legendary, conservative
traffic ➡ business, trade, travel
tragedy ➡ disaster, play
tragic ➡ unfortunate
trail ➡ path, track, course, follow, lag
train ➡ teach, practice, exercise
trained ➡ tame
trainee ➡ student
training ➡ education, experience, discipline, exercise
traipse ➡ walk
trait ➡ quality, detail, habit
traitor ➡ rebel

➡ = synonym cross-reference • ⇨ = antonym cross-reference

trample *vb* tramp, stamp, stomp, tread, flatten, squash, squish, crush

translate *vb* convert, interpret, decipher, decode, paraphrase, render, transcribe, transliterate, paraphrase, transform

translation *n* rendition, paraphrase, adaptation, interpretation, version, transliteration

transparent 1. *adj* clear, see-through, sheer, diaphanous, limpid, lucid, crystalline, translucent
2. *adj* ➡ **obvious**

trap 1. *n* pitfall, snare, catch, hitch
➡ **trick**
2. *vb* ➡ **catch**

trash *n* garbage, rubbish, refuse, waste, debris, litter, rubble, flotsam, wreckage, junk

travel 1. *vb* journey, voyage, tour, cruise, trek, commute, explore, traverse, roam, visit, sail
➡ **go, wander**
2. *n* passage, transportation, traffic, transit
➡ **trip**

traveler *n* tourist, voyager, wayfarer, commuter, fare, pilgrim, wanderer, itinerant, gypsy, vagabond, migrant, nomad ➡ **rider**

tray *n* platter, service, salver, trencher
➡ **plate**

treason *n* treachery, disloyalty, betrayal, mutiny, sedition ➡ **revolution, crime**

treatment 1. *n* care, handling, usage, reception, approach
2. *n* ➡ **cure, dose**

tree *n* sapling, seedling, hardwood, conifer, evergreen ➡ **wood, plant**

If the word you want is not a main entry above, look below to find it.

traitorous ➡ **unfaithful**

trajectory ➡ **curve**

tramp ➡ **beggar, trample, walk**

trance ➡ **dream**

tranquil ➡ **calm**

tranquilizer ➡ **drug**

tranquillity ➡ **calm**

transact ➡ **negotiate**

transaction ➡ **business, sale**

transcend ➡ **exceed**

transcribe ➡ **write, translate**

transcription ➡ **score**

transfer ➡ **move, carry, send, movement, delivery**

transform ➡ **change, translate**

transformation ➡ **change**

transgress ➡ **disobey, sin**

transgression ➡ **crime, disobedience**

transient ➡ **short, mortal**

transit ➡ **travel**

transition ➡ **movement, change**

transitory ➡ **temporary**

transliterate ➡ **translate**

transliteration ➡ **translation**

translucent ➡ **transparent**

transmissible ➡ **contagious**

transmission ➡ **movement, delivery**

transmit ➡ **broadcast, send**

transmittable ➡ **contagious**

transparency ➡ **clarity**

transpire ➡ **happen**

transplant ➡ **plant**

transport ➡ **carry, take, vehicle**

transportable ➡ **portable**

transportation ➡ **vehicle, travel, delivery, exile**

transpose ➡ **change**

trapeze artist ➡ **acrobat**

trash heap ➡ **dump**

trauma ➡ **shock**

travail ➡ **work**

traveling ➡ **abroad**

traverse ➡ **travel**

treacherous ➡ **dangerous, unfaithful**

treachery ➡ **treason**

tread ➡ **gait, step, trample**

treasure ➡ **appreciate, wealth**

treasury ➡ **safe, bank**

treat ➡ **heal, entertain, explain**

treatise ➡ **report**

treaty ➡ **agreement**

treble ➡ **high**

trek ➡ **travel, walk**

tremble ➡ **shake, fear, vibration**

tremblor ➡ **earthquake**

tremendous ➡ **huge, great**

tremor ➡ **vibration, earthquake**

trench ➡ **channel**

trench coat ➡ **coat**

trencher ➡ **tray**

trend ➡ **tendency, fashion**

trendy ➡ **fashionable, new**

trespass ➡ **crime, sin, intrude**

tress ➡ **lock**

tresses ➡ **hair**

trial ➡ **try, tryout, experiment, examination, experimental**

tribe ➡ **family**

tribulation ➡ **hardship**

tribunal ➡ **court**

tributary ➡ **river, branch**

tribute ➡ **monument, tax**

n = noun • *vb* = verb • *adj* = adjective • *adv* = adverb • *prep* = preposition • *conj* = conjunction

trick 1. *n* stunt, illusion, hoax, artifice, ploy, ruse, device, strategem, deception, subterfuge, wile, dodge ➡ **joke, trap, pretense**
2. *vb* ➡ **cheat, betray**

trinket *n* bauble, frippery, gewgaw, trifle, bead ➡ **jewel, novelty**

trip 1. *n* journey, voyage, tour, excursion, expedition, cruise, passage, drive, travel, jaunt, outing, spin, pilgrimage, odyssey
2. *vb* stumble, slip, lurch, sprawl ➡ **fall**
3. *vb* ➡ **dance**

trite *adj* insipid, banal, uninteresting, unexciting, vapid, inane, hackneyed, clichéd, stale, musty, overused, tired, stock ➡ **superficial**

trivial *adj* petty, trifling, unimportant, negligible, frivolous, paltry, piddling, insignificant, meager, small, minute, minor, mere ➡ **superficial**

troop *n* troupe, company, squad, unit, corps, garrison ➡ **band, group, crowd, soldier, army**

tropical *adj* tropic, sultry, torrid, humid, muggy, equatorial, lush ➡ **hot**

trouble 1. *n* difficulty, predicament, plight, problem, matter, quandary, fix, pinch, strait, pickle, jam, spot, ordeal, mischief ➡ **hardship, nuisance**
2. *vb* inconvenience, distress, afflict, ail, harry ➡ **bother, disturb, worry**

truce *n* cease-fire, armistice, stand down ➡ **peace**

truth *n* truthfulness, verity, authenticity, veracity, candor, sincerity, openness ➡ **accuracy, honesty, certainty** ⇨ *lie*

try 1. *vb* attempt, strive, struggle, essay, endeavor, venture, undertake, tackle, take on
2. *vb* test, sample, check, taste, experiment
3. *vb* prosecute, sue, indict, adjudicate, impeach, arraign ➡ **blame**
4. *n* attempt, bid, endeavor, go, effort, trial, shot, stab, whirl

---

If the word you want is not a main entry above, look below to find it.

trice ➡ moment

trickery ➡ pretense

trickle ➡ drop

tricky ➡ sly, delicate

trifle ➡ trinket, bit

trifling ➡ trivial

trifocals ➡ glasses

trigger ➡ start

trim ➡ neat, level, cut, decorate, dress, decoration

trimester ➡ term

triumph ➡ victory, win

triumphant ➡ successful, ecstatic

trophy ➡ prize

tropic ➡ tropical

troposphere ➡ air

trot ➡ run

troubadour ➡ musician

troublemaker ➡ bully

troublesome ➡ inconvenient

trough ➡ channel

troupe ➡ troop

truancy ➡ absence

truant ➡ runaway

truck ➡ vehicle

trudge ➡ walk

true ➡ correct, faithful, sincere, real, straight

truffle ➡ fungus

truism ➡ cliché

truly ➡ certainly, sincerely

trunk ➡ luggage, chest, body, nose

truss ➡ support

trust ➡ belief, duty, monopoly, inheritance, believe, depend

trust company ➡ bank

trustee ➡ guardian

trusting ➡ naive

trustworthiness ➡ virtue

trustworthy ➡ reliable, sincere, faithful

trusty ➡ faithful

truthfulness ➡ truth

trying ➡ hard

➡ = synonym cross-reference • ⇨ = antonym cross-reference

tryout *n* audition, trial, reading, screening, hearing

turn 1. *vb* spin, revolve, rotate, twirl, swirl, whirl, wheel, swivel, pivot, gyrate, wind, coil, hinge, flip ➡ **bend, swing, swerve**
2. *n* ➡ **curve, corner, round**

tycoon *n* financier, magnate, capitalist, industrialist, entrepreneur, millionaire, businessman, businesswoman, businessperson

type 1. *n* kind, sort, class, nature, manner, style, category, species, variety, race, breed, strain, genre ➡ **make**
2. *n* ➡ **print**

Note that **type**, **kind**, *and* **sort** *are close synonyms and are usually interchangeable.* **Sort** *is more often used in negative or critical contexts than* **type** *and* **kind**: *"He's just the* **sort** *of person who would cheat."* **Class** *and* **category** *are more precise in suggesting the nature of the group referred to: "Platypuses are in a* **class** *by themselves;" "These books are divided into two* **categories**—*fiction and nonfiction."*

tyranny *n* oppression, repression, despotism, fascism, totalitarianism, dictatorship, absolutism ➡ **government**

If the word you want is not a main entry above, look below to find it.

tryst ➡ meeting

tsar ➡ emperor

tsarina ➡ empress

tub ➡ barrel, container

tube ➡ pipe, container

tubing ➡ pipe

tuck ➡ fold

tuft ➡ lock, lump

tug ➡ pull

tuition ➡ education

tumble ➡ fall

tumbler ➡ glass, acrobat

tumbling ➡ gymnastics

tummy ➡ stomach

tumor ➡ growth

tumult ➡ noise, excitement

tumultuous ➡ stormy

tun ➡ barrel

tundra ➡ plain

tune ➡ song

tuneful ➡ musical

tunnel ➡ cave, mine, dig

turbine ➡ engine

turbulence ➡ disturbance

turbulent ➡ stormy, wild

tureen ➡ bowl

turf ➡ dirt

turgid ➡ pompous

turmoil ➡ confusion

turn up ➡ appear

turncoat ➡ rebel

turnout ➡ productivity

turnpike ➡ highway

turquoise ➡ blue

turret ➡ tower

tussle ➡ fight

tutor ➡ teacher, teach

twaddle ➡ nonsense

twang ➡ accent

tweak ➡ squeeze

twiddle ➡ tinker

twig ➡ stick, shoot

twilight ➡ evening

twin ➡ duplicate

twine ➡ string, weave

twinge ➡ pain

twinkle ➡ blink, shine, light[1]

twinkling ➡ moment

twins ➡ pair

twirl ➡ turn, swing, bend, hurt, braid, dance

twisted ➡ bent

twisting ➡ indirect

twitch ➡ fidget, jump

two-by-four ➡ board

two-faced ➡ hypocritical

twosome ➡ pair

typescript ➡ print

typhoon ➡ storm

typical ➡ common, normal, model

typically ➡ regularly

typify ➡ embody

tyrant ➡ dictator, bully

tyrannical ➡ dictatorial

tzar ➡ emperor

tzarina ➡ empress

U

ugly *adj* unsightly, repulsive, hideous, grotesque, loathsome, revolting, repellent, repugnant, horrid, grisly ➡ **plain** ⇨ *pretty*

unanimous *adj* undivided, unified, united, universal, common, undisputed, harmonious, concerted

unaware *adj* ignorant, oblivious, obtuse, unmindful, unconscious, unconcerned, blind, deaf, heedless ➡ **naive**

unbelievable *adj* incredible, unimaginable, implausible, improbable, indescribable, unlikely ➡ **impossible, doubtful**

unbreakable *adj* indestructible, durable, rugged, resistant ➡ **strong, tough** ⇨ *breakable*

uncomfortable *adj* ill at ease, discomfited, cramped, painful, distressful, disagreeable, agonizing ➡ **anxious, nervous** ⇨ *comfortable*

unconditional *adj* unrestricted, unqualified, outright, absolute, unequivocal ➡ **complete, certain**

unconscious *adj* insensible, stunned, comatose, out cold, senseless, insensate, inanimate ➡ **asleep, unaware**

If the word you want is not a main entry above, look below to find it.

ubiquitous ➡ universal

ulcer ➡ sore

ultimate ➡ last, best, top

ultimately ➡ finally

ultimatum ➡ rule, order

ultraviolet ray ➡ X ray

umber ➡ brown

umpire ➡ judge

unable ➡ incompetent

unabridged ➡ complete

unaccompanied ➡ alone

unaccountable ➡ impossible

unaccustomed ➡ strange

unadorned ➡ plain, bald

unanimity ➡ unity

unapparent ➡ inconspicuous

unappreciated ➡ thankless

unappreciative ➡ thoughtless

unarmed ➡ vulnerable

unassuming ➡ humble

unattached ➡ single

unattainable ➡ impossible, inaccessible

unattended ➡ alone

unattractive ➡ plain

unavailable ➡ inaccessible

unavailing ➡ useless

unavoidable ➡ certain

unawareness ➡ ignorance

unbalanced ➡ insane

unbearable ➡ intolerable

unbeatable ➡ invincible

unbecoming ➡ improper

unbefitting ➡ improper

unbeliever ➡ skeptic, atheist

unbend ➡ straighten

unbent ➡ straight

unbiased ➡ fair

unblemished ➡ clean, perfect

unbolt ➡ open

unbounded ➡ infinite

unbroken ➡ complete, continual

uncanny ➡ mysterious

uncaring ➡ apathetic, insensitive

unceasing ➡ continual

uncensored ➡ complete

uncertain ➡ doubtful, variable

uncertainty ➡ doubt, suspense

unchanging ➡ continual

uncivilized ➡ primitive

unclad ➡ naked

unclean ➡ dirty

unclear ➡ obscure, doubtful

unclothe ➡ undress

unclothed ➡ naked

uncommon ➡ rare

uncomplicated ➡ plain

uncompromising ➡ resolute, strict

unconcern ➡ apathy

unconcerned ➡ apathetic, unaware

unconfined ➡ free

uncongenial ➡ unfriendly

unconquerable ➡ invincible

unconsciously ➡ accidentally

uncooked ➡ natural

uncoordinated ➡ clumsy

uncouth ➡ rude

uncover ➡ discover, reveal

uncovered ➡ open

uncritical ➡ indiscriminate, superficial

unctuous ➡ self-righteous

uncultivated ➡ wild

uncut ➡ complete

undaunted ➡ brave

undecided ➡ unresolved

undeniable ➡ certain, conclusive

---

under 1. *prep* below, beneath, underneath ⇨ *above*
2. *prep* less than, lower than, inferior to, subject to, subordinate to

underdeveloped *adj* undeveloped, disadvantaged, impoverished, deprived, backward, depressed

underestimate *vb* underrate, undervalue, deprecate, belittle

underground 1. *adj* subterranean, covered, buried, sunken, belowground
2. *adj* ➡ **secret**

undress *vb* disrobe, strip, unclothe, undrape, divest

unemployed *adj* jobless, idle, inactive, unoccupied, out-of-work ⇨ *employed*

unfaithful *adj* false, traitorous, treacherous, disloyal, perfidious, false-hearted, fickle
➡ **dishonest** ⇨ *faithful*

unfortunate *adj* unlucky, unhappy, hapless, disastrous, catastrophic, tragic, adverse, hapless, regrettable, lamentable, deplorable
➡ **sad, poor, pitiful**

unfriendly *adj* quarrelsome, antisocial, unsociable, uncongenial, inhospitable, combative, antagonistic ➡ **belligerent, cool** ⇨ *friendly*

If the word you want is not a main entry above, look below to find it.

undependable ➡ unreliable

underage ➡ young

underbrush ➡ brush

undercover ➡ secret

underfed ➡ hungry

undergo ➡ experience

undergraduate ➡ student

undergrowth ➡ brush

underhanded ➡ sly

underline ➡ emphasize

undermine ➡ weaken

underneath ➡ under

undernourished ➡ hungry

underpinning ➡ basis

underrate ➡ underestimate

underscore ➡ emphasize

undersized ➡ short

understand ➡ know

understandable ➡ articulate

understanding ➡ patient, belief, wisdom, patience, agreement

undertake ➡ try, bear

undertaking ➡ act, work

undervalue ➡ underestimate

underweight ➡ light²

undesirable ➡ bad

undetectable ➡ invisible

undetermined ➡ unresolved

undeveloped ➡ underdeveloped, latent

undeviating ➡ straight

undisciplined ➡ wild

undisputed ➡ unanimous

undisturbed ➡ calm

undivided ➡ unanimous

undo ➡ separate, open

undoubtedly ➡ certainly

undrape ➡ undress

undressed ➡ naked

undulate ➡ swing

undying ➡ eternal

unearth ➡ discover, reveal

unearthing ➡ discovery

unearthly ➡ supernatural

uneasy ➡ anxious

uneducated ➡ ignorant

unending ➡ long, eternal

unequal ➡ different

unequivocal ➡ unconditional

unerring ➡ infallible

unessential ➡ unnecessary

unethical ➡ immoral

uneven ➡ rough, variable, different

unexceptional ➡ average

unexciting ➡ trite

unexpected ➡ sudden

unexplainable ➡ impossible

unfailing ➡ faithful

unfair ➡ prejudiced

unfamiliar ➡ strange

unfashionable ➡ unpopular

unfasten ➡ open

unfastened ➡ open

unfavorable ➡ ominous, destructive

unfeasible ➡ impractical

unfeeling ➡ insensitive

unfettered ➡ free

unfinished ➡ partial, unresolved

unfit ➡ weak, incompetent

unflagging ➡ diligent

unfold ➡ spread

unforeseen ➡ sudden

unforgettable ➡ memorable

unforgiveable ➡ inexcusable

unfounded ➡ superstitious

ungainly ➡ clumsy

ungraceful ➡ clumsy

ungracious ➡ rude

ungrateful ➡ thoughtless

unguarded ➡ vulnerable

unhappy ➡ sad, unfortunate

---

n = noun • *vb* = verb • *adj* = adjective • *adv* = adverb • *prep* = preposition • *conj* = conjunction

unhealthy 1. *adj* unwholesome, harmful, injurious, noxious, unsanitary, toxic, bad
➡ **dangerous**
2. *adj* ➡ **sick**

unify *vb* unite, integrate, merge, fuse, consolidate ➡ **join**

union 1. *n* unification, fusion, amalgamation, coupling, confluence, combination, marriage, merger, consolidation ➡ **link, wedding**
2. *n* association, alliance, federation, league, partnership, guild ➡ **organization**

unique *adj* unprecedented, incomparable, singular, peerless, unparalleled, unrivaled, unsurpassed, matchless, idiosyncratic
➡ **different, special, only**

unity 1. *n* identity, homogeneity, sameness, integrity ➡ **similarity**

2. *n* unison, concord, harmony, unanimity
➡ **agreement**

universal 1. *adj* worldwide, international, global, cosmic
2. *adj* ubiquitous, limitless, catholic
➡ **common, general, unanimous**

unnecessary *adj* needless, unessential, irrelevant, extraneous, superfluous, redundant, optional, gratuitous, pointless, extra, surplus, leftover ➡ **useless, excessive**

unnoticed *adj* unheeded, unobserved, disregarded, unseen, overlooked

unpopular 1. *adj* disliked, despised, unwelcome, friendless
2. *adj* unfashionable, outmoded ➡ **old**

unprepared *adj* unready, unsuspecting, inexperienced, napping, unwary

---

If the word you want is not a main entry above, look below to find it.

unhearing ➡ deaf
unheeded ➡ unnoticed
unhinged ➡ insane
unification ➡ union
unified ➡ unanimous, inseparable
uniform ➡ same, suit
unimaginable ➡ unbelievable
unimaginative ➡ dull
unimpeachable ➡ reliable
unimportant ➡ trivial
uninhabited ➡ empty, abandoned
unintelligent ➡ stupid
unintelligible ➡ illegible
unintentional ➡ accidental, automatic
unintentionally ➡ accidentally

uninterested ➡ bored
uninteresting ➡ dull, trite
uniqueness ➡ novelty
unison ➡ unity
unit ➡ troop, team
unite ➡ join, unify
united ➡ unanimous, inseparable
universe ➡ space
university ➡ college
unjust ➡ prejudiced
unjustifiable ➡ inexcusable
unkempt ➡ messy
unkind ➡ mean
unknown ➡ strange, anonymous
unlawful ➡ illegal
unlearned ➡ ignorant
unlettered ➡ ignorant
unlike ➡ different

unlikely ➡ unbelievable
unlimited ➡ infinite
unlit ➡ dark
unload ➡ empty
unlocked ➡ open
unloose ➡ free
unloosen ➡ free
unlovely ➡ plain
unlucky ➡ unfortunate
unmanageable ➡ clumsy, stubborn, invincible
unmarried ➡ celibate, single
unmindful ➡ unaware
unnamed ➡ anonymous
unnatural ➡ strange
unnerve ➡ disturb, scare, discourage
unnerving ➡ scary
unnoticeable ➡ inconspicuous

unobjectionable ➡ harmless
unobserved ➡ unnoticed
unobstructed ➡ open
unobtainable ➡ inaccessible
unobtrusive ➡ inconspicuous
unoccupied ➡ empty, unemployed
unpack ➡ empty
unpaid ➡ amateur, due
unparalleled ➡ best, unique
unpardonable ➡ inexcusable
unplanned ➡ accidental, spontaneous, arbitrary
unpleasant ➡ bad
unpolished ➡ provincial
unprecedented ➡ unique
unpredictable ➡ arbitrary
unprejudiced ➡ fair

---

unreliable 1. *adj* (*used in reference to persons*) untrustworthy, irresponsible, fickle, undependable ➡ **unfaithful, dishonest** ⇨ *reliable*
2. *adj* (*used in reference to ideas and inanimate objects or things*) deceptive, unsound, misleading, flimsy ➡ **wrong**

unresolved *adj* unsettled, undecided, undetermined, indeterminate, unfinished, pending, incomplete ➡ **doubtful**

unsteady *adj* unstable, wobbly, shaky, insecure, precarious ➡ **variable**

until 1. *prep* till, before, up till, up to, to
2. *conj* till

If the word you want is not a main entry above, look below to find it.

unpretentious ➡ common, humble

unprincipled ➡ immoral, dishonest

unprocessed ➡ natural

unprofitable ➡ useless

unprotected ➡ vulnerable

unqualified ➡ incompetent, unconditional

unquestionable ➡ certain

unquestionably ➡ certainly

unravel ➡ solve

unreachable ➡ inaccessible

unread ➡ ignorant

unreadable ➡ illegible

unready ➡ unprepared

unreal ➡ imaginary

unrealistic ➡ impractical

unrealized ➡ latent

unreasonable ➡ illogical

unrelenting ➡ stubborn

unremarkable ➡ average

unresponsive ➡ apathetic

unrest ➡ disturbance

unrestrained ➡ free

unrestricted ➡ unconditional

unrewarded ➡ thankless

unrewarding ➡ thankless

unrivaled ➡ unique

unruly ➡ mischievous, stubborn, wild

unsafe ➡ dangerous

unsanitary ➡ dirty, unhealthy

unsatisfactory ➡ poor

unsavory ➡ bad

unschooled ➡ ignorant

unscientific ➡ arbitrary

unscramble ➡ solve

unscrupulous ➡ dishonest

unsealed ➡ open

unseat ➡ oust

unseeing ➡ blind

unseemly ➡ improper

unseen ➡ invisible, unnoticed

unselfish ➡ generous

unselfishness ➡ generosity

unsentimental ➡ practical

unsettle ➡ disturb

unsettled ➡ unresolved, variable

unshackled ➡ free

unshaken ➡ faithful

unsharpened ➡ dull

unsociable ➡ unfriendly

unsightly ➡ ugly

unsigned ➡ anonymous

unskilled ➡ amateur

unsoiled ➡ clean

unsolvable ➡ impossible

unsophisticated ➡ naive, primitive, provincial

unsound ➡ unreliable, imprudent

unsparing ➡ generous

unspoiled ➡ new

unstable ➡ unsteady

unsuccessful ➡ useless

unsuitable ➡ improper

unsure ➡ doubtful

unsurpassed ➡ best, unique

unsuspecting ➡ unprepared

unsympathetic ➡ insensitive

untamed ➡ wild, primitive

untangle ➡ comb

unthinkable ➡ impossible

untidy ➡ messy

untie ➡ open

untimely ➡ early, inconvenient

untouched ➡ new

untrained ➡ amateur

untrodden ➡ impassable

untroubled ➡ calm, carefree

untrue ➡ wrong

untrustworthy ➡ dishonest, unreliable, fickle

untruth ➡ lie

untruthful ➡ dishonest

untwist ➡ straighten

unusable ➡ useless, broken

unused ➡ clean, new

unusual ➡ strange, special, striking

unusually ➡ very

unvarnished ➡ plain

unvarying ➡ continual

unveil ➡ reveal

unwary ➡ unprepared

unwavering ➡ resolute

unwed ➡ single

unwelcome ➡ unpopular

unwell ➡ sick

unwholesome ➡ unhealthy

unwieldy ➡ clumsy

unwilling ➡ reluctant

unwind ➡ rest

unwise ➡ imprudent

unwittingly ➡ accidentally

unwrap ➡ empty

unwritten ➡ spoken

unyielding ➡ resolute, tight, strict

up ➡ above, awake

upbraid ➡ scold

upcoming ➡ future

update ➡ renew

upend ➡ upset

upgrade ➡ promote

upheaval ➡ disturbance

uphill ➡ steep

uphold ➡ support

upkeep ➡ support

upland ➡ plateau

uplift ➡ lift

upon ➡ above

upper ➡ best

upset 1. *vb* overturn, capsize, topple, upend, invert, tip
2. *vb, n* ➡ **defeat**
3. *vb* ➡ **worry, disturb, anger**
4. *adj* ➡ **angry**
5. *n* ➡ **shock**

upside down *adv* inverted, topsy-turvy, head-over-heels, reversed

urban *adj* city, metropolitan, municipal, civic, cosmopolitan

urchin *n* waif, ragamuffin, brat, imp, gamin ➡ **child**

urge 1. *vb* coax, encourage, goad, prod, spur, egg (on), press, prompt, push, inspire, incite, instigate, provoke ➡ **persuade, suggest**
2. *n* ➡ **desire, beg**

urgent *adj* crucial, pressing, imperative, compelling, desperate, dire, acute ➡ **important**

use 1. *vb* employ, utilize, wield, practice, exercise, exert, apply, expend, exploit, refer to, resort to ➡ **operate**

2. *vb* consume, deplete, exhaust, expend ➡ **finish**
3. *n* application, utilization, utility, usefulness, usage, purpose, operation, employment, consumption, expenditure, exercise ➡ **function, worth**

useful *adj* helpful, practical, handy, beneficial, desirable, advantageous, profitable, pragmatic, utilitarian, versatile ➡ **efficient** ⇨ *useless*

useless 1. *adj* futile, vain, fruitless, unavailing, hopeless, desperate, abortive, unsuccessful, ineffectual, unprofitable ➡ **unnecessary** ⇨ *useful*
2. *adj* worthless, unusable, ineffective, counterproductive ➡ **broken**

usual *adj* regular, customary, accustomed, habitual, ordinary, normal, set ➡ **normal**

usually *adv* ordinarily, customarily, regularly, normally, generally ➡ **often, regularly**

utopia *n* paradise, Eden, Shangri-la, Camelot, promised land ➡ **heaven**

If the word you want is not a main entry above, look below to find it.

upper class ➡ aristocracy	uptight ➡ nervous	used ➡ old	utilization ➡ use
upper hand ➡ advantage	up till ➡ until	usefulness ➡ use	utilize ➡ use
upright ➡ vertical, post	up to ➡ until	use up ➡ finish	utmost ➡ most
uprising ➡ revolution	up-to-date ➡ modern, new	usher ➡ guide, lead	utopian ➡ idealistic
uproar ➡ noise, disturbance	upward, upwards ➡ above	usurp ➡ take	utter ➡ pronounce, complete
uproarious ➡ loud	urbane ➡ suave	utensil ➡ tool	utterance ➡ remark, speech, word
upscale ➡ expensive	usable ➡ available	utilitarian ➡ useful	
upshot ➡ effect	usage ➡ habit, use, treatment	utility ➡ use	utterly ➡ completely

---

➡ = synonym cross-reference • ⇨ = antonym cross-reference

V

vacation *n* holiday, recess, leave, furlough, sabbatical, respite, rest, R & R ➡ **break, leisure**

vaccinate *vb* inoculate, immunize

valid 1. *adj* sound, convincing, logical, cogent, telling ➡ **fair**
2. *adj* ➡ **legal, official**

valley *n* vale, glen, dell, dale, hollow, gap, basin, lowland ➡ **canyon** ⇨ *hill, mountain*

valuable *adj* precious, dear, cherished, prized, beloved, inestimable, important, worthwhile, priceless ➡ **expensive, rare**

vandal *n* hooligan, hoodlum, hood, tough, punk, thug, delinquent, savage, barbarian ➡ **criminal, bully, pirate**

variable *adj* changeable, unsettled, mutable, erratic, uncertain, uneven, inconsistent ➡ **arbitrary, fickle, unsteady**

vegetable *n* green, produce ➡ **plant, fruit, herb**

vehicle 1. *n* automobile, car, truck, transportation, transport, wheels (*informal*) ➡ **airplane, boat, taxi**
2. *n* ➡ **tool**

If the word you want is not a main entry above, look below to find it.

vacant ➡ empty, blank

vacate ➡ leave, empty

vaccine ➡ medicine

vacillate ➡ hesitate

vacuous ➡ blank, stupid

vacuum ➡ sweep

vagabond ➡ traveler, homeless

vagrant ➡ homeless, beggar

vague ➡ obscure, doubtful

vain ➡ proud, empty, useless

vainglory ➡ pride

vale ➡ valley

Valhalla ➡ heaven

valiant ➡ brave

validate ➡ approve

validation ➡ justification

valise ➡ luggage

valor ➡ courage

valorous ➡ brave

value ➡ worth, importance, appreciate, respect

valve ➡ faucet

van ➡ front

Vandyke ➡ beard

vanguard ➡ front, patrol

vanish ➡ disappear

vanity ➡ pride

vanquish ➡ defeat

vantage ➡ advantage

vapid ➡ trite

vapor ➡ smoke, cloud

variance ➡ difference

variation ➡ change, difference

varied ➡ different

variegated ➡ speckled

variety ➡ assortment, type

various ➡ many, different

variously ➡ differently

varnish ➡ finish

vary ➡ change, differ

vassalage ➡ slavery

vast ➡ huge

vat ➡ barrel, pot

vault ➡ jump, safe, grave

vaulting ➡ gymnastics

vaunt ➡ boast

veer ➡ bend, swerve

vegetate ➡ rest

vegetation ➡ plant

vehemence ➡ strength

vehement ➡ certain

veil ➡ scarf, divider, hide

vein ➡ mood, band, blood vessel

vellum ➡ paper

velocity ➡ speed

velvety ➡ fuzzy

vend ➡ sell

vendor ➡ seller

veneer ➡ coat

venerable ➡ old

venerate ➡ worship

veneration ➡ worship

vengeance ➡ revenge

vengeful ➡ revengeful

venom ➡ poison

venomous ➡ deadly

vent ➡ hole, say

ventilate ➡ fan

ventilation ➡ air

venture ➡ try, bet, adventure, pastime

veracity ➡ truth, honesty

veranda ➡ porch

verbal ➡ spoken

verbalism ➡ word

verbalize ➡ say

verbatim ➡ literal

verbose ➡ talkative

verdant ➡ green

verdict ➡ decision

verge ➡ edge

veridian ➡ green

n = noun • *vb* = verb • *adj* = adjective • *adv* = adverb • *prep* = preposition • *conj* = conjunction

verify *vb* determine, prove, confirm, ascertain, ensure, assure, show, demonstrate, establish, authenticate, corroborate, substantiate, vindicate, defend ➡ **decide**

vertical *adj* perpendicular, upright, erect, plumb ➡ **steep**

very *adv* extremely, unusually, greatly, absolutely, immensely, terribly, awfully, rather, really, quite, most, too ➡ **much**

vibration *n* quiver, quaver, quake, oscillation, tremor, tremble, shake, shock

victory *n* triumph, conquest, subjugation, mastery, overthrow, ascendancy, win ⇨ *defeat*

view 1. *n* sight, glimpse, scene, scenery, vision, panorama, outlook, spectacle, perspective, prospect, vista ➡ **look**
2. *n* ➡ **belief**
3. *vb* ➡ **look, study**
4. *vb* ➡ **believe**

violence *n* brutality, destruction, destructiveness, savagery, aggression
➡ **disturbance, confusion, fight, strength**

violent 1. *adj* savage, fierce, furious, fuming, enraged, berserk ➡ **angry, belligerent, mean, wild, destructive**
2. *adj* ➡ **strong, stormy**

virtual *adj* implied, implicit, practical

virtue 1. *n* integrity, morality, honor, trustworthiness, principle, decency, goodness
➡ **truth, honesty, kindness**
2. *n* innocence, purity, modesty, chastity, virginity
3. *n* ➡ **advantage, worth**

visible *adj* observable, discernible, perceptible, perceivable, visual, optical, graphic, illustrative
➡ **obvious**

If the word you want is not a main entry above, look below to find it.

verification ➡ proof

veritable ➡ real

veritably ➡ really

verity ➡ truth

vermilion ➡ red

vermin ➡ bug

vernacular ➡ dialect

versatile ➡ talented, useful

verse ➡ poem, stanza

versed ➡ expert

version ➡ translation, story

versus ➡ opposite

vessel ➡ boat, bowl

vestibule ➡ hall

vestments ➡ clothes

veteran ➡ soldier

veto ➡ rejection, abolish

vex ➡ bother

vexation ➡ nuisance

viable ➡ alive, possible

viaduct ➡ bridge

vibes ➡ xylophone

vibrant ➡ active

vibraphone ➡ xylophone

vibrate ➡ shake, swing

vicar ➡ priest

vice ➡ fault, dishonesty

vicinity ➡ neighborhood, place

vicious ➡ mean

vicissitude ➡ change

victim ➡ casualty, prey, patient, tool

victimize ➡ abuse

victor ➡ winner

victorious ➡ successful

victuals ➡ food

video ➡ movie

vie ➡ compete

viewer ➡ observer

viewers ➡ audience

viewpoint ➡ perspective

vigil ➡ watch

vigilant ➡ alert

vigor ➡ energy, health

vigorous ➡ lively, strong, healthy

vile ➡ bad

vilify ➡ curse

villa ➡ home

village ➡ town

villain ➡ rascal

villainous ➡ bad

vim ➡ energy

vindicate ➡ revenge, forgive, verify

vindication ➡ revenge, justification

vindictive ➡ revengeful

vine ➡ flower

violate ➡ disobey

violation ➡ crime

violet ➡ purple

VIP ➡ celebrity

viper ➡ snake

virgin ➡ new

virginal ➡ celibate

virginity ➡ virtue

virile ➡ masculine, strong

virtually ➡ practically

virtuoso ➡ expert, genius

virtuous ➡ good

virulent ➡ deadly

virus ➡ disease, poison

visa ➡ ticket

visage ➡ face, appearance

viscid ➡ thick, sticky

viscous ➡ thick, sticky

➡ = synonym cross-reference • ⇨ = antonym cross-reference

visit 1. *vb* call on/upon, stay with, drop by/in, sojourn ➡ **frequent, travel**
2. *n* call, stay, appointment, sojourn, visitation, get-together

visitor *n* guest, caller, company, houseguest, tourist

voluntary *adj* intentional, deliberate, willful, willing, freely, spontaneous, optional

vomit *vb* throw up, retch, regurgitate, gag, heave, puke (*informal*), barf (*informal*)

vote 1. *n* ballot, election, referendum, poll, polls, tally ➡ **choice**
2. *vb* ➡ **choose, decide**

vulnerable *adj* defenseless, unarmed, unprotected, unguarded, susceptible, prone, disposed ➡ **weak**

If the word you want is not a main entry above, look below to find it.

vision ➡ sight, view, foresight, imagination

visionary ➡ idealistic, idealist

visionless ➡ blind

visitation ➡ visit

visor ➡ bill

vista ➡ view

visual ➡ visible

visualize ➡ imagine

visually impaired ➡ blind

vital ➡ lively, alive

vitality ➡ energy, health, life

vivacious ➡ lively

vivid ➡ bright, explicit

vocable ➡ word

vocabulary ➡ dictionary

vocal ➡ spoken, straightforward

vocalist ➡ singer

vocalize ➡ pronounce, sing

vocation ➡ profession

vociferous ➡ loud

vogue ➡ fashion

voice ➡ speech, choice

voiced ➡ spoken

voiceless ➡ dumb

void ➡ empty, space

volatile ➡ inflammable, temperamental

volition ➡ will

volley ➡ flood

voltage ➡ energy

voluble ➡ talkative

volume ➡ size, book, measure, productivity

voluminous ➡ abundant

volunteer ➡ soldier

vomiting ➡ nausea

voodoo ➡ magic

voracious ➡ predatory, greedy

vouch ➡ testify

voucher ➡ ticket

vouchsafe ➡ condescend

vow ➡ promise

voyage ➡ trip, travel

voyager ➡ traveler

vulgar ➡ common, dirty, sensational

vulgarity ➡ rudeness

vying ➡ competitive

wage *n* salary, pay, allowance, fee, tip, compensation, income, earnings, profit, intake, stipend, revenue, return ➡ **pension**

wagon *n* carriage, buggy, cart, coach, stagecoach ➡ **vehicle**

wait *vb* remain, linger, loiter, stay, tarry, await, abide, dally ➡ **delay, hesitate** ⇨ *leave*

wake *vb* wake up, waken, rouse, arouse, awaken

walk 1. *vb* amble, stroll, march, step, hike, stride, trudge, plod, lumber, file, trek, traipse, tramp ➡ **wander, strut, crawl**
2. *n* ➡ **gait**
3. *n* ➡ **path**

wall *n* partition, fence, parapet, stockade, rampart, palisade, barricade ➡ **divider, dam**

wallet *n* billfold, change purse ➡ **bag**

wander 1. *vb* roam, meander, ramble, saunter, rove, range, drift ➡ **walk, travel**

2. *vb* stray, deviate, meander, ramble, digress, diverge

want 1. *vb* wish, desire, crave, yearn, long, pine, hanker, itch ➡ **envy, hope, prefer**
2. *vb* ➡ **need**
3. *n* lack, dearth, paucity, shortage, scarcity, deficiency ➡ **absence, hardship, poverty**

warehouse *n* storehouse, stockroom, depot, depository, granary, grain elevator, silo, armory, arsenal, magazine

warm 1. *adj* lukewarm, tepid, heated, mild ➡ **hot**
2. *adj* ➡ **friendly**

warn *vb* forewarn, caution, alert, tip off, advise, admonish, exhort, counsel ➡ **scare, tell**

warning *n* alarm, signal, admonition, caution, advice, caveat, premonition, forewarning, omen, threat ➡ **notice, sign**

If the word you want is not a main entry above, look below to find it.

wad ➡ pile

waddle ➡ swing

wader ➡ bird

waft ➡ blow[2]

wag ➡ shake

wager ➡ bet, lottery

wagering ➡ gambling

waggle ➡ shake

waif ➡ urchin

wail ➡ cry

wait on ➡ help

wakeful ➡ awake

waken ➡ wake

walker ➡ pedestrian

walk out ➡ protest

walkway ➡ path

wallop ➡ blow[1]

wallow ➡ fumble

wan ➡ pale

wand ➡ stick

wanderer ➡ traveler

wane ➡ decrease

wanton ➡ thoughtless, wasteful

war ➡ fight

warble ➡ sing

ward ➡ neighborhood

ward off ➡ repel

wardrobe ➡ clothes, closet

wares ➡ product

warfare ➡ fight

warily ➡ carefully

warlike ➡ military

warlock ➡ magician

warmhearted ➡ kind

warmth ➡ hospitality, feeling

warp ➡ bend

warped ➡ bent

warrant ➡ promise, guarantee, deserve

warren ➡ den

warrior ➡ soldier

wary ➡ suspicious, careful

wash ➡ clean, cleaning, laundry

washbasin ➡ sink

washcloth ➡ cloth

washed ➡ clean

washing ➡ cleaning, laundry

washroom ➡ bathroom

washstand ➡ sink

---

waste 1. *vb* squander, fritter away, dissipate, misuse, misspend ⇨ *save*
  2. *vb* ➡ **decrease**
  3. *n* ➡ **trash**
  4. *n* ➡ **desert**
  5. *adj* ➡ **sterile**

wasteful *adj* extravagant, lavish, profligate, prodigal, reckless, wanton, spendthrift

watch 1. *n* ➡ **clock**
  2. *n* ➡ **period**
  3. *n* guard, lookout, vigil, surveillance ➡ **attention**
  4. *n* ➡ **patrol**
  5. *vb* ➡ **look**
  6. *vb* ➡ **protect**

wave 1. *n* billow, swell, surge, tidal wave, ripple, breaker, roller, whitecap, comber, surf
  2. *vb* motion, gesture, signal, beckon, flag, salute
  3. *vb* flutter, flap, ripple, sway ➡ **blow, swing**

weak *adj* frail, feeble, infirm, invalid, helpless, powerless, unfit, impotent, puny, delicate, fragile, flimsy, rickety ➡ **breakable, thin, sick, vulnerable** ⇨ *strong*

weaken 1. *vb* flag, wilt, droop, sag, wither ➡ **tire**

  2. *vb* cripple, undermine, impair, sabotage, subvert, erode, incapacitate ➡ **destroy**
  3. *vb* dilute, thin, water down, adulterate, attenuate ➡ **decrease**

wealth *n* riches, affluence, means, opulence, luxury, prosperity, assets, fortune, treasure, hoard ➡ **money, property, abundance**

weather 1. *n* climate, conditions, clime (*literary*)
Use **weather** *to refer to what is happening in the atmosphere at a particular time or in general:* "I don't like this rainy **weather**." "Is the **weather** being affected by global warming?" *Use* **climate** *to refer to the average state of the atmosphere in a place or region:* "Florida has a warm **climate**."
  2. *vb* age, season, wear, endure ➡ **harden**
  3. *vb* expose, overcome ➡ **bear**

weave 1. *vb* braid, knit, interlace, plait, twine, intertwine ➡ **sew**
  2. *n* ➡ **cloth**

weight 1. *n* heaviness, heft, mass, substance, pressure, load ➡ **density, measure**
  2. *n* ➡ **importance**

welcome 1. *vb* greet, receive, salute, address, herald, hail ➡ **call, entertain, appreciate**
  2. *n* greeting, salutation, reception
  3. *n* ➡ **hospitality**

If the word you want is not a main entry above, look below to find it.

wasted ➡ hungry	watery ➡ liquid	weakness ➡ fault	wedded ➡ married
wasteland ➡ desert	waver ➡ hesitate	wealthy ➡ rich	wedding ➡ marriage
watchdog ➡ guardian	wax ➡ shine, finish, grow	weapon ➡ gun	wedge ➡ block, push, embed
watchful ➡ alert	wax paper ➡ paper	weaponry ➡ arms	wedlock ➡ marriage
watchman ➡ doorman	waxy ➡ slippery	weapons ➡ arms	weed ➡ plant
water ➡ liquid, wet	way ➡ course, distance, choice, method	wear ➡ dress, damage, decay, weather	weekly ➡ paper
water down ➡ weaken	wayfarer ➡ traveler	weariness ➡ exhaustion	weep ➡ cry
waterfowl ➡ bird	waylay ➡ attack	weary ➡ tired, tire	weigh ➡ consider, measure
waterpipe ➡ pipe	wayward ➡ mischievous	web ➡ net	weightless ➡ light²
waterspout ➡ gargoyle	waywardness ➡ disobedience	webbing ➡ net	weighty ➡ heavy, important
watertight ➡ tight		wed ➡ marry, married	weir ➡ dam
waterway ➡ channel			weird ➡ strange

   n = noun • *vb* = verb • *adj* = adjective • *adv* = adverb • *prep* = preposition • *conj* = conjunction

welfare 1. *n* well-being, prosperity, good ➡ **health**
2. *n* public assistance ➡ **help**

well 1. *adv* properly, thoroughly, competently, satisfactorily, adequately, excellently, splendidly
2. *adv* favorably, kindly, approvingly, highly
3. *adj* ➡ **healthy**
4. *n* spring, reservoir, cistern ➡ **fountain, source**
5. *n* shaft, bore ➡ **hole**

wet 1. *adj* soaked, drenched, saturated, sodden, soggy, dripping ➡ **damp, liquid** ⇨ *dry*
2. *adj* rainy, drizzly, stormy, inclement, misty, showery, snowy, slushy
3. *vb* moisten, soak, dampen, sprinkle, saturate, drench, douse, water, steep, immerse, rinse

wheel 1. *n* tire, roller ➡ **tool**
2. *n* steering wheel, helm, tiller, controls, reins, driver's seat
3. *vb* ➡ **turn**

whip 1. *n* lash, crop, switch, cane, scourge, cat-o'-nine-tails, bullwhip

2. *vb* spank, paddle, lash, thrash, flog ➡ **hit, punish**
3. *vb* ➡ **defeat**
4. *vb* ➡ **mix**

white *adj, n* ivory, milky, snowy, silvery, snow-white, frosty, creamy ➡ **fair, pale** ⇨ *black*

wicked *adj* evil, malevolent, diabolical, fiendish, demonic, devilish, heinous ➡ **bad, immoral, mean**

width *n* breadth, girth, wideness, diameter, span ➡ **measure**

wig *n* hairpiece, fall, toupee, periwig (*historical*), rug (*informal*) ➡ **hair**

wild 1. *adj* untamed, fierce, ferocious, savage, raging, turbulent, fiery ➡ **violent, mean, rough, stormy**
2. *adj* uncultivated, overgrown, rampant, overrun
3. *adj* disorderly, unruly, obstinate, undisciplined ➡ **stubborn**
4. *n* ➡ **country**

If the word you want is not a main entry above, look below to find it.

weld ➡ join
well-behaved ➡ good
well-being ➡ welfare
well-informed ➡ educated
well-known ➡ famous
well-mannered ➡ polite, good
well-meaning ➡ kind
wellness ➡ health
well-off ➡ rich
well-read ➡ educated
wellspring ➡ source
well-to-do ➡ rich
well-versed ➡ educated, expert
welt ➡ sore

wetness ➡ humidity
whack ➡ blow[1], knock, hit
wharf ➡ dock
wheatfield ➡ field
wheedle ➡ persuade
wheels ➡ vehicle
wheeze ➡ breathe
whelp ➡ dog
wherefore ➡ therefore
whet ➡ sharpen
whiff ➡ smell
whim ➡ fancy, impulse
whimper ➡ cry
whimsical ➡ funny, arbitrary
whimsicality ➡ humor

whimsy ➡ impulse
whine ➡ complain, cry
whir ➡ hum
whirl ➡ turn, dance, swing, try
whirlwind ➡ wind
whisk ➡ sweep
whiskers ➡ beard
whisper ➡ mumble, rustle
whitecap ➡ wave
whiten ➡ bleach
whittle ➡ carve
whiz ➡ hurry, genius
whole ➡ total, complete, all, healthy

wholehearted ➡ sincere
wholesaler ➡ seller
wholesome ➡ healthy
wholly ➡ completely
whoop ➡ cry
wickedness ➡ immorality
wide ➡ broad
wide-awake ➡ alert
widen ➡ spread
wideness ➡ width
widespread ➡ common, general
wield ➡ swing, use
wife ➡ spouse
wiggle ➡ fidget, crawl

➡ = synonym cross-reference • ⇨ = antonym cross-reference

will 1. *n* willpower, determination, resolution, volition, conviction, resolve, willfulness
➡ **ambition**
2. *n* testament, bequest ➡ **inheritance**
3. *vb* ➡ **leave**

win 1. *vb* triumph, prevail, succeed, overcome
➡ **defeat** ⇨ *lose*
2. *vb* score, achieve, earn ➡ **get**
3. *n* ➡ **victory**

wind 1. *n* breeze, gale, tempest, gust, zephyr, draft, blast, whirlwind, blow, puff, breath
➡ **air, storm**
2. *vb* ➡ **bend, turn**

windy *adj* breezy, blustery, airy, drafty, wind-swept ➡ **stormy**

winner *n* champion, victor, hero, medalist, prizewinner, conqueror, champ (*informal*)

wisdom *n* judgment, reason, understanding, appreciation, intelligence, intellect, comprehension, sagacity, perception, discernment, sense, common sense
➡ **knowledge, experience, depth**

woman *n* lady, girl, female, gentlewoman, matron, maiden, gal (*informal*), lass
➡ **human being, humanity, adult**

wood *n* lumber, log, timber, plank, firewood, kindling ➡ **forest**

word 1. *n* term, expression, locution, utterance, vocable, verbalism, articulation, syllable
2. *n* ➡ **talk**
3. *n* ➡ **promise**

If the word you want is not a main entry above, look below to find it.

wilderness ➡ country, desert
wildflower ➡ flower
wildlife preserve ➡ zoo
wile ➡ trick
willful ➡ voluntary, arbitrary
willfully ➡ purposely
willfulness ➡ will
willing ➡ ready, voluntary
willpower ➡ will, discipline
wilt ➡ dry, weaken
wilted ➡ stale
wily ➡ sly
wince ➡ jump
windbreak ➡ hedge
windbreaker ➡ coat
windfall ➡ luck
wind-swept ➡ windy
wind up ➡ finish
wing ➡ limb, branch, fly

wink ➡ blink, moment
winning ➡ attractive
winnings ➡ booty, prize
winnow ➡ sift
wino ➡ drunkard
winsomeness ➡ beauty
wipe ➡ dry, sweep
wire ➡ rope
wiry ➡ thin
wise ➡ smart
wisecrack ➡ joke
wish ➡ want, hope
wistful ➡ thoughtful
wistfulness ➡ desire
wit ➡ humor
witch ➡ magician
witchcraft ➡ magic
with ➡ beside
with child ➡ pregnant

withdraw ➡ leave, retreat, extract
withdrawal ➡ departure, privacy
withdrawn ➡ private
wither ➡ dry, weaken
withhold ➡ subtract, hide, deprive
with-it ➡ fashionable
without ➡ minus
withstand ➡ repel
witness ➡ observer, look
witticism ➡ joke
witty ➡ funny
wizard ➡ genius, magician
wizardry ➡ magic
wobble ➡ shake, swing
wobbly ➡ unsteady
woe ➡ sorrow
woeful ➡ pitiful

wolf ➡ eat
womanhood ➡ maturity
womanly ➡ feminine
women's room ➡ bathroom
wonder ➡ surprise, doubt, miracle, respect
wonderful ➡ great
wont ➡ habit
woo ➡ court
woodcut ➡ print
wooden ➡ prim
woodland ➡ forest
woods ➡ forest
woof ➡ bark
wool ➡ coat
woolly ➡ fuzzy
woozy ➡ dizzy
word-for-word ➡ literal
wordless ➡ dumb

work 1. *n* labor, toil, effort, drudgery, exertion, industry, endeavor, pains, elbow grease (*informal*), travail
2. *n* ➡ **job, profession**
3. *n* accomplishment, undertaking, composition, creation, opus ➡ **act, book, picture, poem**
4. *vb* toil, labor, strive, struggle, slave, strain ➡ **act, do**
5. *vb* work out ➡ **solve**

worker *n* laborer, employee, hand, help, colleague, breadwinner, jobholder ➡ **helper, farmer**

worm *n* earthworm, nightcrawler, angleworm, inchworm ➡ **larva**

worry 1. *n* concern, care, anxiety, apprehension, burden ➡ **fear**
2. *vb* upset, concern, trouble, fret, brood, stew ➡ **disturb, bother**

worship 1. *vb* sanctify, venerate, glorify, exalt, praise, laud, adore, revere, reverence
2. *vb* ➡ **love**
3. *n* devotion, prayer, veneration, adulation

worst *adj* meanest, lowest ➡ **bad, least** ⇨ *best*

worth *n* value, benefit, merit, virtue, estimation ➡ **importance, price, use**

wrap 1. *vb* gift wrap, cover, bind, envelop, shroud, clothe, swathe, sheathe, swaddle ➡ **bandage**
2. *n* shawl, muffler, cloak, cape, mantle, stole ➡ **scarf**

wrapper *n* covering, cover, envelope, jacket, dust jacket, folder ➡ **container**

wrinkle 1. *n* crease, rumple, crinkle, crimp, crumple, pucker ➡ **fold**
2. *vb* crease, rumple, crumple, crinkle, crimp ➡ **fold**

write 1. *vb* inscribe, jot, record, scribble, scrawl, transcribe ➡ **sign**
2. *vb* compose, draft, indite, pen, author, publish, edit, compile ➡ **print**

writer *n* author, novelist, poet, playwright, historian, biographer, essayist, humorist, scriptwriter, screenwriter ➡ **reporter, artist**

wrong 1. *adj* incorrect, false, mistaken, inaccurate, untrue, erroneous, invalid, bad, corrupt, amiss, awry ➡ **improper, illogical, immoral** ⇨ *correct, right*
2. *n* ➡ **crime**

If the word you want is not a main entry above, look below to find it.

working ➡ employed

work out ➡ exercise

workout ➡ exercise

workplace ➡ office

workshop ➡ factory

world ➡ earth

worldly ➡ cosmopolitan

worldwide ➡ universal

worn ➡ old

worn out ➡ tired

worn-out ➡ old

worried ➡ anxious

worsen ➡ relapse

worthless ➡ poor, useless

worthwhile ➡ valuable

worthy ➡ good, noble, praiseworthy

wound ➡ hurt, cut

wraith ➡ ghost

wrangle ➡ argue

wrath ➡ anger

wreak ➡ inflict

wreath ➡ crown

wreck ➡ destroy, collision

wreckage ➡ damage, trash

wrench ➡ pull, hurt

wrest ➡ seize

wrestle ➡ fight

wretch ➡ beggar, rascal

wretched ➡ sorry, poor, awful

wriggle ➡ fidget, crawl

wring ➡ squeeze

wristwatch ➡ clock

writ ➡ order

writhe ➡ fidget

writing ➡ print, handwriting, literature

writing paper ➡ paper

wrongdoer ➡ criminal

wrongdoing ➡ crime

wrongful ➡ illegal

wry ➡ dry

wunderkind ➡ genius

➡ = synonym cross-reference • ⇨ = antonym cross-reference

X-Y-Z

X ray 1. *n* radiation, ultraviolet ray, gamma ray
2. *n* radiograph, encephalogram
➡ **photograph**

xylophone *n* marimba, vibraphone, vibes, glockenspiel

yell *vb, n* call, shout, scream, shriek, screech, bellow, thunder, rant, rave, harangue, boo, hiss, jeer, hoot, squall ➡ **cry**

yellow 1. *adj, n* gold, lemon, sandy, saffron, flaxen, blond, blonde
2. *adj* ➡ **cowardly**

yes *interj* aye, okay, OK, affirmative, amen, yeah (*informal*), yup (*informal*), okey-dokey (*informal*) ➡ **certainly** ⇨ *no*

young *adj* youthful, immature, juvenile, adolescent, boyish, girlish, underage
➡ **childish, new** ⇨ *old*

zero *n* nothing, naught, nought, none, nil, love (*in tennis*), zip (*informal*), zilch (*informal*), goose egg (*informal*), cipher

zigzag *adj* crooked, askew, jagged, oblique, meandering, erratic ⇨ *straight*

zone 1. *n* area, region, district, belt, band, quarter ➡ **place**
2. *vb* ➡ **divide**

zoo *n* menagerie, animal farm, game farm, wildlife preserve, game preserve, aviary, terrarium, aquarium ➡ **park**

If the word you want is not a main entry above, look below to find it.

x ➡ tick
yachting ➡ nautical
yachtsman ➡ sailor
yahoo ➡ boor
yank ➡ pull
yap ➡ bark
yard ➡ property
yardarm ➡ gallows
yardstick ➡ measure
yarn ➡ string, story
yawn ➡ spread
yeah ➡ yes
yearn ➡ want

yearning ➡ desire
yelp ➡ bark
yen ➡ desire
yeoman ➡ farmer
yesterday ➡ past
yesteryear ➡ past
yet ➡ but, more, before
yield ➡ surrender, give, growth
yielding ➡ passive
yip ➡ bark
yo ➡ hello

yoke ➡ team, pair
yonder ➡ far
yore ➡ past
youngster ➡ child
youth ➡ teenager, child, childhood
youthful ➡ young
yowl ➡ cry
yup ➡ yes
zany ➡ funny
zeal ➡ enthusiasm
zealot ➡ extremist

zealous ➡ ambitious, patriotic
zenith ➡ top
zephyr ➡ wind
zest ➡ enthusiasm, spice, excitement
zestful ➡ lively
zesty ➡ spicy
zilch ➡ zero
zip ➡ hurry, energy, zero
zipper ➡ clasp
zippy ➡ lively
zoom ➡ hurry

n = noun • *vb* = verb • *adj* = adjective • *adv* = adverb • *prep* = preposition • *interj* = interjection

Where Did All These Words Come From?

There are hundreds of thousands of words in English. Where did they come from, and why are there so many synonyms? The answers to these questions are found in the history of the English language. Every language has a history, and all languages change over time, as each language is affected by what happens to the people who speak it and by other languages with which they come into contact.

A language or a dialect may change so much that it becomes a new language. For example, the group of languages called *Romance languages* all developed from Latin – the language of the Romans, who spread their language across Europe. The Romance languages include Italian, French, Spanish, Portuguese, Romanian, and a few others. English is a member of a group called the *Germanic languages*. This group includes German, Dutch, Swedish, Danish, Norwegian, and Icelandic.

Old English (600 A.D. to 1100 A.D.)

The English language developed from the seventh to the eleventh centuries after people known as Angles, Saxons, and Jutes invaded and settled the part of the British Isles that is now called England. This early form of English is now called *Old English* or *Anglo-Saxon*. Today Old English looks like a foreign language, as you can see in these lines from *Beowulf*, a long poem about a hero who fought monsters and dragons.

Cwædon þæt he wære wyruld-cyninga,	They said that he was, among the world's kings,
mannum mildust ond mon-ðwærust,	mildest to men and most gentle,
leodum liðost ond lof-geornost.	kindest to his people and most eager for fame.

However, we have been using many of the same words for more than a thousand years, although the spelling or pronunciation might have changed. The letter æ, called "ash," is pronounced like the "a" in "ash" and "that." *Sc* is pronounced like *sh*. The letter þ, called "thorn," is pronounced like "th."

Here are a few Old English words you might recognize:

æfter "after"	niht "night"	þanc "thanks"	scip "ship"	cniht "knight"
song "song"	þoht "thought"	under "under"	wundor "wonder"	

During the Old English period, England was invaded by raiders known to the

English as *vikings*, who came from Denmark and Norway. They spoke Old Norse, the ancestor of modern Scandinavian languages. Old English and Old Norse were closely related. For example, they had the same word for an outer garment: Old English *scyrte* and Old Norse *skyrta*. Old English *scyrte* became **shirt**, and Old Norse *skyrta* became English **skirt**. Other borrowings from Old Norse include many everyday words:

birth	dirt	get	kid	scare	skill
bloom	egg	give	leg	sister	sky

Another important source of new words was Latin. Many of the earliest Latin borrowings came from the language of the Catholic Church:

altar	angel	candle	hymn	noon	organ

There were also many Latin words from other areas of life:

chalk	cup	dragon	mile	pound	wall

Middle English (1100 A.D. to 1500 A.D.)

In the year 1066 A.D. England was conquered by Normans from the north of France. Their leader, William the Conqueror, became king of England, and suddenly French became the language of the king's court, the aristocracy, and the officials who took over the country. English remained the language of the ordinary people, but during the next five centuries it changed so much in its grammar, pronunciation, and vocabulary that we call the language of this period *Middle English*.

Thousands of French words were borrowed into Middle English, especially as the French-speaking upper classes began to speak English, while keeping many of their French words. There are many other food-related terms that come from French:

appetite	boil	dinner	fruit	plate	spice	sugar	taste
biscuit	cream	fry	jelly	salad	stew	supper	toast

Often the words borrowed from French reflect that French speakers were in the ruling classes. Thus, many words relating to government and status are French in origin:

allegiance	court	empire	liberty	majesty	reign	royal	sir

Latin terms of all kinds continued to be borrowed in the Middle English period:

distract	gesture	include	magnify	nervous	polite	quiet	testify

Middle English looks much more familiar to us than Old English. On the following page is a sentence from Geoffrey Chaucer's *Canterbury Tales*, written in the late fourteenth century. Though the spelling may be different, most of the words are still familiar today.

A knyght ther was, and that a worthy man,	*There was a knight, and he was a worthy man,*
That fro the tyme that he first began	*And from the time he first began*
To riden out, he loved chivalrie,	*To ride about, he loved chivalry,*
Trouthe and honour, fredom and curteisie.	*Truth and honor, freedom and courtesy.*

Modern English (1500 A.D. to Today)

By about 1500, more changes in grammar, pronunciation, and spelling had made English very similar to the language of today. This stage of the language is called *Modern English*. Of course, even more changes have taken place since 1500, as they will continue to do as long as the language is spoken and written. Therefore, we call the English of the sixteenth and seventeenth centuries *Early Modern English*.

One of the major events that affected the language was the invention of the printing press in the late fifteenth century. Suddenly large numbers of books could be produced cheaply. This made it easier for more people to get an education, especially members of the middle classes, not just scholars and the aristocracy. Education in the Early Modern English period was still mainly in Latin, with Greek taught in the later school years. Thus, many words were borrowed from Greek into Latin and then from Latin into English. Some, like the following, came straight from Greek:

atmosphere	*chaos*	*enthusiasm*	*skeleton*
autograph	*democracy*	*gymnasium*	*thermometer*

The sixteenth to eighteenth centuries were also a time of great exploration, and Europeans began to travel literally around the world for the first time in history. English travelers came into contact with many people and cultures, and words were borrowed from their languages. The following words from Caribbean and Native American languages are arranged in order of the approximate year they first appeared in English:

1555 hurricane	*1603 moose*	*1608 raccoon*	*1709 barbecue*
1555 canoe	*1604 tomato*	*1634 skunk*	*1757 kayak*

The words below, listed by date, language, and place of origin, came from many different parts of the world. **Note:** The symbol < means "comes from."

1582 mango < Malayalam (southern India)	*1598 coffee < Turkish (Turkey)*
1634 cot < Hindi (India)	*1655 tea < Chinese (China)*
1662 shawl < Persian (Iran)	*1717 sofa < Arabic (Middle East)*
1738 chimpanzee < Kongo (central Africa)	*1755 ski < Norwegian (Norway)*

But new words do not just come from other languages. In Modern English, most new words are formed from existing English words, often by adding a prefix or suffix or by combining words. The following compound words first appear in the works of William Shakespeare:

bedroom   bloodstained   eyeball   outbreak   shooting star   watchdog

Even today more new words are constantly being added to the language. Here are some fairly recent additions, with the year each was first recorded:

1972 slam dunk   1981 snowboard   1984 cell phone   1992 hoodie

1977 download   1983 upload   1988 scrunchie   1992 Web site

Synonyms in English

Some synonyms are more formal than others, and this allows us to express the level of seriousness of what we want to say. In many cases, the formality of synonyms reflects the history of the language. For many concepts, there is an ordinary word from Old English, a more formal word from French, and an even more learned or scholarly term from Latin.

GENERAL, from Old English	FORMAL, from French	LEARNED, from Latin
ask	question	interrogate
fear	terror	apprehension

Here are two entries from this thesaurus showing the languages of origin for the synonyms:

BRAVE	< French < Italian & Spanish	DREAM	< Old English
courageous	< French	reverie	< French
heroic	< Latin < Greek	daydream	< Old English
fearless	< Old English	trance	< French
valiant	< French	daze	< Old Norse
gallant	< French < Germanic	spell	< French < Germanic
bold	< Old English	stupor	< Latin
stalwart	< Old English	study	< French < Latin
daring	< Old English	swoon	< Old English

English is now spoken all over the world. It has become an international language of business, government, technology, music, and entertainment. This global use guarantees that English will continue for many years to create and borrow new words and to develop even more synonyms. This steady growth allows us to communicate the ever-expanding range of information, ideas, and emotions that are necessary for us to understand each other more fully.